PSYCHOPATHOLOGY AND CHILD DEVELOPMENT

Research and Treatment

PSYCHOPATHOLOGY AND CHILD DEVELOPMENT

Research and Treatment

Edited by
Eric Schopler
and
Robert J. Reichler
University of North Carolina at Chapel Hill

Plenum Press · New York and London

Library of Congress Cataloging in Publication Data

Main entry under title:

Psychopathology and child development.

"Based on the First International Kanner Colloquium on Child Development, Deviations, and Treatment, held in Chapel Hill, North Carolina, October 30-November 2, 1973."
Includes bibliographies and index.
1. Autism – Congresses. 2. Schizophrenia in children – Congresses. 3. Developmental psychobiology – Congresses. 4. Child psychology – Congresses. I. Schopler, Eric. II. Reichler, Robert J., 1937-   III. International Kanner Colloquium on Child Development, Deviations, and Treatment, 1st, Chapel Hill, N.C., 1973. [DNLM: 1. Child development – Congresses. 2. Child development deviations – Therapy – Congresses. 3. Autism, Early infantile – Congresses. 4. Child development deviations – Congresses. W3 IN7237 1973c/WS350 I6104 1973c]
RJ506.A9C48   618.9'28'9   75-44351
ISBN 0-306-30870-3

Based on the First International Kanner Colloquium on Child
Development, Deviations, and Treatment, held in Chapel Hill,
North Carolina, October 30-November 2, 1973

© 1976 Plenum Press, New York
A Division of Plenum Publishing Corporation
227 West 17th Street, New York, N.Y. 10011

United kingdom edition published by Plenum Press, London
A Division of Plenum Publishing Company, Ltd.
Davis House (4th Floor), 8 Scrubs Lane, Harlesden, London, NW10 6SE, England

Printed in the United States of America

Foreword

The First International Leo Kanner Colloquium on Child Development, Deviations, and Treatment explores relationships between experimental research, normal development, and interventions, with early infantile autism as a reference model of "relatively unambiguous abnormal development."

Sponsored by the Treatment and Education of Autistic and related Communications handicapped CHildren (TEACCH) Project at the University of North Carolina at Chapel Hill, the colloquium tackled the challenge of facilitating communications among scientists of different disciplines working in a specialized area. The meeting proved successful in generating an interplay and information exchange among scientists of diverse academic and professional orientation, who, if not completely able to agree on common factors, did nevertheless achieve awareness and clarification of their differences.

The TEACCH conference and this volume have implications for all research efforts, within and outside the domain of mental health. This is particularly so at a time of limited dollar resources for research support. The present and foreseeable future represent such a time—one when communication among fields, resource competition between basic and applied research, biomedical versus psychosocial research, and the question of research utilization assume a new commanding significance.

Thus the question of accountability for research has come to the fore. Examples of interest in this topic are found in a series of similar studies undertaken by such research institutions as the Department of Defense, the National Science Foundation, the National Institute of Mental Health—for example, the Report of the NIMH Research Task Force—as well as in the establishment (in 1975) of the President's Panel on Biomedical and Behavioral Research. With some variation in purpose and methodology, each of the studies has retrospectively analyzed various scientific innovations with the aim of shedding light on the process of knowledge development, minimizing duplication of efforts, and facilitating research utilization.

Without exception, the completed federal studies emphasize the importance of interdisciplinary communication. The studies also illustrate, as does this colloquium, the frequent blurring of the line between basic and applied research. As the chapters in this volume suggest, one scientist's basic research may be another scientist's applied research. One option that unfortunately may be selected in times of restricted research investment is to restrict basic studies in favor of applied or targeted research, disrupting the traditional process of knowledge development.

An alternative possibility displayed in this volume is the strenuous task of integrating new areas of knowledge from different disciplines. Such integration can lead to a lessening dependence upon serendipity and time. Although the current slow process of information dissemination and utilization can be seen as a protective system of "checks and balances," steps can and must be taken to facilitate the process.

Exploring the relationships between fields requires crossing barriers of field-specialized jargon, of academic persuasion, and even of personal beliefs (which for some become insular). Dr. Schopler and Dr. Reichler note in the preface the difficulties inherent in attempts to bridge the gap between researcher and clinician, and even to synthesize conceptual models within different areas of study. Yet, the effort, I believe, greatly enhances the potential for payoff of research investments.

In summary, I am proud that the National Institute of Mental Health, through its resources and staff, played an active role in the colloquium. The colloquium itself was the creation of Drs. Schopler and Reichler, and structured as a tribute to Dr. Leo Kanner.

Much of the groundwork that enabled the already apparent payoff of such programs as TEACCH is attributable to the pioneering efforts of Dr. Leo Kanner, to whom the colloquium and this volume are dedicated. As a student, colleague, and friend of Dr. Kanner, as well as an admirer of his companion and wife June Kanner, I take personal pleasure in the efforts as well as pride in the successes of researchers working on behalf of children, their growth and development. This volume represents both effort and success. I look forward to a future of advances forthcoming from application of the crossfertilization model presented by the cadre of researchers and clinicians who made this First International Leo Kanner Colloquium possible.

Bertram S. Brown
Director, National Institute of Mental Health

Contributors

MAGDA CAMPBELL, Department of Psychiatry, New York University Medical Center, New York, New York

ELAINE CARUTH, Department of Child Psychiatry, University of California at Los Angeles, Los Angeles, California

STELLA CHESS, Department of Psychiatry, New York University Medical Center, New York, New York

MARIAN K. DeMYER, Institute for Psychiatric Research, Indiana University Medical Center, Indianapolis, Indiana

SPYROS A. DOXIADIS, Institute of Child Health, Incorporated, Aghia Sophia Children's Hospital, Athens, Greece

RUDOLF EKSTEIN, Childhood Psychosis Project, Reiss-Davis Child Study Center/Department of Medical Psychology, University of California at Los Angeles, Los Angeles, California

DAVID ELKIND, Department of Psychology, University of Rochester, Rochester, New York

CARL FENICHEL, The League School, Brooklyn, New York (Deceased)

JAMES J. GALLAGHER, Frank Porter Graham Child Development Center, University of North Carolina at Chapel Hill, Chapel Hill, North Carolina

LIBBY GOODMAN, Department of Special Education, Montgomery County Intermediate Unit, Blue Bell, Pennsylvania

WILLARD W. HARTUP, Institute of Child Development, University of Minnesota, Minneapolis, Minnesota

LEO KANNER, Department of Child Psychiatry, The Johns Hopkins University, Baltimore, Maryland

HERBERT KAYE, Department of Psychology, State University of New York, Stony Brook, New York

ROBERT L. KOEGEL, Department of Psychology, University of California at Santa Barbara, Santa Barbara, California

O. IVAR LOVAAS, Department of Psychology, University of California at Los Angeles, Los Angeles, California

BOYD R. McCANDLESS, Psychology Department, Emory University, Atlanta, Georgia (Deceased)

ARNOLD J. MANDELL, Department of Psychiatry, School of Medicine, University of California at San Diego, La Jolla, California

LESTER MANN, Department of Special Education, Montgomery County Intermediate Unit, Blue Bell, Pennsylvania

PAULA MENYUK, School of Education, Boston University, Boston, Massachusetts

EDWARD M. ORNITZ, The Center for the Health Sciences, University of California at Los Angeles, Los Angeles, California

HERBERT L. PICK, JR., Institute of Child Development, University of Minnesota, Minneapolis, Minnesota

ROBERT J. REICHLER, Department of Psychiatry, School of Medicine, University of North Carolina at Chapel Hill, Chapel Hill, North Carolina

MARK R. ROSENZWEIG, Department of Psychology, University of California at Berkeley, Berkeley, California

ERIC SCHOPLER, Department of Psychiatry, School of Medicine, University of North Carolina at Chapel Hill, Chapel Hill, North Carolina

LAURA SCHREIBMAN, Department of Psychology, Claremont Men's College, Claremont, California

RONALD WIEGERINK, Developmental Disabilities Technical Assistance System, University of North Carolina at Chapel Hill, Chapel Hill, North Carolina

Preface

This book is based on the First International Leo Kanner Colloquium on Child Development, Deviations, and Treatment organized by the Child Research Project of Division TEACCH in the Department of Psychiatry of the University of North Carolina School of Medicine at Chapel Hill.

The purpose of the colloquium was to provide a forum for discussing some of the relationships between experimental research (including both biological processes and child development) and interventions for deviant behavior. The difficulties of interdisciplinary communication are well known. With the increase of specialized information and technical language, even understanding among investigators in the same area has become difficult. The researcher often stereotypes the clinician as being fuzzy-headed and intellectually undisciplined. Conversely, the clinician often caricatures the researcher as preoccupied with trivial or socially irrelevant issues.

We tried to identify areas of common interest and to clarify differences. Participants accepted the challenge to present an overview of the area of research or intervention in which each had demonstrated leadership.

The colloquium was divided into three sections: biological research, developmental research, and intervention models. The biological papers, some of which used animal subjects, while others used human autistic subjects, were reviewed and considered for application to intervention. The developmental papers focused on the socialization process in normal children with consideration of implications for maladjustment. Intervention models were reviewed with special interest given to their use of developmental knowledge.

The discussions of deviant development were focused on autism though not confined to it. What this disorder may lack in epidemiological significance is made up for by its representation of relatively unambiguous abnormal development. The clarity of autistic children's clinical features can be attributed, largely, to Leo Kanner's discovery of autism. It was to his pioneering work in child psychiatry that this meeting was dedicated.

To meet the purposes of the colloquium, the most knowledgeable people available in each area were invited to participate. Since several technical areas are included, considerable effort was made to edit all presentations for under-standing by a general audience, without impairing the intent of the authors. In some instances, technical language has been transformed into colloquial English. Where technical jargon was essential, the author was encouraged to provide some definition in ordinary language.

It is difficult for us to evaluate the extent to which the aims of the colloquium were met. It did suceed in bringing together, for the first time, experts from several areas of research and leaders in various intervention ap-proaches. The discussion sessions succeeded in pointing out some general integra-tive issues among the three areas. The decision was made to include only a brief summary of the main points from the discussion, and to confine this review to the issues related to the purposes of the colloquium. The more general integra-tive issues are reported in the three discussion chapters.

Any success in achieving the aims of the colloquium was due to the efforts of our illustrious contributors. The editors take full responsibility for having set so broad a task as to almost assure only incomplete realization of goals. Likewise, we may have missed some important areas of integration from the meeting's discussion. However, we believe the task of integrating related areas of knowledge is sufficiently important that even the partial approximation achieved will encourage the process to be refined and continued in the future.

Chapel Hill   Eric Schopler
January, 1976   Robert J. Reichler

Acknowledgments

We gratefully acknowledge the support of the National Institute of Mental Health for both the clinical work and research with autistic children conducted by the Child Research Project. Not only did grant #5R01 MH 15539 in part support this work; more importantly, the Institute provided continued interest in the relationship between research and application, which led to this colloquium.

Ms. Margie Bird of the Division TEACCH gave invaluable assistance in the arrangements for the meeting as did Ms. Edwina Bentz. Important editorial help was contributed by Ms. Anne Poole, Ms. Nancy Park, and Dr. David Park. Ms. Connie Brite contributed her patient assistance by typing and proofreading the many drafts required.

We are grateful to each member of our unusually competent staff, who maintained the operation of our clinical program during our preoccupation with this volume and also made important contributions to our conceptualizations. Finally, we are indebted to our autistic children and their parents who taught us much of what we know, and whose constant challenge stimulated this colloquium. It is our hope that they will be the ultimate beneficiaries of this effort.

Contents

Part II
Developmental: Development of Social Behavior and Deviations

Introduction

STELLA CHESS

The mental health professional who works with children has to keep abreast of new research findings in child psychopathology. This is a difficult task because of the extraordinary complexity of even the infant's social, motor, visual, linguistic, and other functioning. As our understanding of these factors expands, it becomes more and more evident that we must know their orderly normative development if we are to deal with their pathological deviations.

We know that pathological development takes many diverse directions. This is just as true for normal development, which is the response of an organism with very different though limited capacities for expansion and refinement in response to specific environmental stimuli. Here, too, the range of normal environment is also quite varied for any sociocultural group, let alone different groups. The assessment of developmental patterns, therefore, also requires an identification of the normal as contrasted to the abnormal and stressful environment.

Vulnerability to stress also varies from one child to another. Some of these vulnerabilities represent variations within the normal range. The sensitivities to stress of other children are so extreme that they can adapt only to specific and limited environments. When these limits are sufficiently restricted, this in itself defines a significant abnormality of the organism.

The above general principles are simplistic as stated. It is in their exposition that the complexity of child psychopathology becomes evident. Thus, it is not enough to assemble a time-table of motor, visual, linguistic, and adaptive milestones for any population with their usual range of normal variability. Such milestones assume normal limb intactness, and the presence of hearing and

STELLA CHESS · Department of Psychiatry, New York University Medical Center, New York, New York 10016

1

eyesight. The phocomelic, deaf, or blind infant and child may not reach these milestones even in his intact functions, due to a crossover effect. For these children, it becomes necessary to use as reference points totally new sets of norms for each type of handicapped child, some of which have not as yet been determined.

There are ranges, in children with intact limbs and sensory organs, of normal auditory, visual, haptic, tactile, and olfactory capacities for increasingly subtle differentiations with age. The development of abilities to make such differentiations and to utilize intersensory discriminations depends very much on the life history of the individual and the nature of his environment. As a result, it is no simple matter to interpret the meaning of any single item of perceptual data and its significance for remedial programs.

Information regarding normal and abnormal biochemical functioning of children is now emerging. As has been true of most areas of investigation, data on adult functioning is considerably more advanced than is the case for children, where we are particularly concerned with the biochemical adaptive mechanisms at varying ages and what intrinsic and environmental factors might be responsible for developmental changes. Knowledge moves from adult definitions to the immature variations of children, and from gross metabolic and biochemical faults to the study of partial syndromes. We have barely begun to explore the question of behavioral concomitants of specific biochemical faults, their variability, and the pathways that explain their occurrence.

The identification of genetic bases for some behavioral pathologies has opened still another rapidly expanding field of knowledge in child psychopathology. Genetic faults that result in morphological, metabolic, and/or sexual deviations have a high probability of resulting in mental retardation. Other behavioral deviations have also been implicated, although great variability occurs due to the reinforcement or buffering action of the final chromosomal mix and the presence or absence of potentiating factors in the child's environment. The clinician must be able to identify indications for a genetic study that, even if not providing therapy for the afflicted child, may point to the need for genetic counseling.

The complexities of understanding the child organism itself are matched by those issues that arise in the study of the rules of social behaviors and the demands they make on the child at one age period after another. Whether the society involved is that of peers—infant, preschooler, school age, adolescent—or parents, or educational setting, or the wider authorities, there are rules of adaptation that hold sway. Understanding these demands and the societies to which the child has been exposed in his lifetime is still another essential element in determining whether a child's behavior is in itself normal or pathological, and in devising useful intervention for troubled and/or troublesome behavior.

Criteria of normality in child behaviors have been derived for the most part from the middle class. At the same time, there is a growing body of data dealing with the adaptive behaviors of children of lower socioeconomic families. These studies have dealt in part with the essential distinction between healthy adaptations to a given life style as opposed to the behavioral consequences of stressful events. Chronic malnutrition, racial prejudice, educational inadequacy, and poor medical care will all have adverse potentialities behaviorally. On the other hand, linguistic patterns, styles of person-oriented rather than task-oriented functioning, attentional habits, and meaning of certain conventions of social relatedness may be merely different from middle-class expectancies without being intrinsically either better or worse. To competently diagnose and treat child psychopathology, the middle-class clinician must be well versed in making such distinctions.

Cognitive and linguistic developmental issues are involved in all of the above, sometimes closely linked with each other as in retardation, but not infrequently showing diverse and seemingly unrelated developmental rates. These developmental graphs, and the points at which they approach or diverge, in fact the total pattern of interrelatedness may often be the key to identification of the syndrome of psychopathological development. The wealth of studies and discussions of basic issues in linguistics and cognition by research workers in these fields makes it increasingly possible for us to identify and analyze deviant patterns of language and thinking in individual children.

The above survey of the various issues in child psychopathology, even though incomplete, indicates the scope and range of scientific approaches that are relevant. The Kanner Colloquium, whose papers are collected in this volume, was an attempt to bring these different but interrelated bodies of knowledge together.

In his introduction to this conference that bears his name, Leo Kanner stated his own devotion to the study of the living, breathing child as the starting point for any examination of his pathology. Repeatedly in this introductory statement, as in his own lifetime style of work, Dr. Kanner points out that discussion that seeks mainly to prove or disprove a specific theoretical approach without constantly returning to the child himself will do little to help him.

The number and type of questions placed before the participants in the Kanner Colloquium do indeed indicate that we were gathered for the purpose of examining a diversity of ways of adding new insights on children's malfunctioning. These were presented by individuals, each of whom has studied his area in depth. The mandate was to present one's own researches and experience as clearly as possible for the benefit of the other participants so that all might meaningfully consider its validity and implications. As a consequence, this collection of papers will be of use to a reader who wishes to gain a view of the current state of knowledge regarding child psychopathology. Thus, the papers include consideration of residential care of normal babies, biochemical adaptive mechanisms and interventions, and considerations of language development and of perceptual development and interventions. Autistic children's capacities and deviances were examined, as were the possibilities of utilizing their environments to enhance positive development. The influence of the environment on different children was considered in terms of socialization of individuals, of peer groups, and through planned behavior modification techniques.

Thus, the ideas explored covered a very wide range and provided an experience of cross-fertilization of ideas that was both gratifying and challenging. It is very comfortable to get into a groove of familiar concepts and dig deeper in the company of one's peers, yet it brings in some ways a greater need to explore new areas of investigation and see that these concepts may fill gaps or explain pathologies quite as well as those with which we have come to be familiar. Vistas of explanation for some as yet unanswered questions can be imagined. On the other hand, skepticism was also very much present in the conference sessions, as contradictory theoretical concepts were considered.

It is an interesting phenomenon that new approaches are usually subjected to more rigorous scrutiny, requiring more precise methodology and explanations of greater precision than standard accepted theoretical positions. While this is reasonable as far as a scientific standard for the introduction of new ideas is concerned, such an exchange of ideas brings to one's awareness the fact that the same standards for exposition should be extended to ideas with which we are more familiar. Such equalizing of demand on new and old concepts, the arguing of opposing logics, and the indices of applicability of presented data to the clinical facts are enhanced by the face-to-face exposure of divergent patterns of thought. At the very least, it will enable us to read and think about papers in heretofore poorly understood areas with better understanding so that the possibility of rational understanding, exploration, agreement, and/or disagreement now exists. More important, one can now keep abreast of developments in such areas. Even if the surface is only skimmed, one is still better able now to fulfill the responsibility of knowing these new areas of research.

The dilemma between the dangers of premature application of insufficiently tested clinical interventions because of oversell of a useless or even harmful approach, and the overlong withholding of genuinely useful therapies is a constant issue that has no simple solution. Desperate parents with children whose chronic behavioral disabilities interfere with meaningful interpersonal development for the youngsters and disruption of family living for sibs and the parents themselves grasp eagerly at each new treatment advocated. Statements of caution in accepting an incompletely validated treatment program are hardly comforting. New approaches that hold promise can be tried; it is said, What is the loss? Sometimes there is no loss—simply disappointment. On the other hand, the new procedure may involve considerable diversion of funds and energies for little or no improvement. At times the child's status may in fact be worsened. However, the balance between careful assessment of new approaches—their solidity of theoretical base, the balancing of benefit against side reaction, whether pharmacological or emotional—must be done with care. Having worked this out on a large-scale basis, there will always remain the identical questions to be answered for the individual case. Occasionally a true breakthrough is treated with undeserved scientific scorn. More often the reverse is true: A technique is blown up by premature exposure and applied before adequate exploration. The jump between an idea worth exploring and an elaborate treatment technique can be made with undue rapidity with, at times, disastrous consequences. The dedication of a scientific community to open discussion of new concepts will do much to increase the probabilities that important ideas will be given adequate exposure and subjected to productive discussions that may illuminate serious inadequacies or highlight directions of further useful exploration.

For those participants in such discussions who are involved in clinical situations, the mandate to keep abreast is most demanding. The sophisticated parent will inquire about a new drug or other healing regimen he has heard about. While others may not challenge his awareness of publicized reports, the clinician has a responsibility to see to it that his patients have available a reasonable range of the therapeutic modalities that may be appropriate to their particular needs, without an undue time lag between indications of the value of new developments and their clinical application.

Certain research questions must be separated from the immediate issue of provision of service. Questions of whether certain biochemical correlates of syndromes of behavioral deviation are specific to these syndromes or have more general implications are many steps away from a clinical application of the data. It is of the utmost importance in such investigations to permit the identification and careful examination of the in-between steps. Other research questions are associated with delivery of service by their very nature. To take one example, studies of perceptual norms and their variability immediately raise such questions as the following: (a) Are deviations in ability simply normative variability that ought to be taken into account in programs for teaching normal children? (b) Are the variabilities the results of differences in prior experience and training and not of perceptual disability, thus requiring an educational plan based on this judgment? (c) In those cases where there is difficulty in making visual, auditory, or other perceptual distinctions, to what extent are remedial measures best directed toward training the weakness, and to what extent is it best to teach basic learning through the child's intact and usable abilities? (d) Which training procedures are in fact useful? For example, should one train through the activities to be learned such as reading and writing itself, or is it better to train eyes, hands, and ears through exercises not directly related to reading and writing? These types of questions can only be answered through services that are assessed and evaluated in a controlled manner.

There are still other research questions that do not require a direct link to service, but nevertheless the children being studied require special programs of care and treatment. Having defined these special needs in the course of the research, the researchers are in fact in a better position to explain and advocate the necessary programs than some other service agency. To fulfill this function, it becomes necessary to plan for these service issues from the beginning of the research project. Otherwise, both research and service are short-changed by virtue of insufficient funding, insufficient and wrong personnel, and a feeling that the research and service demands are in conflict with each other. On the other hand, if service is planned into the research design, it often illuminates pertinent issues and adds to the value of the data.

The interdependence of research and clinical service has been a highlight of the work of Dr. Leo Kanner himself throughout his lifetime. His dedication to both also helped to make him the great teacher who has inspired so many students.

The dry statistics of his official biography—his publications and teaching posts—fail to include the details that explain this man's greatness. Those of us who are familiar with his work know his mind and thought to be free and independent, and though superbly disciplined, never pedestrian. As a result of his World War I experiences in the Austrian army, he developed an abhorrence of the military mind, an abhorrence that has expressed itself not only in his concern for the individual, but also in his refusal to wear a uniform of *any* kind, either real or symbolic. As a result of this strong personal conviction, he has declined to march in an academic procession, or to participate in any kind of the lock-step rituals of our society. There has been a price, though, for such liberated thinking. Together with so many of our other distinguished citizens, he found that he had been elected to Senator Joseph McCarthy's dubious honor roll.

One interesting footnote to this man's career may serve to demonstrate his refusal to be fettered in his work and thought. Although Dr. Kanner has been continuously engaged in research for over fifty years (since 1924), he has never, to use his own words, "grunted for grants." He has never applied for a grant! He states that if anyone had been able to prove to him that he could have done better work with a grant, he would have applied. In our scientific community of grantmanship (and I speak as one who has written *many* a grant proposal), such an attitude is the epitome of the rebel—or should we say, free spirit?

It is indeed a humbling experience to introduce a man of Leo Kanner's moral and intellectual stature. When we remember that it is only recently that we have begun to see in our society any general acceptance of understanding of the emotionally disturbed child, that even ten years ago to speak publicly of psychosis in childhood was to violate the sancity of the nursery, it becomes all the more important to recognize the vision and endeavor of Leo Kanner, a dedicated researcher who has devoted half a century to the understanding of deviant child development.

Historical Perspective
on Developmental Deviations

LEO KANNER

Almost invariably, people devoting the major part of their professional lives to some specific offshoot of science have been known to round up their careers by looking back to the origins, sproutings, and ramifications of such offshoots. They find themselves fascinated by the historical aspects of something that they had experienced as an ongoing contemporaneous concern. This cannot be done without a degree of biographic self-involvement. Haunting questions arise: What was the shape of things when my generation came of age? What has been done since then? Can it be said that, as a result, we have arrived at some resting points of satisfaction? If so, what are they? What can be put down by now as reliable underpinnings to support a solid edifice? What, indeed, can be gleaned from retrospect?

Johann Wolfgang von Goethe, whose portrait hangs over my desk next to that of Adolf Meyer, comes to the rescue. Embedded in his treatise on mineralogy and geology is the following statement: "The history of science is science itself, the history of the individual is the individual." There is much wisdom in this aphorism, which has more depth than may appear at first glance. There is, of course, no scientific enterprise that does not have its own dynamic background, just as there is no individual who, like the *deus ex machina* of ancient drama, pops up suddenly without a developmental past of his own. The juxtaposition of science and individual is a realistic reminder of the interdependence of the two; it tends to put aside the age-old "Which came first?" controversy, which no historian thus far has been able to settle to anybody's satisfaction.

LEO KANNER · Department of Child Psychiatry, The Johns Hopkins University, Baltimore, Maryland 21218.

This must be kept in mind in an attempt to gain a clear historical perspective on developmental deviations. There would be no new trails without assiduous trailblazers and there can be no blazing without anteceding events guiding the blazers to prospective trails.

How far back do we have to go to discover the earliest traces of scientific curiosity about child development? It would hardly be astonishing news to professionals that it takes but a few short steps to trace the embryonic state, nascency, and infancy of such interest. Three centuries ago the concept itself was not even a gleam in anybody's eye. There were no trails and no blazers. The circumstances were not ready for either; they could not be ready at a time when the notion of behavior was dominated by the postulate of a bipartition of man into body and soul. When the prevailing theocracies persisted in claiming for themselves the supreme sovereignty over the soul, some philosophers sought to liberate it by changing it into a "vital force," still maintaining the division into a somatic constituent and something different, more or less imponderable. Thus we have a dualism, in which the one component may be studied with regard to its morphology, physiology, and structural peculiarities, and the other can be reached through speculation and dialectics only.

Along with the Renaissance came a tendency toward the unification of man. But the resulting monistic doctrines fell mostly into the extremes of annihilating either "matter" or "mind." On the one hand, "matter" was reduced to particles of "mind-stuff" or "an incidental aspect of reality in our sensation." On the other hand, consciousness was declared to be nonexistent or emanating from the brain in the same sense as the squeaking noise made by the axle of an insufficiently greased cartwheel. Some thinkers preached a compromise, dubbed "psychophysical parallelism," which assumed a coincidental running together of a mental and physical aspect.

What does all this have to do with the study of child development and its variants? It is evident that we can expect little practical benefit from trying to decode a detachable soul, a vital force, or a physical or mental aspect. The adherents of the various doctrines did not bother to ask what sort of evolution, if any, the soul or the aspect undergoes before the person in whom it dwells has reached maturity. This kind of setting did not lend itself to the idea of personality development; abstractions were meant to take care of the individual, instead of being derived from the summation of experiences with observed individuals.

According to an anecdote about the birth of objective science, a council of medieval savants was debating about the number of a horse's teeth. Some tried to find an answer by computing the equine references in the Bible, some by counting the words in the sentence in which a horse is mentioned in Genesis for the first time. Other theories were brought up until there was confusion and quarreling. Just then a lowly janitor, who rushed in to find out what the argument was about, informed them humbly that there was a stable nearby and suggested that the learned gentlemen go there and count for themselves. This they did, and an uncontroversial fact was added to man's treasury of knowledge.

For a long time, it did not seem to occur to the philosophers that very close to the armchairs and desks of their thinking chambers fellow humans could be observed as feeling and behaving individuals. In their way of thinking, people were merely to be pondered and talked about but not to be seen or heard. To them, to paraphrase Gertrude Stein, a person was a person was a person was a person.

The first inkling that children differ among each other and that this has something to do with the way they develop came to some of the early pioneers in education. The barest rudiments can be traced to the Moravian bishop Jan Amos Komenský (or Comenius), who in several books, written in the turbulent days of the Thirty Years' War, advocated a *gradual* instruction in habits, diction, and grasp of the environment. Soon thereafter, in 1690, the British philosopher John Locke insisted that education should be based on "native instincts and capacities," and that it therefore was important to make a careful study of each child's equipment. In France, seventy-two years later, Jean Jacques Rousseau was probably the first writer to make a direct plea for the recording of children's progress from the time of birth onward. Rousseau initiated an era of more or less naïve, unsystematized jottings about the doings of the various authors' offspring during the early stages of growth. Most of these writing still carried a heavy ballast of reflections, some admixture of mysticism, and conclusions based on pious idealism rather than on factual data. But in the subsequent decades the attention of the diarists was focused increasingly on sober empiricism. Their notes were limited to data gathered from only one child or, at the most, from a small number of siblings, invariably the progeny of highly sophisticated people. A desire to expand the information led Stanley Hall in the 1880s to ask thousands of parents to fill out questionnaires on the actual observations of their children, and he presented the facts thus obtained in terms of percentage calculations.

Thus, following centuries of total neglect, a sudden spurt led to the seeding and sprouting of developmental psychology. Sporadic beginnings burgeoned into a wealth of activities in the last three decades of the nineteenth century. The groundwork was laid, questions were formulated, methods were worked out, and concerted efforts began to yield a few incontestable verities.

All this, of course, did not just happen in a cultural vacuum. It fitted in tightly with an overall stirring and rumbling in the ranks of Western civilization. There was a growing awareness of the harsh discrepancy between the preachments of brotherly love on the one hand and the practices of cruel inhumanity on the other. An unprecedented change began to assert itself with regard to the role of the individual in society. The regimented subjects of feudal lords, the helpless pawns of ecclesiastic and laic autocracy found spokesmen who encouraged them to view themselves as citizens entitled to respect and self-respect. True liberalism became a popular movement fostered by the satires of Voltaire and Montesquieu, the serious expositions of the French encyclopedists, and— wafted across the Atlantic Ocean—the ideas propagated by Jefferson and Paine.

As a result of these new sentiments, we encounter active sympathy for those human beings who until then had been neglected, sometimes treated with contempt, and often brutally oppressed. Voices were raised in England against the horrors of the slave trade in the colonies and the cruel treatment of prison inmates. Pereire, a refugee from Spain to France, demonstrated that deaf mutes could be taught to communicate with their fellow-men. In 1784 Haüy opened in Paris the first school for the education of the blind. Itard and Seguin developed methods that made it possible to reach children with severe mental retardation.

It takes time before new concepts are accepted by the public. So revolutionary was the idea of personal worth that it had a slow and laborious uphill struggle. It was supported by two major developments that were destined to alter the trend of Western society—the toleration of individual differences and the extension of equality to include the feminine gender.

In the past, man had been dealt with in the aggregate, as though the species were a homogeneous category. Philosophers discoursed summarily on the mind of man, his ways of thinking and perceiving, and his moral obligations. Physicians centered their interest on organs and diseases; the patient was viewed mainly as a pair of lungs and kidneys lying between two bedsheets. Educators limited their preoccupations to rigid curricula to be imposed on students without regard to personal aptitudes.

With the new gospel of individual worth came the acknowledgment of the heterogeneity of the members of any group. Being different ceased being regarded as a curse, a whim of mysterious forces, or a reason for ridicule. It rather came to be viewed as an invitation to scientific curiosity. The scientists stepped out of their monastic seclusion and went among the people. This led, among other things, to the study of the patterns of mental illness and to the concept of special education of children who could not conform to the regular curriculum. Breathtaking discoveries in the areas of pathology and bacteriology led to the idea of prevention of disease and brought a new dimension to medicine. Politically, too, there was ferment in the autocratic countries, culminating in the revolts of the masses in the year 1848.

Society had changed, indeed. But, after two steps forward, it had to take a step backward. "Kautsky's law" asserted itself. The ambivalences came to the fore in the form of reactionary obstacles. The revolts of 1848 were suppressed. Children were still chattel; the story of Oliver Twist was fiction based on stark reality. Unrestricted child labor sucked health and spirit out of impecunious youngsters. The Prussian police closed Froebel's kindergartens, which were denounced as hotbeds of atheism and socialism.

Nevertheless, things were no longer the same. The spirit of freedom, once aroused, could not be squelched by bayonets. One of the two forward steps could not be pushed back, and the urge for further progress went on.

A substantial portion of humanity, treated as subordinate, made its claim for equality. In a society dominated by adult males, women had been relegated to the triad of "children, kitchen, and church." When the first cautious attempts were made to challenge this premise, Möbius, a renowned German neurologist, issued a battle cry against the new trend in the book entitled *The Physiological Weak-Mindedness of Women.*

On the forefront of the feminine struggle for equality stood the Swedish sociologist, Ellen Key. By the turn of the century, she felt that women were well on the way toward this goal. The more secure among the males, having no cause to be jittery about their status, were in favor of opening to women the doors of the halls of learning and to remunerative occupations. The story of Nora Helmer, dramatized forcefully in Ibsen's *A Doll's House,* resounded like a bombshell in Northern, Central, and Western Europe.

Ellen Key, heartened by these developments, foresaw a further area of progress in man's relations to man. In a book published in 1900 she predicted that the twentieth century was destined to be "the century of the child." Her prophecy was proved to be correct.

A new scenario was in the making. The stage was set. The props were being installed. The cast began to line up for rehearsals. In about a hundred years circumstances had arisen that made it possible to press toward enactment. The child was the central *dramatis persona* of the plot. The medical academicians at first grudgingly, then condescendingly, and finally with conviction accepted pediatrics as a bona fide speciality. Education had become a governmental concern when provisions for school attendance were recognized as a legislated public responsibility. Wundt's introduction of experimentation as a method of psychological inquiry invited an extension of Stanley Hall's round robin. For the first time in history, Binet and Simon, by letting live children come unto them, devised a tool for measuring the heterogeneity of human beings, at least so far as adaptation to established curricular requirements was concerned; the first draft was published in 1905.

That psychiatry has so far not been mentioned is not an intended oversight. Psychiatrists had limited their attention to the extremes of mental aberration, mostly in intramural settings. Pinel's insistence on removing the shackles and strait-jackets from some of the inmates was an innovation that startled his contemporaries around the time of the French Revolution. "Insanity" was seen as a unitary affliction that "came upon" a person, never mind whence or how. Eventually, some specific syndromes were lifted out of the nondescript jungle of insanity. Kraepelin, in his monumental work published in 1894, did a systematic job of describing, itemizing, and classifying different patterns of mental illness.

The great significance of his accomplishments is in no way minimized by the fact that in all four volumes of his opus there is hardly any mention of problems presented by children. Children just were not then an object of psychiatric curiosity.

Henry Maudsley may well be regarded as the first psychiatrist who paid serious attention to childhood psychoses at a time when most of his colleagues emphatically denied their existence. In 1867, in his *Pathology of Mind,* he included a thirty-four-page chapter on "Insanity of Early Life." In it he attempted to correlate symptoms with the patient's developmental status at the time of onset and suggested an elaborate classification. He was so severely criticized that in the second edition of his book (1880) he found it necessary to preface the chapter with an explanatory, rather apologetic-sounding paragraph.

In this country, in his textbook published in 1889, Spitzka devoted considerable space to the mental illness of children, which he declared to be caused by heredity, fright, sudden temperature changes, or masturbation. In the subsequent two decades the number of case reports on children in psychiatric periodicals increased perceptibly. Four textbooks appeared that dealt exclusively with the subject—one in Germany (1887), two in France (1888, 1889), and one in the United Kingdom (1898).

One might think that thus the door, barely ajar, was opened widely to children by the psychiatrists of the day. The educators, who had to deal daily and directly with problematic youngsters, thought so too. They looked to the "experts" for enlightened guidance. When none was forthcoming, they decided to go it alone. They originated the movement of *Heilpädagogik* (remedial education) in Central Europe under the leadership of Theodor Heller, a Viennese teacher whose name is familiar as the man who in 1908 first described dementia infantilis, commonly known as Heller's disease.

Here I must point out that until then the psychiatrists had shown little concern about a major segment of developmental variations that for sometime had captivated the attention of the public. I refer to the forms of defective, fragmentary, or lagging development subsumed under the heading of "amentia," "feeblemindedness," or nowadays more mellifluously as "mental retardation." Itard's efforts with the "savage boy of Aveyron," regarded as doomed to failure by the eminent Pinel, were applauded by the French Academy of Science "because he was capable of furnishing science with new data, the knowledge of which can but be extremely useful to all persons engaged in the teaching of youth." The very first institution for the treatment and education of severely defective children was opened in 1841 on the Abendberg near Interlaken in Switzerland by young Jean-Louis Guggenbühl, who wished to do something about the deplorable status of endemic cretinism in the valleys of the Alps. Its fame spread throughout the Western world. Statesmen, physicians, writers, and philanthropists came to see, learn, and start similar enterprises in their own countries. Samuel Gridley Howe, founder of the Perkins Institute for the Blind and the husband of abolitionist Julia Ward, was one of the pilgrims. On his return to Boston in 1848, Howe succeeded in persuading the legislature of the Commonwealth of Massachusetts to allot twenty-five hundred dollars annually for three years for the training of idiotic children. This was the nucleus of the first American publicly supported institution for intellectually handicapped children, whose care, study, and rearing became the domain of a separate civic-minded group that had little contact with, and little inspiration from, academic psychiatry. They had their own spokesmen, their own periodicals, their own textbooks, their own meetings.

It was not until the turn of the century that psychiatrists became aware of children as a part of their professional responsibility. This, in a rather circuitous way, was accomplished by two trailblazers: Adolf Meyer in this country and Sigmund Freud abroad. Though guided by different premises, both could show that many of their adult patients' symptoms did not just happen as if they had come unheralded from a clear sky, and were not merely partial ingredients of a duly catalogued disease but were rooted in the life histories of the patients themselves. Thus, an appetite was whetted for the study of the onset and course of behavioral difficulties. As a result, mental illness came to be evaluated as the culmination of problems that had been developing within a patient as his individual reaction to his particular life situation. The logical next step was a desire not just to wait until something happens and then to look back to probable beginnings, but to try to recognize and deal with the beginnings right then and there.

Circumstances thus rendered inevitable the start of a movement that urged psychiatric convergence on children. The time was ripe for a new way of reasoning: If we get to know the elements that make for psychopathology, we might learn how to remedy them at the earliest possible time—"nip them in the bud," so to speak. This novel idea of prophylaxis found concrete expression in the foundation in 1909 of the National Committee for Mental Hygiene by a young law school graduate, Clifford Beers, with the blessings of leading American psychiatrists, psychologists, and educators. It did not take long for the movement to spread throughout the Western world. Its slogan was the prevention of insanity and delinquency.

The coming decade witnessed a number of innovations, directed mainly against the plight of children who were glaringly neglected, brutally mistreated, conspicuously handicapped, obviously misbehaving. Special education, juvenile court probation, and supervised foster homes became established features of the culture.

In 1921 Douglas Thom opened in Boston an ambulatory station to which parents, teachers, and social agencies could refer for treatment children who presented problems of behavior. It proved so successful that in 1922 the

Commonwealth Fund set up similar units, called Demonstration Child Guidance Clinics, in several communities that, if satisfied, would take over the administrative and financial responsibilities. These clinics deserve credit for three major innovations:

1. They introduced the concept and practice of collaboration of disciplines, which previously had barely more than a nodding acquaintance with each other; though this was initially limited to the so-called team of psychiatrists, psychologists, and social workers, a point was consequently reached when the work was also shared with pediatricians, neurologists, educators, jurists, public health workers, and everyone else who could lend a hand in rehabilitation.

2. They opened their doors to any child whose behavior puzzled, worried, or annoyed parents and teachers. A child was treated not with the dreaded projection onto future calamity, but with a feeling that unwell children deserve treatment of what bothers them because it bothers them *now*.

3. They embarked on a study of a set of agents responsible for health not until then given its proper regard in medical formulations. While knowledge of chemical, mechanical, thermal, and bacterial agents was seen rightly as an intrinsic part of training and practice, the clinics also examined the impact of attitudinal agents, the influences that attitudes of adults exerted on a child's emotional development. Previously, child study had been restricted to factors of internal organization, matters of perception, intellectual endowment, inherent instincts, and bodily configuration. Thanks to the clinics, interpersonal relationships, with all their varieties and complexities, became a significant feature in the evaluation of health and its deviations.

Since these clinics were essentially community oriented, they were for the most part remote from medical centers. In 1930 a children's psychiatric service was opened at the pediatric department of the Johns Hopkins Hospital and many such units are now in existence in this country and abroad. Residential treatment centers have been established for children in need of twenty-four-hour-a-day care. Facilities have been extended to the very young in day-care centers and in therapeutic nursery schools.

As I look back to the days when I began my professional career just about a half century ago, I discern the bare rudiments of some of these innovations and realize that some had not then begun to exist even in the nascent state.

Is one who has lived through these remarkable changes and has actively participated in some of them entitled to sit back in a spirit of jubilation? Would it be wise to say glowingly, Just look how much further we got in so short a time. Behold! Child psychiatry, nonexistent a few decades ago, has emerged from its neonatal stage when nobody was certain about its legitimate parentage. I recall the 1930 White House Conference on Child Health and Protection, at which psychiatrists and pediatricians had vociferous squabbles about who should adopt the infant and be responsible for sheltering it. In fact, it was even nameless. It was not until May 19, 1933, that at a meeting of the Swiss Psychiatric Society one of the trailblazers, Maurice Tramer, advocated the name *Kinderpsychiatrie,* the German equivalent of child psychiatry, to serve as a designation for a scientific discipline that had reached a point where it could stand on its own feet and work out its own, sufficiently delineated areas of research, therapy, prevention, and teaching. In 1935, I made the name popular in the United States when I chose it for the title of my textbook. In 1937, when the French pioneer Heuyer called together the first International Congress in Paris, he suggested the analogous term *psychiatrie infantile,* which was accepted, but only after considerable debate. Child psychiatry is now an accepted feature of the social scene. Clinical empiricism and an increasing mass of experimentation have produced many significant insights. We are still far removed from knowing all the answers but we do know some and, what is equally important, we know how to ask pertinent questions for further research and for further therapeutic and preventive amelioration.

But there is still a danger of smug contentment with that which has been achieved. It is not too difficult to perceive the direction of dissatisfactions and challenges as guides to further progress and to the avoidance of entrenchment and stagnation. I should like to spell out the most obvious pitfalls besides that of unquestioning adherence to the status quo:

1. Child psychiatry has started out as a number of clusters of building stones, each at first removed from the others in none-too-splendid isolation. Eventually all these clusters were put together and used to erect a unified edifice under its own roof. On the whole, the battles between the different "schools," each claiming what Dr. Meyer has referred to as "exclusive salvation," have become less heated. Nevertheless, we still have different "orientations," and those who have been exposed to more than one of them know how confusing this can be.

2. It is the job of child psychiatry to help children who are in need. It is not its primary job to prove or disprove this or that theory. There is still too much method-centered instead of patient-centered child psychiatry. I am rather impatient with the notion that there are different "approaches." We do not approach a child; it is he who approaches us with his specific problems and his need for help. I am aware of the contempt in which the idea of common sense is held by the more obsessive adherents of some of the so-called approaches. I remember the time when, in the discussion of a talk I once gave to a group of ultra-sophisticated matrons, a lady asked indignantly, "Do you mean to say that we should go back to common sense?" I replied, "No, ma'am, I mean to say that we should go *forward* with common sense"—informed and experienced common sense, that is.

3. The progress of child psychiatry depends heavily on the progress of all spheres of society. It owes its very existence to advances in the attitudes of man

toward his fellow-man in the past two centuries. Sympathy and empathy are—and should be—the primary motivation of its practitioners and collaborators. This should be stressed more in the education of those who wish to enter the profession. What good is indoctrination that in more or less solemn lectures and seminars feeds to the novices theories and clichés to be accepted at face value and repeated parrotlike on examinations without kindling the warmth of compassion and friendliness?

The study of the natural history of human development, its deviations, and treatment is a ramified, objective, pluralistic, relativistic, and melioristic science. In its present state, and hopefully in the future, such study will be what I like to call a science dunked in the milk of human kindness.

SELECTED LIST OF THE AUTHOR'S PUBLICATIONS DEALING WITH THE HISTORY OF CHILD PSYCHIATRY

1933 The significance of a pluralistic attitude in the study of human behavior. *Journal of Abnormal and Social Psychology, 28,* 30–41.

1944 The origin and growth of child psychiatry. *American Journal of Psychiatry (Centennial Anniversary Issue), 100,* 139–143.

1950 Adolf Meyer: In memoriam. *Quarterly Journal of Child Behavior, 2,* 348–349.

1952 Critical evaluation of the present state of child psychiatry. *American Journal of Psychiatry, 108,* 490–492.

1954 August Homburger: Pioneer in child psychiatry. *American Journal of Psychiatry, 112,* 146–148.

1954 A matter of historical perspective. *American Journal of Psychiatry, 11,* 387–388.

1955 The status of historical perspective in psychiatric instruction. *Bulletin of the History of Medicine, 29,* 326–336.

1958 History and present status of childhood schizophrenia in the U.S.A. *Acta Paedopsychiatrica, 15,* 138–149.

1958 Trends in child psychiatry (The 33rd Maudsley Lecture). *Journal of Mental Science, 105,* 581–593.

1958 Centripetal forces in personality development (The 7th Karen Horney Lecture). *American Journal of Psychoanalysis, 19,* 123–133.

1960 Jean-Louis Guggenbühl und der Abendberg. *Bulletin of the History of Medicine, 33,* 489–502.

1960 Itard, Seguin, Howe—three pioneers in the education of retarded children. *American Journal of Mental Deficiency, 65,* 2–10.

1960 Child psychiatry—retrospect and prospect. *American Journal of Psychiatry, 117,* 15–22.

1960 Arnold Gesell's place in the history of developmental psychology and psychiatry. *Psychiatric Research Report, 13,* 1–9.

1962 American contributions to the development of child psychiatry (The Hutchings Memorial Lecture). *Psychiatric Quarterly* Supplement, Part 1, 1–12.

1962 An early mental deficiency periodical. *Bulletin of the History of Medicine, 36,* 532–534.

1963 A tribute to Maurice Tramer. *Acta Paedopsychiatrica, 30,* 281–284.

1964 *A History of the Care and Study of the Mentally Retarded.* Springfield, Ill.: Charles C Thomas.

1964 The future of child psychiatry. In D. A. van Krevelen (ed.), *Child psychiatry and prevention.* Huber, Bern.

1967 Child psychiatry in the framework of Western civilization. *Acta Paedopsychiatrica, 34,* 1–34.

1967 Medicine in the history of mental retardation. *American Journal of Mental Deficiency, 72,* 165–170.

1967 History of child psychiatry. In A. M. Freedman and H. I. Kaplan (Eds.), *Comprehensive textbook of psychiatry.* Baltimire: Williams and Wilkins. Pp. 1313–1315.

1969 The removal of national barriers in child psychiatry. *Acta Paedopsychiatrica, 36,* 313–317.

1971 Childhood psychosis: a historical overview. *Journal of Autism and Childhood Schizophrenia, 1,* 14–19.

1971 Approaches: retrospect and prospect. *Journal of Autism and Childhood Schizophrenia, 1,* 453–459.

Part I
Biological: Normal Development
and Deviations

1

Neurobiological Mechanisms of Adaptation in Relation to Models of Psychobiological Development

ARNOLD J. MANDELL

Once defined by anatomical features or electrical activity, neural systems in the brain can now be discriminated by neurochemical techniques. The neurons in each system synthesize and release or store specific chemicals to excite subsequent cells in their respective pathways. For several years my colleagues and I (and others in other laboratories) have been studying a number of macromolecular adaptive changes affecting the function of adrenergic and serotonergic transmission in the brain. In the former, norepinephrine is thought to be related to states of arousal, attention, and perhaps to mood; in the latter, serotonin has been implicated in involuntary vascular functions, emotional memory, and moods of sexuality and rage.

Like the changes involved with nutritional processes in the liver, adaptations in the central nervous system appear to be organized to return its function to normal in response to perturbations: they can be induced by drugs, nutritional loads, or radical environmental alterations. The particular neurochemical changes and the extent of their effects are functions of many variables, including the genetic strain of the experimental animals. In young adult rats, induced changes manifest various latencies (from minutes to weeks) and various durations (from hours to months). They can involve various parts of the neurons,

ARNOLD J. MANDELL · Department of Psychiatry, School of Medicine, University of California, San Diego, La Jolla, California 92037.

from the apparatus for protein synthesis in the cell bodies to the synthesis, storage, and release of transmitter in the nerve ending, and even to the receptor function.

Adaptive neurochemical changes can be related to emerging knowledge about the mechanisms of regulation in mature animals versus those in developing organisms. It appears that, at least in some systems, an adult organism manifests situation-bound, transient adaptive changes. It is as though a mature organism has the capacity to maintain its baseline state in response to the realities of the environment. Deviation from the usual conditions of that external or internal environment are responded to as unusual and temporary, and reversible mechanisms are invoked. When the inciting source of irregularity is removed, the half-life of the adaptive macromolecular change is manifest by return to the baseline state.

In developing organisms, perturbation-induced changes appear to be more lasting. The unusual circumstance may be responded to as "reality," and the baseline state of the developing macromolecular mechanism could become a function of that distorted environment. If this happens, a return to normal environment would then be responded to as if it were a deviation from "reality." Subsequent adjustments to *that* reality might then be transient, with a return to what we could call a maladaptive baseline state. Before reviewing some neurobiological adaptive mechanisms that might be affected by perturbations during development, I will describe two experiments that dramatize the contrast between transient adaptive change in an adult neurotransmitter system and permanent adaptive change in a developing nervous system.

A good example of transient adaptation is the sequence of changes in the serotonergic system in the brains of adult rats that have been treated daily with lithium (Knapp and Mandell, 1973a). The lithium *initially* stimulates conversion of the amino acid tryptophan to the neurotransmitter serotonin in tissue samples prepared from regions of the brain in which serotonergic nerve endings predominate (Figure 1). We have shown that the stimulation results from the activation of a high affinity uptake system for tryptophan in those regions, i.e., one that functions in the presence of low concentrations of the substrate tryptophan. However, with *chronic* lithium treatment there appears to be a compensatory decrease in the specific activity of tryptophan hydroxylase, the presumed rate-limiting enzyme in the biosynthesis of serotonin, in regions of the brain in which serotonergic cell bodies predominate. We see this as either a decrease in the synthesis of the enzyme itself or (less likely) as an increase in the rate of hydrolysis of the protein molecules. The tryptophan hydroxylase molecules, their ranks depleted, move by slow axonal flow to the nerve endings. In our lithium experiments we observed decreased conversion of tryptophan to serotonin in the nerve endings about two weeks after initiation of daily lithium treatment. This decreased synthesis of transmitter *and* the maintained increase in

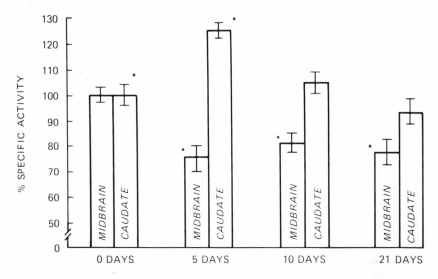

Figure 1. The effects of daily lithium treatment on rat midbrain tryptophan hydroxylase activity and striate synaptosomal conversion of tryptophan to serotonin, expressed as percent of control (0 days) specific activity ± SEM. There were 15 rats in each group. As early as 3 days (data not shown) after initiation of treatment, both enzyme and conversion activity changed significantly. By 10 days synaptosomal conversion activity had returned to control levels and remained there. The decrease in midbrain enzyme activity persisted throughout the experiment. * $p < 0.02$ (Mann–Whitney U test).

the relative velocity of the high affinity uptake of substrate combined, we think, to achieve a return to the baseline state of activity that had existed before treatment was begun. All the parameters returned to normal within two weeks after the cessation of daily lithium treatment.

We have shown, then, that an initial increment in serotonergic neurotransmission associated with a (lithium-induced) increase in the rate of substrate uptake was followed by a decrease in production of biosynthetic enzyme that resulted in decreased synthesis of transmitter, compensating for the original enhancement of transmission, and that when the incitement (the lithium) was removed the mechanisms returned to their usual level of function.

A comparable experiment involving a developing organism was conducted by Samuel Eiduson at UCLA (1969) with the chick embryo, with very different results. Eiduson's work was done before there was a good assay for tryptophan hydroxylase, and the measure of serotonergic biosynthetic capacity at that time was the level of serotonin in whole brain. Eiduson found that when 5-hydroxytryptophan was injected into the yoke sac of the chick embryo at a critical point in prenatal time, the initial embryonic increase in serotonin was followed by a postnatal decrease in levels of the transmitter, and the lowered level of serotonin remained into adulthood. Since Eiduson had ruled out factors relating to substrate supply and to the activity of other catalysts in the serotonergic pathway (hydroxytryptophan decarboxylase and monoamine oxidase), he deduced that the decrease in the amount or activity of tryptophan hydroxylase was permanent and probably irreversible.

A comparison of our lithium experiments with Eiduson's work with the chick embryo illustrates a difference between the adaptation of an adult and that of a developing organism. The distinction is reminiscent of the contrast between the permanent production of enzyme that can be induced in bacterial cultures and the transient production of enzyme inducible in adult mammalian hepatic tissue, for example.

The contrast between the net results of metabolic regulation in the developing versus the established system has incredibly broad implications for the clinical aspects of developmental neurobiology, particularly since the human nervous system emerges into the environment in such a primitive, immature state. The implications extend from the psychological state (reflected in blood hormones) and drug experience of the mother during pregnancy to the psychopharmacological and environmental experiences of the neonate and young child. The area of behavioral teratology is vast and virtually unexplored, and I would venture to guess that investigators from now disparate disciplines, e.g., neurochemistry and clinical psychology and psychiatry, will be moving toward one another across that distance with increasing rapidity over the next several years. More of the techniques and approaches that are yielding information about adaptive regulation need to be applied to the study of developing nervous systems.

I would like to offer some other examples of adaptive regulation in the brain of the young adult rat that might have the potential of permanency if they were invoked during critical developmental periods. In studying the responses to pharmacological or environmental stimuli made by adaptive mechanisms in one or another of the neurotransmitter systems, we see a constellation of neural processes that appear to act in concert to regulate those responses (Figure 2).

ALTERATIONS IN RECEPTOR FUNCTION

There are precedents for the assertion that central nervous tissue responds to denervation by becoming supersensitive, and David Segal and Mark Geyer in our laboratories have designed experiments that demonstrate this response in adrenergic pathways. They infused 6-hydroxydopamine, which is incorporated by catecholamine nerve endings and destroys them, to the brain ventricles of

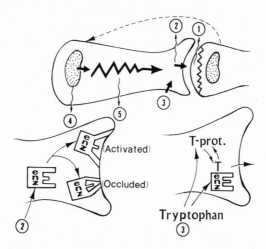

Figure 2. Adaptive mechanisms involved in the regulation of neurotransmitter synthesis and efficacy. (1) The receptors are thought to increase or decrease in sensitivity to infused neurotransmitter. (2) Enzymes in the nerve ending may be inhibited by occlusion or activated by alterations in physical conformation that can improve the quality of the molecular bond between the enzyme and a substrate (increase affinity), or improve the efficiency of the catalysis itself (increase the maximal velocity of the reaction). (3) Uptake is thought to involve a drug-sensitive mechanism, a storage pool, and a direct conversion pathway. (4) Nuclear enzyme synthesis or degradation is probably affected by intra- or interneuronal feedback communication. (5) Axoplasmic flow accounts for the latency of the appearance of increased or decreased enzyme at the nerve ending.

rats. Three weeks later they began chronic infusions of low volumes of the adrenergic transmitter norepinephrine. The response of the experimental rats to the norepinephrine was significantly greater than that of control animals, as reflected by spontaneous exploratory behavior. The increase seems to be due to functional supersensitivity of the catecholamine receptors. The presynaptic apparatus that removes active transmitter by taking it up again into the nerve endings was also destroyed by the 6-hydroxydopamine, so it was possible that the behavioral potentiation was caused by a loss of transmitter deactivation. To rule out that possibility, we infused catecholamines to the brains of rats that had received chronic treatment with alpha-methyltyrosine, which inhibits catecholamine synthesis by blocking the uptake of substrate and inhibiting the activity of the biosynthetic enzyme tyrosine hydroxylase. Again later response to infused transmitter was potentiated (Geyer and Segal, 1973). When the functions of central synapses are affected by drugs, and the normal interactions between biogenic amines that serve as transmitters and their receptors are impaired, the receptor function is capable of compensatory alterations in sensitivity.

ALTERATIONS IN ENZYME CONFORMATION AND ACTIVITY

By maintaining the integrity of the nerve endings during homogenization of tissue from the rat striatum, we have studied the rate of conversion of substrate to transmitter as a function of the physical state of tyrosine hydroxylase, the enzyme that is believed to limit the rate of catecholamine biosynthesis. When we examined the brains of rats to which we had administered methamphetamine, we found a progressive, dose-dependent shift in the subcellular distribution of tyrosine hydroxylase. The observable effect of 1 mg/kg lasted 4 hours; that of 5 mg/kg lasted 8 hours. A portion of the measurable tyrosine hydroxylase activity shifted from the supernatant (soluble) fraction to the pellet; there was no change in total measurable enzyme activity. Ronald Kuczenski has shown that the presence of the specific sulfated mucopolysaccharide heparin (mucopolysaccharides characteristically form part of cell membranes) can alter the conformation of tyrosine hydroxylase, thereby increasing its affinity for a nitrogenous cofactor and increasing the rate of the reaction (Kuczenski and Mandell, 1972a, 1972b). Membrane binding might have a similar effect on the rate at which the enzyme catalyzes the rate-limiting step in the synthesis of catecholamine transmitters. When heparin was added to the assay of synaptosomes, i.e., to the tissue in which the nerve endings were intact, the enzyme activity did not increase. Moreover, it appears that membrane binding might serve to decrease the activity of the enzyme by occluding it instead of activating it: By varying the ionic composition in media containing soluble tyrosine hydroxylase and membrane components, we have shown a decrease in enzymatic activity. The evidence tempts us to relate drug-inducible shifts in the physical state of the enzyme to increases or decreases in its activity. We do not know whether binding is regulatory or whether it might be the normal end state in a process by which soluble enzyme is transported down the axon that connects the cell body (where it is produced) to the terminal (where it functions).

ALTERATIONS IN SUBSTRATE UPTAKE

In the serotonergic neuropathways, we have found that morphine inhibits tryptophan hydroxylase activity in nerve endings without changing the rate at which the nerve endings take up the substrate tryptophan. However, a number of other drugs or treatments do alter tryptophan uptake into nerve endings (Knapp and Mandell, 1973b). Of the two systems that take tryptophan up into the nerve endings, the one with higher affinity for the substrate (requiring lower concentrations of tryptophan) is more sensitive to drugs. As I have already described, lithium appears to increase serotonin biosynthesis in synaptosomes from rat brain by stimulating the high affinity uptake of tryptophan. Cocaine, on the other hand, inhibits the high affinity uptake, thereby reducing the rate of conversion of tryptophan to serotonin (Knapp and Mandell, 1972a). The relationship between substrate uptake and conversion to transmitter in the serotonergic system is not precisely explicated. After 15 minutes of incubation in substrate and the disruption of synaptosomes, almost 90% of the radioactive tryptophan in our assay remained unconverted to transmitter. This suggests to us that there may be an intrasynaptosomal storage pool of substrate. We wonder if there is a tryptophan-binding protein in the synaptosomes for storage of substrate like that which has been demonstrated in bacteria (Wiley, 1970).

LONG-LATENCY ALTERATIONS IN ENZYME AMOUNT OR ACTIVITY

The mechanisms that appear to regulate neurotransmission in the brain are affected differentially by *chronic* versus *acute* administration of psychoactive drugs. When normal transmission is persistently perturbed by the chronic presence of a drug, the mechanisms apparently shift to counteract the effects of the initial administration. For example, we administered reserpine, a drug known to deplete catecholamines in the brain, to rats for nine days. By the ninth day, there was an increase in tyrosine hydroxylase activity in various areas of their brains (Segal, Sullivan, Kuczenski, and Mandell, 1971). The increase in brain enzyme was comparable to that induced by others with reserpine in the peripheral sympathetic system (Thoenen, Mueller, and Axelrod, 1969). Data from similar experiments indicate that the chronic administration of amphetamine and monoamine oxidase inhibitors decreases midbrain tyrosine hydroxylase activity. Again, in the serotonergic system we have demonstrated a delayed increase in the activity of the rate-limiting enzyme tryptophan hydroxylase in the chronic presence of morphine, which, upon being taken into the synaptosomes, inhibits the enzyme (Knapp and Mandell, 1972a). Immediately upon inhibition of serotonin biosynthesis in the nerve ending, there was an increase in cell body enzyme activity that was seen later at the nerve endings. These compensatory changes in tryptophan hydroxylase activity are directly opposite to those we observed with chronic administration of lithium.

We have come to believe that the reflexive alterations in enzyme levels may be consistent adaptations to chronic administration of drugs that alter synaptic function. Induced changes in neurotransmitter dynamics at the nerve ending probably alter enzyme activity by modifying the rate of enzyme synthesis under prompting by intra- or interneuronal communication of some sort. The cell body region of the biogenic amine system is first to manifest this adaptive change. The *amount* of enzyme seems to be involved because the alterations induced in the cell body regions are seen later in nerve-ending regions of the brain.

AXOPLASMIC FLOW OF ENZYMES

The consistent latency that we have observed between alterations in the enzyme activity in the cell body and those in nerve-ending regions suggests that the alteration moves to the nerve ending with the axoplasmic flow of either increased or decreased enzyme. Previous work on axoplasmic flow rate suggests that particulate enzyme moves with "fast flow" and soluble enzyme moves with "slow flow." In an effort to describe the flow rate of an enzyme, we have inhibited tryptophan hydroxylase with parachlorophenylalanine and followed the defective enzyme activity as it moves from the midbrain to the septum of the rat brain (Knapp and Mandell, 1972b). It appeared to leave the midbrain and arrive at the septum in appropriate temporal sequence; the rate was calculated as 1 to 2 mm per day, or "slow flow." We wonder if the latency to action of some psychotropic drugs and the time required for the development of tolerance and withdrawal to chronic addictive drugs might be functions of this inevitable delay. The delay between trauma and severe clinical response (loss leading to depression, for example) usually amounts to a few or several days ("until it sinks in").

As I have noted, these adaptive mechanisms are triggered not only by drugs and nutritional manipulations, but by environmental changes as well. Figure 3 graphs the effects of increasing periods of sensory isolation on rate-limiting transmitter biosynthetic enzymes in the brains of rats. There was an immediate and progressive increase in midbrain tyrosine hydroxylase activity and an immediate decline in septal tryptophan hydroxylase (as indicated by synaptosomal conversion of tryptophan to serotonin). The magnitude of these responses is comparable to that of reactions induced by acute or chronic treatment with relatively large doses of psychotropic agents (Segal *et al.,* 1973). Isolation has the same effect on regional brain tyrosine hydroxylase as the administration of agents that depress mood, such as reserpine (Segal *et al.,* 1971) or propranolol (Sullivan *et al.,* 1972). It is tempting to suggest that the psychopathology induced in infants by social isolation, first popularized by the work of Rene Spitz (1945, 1946) may have such a mechanism as a neurobiological substrate. Moreover, as suggested by studies of induced regulatory changes in a developing organism (Eiduson, 1969), such changes may become permanent.

A second aspect of neurobiological adaptation (other than the "temporary-permanent" dichotomy in regulatory changes during adulthood and infancy) has

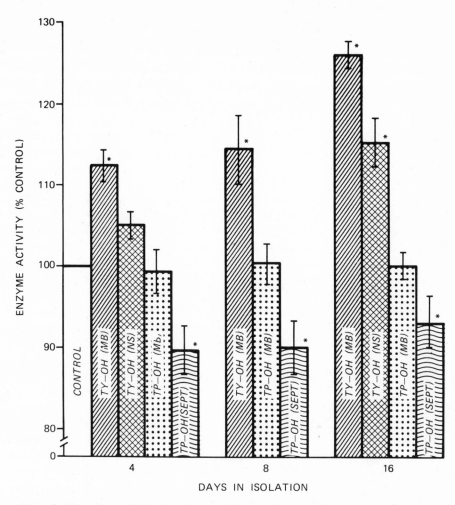

Figure 3. The effects of isolation of rats in individual, sound-attentuated, darkened chambers for 4, 8, or 16 days on midbrain (MB), neostriatal (NS), and septal (SEPT) tyrosine hydroxylase (TY-OH) and tryptophan hydroxylase (TP-OH) activities, expressed as percent of control specific activity ± SEM. There were at least 10 rats in each group. There was an immediate and progressive increase in midbrain TY-OH, a delayed increase in neostriatal TY-OH, and an immediate decrease in septal TP-OH. * $p < 0.05$ (Mann–Whitney U test).

implications for an understanding of developmental deformation, and is represented by the contrast between our work and that of Rosenzweig, presented in this volume. Measuring brain weight and cortical enzymes (e.g., acetylcholine esterase), Rosenzweig concludes that the development of the rat brain can be enhanced by enrichment of environmental stimuli. Our studies, in which we focus on subcortical neurotransmitter systems, would suggest that stimulation, or perhaps overstimulation, might lead to a compensatory *decrease* in the function of some enzymic systems in the brain.

There are at least two ways to resolve these differences as they relate to developmental implications. The first might be to consider the extent of the deviance of the experimental environments. Perhaps progressive sensory isolation and powerful drugs are not comparable to enriched "normal" environments. The two kinds of pathogenic environments that have been posited for unresponsive children (understimulation and overstimulation) seem more relevant to our examination of isolation versus chemical stimulation than they do to the more normative environments used in the experiments Rosenzweig reports. Another possibility is that cortical development might operate differently than subcortical functions development with regard to response to environment, i.e., the subcortical functions affecting mood and autonomic processes may require stability, and therefore they may manifest compensatory vigor beyond that required by cortical systems which subserve intellectual scanning, learning, and memory.

The general premise that what may be a permanent adjustment to environmental abnormality when experienced during development contrasts to the transient adjustments made in adulthood has intuitive validity for observers of children. It is hoped that some of our studies of neurobiological mechanisms of adaptation offer to the field a quantitative locus for this intuitive observation. Future work on developing versus adult organisms that incorporates definable and measurable parameters should provide much food for thought for developmental psychologists and psychiatrists.

REFERENCES

Eiduson, S. The developmental-biochemical approach in man. In A. J. Mandell and M. P. Mandell (Eds.), *Psychochemical research in man.* New York: Academic Press, 1969. Pp. 147–159.

Geyer, M., and Segal, S. Differential effects of reserpine and alpha-methyl-p-tyrosine on norepinephrine and dopamine induced behavioral activity. *Psychopharmacologia,* 1973, *29,* 131–140.

Knapp, S., and Mandell, A. J. Narcotic drugs: effects on the brain's serotonin biosynthetic systems. *Science,* 1972, *177,* 1209–1211. (a)

Knapp, S., and Mandell, A. J. Parachlorophenylalanine: its three phase sequence of interactions with the two forms of brain tryptophan hydroxylase. *Life Sciences,* 1972, *2(16),* 761–771. (b)

Knapp, S., and Mandell, A. J. Short- and long-term lithium administration: effects on the brain's serotonergic biosynthetic systems. *Science,* 1973, *180,* 645–647. (a)

Knapp, S., and Mandell, A. J. Some drug effects on the functions of the two physical forms of tryptophan-5-hydroxylase: influence on hydroxylation and uptake of substrate. In J.

Barchus and E. Usdin (Eds.), *Serotonin and Behavior.* New York: Academic Press, 1973, Pp. 61–71. (b)

Kuczenski, R., and Mandell, A. J. Allosteric activation of hypothalamic tyrosine hydroxylase by ions and sulfated mucopolysaccharides. *Journal of Neurochemistry,* 1972, *19,* 131–137. (a)

Kuczenski, R., and Mandell, A. J. Regulatory properties of soluble and particulate rat brain tyrosine hydroxylase. *Journal of Biological Chemistry,* 1972, *247,* 3114–3122. (b)

Segal, D. S., Sullivan, J. L., Kuczenski, R. T., and Mandell, A. J. Effects of long-term reserpine treatment on brain tyrosine hydroxylase and behavioral activity. *Science,* 1971, *173,* 847–849.

Segal, D. S., Knapp, S., Kuczenski, R. T., and Mandell, A. J. Effects of environmental isolation on behavioral and regional rat brain tyrosine hydroxylase and tryptophan hydroxylase activity. *Behavioral Biology,* 1973, *8,* 47–53.

Spitz, Rene. Hospitalism. An inquiry into the genesis of psychiatric conditions in early childhood. In A. Freud *et al.* (Eds.), *The psychoanalytic study of the child.* New York: International Universities Press, 1945, Pp. 53–74.

Spitz, Rene. Anaclitic depression. In A. Freud *et al.* (Eds.), The psychoanalytic study of the child. New York: International Universities Press, 1946. Pp. 313–342.

Sullivan, J. L., Segal, D. S., Kuczenski, R. T., and Mandell, A. J. Propranolol-induced rapid activation of rat striatal tyrosine hydroxylase concomitant with behavioral depression. *Biological Psychiatry,* 1972, *4,* 193–203.

Thoenen, H., Mueller, R. A., and Axelrod, J. Trans-synaptic induction of adrenal tyrosine hydroxylase. *Journal of Pharmacology and Experimental Therapeutics,* 1969, *169,* 249–254.

Wiley, W. R. Tryptophan transport in neurospora crassa: a tryptophan-binding protein released by cold osmotic shock. *Journal of Bacteriology,* 1970, *103,* 656–662.

2
Effects of Environment on Brain and Behavior in Animals

MARK R. ROSENZWEIG

Since 1960 it has become increasingly clear from animal research that environment and experience affect not only behavior but also the nervous system. It is tempting to try to use some of the findings of this animal research as models for child development and its deviations, and even to suggest treatments by extrapolating from experimental results. Such attempts may be fruitful, but they are also hazardous because each species has its own peculiarities, and results obtained with one species cannot safely be transferred to another. Such results should be used only as a source of ideas for research with other species. The dangers of uncontrolled extrapolations are particularly great when specialists from different fields or backgrounds attempt to communicate with each other, because one may not understand the preconceptions and limitations of the results of the other.

Two rather different kinds of research will be discussed in this paper: (a) experiments in which animals are given enriched or impoverished experience that involves a variety of sensory modalities, and (b) experiments involving only a single sensory modality. In this second type, certain subjects may be totally deprived of visual input, or they may receive only highly specific or distorted input. The first type, (a), will receive greater emphasis, both because it seems more likely to be related to general developmental abnormalities, and because it is the subject of research that my collaborators and I have been conducting for a

MARK R. ROSENZWEIG · Department of Psychology, University of California at Berkeley, Berkeley, California 94720.

number of years. We will see that investigations of the two types, (a) and (b), show some systematic differences in results, but these may be due in part at least to the fact that different species have usually been employed in these two kinds of research.

EFFECTS OF DIFFERENTIAL EXPERIENCE
ON BRAIN AND BEHAVIOR

In the late 1940s and early 1950s, it was shown that experience in an enriched environment improves subsequent problem-solving behavior of rats (e.g., Hebb, 1949; Forgays and Forgays, 1952; Hymovitch, 1952). "Enriched experience" in these studies meant that the rats lived in a group in a relatively large cage furnished with a variety of stimulus objects.

In the late 1950s my colleagues and I found evidence that formal training altered the brain chemistry of rats. In an attempt to increase the size of the effect, we decided to give animals prolonged differential experience, along the lines of the experiments of Hebb and his students (Rosenzweig, Krech, and Bennett, 1961). The main experimental conditions are shown in Figure 1. We soon found that not only brain enzymes but also the weight of the cerebral cortex was modified significantly by differential experience that started at weaning (about 25 days of age) and that continued for 80 days (Rosenzweig, Krech, Bennett, and Diamond, 1962). The cortex becomes significantly heavier in enriched condition (EC) rats than in their littermates in the impoverished condition (IC), but the rest of the brain shows little effect, so the cortical/ subcortical weight ratio furnishes a particularly reliable and significant measure. (It should be pointed out that the person who dissects the brains, and the people who perform later chemical or anatomical measures do so without knowledge of the condition from which any particular animal came. We are careful to insure that preconceptions or hypotheses do not bias our results.)

In the early experiments, we put the rats into the differential conditions at weaning (thinking that only the young brain might be plastic), and we kept them there for a prolonged period (since no one had previously shown that experience could produce measurable changes in the brain). We were surprised at the clear effects that rather natural and gentle treatment could produce, and other investigators were properly skeptical. It had become dogma around the start of this century that the brain is a particularly stable organ and that it cannot be altered by experience. Cragg (1972) has commented on the reception accorded our findings:

> Initial incredulity that such differences in social and psychophysical conditions could give rise to significant differences in brain weight, cortical thickness, and glial cell

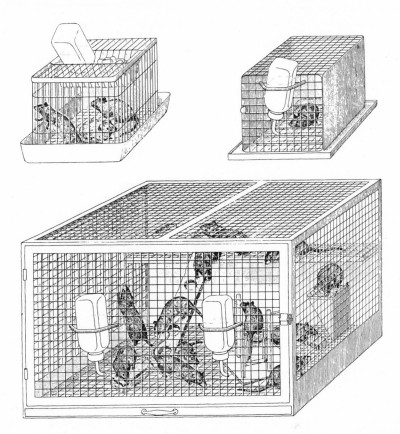

Figure 1. Environmental conditions used to study effects of experience on brain and behavior in rats. The standard colony (SC) condition is shown at the upper left. This provides a baseline, since most laboratory rats live in such conditions. An impoverished condition (IC) is obtained simply by caging each rat singly, as shown at the upper right. We formerly used cages with solid side walls, as shown here, but that proved unnecessary. The enriched condition (EC) in our laboratory consists of a large cage furnished with varied objects that are changed daily from a pool of about 25 objects; usually 10 to 12 rats are placed in EC together. (From "Brain Changes in Response to Experience," by Mark R. Rosenzweig, Edward L. Bennett, and Marian Cleeves Diamond, *Scientific American,* February, 1972. Copyright 1972 by Scientific American, Inc.)

numbers seems to have been overcome by the continued series of papers from Berkeley reporting consistent results. Some independent confirmation by workers elsewhere has also been obtained, as mentioned below (p. 42).

In later experiments we found it was easier to induce such cerebral changes than we had supposed. For one thing, the differential experience need not begin at weaning. We reported in 1964 (Bennett, Diamond, Krech, and Rosenzweig)

Table 1

EC-IC Percentage Differences in Brain Weights and Body Weights in Experiments with Different Starting Ages and Different Durations

Age at start	Duration (days)	30	60	80	130	160
	N (pairs)	201		206	46	22
25	Occipital cortex	9.7***		7.3***	6.8***	11.4***
	Total cortex	5.5***		4.2***	6.6***	2.5**
	Rest of brain	0.6		−0.8*	1.4	−3.3**
	Total brain	2.7***		1.2***	3.5***	−0.9
	Cortex/rest	4.9***		5.1***	5.2***	6.1***
	Body weight	−9.0***		−7.7***	−9.4***	−6.8*
	N (pairs)	109				
60	Occipital cortex	7.6***	−	−	−	−
	Total cortex	5.4***				
	Rest of brain	1.8***				
	Total brain	3.3***				
	Cortex/rest	3.5***				
	Body weight	−1.3				
	N (pairs)			45		
105	Occipital cortex	−	−	10.9***		
	Total cortex			5.4***		
	Rest of brain			1.7*		
	Total brain			3.2***		
	Cortex/rest			3.7***		
	Body weight			−0.1		
	N (pairs)	21	21			
185	Occiptal cortex	6.0**	3.6*	−	−	−
	Total cortex	3.2**	4.7***			
	Rest of brain	1.1	2.9***			
	Total brain	2.0	3.6***			
	Cortex/rest	2.1**	1.7*			
	Body weight	0.6	0.7			
	N (pairs)	21	23			
290	Occipital cortex	4.8***	9.6***	−	−	−
	Total cortex	2.7**	5.8***			
	Rest of brain	0.2	2.1*			
	Total brain	1.2	3.6**			
	Cortex/rest	2.5**	2.6**			
	Body weight	−4.3	4.0			

*P < .01.
**P < .01.
***P < .001.

that even young adults showed clear cerebral effects of differential experience, and Riege (1970) found similar effects with 300-day-old rats. There is no critical period for these effects of experience. For another thing, the differential experience does not have to last as long as the 80-day period that we employed in our initial experiments; even a few days can produce significant effects. Furthermore, 2 hours per day of enriched experience over a 30-day period yields significant effects (Rosenzweig, Love, and Bennett, 1968). Table 1 shows brain weight effects as a function of starting age and duration of differential experience.

The Variety of Cerebral Effects

A large number of aspects of brain chemistry and brain anatomy have by now been found to respond to differential experience, and many more dimensions of change will undoubtedly be discovered in further research of this sort. EC rats come to differ from their IC littermates in activities of the enzymes acetylcholinesterase (AChE) and cholinesterase (ChE) and in the RNA/DNA ratio. Anatomically we have been measuring more and more detailed effects. We first found that thickness of cerebral cortex becomes greater in EC than in IC (Diamond, Krech, and Rosenzweig, 1964), and this was later confirmed by Walsh, Budtz–Olsen, Penny, and Cummins (1969). The increase of ChE activity in EC led us to make counts of glial cells, since ChE occurs in glia and in capillaries but not in neurons; we found significantly more glia in the cortex of EC rats than in IC (Diamond, Law, Rhodes, Lindner, Rosenzweig, Krech, and Bennett, 1966). Using electron microscopy, dimensions of the synaptic junction were found to differ significantly between EC and IC (Møllgaard, Diamond, Bennett, Rosenzweig, and Lindner, 1971; West and Greenough, 1972). Numbers of dendritic spines also differ significantly between EC and IC (Globus, Rosenzweig, Bennett, and Diamond, 1973).

Effects of EC and IC on brain weights and brain enzymes have been found in other species of rodents besides the rat—mice (La Torre, 1968), gerbils (Rosenzweig and Bennett, 1969) and peromyscus (Rosenzweig and Bennett, unpublished). Similar experiments have not yet been extended to other orders of mammals, although behavioral effects of experience have been demonstrated in carnivores and primates.

Persistence of EC-IC Differences

How persistent are the cerebral differences induced by experience in the EC or IC environments? No single answer can be given to this question, because many factors affect the result, as we will see.

Earlier research had shown that effects on problem-solving behavior last for a month or more after rats have been removed from differential environments and placed in colony conditions. Brown (1971) reported, however, that differences in brain enzymes disappeared within a few days after she removed rats from an enriched condition (where they had spent 80 days) and returned them to the colony condition. She therefore concluded that the changes in brain enzymes could not be related to memory mechanisms, since the chemical changes disappeared rapidly while memory for the differential experience could be shown to persist.

We have recently obtained quite different results from Brown in more extensive experiments (Bennett, Rosenzweig, and Diamond, 1974). Rats in some groups were removed from EC and placed into IC for varying periods of time; these were called EC·IC, while those that remained in the original conditions were called EC·EC and IC·IC. After a 30-day period of EC, differences between EC·IC and IC·IC were still significant 7 days after the changeover but they became nonsignificant by 14 days. Much greater persistence was found after the 80-day initial period. Significant differences between EC·IC and IC·IC were still found after 47 days, the longest interval that was tested. Different measures of brain weights and brain enzymes showed different rates of change. Activity of ChE per unit of tissue weight showed particularly persistent effects of prior experience; in several experiments, ChE values of EC·IC actually exceeded those of EC·EC. While we are not convinced that cerebral weights and enzymatic measures are directly related to memory mechanisms, we cannot accept Brown's conclusion that lack of persistence rules them out.

A rather different picture of persistence is found when we ask whether effects of environmental impoverishment last after animals are removed from IC and placed into EC. We found sometime ago that when rats were removed after 80 days in an extremely impoverished environment and placed for 50 days in EC, cortical weights of the IC·EC rats exceeded those of EC·EC in one experiment and matched those of EC·EC in another (Rosenzweig, Bennett, and Diamond, 1967). Also, when rats from EC and IC are tested in mazes, the EC rats perform better at first, but the ICs catch up within a few days; several studies in which this has been observed are cited in Rosenzweig (1971, p. 321). In an experiment conducted in Australia, rats were kept for 500 days in EC or IC and then were tested on the Lashley III maze. During 3 weeks of training and testing, IC brain weights moved significantly closer to EC than in rats killed without Lashley maze experience (Cummins, Walsh, Budtz-Olsen, Konstantinos, and Horsfall, 1973). It appears from these studies that deficits caused by IC in both brain and behavior of rats are readily overcome by enriched experience. (It should be noted that these experiments are possible because laboratory rats of most strains can be handled and tested easily even after prolonged isolation. They do not become savage during isolation as do male mice of many strains. This example of clear differences in behavior between related species should warn against untested extrapolations from one species to another.)

The Interpretation of Cerebral Effects

As soon as we began to find cerebral effects of differential environments, we began to test whether the effects were due to experience and learning or whether they could be accounted for in terms of other variables. In our first publication on effects of differential environments on brain enzymes (Krech, Rosenzweig, and Bennett, 1960), we showed that the effects were not due to differential handling or to differential locomotor activity. Subsequent experiments demonstrated that the cerebral effects are not due to stress (Riege and Morimoto, 1970). We have also found that social stimulation is not required; rats exposed to EC individually for 2 hours per day develop typical EC brain measures, if they are primed to interact with the stimulus objects (Rosenzweig and Bennett, 1972). Mere exposure to the complex environment is not enough to induce the cerebral changes. Rats kept in small mesh cages within the larger EC cages show brain weights that differ significantly from their EC littermates but that do not differ from IC values (Ferchmin, Rosenzweig, Bennett, Morimoto, and Hebert, 1975). Apparently active and direct interaction with the enriched environment is necessary for production of the cerebral changes; passive and indirect contact is not enough. No particular sensory modality appears to be required: Rats develop EC-IC differences if they are blind (Rosenzweig, Bennett, Diamond, Wu, Slagle, and Saffran, 1969) or if they are anosmic (Rosenzweig, Bennett, and Wallen, unpublished).

We have found prolonged formal training to produce changes in brain weights and in brain AChE and ChE activities, but these effects tend to be small in comparison with those induced by informal experience. The enriched environment may afford much more opportunity for learning than does a formal training situation. At present, we are preparing to test further the hypothesis that the cerebral changes induced by differential experience are due, in large part, to learning. Experiments for this purpose will involve intensive formal training in two new sorts of apparatus.

EFFECTS OF SENSORY RESTRICTION OR DISTORTION ON NERVOUS SYSTEM AND BEHAVIOR

Since the early 1950s, a number of studies have been made on the role of sensory stimulation on development of the nervous system and behavior. Most of these studies have been done on vision, and most have employed cats or monkeys as subjects. Early visual deprivation in these species has marked effects, but similar treatment has little effect in the rat, so once again we must be concerned about species differences when we wish to extrapolate.

An important current research technique is the recording of electrophysiological activity in single cells of the visual cortex. Most neurons in the visual cortex of the rat are binocular; that is, they can be activated by stimulation of either eye. But if one eye of a kitten is covered for even a few days within the critical period of about 4 to 8 weeks of age, that eye loses the power to make cortical cells respond (Gantz, Fitch, and Satterberg, 1968; Hubel and Wiesel, 1970). It is as if there is competition between the two eyes for synaptic sites on the neurons, and the covered eye loses out. A similar result occurs if one eye is caused to change its direction of regard by cutting one of the extraocular muscles (Hubel and Wiesel, 1965). In both cases, the cats are virtually incapable of shape discrimination in the eye that has lost its cortical connections, and there is only a little recovery over months or years (Dews and Wiesel, 1970; Ganz and Fitch, 1968). In human beings, a divergent eye can similarly lose its acuity (amblyopia ex anopsia). It should be noted that although changes can be induced readily in kittens, similar treatments have no effects on connections in adult cats. There has been some disagreement as to whether normal stimulation in kittens induces neural connections or whether it "confirms" connections that are determined innately.

Selective restriction of vision in a kitten can also alter the properties of its cortical neurons strikingly. Hirsch and Spinelli (1970) outfitted kittens with special goggles so that one eye saw only vertical slits and the other, only horizontal slits. Experience was given during a daily period, and the kittens spent the rest of the day in the dark. Almost all cortical cells were later found to be monocular, and the preferred orientation of stimuli for arousal of cells corresponded to the orientation to which the eye had been exposed. Blakemore and Cooper (1970) allowed kittens to use both eyes, but restricted their visual experience to the interior of a cylinder that, for some kittens, had vertical stripes, and for others, had horizontal stripes. The kittens spent a few hours a day in this apparatus; otherwise they were in complete darkness. Their cortical cells were later found to have the orientations of their receptive fields markedly biased in favor of the directions of the lines they had experienced. When they were first released into a normal visual environment, such kittens experienced considerable perceptual deficits. A cat that had experienced only vertical stripes would not respond if the experimenter thrust at it a transparent pane with thin horizontal stripes painted on it. It would respond if the pane was rotated so that the stripes were vertical. If the cat was held around the trunk and lowered toward the pane, it would stretch out its paws in anticipation of contact only if the stripes were vertical. When the experimenter held out a wooden stick, the cat would come and play with it only if the stick was in the orientation that the cat had experienced as a kitten. Eventually, the cat would fixate the tip of the stick and then rotate its head to bring the stick into the preferred orientation. Further work has shown that such kittens improve their performance in finding their way visually and avoiding obstacles, but physiological deficits and decreased acuity are still present after 2 years of normal visual exposure (Spinelli, Hirsch, Phelps, and Meltzler, 1972; Muir and Mitchell, 1973).

To test the generality of such effects over species, Mize and Murphy (1973) duplicated with young rabbits the conditions that Blakemore and Cooper had employed with kittens. The rabbit was chosen because its visual system combines properties seen in both "higher" and "lower" mammals. As in the case of the cat and monkey, there is a high degree of encephalization of function in the visual system of the rabbit. But, as in the case of the ground squirrel, complex analysis of specific stimulus features occurs in the retina of the rabbit. Selective visual experience with vertical or horizontal stripes was found not to modify the receptive fields of neurons in primary visual cortex of the rabbit, "which suggests that the rabbit may lack the neural plasticity seen in some other mammals." Here again, the species studied is a major factor in determining the result.

Should the effects of selective experience be interpreted as reflecting degeneration of unused units or reorganization of units? That is, do units drop out or are they reassigned? Kittens given experience with lines of a single orientation do not show fewer active cells per electrode track than normal kittens. They show a normal number of cells, but most of these show the specific orientation presented. This suggests reorganization rather than loss.

Further evidence comes from an experiment in which kittens saw only point sources of light and no lines (Pettigrew and Freeman, 1973). The first of these kittens was kept in complete darkness for 28 days. Then for 13 days it spent 3 hours a day in a sort of small planetarium—a black sphere with small holes bored in the upper hemisphere and lights outside. After another week in the dark, recordings were made from cortical cells. Most cortical cells in normal cats are line detectors. In this kitten, most cortical units were "spot detectors"; they responded best to small targets. Again the results indicate that the specialization of cortical cells is largely derived from early visual experience.

The effects found in cats and monkeys provide a model for the deficit of acuity found in many astigmatic people even when their refractive errors have been completely corrected with lenses (Freeman and Thibos, 1973). An astigmatic person has usually been astigmatic since infancy, but it is a rare child in whom astigmatism is corrected during the first years of life. As a consequence, input is blurred in a particular orientation, and development of the visual system suffers from a relative lack of stimulus input in that orientation.

> Evidently, a complex nervous system does not develop to functional perfection solely through genetic control. There must be a period of plasticity during which [an individual's] experience helps to determine the connections of [his] neural network (Freeman and Thibos, 1973, p. 878).

Uncorrected astigmatism during childhood appears to result in neural defects that then are not overcome during years of corrected vision during adolescence and adulthood. It is not known how early in life a child's vision must be corrected in order to prevent or repair the neurological defect, but Freeman and Thibos report:

> Two subjects we have examined so far, who were corrected at 2 and 3 years of age, respectively, showed no orientation effects in spite of considerable astigmatism (p. 878).

In this case it appears that early detection and correction of an optical defect may prevent the development of a permanent neural defect.

Before leaving this section, we should note that the same symptoms caused by environmental conditions can also be caused by hereditary factors. The studies just cited were influenced by earlier reports of Hubel and Weisel that an eye of a kitten becomes blind for shape discrimination if it is covered during the critical period (see review by Hubel, 1967), or if the eye is made to diverge by cutting one of the extraocular muscles (Hubel and Weisel, 1965). In these cases, as in those cited above, a change in sensory input has repercussions on the neurophysiology of the visual system. But the interaction does not necessarily occur in only one direction. Just as an abnormal sensory input can lead to defective neural development, so can defective neural pathways lead to changed sensory input to the brain, and this in turn can affect further neural development.

In the last few years it has been found that the neuroanatomical projections from the retina to the thalamus are abnormal in albino individuals of all species that have been studied in this respect (Kaas and Guillery, 1973). The details of this abnormality are best known for the Siamese cat, and there have been several studies of the Siamese cat in this regard (e.g., Kalil, Jhaveri, and Richards, 1971; Kaas and Guillery, 1973). These defects are seen at an early age and are presumably hereditary. Nonalbino kittens are born with a large strabismus and develop visually guided behavior and normal ocular alignment during their second postnatal month (Sherman, 1972). Because of its abnormal visual pathways, the Siamese cat has only limited ability to process interocular information and consequently does not have stereoscopic depth perception. There is thus inadequate information to guide coordinated symmetrical movements of the eyes. The lack of coordinated binocular input also entails further consequences for the formation of the receptive fields of cortical cells.

Although misalignment of the eyes and nystagmus—symptoms that are frequently seen in Siamese cats—have usually been considered to be defects of the oculomotor system, in albinos they now appear to arise from a hereditary defect in the primary visual pathways. The human albino commonly has a strabismus but even more often shows nystagmus; it seems probable that the human albino has hereditary defects of the visual pathways similar to those found in the albino cat, although this interspecies extrapolation has not yet (to my knowledge) been tested directly.

ENRICHED EXPERIENCE AS THERAPY

A small amount of evidence is available that supports the hypothesis that enriched experience can help to overcome insults to the nervous system; it supports as well the obverse hypothesis that impoverished experience can aggravate neural deficits. One relevant study is a frequently cited but never replicated animal experiment by Schwartz (1964). Schwartz made cortical lesions in some rats during their first day after birth; others were sham operated. Some litters were then raised in enriched environments and others in impoverished environments; when the mothers were removed at weaning, enrichment or impoverishment were maintained until about 96 days of age. Pretraining was then begun for testing in the Hebb—Williams multiple-problem maze. Mean error scores of the four groups are given in Table 2. Note that the rats that had brain lesions but that were raised in the enriched environment made fewer errors than non-lesioned rats from the improverished environment. That is, the enriched environment appeared to overcome the effects of brain lesions. On the other hand, the worst scores were made by rats that suffered both from brain lesions and environmental impoverishment. [*Note added in proof:* We have recently confirmed that enriched experience can largely overcome effects of cortical lesions made not only at birth (Will, Rosenzweig and Bennett, in press) but also after weaning (Will, Rosenzweig, Bennett, Hebert, and Morimoto, in press), and even in adult rats (Will and Rosenzweig, in press).]

Table 2

Mean Errors on Hebb—Williams Maze as Function of Neonatal Cortical Lesions and Environment [a]

Environment	Brain status	
	Lesioned	Normal
Impoverished	205	125
Enriched	95	65

[a]Means estimated from Figure 1 of Schwartz, 1964.

Table 3

Percent of Children Retarded at Age Four as Function of Neurological Status at Age One and Social Class[a]

	Status at age 1	
Socioeconomic class	Neurologically abnormal[b]	Normal
Lower	35	14
Middle and upper	5	0

[a]From Holden and Willerman, 1972.
[b]Children with Down's disease were excluded from this comparison.

This experiment of Schwartz provides a model that can be used to consider the study of Holden and Willerman (1972) concerning development of children diagnosed as being neurologically abnormal at age 1. The children were part of the large national Collaborative Study, and their families were rated on a socioeconomic index. Of the infants from lower-class homes who were diagnosed as neurologically abnormal, 35% were retarded (scored less than 80 on an IQ test) at age 4. (Children with Down's disease were excluded from these comparisons.) Fourteen percent of the lower-class children who were normal neurologically at age 1 had IQ scores under 80 at age 4 (see Table 3). In contrast, among the children from middle- and upper-class homes only 5% of those

Table 4

Mean Errors on Hebb–Williams Maze as Function of Early Diet and Environment [a]

	Diet (protein)		
Environment	Low	Restricted	High
Impoverished	263	229	182
Enriched	166	159	135

[a]From Wells, Geist, and Zimmermann, 1972. The means are not given in the article but were furnished by Dr. Zimmermann.

neurologically abnormal at 1 showed retarded IQ scores at 4, and none of the neurologically normal were retarded. Note that the neurologically abnormal middle-class children were less likely to show low IQ scores than were the normal children from lower-class homes.

When children or young animals suffer from malnutrition, the effects on subsequent behavior may be compounded by the apathy that the malnutrition causes. This is especially apt to occur in a restricted environment. Such effects were demonstrated in a recent animal experiment by Wells, Geist, and Zimmermann (1972). The upper row of results in Table 4 shows that error scores on the Hebb–Williams maze are related to protein diet among rats kept in an environment that lacked stimulation; the low-protein-diet rats made about 40% more errors than the rats with a good diet. But when similar groups were kept in a complex environment, all groups made fewer errors, and the low-protein group made only about 20% more errors than the high-protein group. Notice that the high-protein rats that had impoverished experience actually performed worse than the low-protein rats with enriched experience. In this case, environmental complexity made up for nutritional deficiency. Clearly, the best performance was shown by rats that had both a good diet and a complex environment. This experiment demonstrates that for optimal performance, both environmental stimulation and good nutrition are important.

Two studies in the 1940s showed that stimulant drugs aided recovery of motor coordination in monkeys after lesions of motor cortex (Ward and Kennard, 1942; Watson and Kennard, 1945). A recent bulletin on *Neurochemistry in the Soviet Union* (Tower, 1969) reports some relevant material from studies of recovery of animals from closed head trauma conducted by M. Sh. Promyslov of Moscow. Promyslov is reported to recommend, on the basis of biochemical studies of the brains of animal subjects, that human patients suffering from craniocerebral trauma should never be narcotized but should be treated by stimulants. Nevertheless there does not seem to be any consensus among American neurologists as to whether stimulant drugs should be employed to promote recovery.

We have found that small doses of methamphetamine enhance EC-IC differences in brain weight measures (Rosenzweig and Bennett, 1972; Bennett, Rosenzweig, and Wu, 1973). The drug has no effect on brain measures of IC rats, but it alters behavior and brain in EC. Pharmacological and environmental determinants of recovery from cerebral trauma have been investigated by a number of workers (see the review by Rosner, 1970), but the possibility of interaction between drugs and environmental stimulation seems scarcely to have been envisaged. We plan to do further research on this question by adding drug conditions to the environments studied by Schwartz (1964) as factors determining recovery from brain damage.

CONCLUSIONS

Animal research has demonstrated the importance of both general stimulation and modality-specific stimulation for development of brain and behavior in several species. General stimulation (or richness of the environment) can affect brain measures of rats at any age; there is no critical period, although somewhat larger changes can be induced in younger than in older animals. Mere exposure to an enriched environment does not suffice to produce cerebral effects; direct and active participation is required. Cerebral results of environmental enrichment are relatively persistent, but results of impoverishment appear to be rather readily overcome. Research on cerebral consequences of general stimulation has so far been confined to rodents. It will be important to extend this research to carnivores and primates in order to generalize it and to favor extrapolations to man. Modality-specific stimulation appears to be required during a critical period in infancy in order to confirm innate but labile neural connections. If such stimulation is not available during the critical period, then enduring deficits will result. Research done with any one species can afford valuable clues and techniques for research with other species, but the results cannot simply be transferred from one species to another.

ACKNOWLEDGMENTS

The research for the project reported here received support from the National Science Foundation, Grant GB-30368X, and also from the U.S. Atomic Energy Commission.

REFERENCES

Bennett, E. L., Diamond, M. C., Krech, D., and Rosenzweig, M. R. Chemical and anatomical plasticity of brain. *Science,* 1964, *146,* 610–619.

Bennett, E. L., Rosenzweig, M. R., and Diamond, M. C. Effects of successive environments on brain measures. *Physiology and Behavior,* 1974, *12,* 621–631.

Bennett, E. L., Rosenzweig, M. R., and Wu, S.-Y. C. Excitant and depressant drugs modulate effects of environment on brain weight and cholinesterase. *Psychopharmacologia* (Berl.), 1973, *33,* 309–328.

Blakemore, C., and Cooper, G. F. Development of the brain depends on the visual environment. *Nature, London,* 1970, *228,* 467–468.

Brown, C. P. Cholinergic activity in rats following enriched stimulation and training: Direction and duration of effects. *Journal of Comparative and Physiological Psychology,* 1971, *75,* 408–416.

Cragg, B. G. Plasticity of synapses. In G. H. Bourne (Ed.), *The structure and function of nervous tissue* (Vol. IV). New York: Academic Press, 1972. Pp. 2–60.

Cummins, R. A., Walsh, R. N., Budtz-Olsen, O. E., Konstantinos, T., and Horsfall, C. R.

3

Some Suggestions for Reclassification of Ontogenetically Relevant Early Psychomotor Behavior

HERBERT KAYE

INTRODUCTION

In psychology "responses," or action patterns (or other descriptions of movement), form the operational basis on which the science has been built. Developmental psychology attempts to describe the ontogenetic changes in these patterns and their underlying processes. However, this is complicated by the fact that in addition to changes brought about by experience, there is evidence to suggest that the child's behavioral "base" is changing. Because these changes have gross systematic species characteristics, it is tempting to talk about basic, age-related motor patterns as though these existed as entities independently of theoretical and methodological constraints. This is, in some respects, similar to the way psychology previously approached the description and measurement of sensory processes. That is, the procedures employed were built on the assumption that the minimal sensitivity of the sensory organs could be estimated independently of the person's motivation, cognition, learning, perceptual strategies, etc. (Corso, 1963). However, with recent signal detection models (Swets, 1961), these factors have all been

HERBERT KAYE · Department of Psychology, State University of New York at Stony Brook, Stony Brook, New York.

shown to play a role in the production of the levels of behavior that index "when" a signal has been sensed.

The developing child's motor repertoire is also undoubtedly affected by the psychological "milieu" (procedural and theoretical) in which it is embedded. This is not an atheoretical process. It is not possible to make any decision on behavioral measurement, organization, or categorization without explicitly invoking a theory or, as is more often the case, implicitly suggesting one. However, the current status of psychology does not provide us with a singular view of human behavioral organization. There are many different theories and, within each theory, many different procedures for examining the same behavioral indices. On the other hand, the same response pattern may play a different role for different theories and procedures. In light of this, it would seem difficult to define any of the child's response patterns in a nonarbitrary manner without placing them in the context of some theoretical and methodological framework. Historically, with adults, older children, and to some degree, in animal research, the context is made relatively obvious when a given response pattern is described in terms specific to a given theory. But occasionally for these varying age and species groups, and often for younger children and infants, the abstract topographic description of the behavior stands as the simple protocol for the subject's ability. But there is some decision that goes into dividing the ongoing stream of behavior that requires a rationale; and whether one wishes to confront this issue or not, the rationale is a part of a theoretical system. In light of this, it would seem inappropriate that the behavioral attributes of any organism be approached on a purely descriptive level, since this does not make explicit the rules for description. As was suggested, this seems most often to be the case when describing the infant's and young child's response patterns. For the young subject or patient, atheoretical behavioral protocols serve to define both: (a) the biological, motoric maturation processes; and (b) the psychological, process development. This is considered only one of many questionable blendings of biologically and psychologically based systems.

The "merging" of the psychological and biological process indicators in organizing the behavioral attributes of children has seemed heuristically "sound," given that life is relatively fragile and the young child's behavior seemingly unsophisticated. Because of the infant's time-limited experience, survival and adaptation are often felt to rest on built-in, genetically coded species-related characteristics. This appraisal seems to have biased much of the research and theoretical approaches to early developmental studies. But in this "Darwinian" merging, there is a seldom acknowledged bringing-together of two different theoretical and procedurally based systems, and this has often allowed developmentalists the luxury of not having to relate the changing behavioral attributes of the growing child to some theoretically uniform system. Thus, often the young child's evolving behavior has been looked upon as though it had to reflect one or another biologically based shifts in capacity that occur with increased neuromuscular or sensory-motor, or higher central-nervous-system control; i.e., biological maturation. Experiential contributions often have been limited to the fine tuning of these maturational species characteristics, and to the few identifiable culturally related early attributes. Any suddenly emerging, relatively universal category of behavior has been more readily included in the biologically based grouping. It should be stressed, however, that the sorting of behaviors into species-related and experience-related characteristics is also not an atheoretical process. Nor is the problem made trivial by taking an interactionist position. The same behaviors will be defined and sorted in different ways within different theories. (Vocalizations, to use a simple example, may or may not be considered related to speech according to one's theoretical bias.) Furthermore, having available a category whose only procedural demands are age-related behavioral description has often led to an uneven or differentially stringent sorting criterion. This has also led to semantically loose, cross-discipline theoretical relationships, which were neither warranted by the data, nor logically appropriate to the systems implicated in the process.

DEVELOPMENTAL NORMS

In describing the trajectory (projected course) of developmental progress, researchers have often focused on response patterns felt to be indicative of culturally relevant or developmentally important attributes. These patterns serve the purpose of providing landmarks in the increasingly complex life of the developing child. Thus, for young infants, the attaining of a given behavioral landmark, most often an atheoretical but reliable description, is taken as evidence for both a grossly intact biological and psychological system. The assumption underlying the selection and use of a particular developmental landmark as an index of the developing system seems to be that the behavior of note fits a relatively autonomous, biologically based, age-related sequence that is generally invariant, given a wide range of nondestructive environments. The behavioral norm often achieves a status where it "speaks for itself." The age at which a child walks, talks, can pick up a cube and build a "bridge" provides the examples of "normalcy." Concurrently, it has been felt that *if* the child's underlying physiology or experiential history were inadequate, then these would be reflected in the lack of performance in one or another motoric or behavioral patterns. These two assumptions arise rather directly from the biological axiom, "All structures subserve some meaningful biological function" (Dennenberg, 1972); and the often assumed obverse, "For every function there is an identifiable set of structures." This sort of symmetry is heuristically appealing, but adds an implicit assumption about landmark characteristics; that is, they are not only *sufficient,* but also *necessary* indicators of an intact system. This latter assumption may seem to be a reasonable working hypothesis, and for many researchers and practitioners it has served just this purpose. It is at the point that this hypothesis assumes the power of an absolute and empirically sound organizational principle that it creates a number of problems. The author suggests that for much of the assessment work with children, and to one degree or another in many developmental theories, there has been an implicit assumption concerning the correlation of underlying structure and external behavior. This has operated across disciplinary boundaries to foster relationships not valid to either of the systems whose methods generated the quantitative or qualitative data. These problems, the author suggests, have reverberated, to some degree, throughout the whole subdiscipline of developmental psychology. The following represents a brief look at aspects of this problem.

Establishing "Landmark" Behaviors

In light of what was previously stated, the first question might be, What evidence needs to be assembled to support the notion that behavioral landmarks are necessary and sufficient indicators of "successful" or adequate developmental progress? It would seem that there are two: The first would be to support the notion that *the behavior* is a necessary attribute of a currently "adaptive child." That is, if it could be shown that without a given behavior the child is currently limited in some nonarbitrary systematically adaptive manner, or that the child's likelihood of staying alive is reduced by the adaptive inadequacy signaled by the absence of this behavior, then one could logically support the specific behavior as a relevant landmark to successful development. For example, a baby's inability to turn over when prone and face down might, over a period of some weeks, create a severe threat to the infant's life, and thus, this might qualify as an important response attribute. However, its meaningful integration into any theory would still be moot. (Certainly, all critical survival behaviors are not included in any current system.) A second sort of example of a potential landmark behavior might be a series of actions denoting the presence of "passive" language understanding in the year-old child. If the child exhibiting this failure is being raised in the "usual" manner, the lack of this integrative skill might well limit the ongoing cognitive and social basis of, say, parent–child inter-action.

The second support for the use of a given behavior as a landmark to development, would come from showing that the presence of the behavior at a certain point in time, or in a given sequence, signals the later development of adaptive characteristics. Thus, indirectly, the presence of trans-midline reaching in the 1-year old might provide the signal that some later characteristics for the encoding or decoding of complex perceptual information will be present, while the absence of this behavior might be associated with alternate forms of information processing. These alternate forms may be considered less "adaptive." It should again be pointed out that this correlation may not "make sense" in terms of the theoretical system in which each of the to-be-correlated measures is organized. If so, its functional value is, at best, limited, and the generalization from the specific measure to a response class is inappropriate. For example, using the last correlation, "reaching across the midline," and "encoding of complex perceptual information" are each made up of many behavioral components. Reaching includes eye movements, arm movements, hand movements, etc. The correlation of any of these with the predicted response of "encoding" ability may account for all of the correlation. Unless the behavior is thought of in the context of some theoretical system both from a functional and systematic point of view, the response's class affiliation or category is not defined. Under these circumstances, the selection of various forms of measurement and the inclusion of various aspects of movement is arbitrary.

The term "adaptive" has been used in several places. The issue of what is "adaptive" is itself, however, as much a theoretical as an empirical issue, and must also be dealt with in a theoretical context. Developmental theory typically consists of a sequence of age- or experience-related hierarchical organizations. Each level of the hierarchy explicitly or implicitly provides a structure whose characteristics either subsume the preceding structure, or whose level of increased ability subsume prior abilities. Each theory limits, by design or by chance, the range of responses that will be included in its hierarchical organization. Similarly, each theory suggests tasks that should be able to be carried out at any level of organization of the system. *Adaptiveness concerns the relationship between the scaled level of the individual and the expected competency within that level of organization.*

In addition, any theory should contain the rules for testing or assessing these relationships. Within a system or theory, procedures appropriate to describing the structure of behavior at a given age, or the antecedents to a given behavior change, should have means for defining the limits to a given behavioral attribute or response pattern. However, at the current state of the art, these limits are usually only loosely stated. Such commonly used developmental responses as walking, reaching, looking, saying, may seem operationally trivial. However, since there are several ways of describing a behavior at any point in time, and since the description of a behavior must arbitrarily segregate a portion of the ongoing stream of activity, it is unlikely that the same set of events will be measured similarly by individuals having different theoretical positions. More than this, it is unlikely that two theoretical or "world" views will purposely focus on the same portions of the behavioral stream as indexing some adaptive landmark.

This means that aside from the occasional critical landmark denoting life-death aspects of concurrent or future "adaptation," each theoretical position will most likely suggest a different criterion for noncritical "adaptation" and a different focus on what the "important" current and predictive characteristics of ongoing behavior are. In infancy, Piagetian theory will look for signs of the coordination of previously independent schemas, while learning theory will look for signs of increased use of responses to control aspects of the environment. The concurrent validity of the notion of noncritical adaptation therefore becomes theoretically circular, having been chosen, in part, to fit into the system, or to "complete" the systematic aspects of the theory. However, it should be possible to check the predictive validity of a landmark by showing that the level of an early behavior is related to a theoretically relevant level of later adaptive behavior. By showing that an early occurring response pattern is systematically correlated with the occurrence of a later behavior, one strengthens both the theory and the choice of the specific early pattern as a relevant landmark. The prediction, however, must be deducible within the theory, and both the index behavior and the predictive behavior must be measured within the accepted procedures of the theory.

The author feels that the above analysis suggests that the valid use of "landmarks" to describe behavioral development is dependent on two considerations: The first is that the occurrence of the initial index (landmark) behavior is describable within the constraints of a scientifically acceptable theoretical system; and the second is that the occurrence of the index behavior holds some predictive relationship to other theoretically consonant behavioral descriptions.

The development theories currently in vogue include, most prominently, those of Piaget, Werner, Erickson, Bijou, and Baer, and a host of eclectic systems. To one degree or another, each of these deals with behavior in the context of a strict theoretical interpretation, but each also hedges on the boundaries between behavior as an abstract description and behavior as a theoretically constrained organizational component. Unfortunately, the empirical likelihood of predicting developmental characteristics within the context of current theories is only at a low and most general level, and the significant (though low) correlations of early with later developmental characteristics are more often functionally valid than theoretically sound. That is, where prediction is possible, the reasons are often vague.

There are, in fact, some strong suggestions in current developmental literature that theoreticians abandon the older notions of developmental *continuity* (Kagan, 1973). However, this would severely change the concept of developmental psychology. On the one hand, the difference between *development* and *acquisition* would become trivial. From a different perspective, the notion of *individual differences* would become specific-task-limited. At this point, it would seem a more productive tack to assume that the current developmental theories are relatively weak and much developmental data either unavailable, ambiguous, or not very robust.

Developmental Continuity

It is suggested that most current developmental theories presume some degree of continuity in the child's developing characteristics, and without this concept many of the other constructs in both the pure and applied developmental area would become uninterpretable. Continuity is not an easily defined term, and is perhaps best "converged upon" with the following examples:

1. Continuity is represented by the prediction of later performance of competency on the basis of early performance or competency in systematically appropriate prerequisite areas.
2. Continuity is implied if it is shown that one may maximize certain later competencies with various environmental manipulations.
3. Continuity is partially defined by the systematic necessity for the inclusion of prior modes of operating in successively more adaptive modes.
4. Continuity is the ability to consistently organize internal or external events in one of several alternative modes.
5. Continuity means, in part, consistent individual differences.
6. Continuity is a correlative relationship across time between attributes whose sequential theoretical relationship is meaningful.

But, as was pointed out, there exists a gap between the belief in continuity and the empirical evidence one can gather to support the notion. In the following six points, the logical and empirical problems that may have led to this difficulty are explored, and some suggestions are made for their rectification.

1. First, predictive statements designed to relate the child's early to his/

her later behavior do not specify parameters for the varying environmental events under which the current trait was nurtured. In addition, prediction often does not specify subsequent expected outcomes in terms of the varying conditions within which the behavior will be embedded. A given level of competency may be elaborated in many ways, each potential outcome being related to the relevant circumstances of its nurturance. Thus, for example, boys and girls having similar early levels of mathematical competency may develop differently within a sexist society, but similarly within a nonsexist society. With respect to the differential character of one's history, a current level of performance will seldom reflect in any simple manner the bias attached to it from the experiential circumstances within which it was nurtured. For example, the child exhibiting a given level of competency in one language, but who has been reared in a multilingual home, may find it difficult to deal with certain types of logical constructs. These may show up in selected situations, or in attempts to learn a third language. (Third-language learning is more frequent in countries other than our own.) This latter effect might be still further complicated by the consistency of the child's previous language training or usage, and the child's age or experiential point at which the new demands are introduced.

Thus, in attempting to empirically support continuity between behaviors at two ages, it would seem important that predictive equations, whether qualitative or quantitative, include: (a) variables that relate to the range of expectations given various nurturing situations; and (b) variables that describe the characteristics surrounding the emergence of the initial performance level. To a degree, and within some broad species-relevant constraints, experience is relative, not absolute.

2. Second, as developmental research and description shift from younger to older children, developmentalists tend to shift their focus from specific behavior topographies (e.g., muscular rigidity; prehensile versus palmar grasp; phonemic universe, etc.) to behaviors as means-ends relationships (reaching, pointing, telling, problem-solving, etc.). Since there is a correlation between growth, experience, and cultural expectations, the broad sequences that are implied in the emergence of certain attributes suggest a structural invariance similar to the biologically constrained invariance in embryonic development. Because the infant has been described as having *a factori* a primitive repertoire, this invariance is assumed to be "reflexively" or in other ways biologically programmed. If this is taken to be the case, then the potential psychological content of these behaviors can be, and often is, ignored. Further, when this continues to be an operating assumption, then the likelihood of describing an early behavior in ways that will correlate with the later description of behaviors is low. As it turns out, it is often the case when describing the relationship between the behavior patterns of infants

and young children, that there is not only the shift in descriptive system from response pattern to response "purpose," but also (as was stated in the previous section) from a biological to a psychological frame of reference. The moving across disciplinary lines makes it nearly impossible to empirically support a notion of continuity.

With respect to this problem, it would seem a better strategy to look upon the child as continuously adaptive within each of its operating modes; for example, in its learning mode, or perceptual mode, or cognitive mode, etc. This need not at any point in time include all the attributes of the mode. Rather, development would consist of the hierarchical expansion of adaptiveness within a given mode. The child, for example, may be looked upon as conditionable within both the classical and instrumental conditioning paradigms without necessarily presuming the ability to utilize time durations beyond a certain level. The young infant may be able to use binocular cues for depth but not certain monocular cues. The child may respond to all distinctive features in a limited set of what will subsequently be a much finer set of auditory-perceptual categories. The young infant may be able to relate current events to visual and bodily images, but not to abstract thoughts. Memory apprehension may be organized on a principle of 3 plus or minus 1, and 5 plus or minus 1, before it grows to "7 plus or minus 2."

By casting the child's activity into an operating frame of reference, even the youngest infant's behavior takes on a means-end or interactive characteristic. More important, it becomes possible to correlate topographically different behaviors because of their functional class relationship within a given paradigm. A *landmark* then takes on a process-related characteristic, and the number of behaviors that may play a role in any process can be better defined. For example, sucking need not be thought of uniquely as a tension reducer for the infant, but could become one of a class of behaviors whose role in a given system would have a certain functional and systematic goal. The same would be true of various aspects of play, movement, etc.

3. Third, the boundaries between different theoretical positions are seemingly less often "honored" in work with younger than with older children. For example, biobehaviorists, instrumental conditioners, cognitivists, and those espousing various approaches to perception will often freely mix infant data outcomes when supporting the interpretation of their own various findings, regardless of the methods with which these data were gathered. However, this becomes less likely when the data comes from older children and adults. For example, it is unlikely that methods related to the use of the term "lapse of memory" would be appropriate to describe the classic Ebbinghaus function, just as it would not be likely that the contrast of instrumental schedule effects would be used to explain a weak ego function. In point (2) above, it was suggested that the biological principles used

to organize infant behavior as opposed to the psychological principles employed for older children make it difficult to empirically support a notion of developmental continuity. The same is true when one moves, within the discipline of psychology, across philosophical lines. The philosophy, terminology, and methodology employed by "Skinnerians" in some cases is contradictory to, and more often orthogonal to those employed by "Piagetians." These differences become more obvious as the child gets older. There may be a future merging of these theoretical positions, but it is suggested that by not clearly articulating the basis on which data are being collected and interpreted, and by adding "apples and bananas," the likelihood of creating clear relationships between early and later attributes is further decreased.

4. Fourth, several theorists have suggested that the infant is a more "wholistic" creature than the adult (see Harris, 1963), one whose traits or attributes are interdependent. For the adult or older child, attributes and trait organization have boundaries provided either by the specific theory or general system within which the measurement is taking place. For much of developmental psychology's history, variations in the fine-grained aspects of infant behavior have been dealt with as psychologically trivial. Focusing back on the previous section for a brief moment, it should be mentioned that from a clinical, neurological point of view, these same fine-grained characteristics have been seen as potentially meaningful to the assessment of the child. The neurological assessment is ultimately validated in terms of its behavioral correlates. Thus, there have been discipline differences in approach to the infant. Looking, then, at the process of development, there are neurologically differentiated sets of reflexes that are slowly being built into a hierarchically complex, interrelated, and subtly integrated system; while from the point of view of psychological development, the primitive behavioral mass is slowly differentiated into a finer and finer set of independently controlled attributes. These alternate views only complicate the general approach one brings to the study of the young infant. Certainly there is extraordinary variety in the infant's behavior. Perhaps one of the conceptual limitations is related to the idea that a categorically defined infant behavior may participate in only one organizational system at a time. However, the inclusion of behavior in any developmental theory is determined by the theory's rules of inclusion. For example, Piaget (1972) and Wohlwill (1970) have chosen to *exclude* the majority of the phenomena that Bijou and Baer (1965) and Statts (1968) *include* in their assessment of developmental processes. Moreover, it is possible for differently oriented theories to simultaneously utilize an ongoing segment of the behavioral stream in many different ways. In a simple example, the child, while feeding, may be engaging in many modes of interaction with his/her environment. He/she is responding reflexively, is learning about contingencies, is organizing percepts,

is socializing, is "thinking" and mapping and planning. Only certain aspects of the feeding behavior may reflect all of these organizing characteristics, and some aspects of the child's activity may independently represent one or another of these organizational modes. For example, the coordination of mouth parts may be reflexive, the burst and pause pattern may indicate the contingencies, and pause duration may correlate with the perceptual organization characteristics, etc. To the degree that the young child is assumed to be a psychologically undifferentiated mass, and the older child and adult a finely differentiated organism, it will continue to be difficult to tease out the variables that show aspects of continuity over development. Young children may show less stable patterns. (We assume that this is so, but the proof of it is, at best, thin.) The variability in the child's behavior may suggest organizational inadequacy, small term shifts in adaptive behavior (which might be called adaptive tracking), or the inadequacy of the researcher's conceptualization of what are the key characteristics that should be measured. The fine-grained behavior may be embedded in a good deal of procedural "noise," which arises from lack of adequate experimental control. This is not meant to suggest "the absurd." Certainly, given some standardized setting, many modes of older child and adult behavior are more highly organized than those of infant. However, this does not require that the infant's behavior be less differentiated, nor less complex.

5. Fifth, at any point in the human's life, the circumstances determining "appropriate" behavior include some combination of those characteristics that are to be of continuing importance, and those that are momentarily adaptive but somewhat arbitrary. The latter may be abandoned by the child at points when the situational circumstances or the child's needs change. These currently adaptive behavioral attributes may add further "noise" to the assessment of individual differences and developmental continuity. Thus, it is necessary to keep track simultaneously of those behavioral attributes that may be shifted both easily and trivially, and those that are individually invariant and prerequisites for various levels of future performance. This has often been the pursuit of developmentalists, although it often becomes entangled with attempts to separate the dimensions of *nature* from those of *nurture*. The nature–nurture issue has been verbally relegated to the status of a *pseudo* issue (Anastasi, 1958), but continues to maintain a presence in the study of various aspects of developmental psychology. Only recently, the issue of nature and nurture has been raised with respect to the development of language (Lenneberg, 1967) and the categorical perception of phonemes (Eimas, Siqueland, Jusczyk, and Vigorito, 1971). Some researchers have interpreted the language-related data in ways that suggest the older dichotomy. However, as was indicated earlier in this chapter, characteristics that are environmentally structured may be universal and need not be mutable. On the other

hand, attributes that are predominantly biologically structured need not be considered immutable. (The current interactionist position, which states that all characteristics are a blend of an individual's heritage nurtured in a unique environment, does not, unfortunately, resolve the issues of human variability and individual differences.) The necessity to continuously separate concurrent transient characteristics from lasting structural organizations and operating strategies may prove the most difficult problem for an empirical approach to continuity. A beginning would be to assess the microstructure of the environmental demands as an ecological system within the boundaries of an explicit theoretical system. For example, it has been tentatively concluded that a child raised for much of its infancy on a carrying board shows little deficit in later locomotive activity. By examining the microstructure of the child's behavior within the context of a perceptual learning framework, this outcome may be understandable. But if one approaches walking as purely instrumental behavior, requiring practice and task-specific feedback, this outcome may be difficult to explain. In addition, it should generally be kept in mind that many behaviors exhibit characteristics that suggest a coming-together of several previous behaviors. (Speech is the obvious example.) At any given age, children reared sequentially differently may still have acquired similarly relevant attributes for behaving in certain ways. The *sequential necessity* of certain classes of experience requires empirical support different from the *absolute necessity*.

6. Finally, historically there have always been differences in the availability of various-aged populations for research purposes. Often, studies of infancy, early childhood, middle childhood, adolescence, and adulthood have been carried out on demographically different samples. This has not insured randomness, and thus, has limited the generalizations that could be made from the data. These limitations may so confound the transient and lasting characteristics of an age or cohort group that the likelihood of sorting the behavioral stream into appropriate units is nearly impossible (see Schaie, 1970). It would seem at this state of the art, that generalizations across populations should be made with the utmost caution rather than to try to smooth out these potential differences through statistical procedures. In line with this, and to the author, even more important, is the feeling that continuity will continue to be a problem unless nonpsychological classificatory systems for matching test populations are abandoned. Instead, behavioral and systematically relevant variables should be employed for these purposes. Specifically, by separating populations on the basis of sex, "race," and social class, an aura of control is suggested that often has little if any specific basis for explanation in the various systems within which behavior is studied. For example, although psychoanalytic theory suggests basic differences between males and females, most cognitive and learning approaches do not. This is not to say that males and females are not treated differently,

but rather, that they are not different with respect to the manner in which they process or act on common information. The current trend to analyze all data for sex, "race," and social class, is not seen as clarifying issues, but rather as giving a false sense of clarity. The fact that there are separate average performance characteristics among these categories does not negate the huge overlap typically found in the distributions for any trait, especially when the trait is studied in young children. By monitoring these classificatory systems over age, the ability to focus on common mechanisms underlying all behavioral outcomes is made difficult by the highlighting instead of categorically related attributes. There is not sufficient space to argue this issue. To state it most strongly, *gender* is a biological variable whose psychological boundaries are at best vague; "race" is an outmoded anthropological concept, even less objective; and social class represents, at best, a weak classification whose characteristics change at least each decade, and whose classificatory system is not stable within any family or individual.

SUMMARY TO THIS POINT

The preceding materials and speculations have taken a broad view of what is, at best, a highly complex set of issues. Approaching the problems of developmental psychology as a science has fostered several strategies (see Chapter 1, Reese and Lipsitt, 1970). The positions outlined above provide one approach to the broad spectrum of developmental phenomena. Before the author presents some data collected on newborns that represent aspects of the above strategy, it might be of value to reiterate the major points.

1. In psychology, behavior can only be dealt with in the context of the procedures and hypothetical processes of which it is a part. It cannot be studied as an operationally descriptive topography.

2. The notion that developmental behavioral landmarks are sufficient signs of normal development requires that these be correlated with concurrent and/or predictive adaptive behaviors, or that the landmarks themselves be shown to serve these purposes. Additionally, the absence of a landmark can only be considered an indicator of developmental inadequacy if it is shown that the presence of the behavior is necessary for normal development.

3. The issue of prediction in developmental theory is related to the concept of continuity, a concept that underlies most pure and applied aspects of the discipline.

4. But developmental continuity is difficult to support empirically. There are several reasons for this: (a) Prediction is relative to the history preceding the

response and the circumstances intervening between the predictor and the outcome; (b) developmentalists tend to focus on early behavior in terms of its topography and later behavior in the context of means-ends relationships; (c) philosophical, theoretical, and methodological boundaries are not separated as clearly in early childhood study as in older child and adult studies; (d) infants are not studied in as refined a manner as are older children and adults; (e) the young child's behavior is often approached as if it were immutable, or at best, moderately plastic, while that of the older child is considered much more changeable (the nature–nuture demands are differently applied as the child develops); (f) different populations often supply the data for variously aged subjects.

Applying these issues to the topic of this paper, it is suggested that the early psychomotor behavior include:

1. Casting any behavior of interest into a theoretical framework so that it functions as one of a class of behaviors in some organizational or adaptive role.
2. Ignoring behaviors that do not play such a role.
3. Being sure that the methods for assessing and defining all behavioral units when testing concurrent or predictive relationships have common theoretical basis before the behaviors are systematically organized.
4. Considering the child as a multiply operating system whose parts need not be interrelated simply because they coexist in time. The interrelating of various attributes of behavior should be a constructive empirical process.

THE RELEVANCE OF THESE ISSUES TO NEONATE AND INFANT RESEARCH

For the last 13 years the author has studied newborn babies, with the major purpose of his work being the understanding of adaptive characteristics that the human "brings into" the world.

The newborn infant is, at first, deceptively simple. It does so little that relates to the everyday life of adults that there is a tendency to classify its activity in gross fashion—eating, sleeping, eliminating, startling. However, changes in behavior occur very rapidly, and the regularization and accumulation of both self-generated behavioral experience, and/or the organization of environmental input, is still poorly understood. Researchers interested in the early occurrence of various adaptive characteristics have tried to work with younger and younger infants, but the specific methodological problems and the difficulties in generalizing procedural analogues have slowed the process.

Lipsitt, in his review of the literature, "Learning in the First Year of Life" (1963), provides ample proof that as technology has advanced, it has been possible to show environmental adaptation in younger and younger organisms. It was with this belief, and under Lipsitt's tutelage, that the author focused much of his work on the methodological problems of working with newborns. It was assumed that theoretical biases would both fall in line behind and/or be shaped by coherent data. It has become obvious to the author that behavioral theory often shaped the research design and data interpretation. The research initially centered on showing that the traditional paradigms of habituation, classical and instrumental conditioning, were viable ways of approaching early infant behavior change (Lipsitt, 1963; Kaye, 1967). It was in the context of this conditioning research that the complexity of motor behavior began to be manifested.

For a number of reasons, the process of conditioning has not been easily shown in the newborn. The first difficulty has been that of isolating treatment effects from the continuous waxing and waning of movement patterns as the infant goes through his or her "daily" circadian cycles (Wolff, 1966). Related to this has been the issue of how to structure the critical variables in these cycles. The second difficulty has been related to picking a timing arrangement that maximizes the likelihood that all the information upon which a conditioned response will be built can be processed (Little, 1971). Third has been the difficulty of picking stimuli that do not produce competing responses. This latter problem has necessitated the use of many control groups in infant studies (Kaye, 1967); and the controls often compound the methodological and/or interpretation difficulties. Finally, it appears that the initial simplistic approach to response description employed in the author's research has been, in many cases, inadequate. The specific response characteristics of the infant must be "teased" out of the general response class to which it appears initially to belong (Brassell and Kaye, 1974).

It is important to keep in mind that a single operational definition may be inadequate for all functions to which the loose notion of "the response" may be applied. Whenever a response is quantified, a great number of arbitrary decisions are made concerning which correlated components will be measured, what numerical system or quantification level will be employed, and over what period of time the correlated relationships "make sense." In addition, all response classes are not formed in the same manner. A *class name* may serve to describe the interrelationship of the flexion and extension of several muscle groups; or it may relate only to the byproduct of this action; or it may include some combination of the two. (Respectively, these would be typified in the newborn by the usual operations for defining the responses: "startle," "cry," and "grasp.") It is possible that different classes of response operate on different process bases.

Early Infant Reflexes

The newborn moves all parts of its body, both separately and in combinations. These movements have been divided, typically, into two observational classes. There are those responses whose underlying structure is assumed to be a simple neuronal arc, *the reflex;* and there is the other major class, called spontaneous behaviors, implying a more random, nonpurposeful, emitted behavior. Unfortunately, neither the term, the model, nor the concept of the reflex has been used in a consistent manner, and since the alternate term has covered all other behaviors, its fate has been dependent on the definition of the reflex. Again there is the confusion produced by freely using a term fostered in one discipline in a second discipline.

Sherrington's classic research (Sherrington, 1906) on the reflex centered on the knee jerk. Even when showing that there were many levels of control of this movement pattern, his model was linked to anatomical imperatives (Swazey, 1969). The neurologist still uses this model. For example, Taft and Cohen (1967) explain: "The reflex performance of an infant is dependent not only on the structural and metabolic integrity of the central nervous system, but on physiological conditions at the time of examination" (p. 81). For these authors, the reflex is a response that describes the underlying neuroanatomical structure. But for the psychologist, the reflex is usually approached as a behavioral unit. The reflex model requires the presentation of one of a class of stimuli (usually) directed at a specific sensory mode, and the measurement of one of a class of responses within a limited amount of time following the stimulus. The unit has an S–R framework independent of the physiology underlying the relationship. The validity of defining an S–R relationship as a reflex depends on its elicitation characteristics and its operational definition, not its anatomical analogue. These stimulus-response sequences are then fitted to larger systematic formats such as "conditioning," "circular reactions," "pleasure seeking," and "arousal." The reflex defines a certain portion of infant behavior. However, a brief time spent with even the newborn baby provides ample evidence that the infant's initial repertoire contains a large number (perhaps the majority) of responses that are not easily included under the simple reflex rubric. It would be quite arbitrary to suggest that these are "unimportant responses" or "incomplete reflexes." Nor does the lack of an identifiable stimulus mean that these responses are not the product of some sensory "input." Thus, for this particular problem the question of "boundaries" is critical; i.e., what movement and/or outcome characteristics are relevant to each response class and how should they be quantified?

Starting at a descriptive level, one would assume that if a reflexive response contains several components, then it cannot be described in terms of any of the components alone. For example, if a loud noise produces "a reflexive response" whose components are said to include leg, arm, face, and trunk components, as well as autonomic changes, then any of these might be adequate as an indication that the "sound has occurred." However, the organization of these components into the unit called "a startle" must have some theoretical or other systematic significance. It has been suggested that any recurrent pattern has *a priori* significance (Hutt, Lenard, and Prechtl, 1969), but then one is faced with the likelihood of definitional circularity. Even if it were granted that repeatable patterns should receive special attention, the infant researcher is confronted with the fact that few (if any) early emerging behavioral patterns have highly correlated attributes (Turkewitz, Moreau, Birch, and Davis, 1971).

It would seem appropriate in light of this, that components should be organized into categorical groupings only on the basis of evidence that these groupings, when applied transsituationally, are of value in the understanding of some aspect of the phenomenon with which one is interested. For example, when a child is presented with a loud sound, he or she goes through a series of movements, often called a startle. However, it is possible that the effective intensity of the sound is only reflected in the latency of the eye blink, the amount of leg flexion, and the amount of air exhaled in the three breaths following sound onset. These may also be correlated, to varying degrees, with body movement, heart rate change, and head movement. In order to arrive at the appropriate response indicator of stimulus intensity sensitivity (of interest in assessing the newborn's hearing), these latter most obvious response characteristics (body movement, etc.) must be ignored. In order for the combination of eye blink latency, leg flexion, and exhalation volume to be validly considered, a new response combination—called, say, a *blurb*—these must be found to signal some aspect of stimulus dimensionality in other modes, such as vision.

As difficult as it may seem, this transsituational validation must be considered as part of the process involved in *deriving theoretically sound functional behavioral classes.* In reality, of course, this is not a totally open-ended search. As the child grows, the organizational process becomes a bit easier. This is in part because as the child grows the construct with which one is working can be related to motivational or other dynamic aspects of a given theoretical system. But with infant research this is seldom the case.

From another perspective, the determination of *when* an infant's response occurs is often definitionally arbitrary and the *determining* events may be as much the unmentioned "setting" conditions as the immediate stimulation.

Taking a simple response pattern such as the infant's "rooting response" will provide an adequate example. "Rooting" is typically described as a relationship between a tactile stimulation of the perioral area of the infant and an ipsilateral movement of the head accompanied by mouth opening and a downward movement of the ipsilateral side of the lip and tongue. It appears that the likelihood of this response has both a cyclical occurrence tied to the feeding and food deprivation schedule, and a second "activation" system related to general activity. Thus, without control or knowledge of at least these two systems with which it is correlated, direct stimulus control of the rooting response is, at best, varied. In addition to their considerable dependence on nonimmediate stimulus factors, these response components also occur separately both in the presence of "cheek stimulation" and without it. The relationship of stimulus-produced responses to spontaneously occurring responses may thus be complicated by the differential rate of spontaneous responding for each of the components. But if the components occur spontaneously, according to instrumental conditioning theory, then they may also be progressively modified. This would mean that for an individual child there may also be experiential determinants for the components of some so-called reflexive responses. Examining one dimension of the "rooting" reflex, Papousek (1961), and Siqueland and Lipsitt (1966), in rather complex designs, focused not on the whole behavior but rather only on the ipsilateral head turn. This component could be easily measured, but even with this simplification, a number of decisions had to be made for which there was little or no relevant data. First, how long and with what strength should the stroke-to-the-cheek stimulus be applied? Second, over what period of time should the head-turning response be minimally required to occur to be considered related to the stimulus? And, most important, how much turn is a "head turn"—10 degrees, 30 degrees, 60 degrees? Siqueland and Lipsitt were well aware of the effect that different criteria could have on the outcome, but nevertheless, employed a 10-degree turn for their criterion, whereas Papousek required 30-degree turns. The results of the two studies suggested some different conclusions about the ontogeny of the infant's learning attributes, but the differences were not easily reconcilable because of the criterion differences.

The message in these studies is not a new one. It has been summarized in a number of studies compiled by Fitzgerald and Brackbill (1973). It may be stated as follows: *How* one decides upon and measures the parameters of responding when the response is imbedded in a given procedure is critical to the conclusions one can draw from its measurement. Very often one starts at an arbitrary or common-sense point. However, ultimately one should test a range of criteria for the response, just as the careful researcher tests a range of stimuli. This has been progressively more obvious to the author in his studies of sucking behavior, its concurrent attributes, and its modification.

Sucking Behavior and Its Modification as an Example of the Complexity of Infant Response Patterns

The feeding response is perhaps the most proficient and consistent movement pattern the baby produces. In addition to consistency, it has a large number of measurable parameters. Teasing apart these components has (for the author) provided some of the methodological sophistication important for understanding what the newborn brings into the world in the way of both species-specific and individual characteristics. Sucking consists of rhythmic movements of jaw, tongue, palate, and glottus, which produce negative pressure in the mouth if the lips are sealed around a nipple (Bosma, 1972). The response can be described in terms of number of single responses per unit time, number of bursts (a burst being a series of single sucks occurring with small interresponse times), interburst intervals, and a host of combinations of these parameters. However, prior to the organizing of these larger units, the researcher must decide on some timing and amplitude requirements for a single response. (These have been suggested by Kaye, 1967, in a review of the research on sucking characteristics.) In addition to its many parameters, sucking is a behavior that perhaps best approximates the characteristics of what is typically thought of as "mature" responding, i.e., it is a highly organized and a seemingly efficient and repeatable pattern, and thus has the prospect of allowing the researcher or theoretician to escape the almost inevitable conceptual "drag" of thinking about the infant as universally immature.

In 1964, Lipsitt and Kaye carried out a classical conditioning study with 3-day-old newborns in which they paired sucking on a nonliquid-producing nipple with a 300 hertz square wave tone. The response used as an indication of conditioning was suckinglike jaw movements made in the absence of the nipple and in the presence of the tone. (Jaw movements are the most easily observed correlate of what is typically called sucking.) The conditioning was successfully carried out in a 45-minute procedure that showed that sucking movements in the presence of a tone alone increased when the tone was previously paired with a nipple, as compared to an unpaired time-separated tone and nipple sensitization (stimulus excitation) group. In some subsequent variations on this procedure (Kaye, 1967) the results were replicated. Again, what was conditioned in these studies was the jaw movement component, a dependent variable that encompasses only a small number of the attributes typically described as sucking. Jaw movements correlate with negative-pressure production over a wide range, varying from close to zero to almost 1.0. The factors affecting this relationship are both the type of stimulus and the amount of time per "sucking" opportunity or trial. For the regular commercial nipple employed in the above study, short time periods (15 seconds) were employed, weakening the correlation of jaw movements and negative pressure. These limitations produced legitimate questions about the generalization of these results to the usual liquid feeding situation, which requires negative or suction pressure. Aware of the value of extending the jaw movement conditioning procedure to the pressure component, these authors began to try to produce changes in the pressure frequency characteristics of the pacifier nipple by rewarding various aspects of the response. This was carried out in the instrumental conditioning paradigm. It was anticipated that if various "rewards" were made contingent on characteristics of the burst and pause pattern, these might change the sucking rhythm, and this would provide an example of the instrumental conditionability of very early feeding behavior. This was found to be extremely difficult because even prior to conditioning, the regular pacifier nipples appeared to produce sucking at the highest rate the infant could generate. Because of this effect, these researchers turned to non-maximal sucking elicitors (Lipsitt and Kaye, 1965; Kaye, 1972), in hopes of finding stimuli that would not produce ceiling responding and would thus allow conditioned increases in sucking rates to be more obviously produced. These nonmaximal sucking stimuli came in several forms, but reduced to those that provided either reduced lip stimulation, such as tubes, or reduced tongue stimulation, such as blunted nipples. In the first of these studies, tube and regular nipple-elicited sucking was compared. However, because of the exploratory nature of the study, jaw movements continued to be used as the indicator response, the issue of pressure sucking being momentarily laid aside. The infants sucked at different rates for the different-shaped nipples (Kaye, 1972, for review). Having the nonmaximal elicitor allowed the infant's sucking response to be positively rewarded. Learning effects were shown through an increase in sucking rate (Lipsitt, Kaye, and Bosack, 1966). Still, the measure was jaw movement rate, and its generalizability to suction responding was an open question.

At the same time that he was involved in this study, Kaye was carrying out some research with infant rhesus monkeys using instrumental conditioning procedures to bring their feeding behavior under control. These studies were, in part, designed to examine auditory characteristics of the youngest possible subjects. Seltzer and Kaye (see Kaye, 1967) found that there were several ways of assessing the effects of auditory conditioning in these infants. However, each mode of assessment gave a different ontogenetic picture of conditionability. In a situation where the infant rhesus was fed only if it sucked during the time when a certain tone was on, auditory control showed first in the measure of latency between tone onset and approach to the nipple. The second indicator, the average number of responses per feeding opportunity, showed a significant effect several sessions later. And finally, the rate of sucking while sucking began to come under auditory control still later. From these data, one may speculate that these monkeys had "learned" something about the relationship of tone to feeding, but that this was expressed in only some aspects of their behavior patterns at any point in time. For example, had the individual pressure durations been the only parameter measured, the earlier-appearing learning effect would not have been found.

Keeping this in mind and returning to the newborn human, a colleague, Brown, who was working with the author while at Emory University, began to explore the possible rewarding characteristics that contingent sucking on a high probability elicitor might have on prior sucking on a low probability elicitor (1972). She abandoned the jaw movement and utilized instead a 6 mm Hg. negative pressure criterion for defining the single sucking response. All stimulus presentations consisted of nonliquid air sucking. Following Premack's paradigm, she set up a response-reward dependency in the following way. For one group, if (within 90 seconds) the infant responded a certain number of times on a blunted nipple, he or she was given access to the regularly shaped pacifier for 30 seconds. For a second group, responding a certain number of times to the regular nipple was followed by 30 seconds of access to the blunted nipples. Control groups were given regular-nipple—regular-nipple, or blunted-nipple—blunted-nipple sequences of the same response-reward contingencies. The blunted nipple had been found previously to yield much lower levels of responding than the regular nipple. *The prediction was that sucking elicited by the regular nipple* (the operant) *when followed by the presentation of the blunted nipple* (the "reward") *would decrease in its response frequency; and that sucking elicited by the blunted nipple when followed by the regular nipple would increase its frequency* when each was compared to its control group. This turned out to be the case for both regular- and blunted-nipple sucking frequency. In addition, latency from acceptance of the nipple to first response showed an even stronger treatment effect in the expected directions. Brown's procedure was extended over two one-hour sessions, one each on the third and fourth days of life. Brown hypothesized that the lack of a first-day effect was due to the novelty of the blunted nipple, which perhaps required some initial adaptation.

An additional finding by Kaye (1972) on some data collected by Brown (1972) suggested that the various aspects of the rate of sucking were controlled by various components of the intraoral stimulation. Specifically, interburst interval was an inverse function of the "sum" of the intraoral stimulation, while burst length was inversely related to the tongue—nipple contact area. This is illustrated (along with a picture of each nipple) in Figure 1.

The differential control of parts of the sucking response by parts of the nipple provided an opportunity for the separation of sucking behavior into its various instrumental and rewarding components. If the parts of the response, such as burst length, interburst interval, or some combination of these, could be

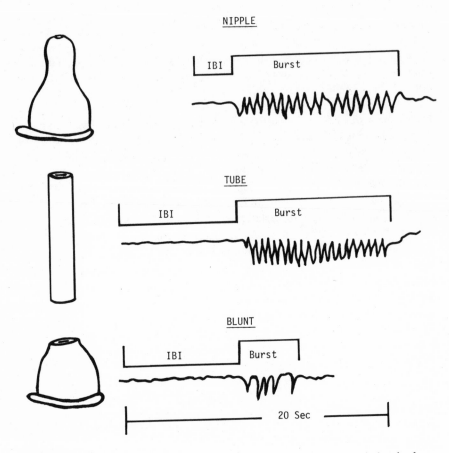

Figure 1. The left-hand column represents a tracing of the 3 devices. The right-hand column represents first a schematic of the relative durations of interburst intervals and burst length (IBI and Burst respectively) and a tracing of an actual sucking record generated by each of the 3 devices. The time scale is represented on the bottom.

purposefully varied, then part of the behavior that was "rewarding" could be pulled from this complex behavior. With this in mind, and with the desire to restructure Brown's procedure so that it could be carried out in a single day, Brassell and Kaye (1974) designed the following experiment. First, each new-born was adapted to all the nipple shapes they were likely to experience in the procedure, i.e., the tube, the blunt, and the "regular." Each infant then received one of six treatments (training procedures). Three of these consisted of the regular nipple used to initiate operant sucking, followed either by the regular, tubular, or blunted nipple, considered the "reward." The other three groups received the blunt nipple first to elicit the operant sucking, followed by one of the three rewarding nipples. The following hypotheses were made:

1. If density of responding (i.e., responses per unit time) was the effective reward component, then the three nipples would be decreasingly effective in the following order: regular, tube, blunt.
2. If interresponse time were negatively correlated with reward effectiveness, then the nipple would be most rewarding and the tube and blunt (which have equal interburst intervals) would be equivalent.
3. If burst length were the effective reward component, then the nipple and tube would be equal and both would be better rewards than the blunted nipple.

The results suggested that for sucking pressure, *response density* elicited by the reward was the key reinforcing characteristic for changing both instrumental response rates and initial response latencies. However, Brassell and Kaye also kept track of jaw movements, and for this instrumental response, *burst length* appeared to be the effective reward component. *Thus, for different measurable aspects of the response, there were different effective rewards.* This was not the first time that the jaw movement and pressure components of sucking were shown to be separable. Sameroff (1968) had reinforced either one or the other components of sucking behavior and partially supported his position that one rewarded component could be changed independent of the other. However, what Brassell and Kaye's findings suggest is that for the newborn, different components or definitions of a class of responses may be simultaneously but differentially affected by different aspects of the rewarding stimulus. Approached (speculatively) from a slightly different perspective, perhaps the jaw movement characteristic represents the stimulus imperatives of the situation that is the "reflexive" dimension of sucking. Pressure, it is known, never occurs in the absence of jaw movements, but the obverse does not hold. Perhaps an infant whose tongue is being stimulated cannot help but "chew" on the stimulus. On the other hand, perhaps the pressure response is a low probability initial correlate of sucking, one whose likelihood rises as a function of the negative pressure necessary during the normal feed. One might then look upon the sucking response as being made up of an elicited component, the jaw movement, and an emitted component, the pressure response. Perhaps this latter emitted component can only be strengthened or weakened in its general characteristics by the nature of consequent stimulation; but the elicited component is affected by the response-relevant characteristics of the unconditioned response with which it is paired.

The suggestion that pressure sucking increases over the first few days of life is born out in a study by Karp and Kaye (1973). Using a −7 mm Hg criterion for defining a suck, they showed first a large increase in general frequency from day 1 to day 2 postpartum age; and secondly, that the infant who is breast-feeding during the first 4 days of life will begin to decrease his or her burst length to a standard air nipple. This change is reasonable if one takes into account the fact that the breast will yield milk on a "ratio" basis, wherein 3 or 4 sucks will release some liquid, then a pause will allow the milk to be set up for the next few sucks. In contrast to this, bottle-feeding provides a continuous, suck-related stream of liquid, one suck drawing one "squirt."

SOME CONCLUDING THOUGHTS

For many years the inadequate feeding response has been taken as one of the pediatric signs of abnormality. The sick child, the genetically anomalous child, and now, the heroin- and methadone-addicted infant, all reflect aspects of their problem in the breakdown of various components of sucking behavior. Many premature infants, especially those who have been sustained by tube feeding for long periods of time have difficulty adapting to the usual methods of suckle-feeding. Perhaps results such as those above might suggest how to separate the fine-grained motor components of the feeding response in such a manner that one could focus on both the "built-in" stimulus elicited and experientially determined properties of the response. This might provide the individualized training mode required to help variously inadequate feeders adapt or readapt; and might provide a meaningful scale for monitoring the disruptive event. For example, one might be able to monitor the effects of various drugs on the reduction of withdrawal symptoms for the addicted baby.

Relating the above work to the earlier sections of the paper is constrained by the fact that the sucking research has been carried out during the first 3 to 4 days of life. And yet, there are some strategic decisions implicit in the ways that this research has been approached that do relate to the prior suggestions.

For example, the sucking behavior was examined in terms consonant with conditioning theory, a theoretical framework built around the notion of ecological adaptation on the basis of information or reward feedback. The immediate adaptive attributes of this response mechanism are easily generalized from these sorts of data, although the potential role that this type of contingency learning may play in later development can only be guessed at. Secondly, the suckle response was viewed as a multiply operating system whose components may be simultaneously responding to different parts of the environment. Out of this has come a view of the newborn as a complex organism whose behavioral attributes may well provide the many dimensions necessary for analyzing individual differences in a manner relevant to understanding the continuity underlying human development.

REFERENCES

Anastasi, A. Heredity, environment and the question "how." *Psychological Review,* 1958, *65,* 197—208.

Bijou, S. W., and Baer, D. M. *Child development II: Universal stage of infancy.* New York: Appleton—Century—Crofts, Meredith Corp., 1965.

Bosma, J. Form and function in the infant's mouth and pharynx. In J. Bosma (Ed.), *Third symposium on oral sensation and perception: The mouth of the infant.* Springfield, Ill.: C. C. Thomas, 1972.

Brassell, W. R., Jr., and Kaye, H. Feedback from the sucking environment and subsequent modification of sucking behavior in the human neonate. *Journal of Experimental Child Psychology,* 1974, *18,* 448–463.

Brown, J. Instrumental control of the sucking response in human newborns. *Journal of Experimental Child Psychology,* 1972, *14,* 66–80.

Corso, J. F. A theoretico–historical review of the threshold concept. *Psychological Bulletin,* 1963, *60,* 356–370.

Dennenberg, V. H. *The development of behavior, papers selected by Dennenberg.* Stamford: Sinaur Assoc., Inc., 1972.

Eimas, P. D., Siqueland, E. R., Jusczyk, P., and Vigorito, J. Speech perception in infants. *Science,* 1971, *171,* 303–306.

Fitzgerald, H. E., & Brackbill, Y. Stimulus-response organization, state, and conditionability during early infancy. Paper presented at S.R.C.D. meeting, Philadelphia, 1973.

Harris, D. B. Child psychology and the concept of development. In D. S. Palermo and L. P. Lipsitt (Eds.), *Research readings on child psychology.* New York: Holt, Rinehart, and Winston, 1963.

Hutt, S. J., Lenard, A. G., and Prechtl, H. F. R. Psychophysiological studies in newborn humans. In L. P. Lipsitt and H. W. Reese (Eds.), *Advances in child development and behavior* (Vol. 4). New York: Academic Press, 1969.

Kagan, J. Cross-cultural perspectives in early development: A progress report. Unpublished manuscript, Harvard University, 1973.

Karp, E. J., and Kaye, H. The effects of early feeding experience on the sucking patterns of neonates. Unpublished manuscript, 1973.

Kaye, H. Infant sucking behavior and its modification. In L. P. Lipsitt and C. C. Spiker (Eds.), *Advances in child development and behavior* (Vol. 3). New York: Academic Press, 1967.

Kaye, H. Effect of variations of oral experience upon suckle. In J. Bosma (Ed.), *Third symposium on oral sensation and perception: The mouth of the infant.* Springfield, Ill.: C. C. Thomas, 1972.

Lenneberg, E. *Biological foundations of language.* New York: Wiley, 1967.

Lipsitt, L. P. Learning in the first year of life. In C. C. Spiker and L. P. Lipsitt (Eds.), *Advances in child development and behavior* (Vol. 1). New York: Academic Press, 1963.

Lipsitt, L. P., and Kaye, H. Conditioned sucking in the human newborn. *Psychonomic Science,* 1964, *1,* 29–30.

Lipsitt, L. P., and Kaye, H. Changes in neonatal responses to optimizing and non-optimizing sucking stimulation. *Psychonomic Science,* 1965, *2,* 221–222.

Lipsitt, L. P., Kaye, H., and Bosack, T. N. Enhancement of neonatal sucking through reinforcement. *Journal of Experimental Child Psychology,* 1966, *4,* 163–168.

Little, A. H. Eyelid conditioning in the human infant as a function of the I.S.I. Paper presented at S.R.C.D. meetings, Minneapolis, 1971.

Papousek, H. Conditioned head rotation reflexes in infants in the first months of life. *Acta Paediatrica,* 1961, *50,* 565–576.

Piaget, J. Development and learning. In C. S. Lavatelli and F. Stendler (Eds.), *Readings in child behavior and development* (3rd ed.). New York: Harcourt Brace Jovanovich, 1972. Pp. 38–46.

Reese, H. W., and Lipsitt, L. P. *Experimental child psychology.* New York: Academic Press, 1970. Chapter 1.

Sameroff, A. J. The components of sucking in the human newborn. *Journal of Experimental Child Psychology,* 1968, *6,* 607–623.

Schaie, K. W. A reinterpretation of age-related changes in cognitive structure and functioning. In L. R. Goulet and P. B. Bates (Eds.), *Life-span developmental psychology: Research and theory.* New York: Academic Press, 1970.

Sherrington, C. S. *The integrative action of the nervous system.* New Haven: Yale University Press, 1906, 1948.

Siqueland, E. R., and Lipsitt, L. P. Conditioned headturning in human newborns. *Journal of Experimental Child Psychology,* 1966, *3,* 356–376.

Staats, A. W. *Learning, language, and cognition.* New York: Holt, Rinehart, and Winston, 1968.

Swets, J. A. Is there a sensory threshold? *Science,* 1961, *134,* 168–177.

Swazey, J. P. *Reflexes and motor integration: Sherrington's concept on integrative action.* Cambridge: Harvard University Press, 1969.

Taft, L. T., and Cohen, J. H. Neonatal and infant reflexology. In J. Hellmuth (Ed.), *Exceptional infant, Vol. 1: The normal infant.* New York: Brunner–Mazel, 1967.

Turkewitz, G., Moreau, T., Birch, H. G., and Davis, L. Relationships among responses in the human newborn: The non-association and non-equivalence among different indicators of responsiveness. *Psychophysiology,* 1971, *7,* 233–247.

Wohlwill, J. F. The age variable in psychological research. *Psychological Review,* January 1970, *77,* 49–64.

Wolff, P. H. The causes, controls and organization of behavior in the neonate. *Psychological Issues,* 1966, *5,* 17.

4

Development in
Complex Perceptual Activities

HERBERT L. PICK, JR.

Let us begin by examining the development of some very simple perceptual functions in normal children. Consider visual acuity as a first example. A number of studies using various methods (Fantz, Ordy, and Udelf, 1962; Gorman, Cogan, and Gillis, 1957; Dayton, Jones, Aiu, Rawson, Steele, and Rose, 1964) find the visual acuity of infants between zero and 1 month of age to be between 20/150 and 20/400 Snellen. It increases over the first several months of age and then rapidly through childhood, reaching maximum (20/20 to 20/15 Snellen) about the age of 10 years (Weymouth, 1963). Consider auditory acuity as a second example. Steinschneider, Lipton, and Richmond (1966) found neonates sensitive to sounds of 70 db or more. Bartoshuk (1964) found that the function relating responsivity and intensity of sound in neonates was similar to that of adults, and Eagles, Wishik, Doerfler, Melnick, and Levine (1963) found auditory acuity increasing slowly and gradually between 5 and 13 years with a slight decrease in sensitivity at 14. Even somewhat more complex perceptual functions such as those involved in size constancy seem to show gradual improvement with age. Typical of these studies is one by Zeigler and Leibowitz (1957). Children between 7 and 9 years of age showed less constancy than a group of adults in adjusting a rod 5 feet away to match the size of one varying from 10 to 100 feet away.

Such evidence as this led my wife and me (Pick and Pick, 1970) to conclude that at that time there was no evidence for qualitative changes in the develop-

HERBERT L. PICK, JR. · Institute of Child Development, University of Minnesota, Minneapolis, Minnesota 55455.

ment of perception similar to those found in cognitive development. Since that time no data have been described that leads me to change that conclusion. Moreover, research has been accumulating that suggests that infants are more perceptually precocious than ever imagined. For example, Ball and Tronik (1971) found infants as young as 2 weeks of age sensitive to the looming visual field of an approaching object. They showed that infants reacted to an expanding shadow (which is perceived as rapidly approaching by adults) in the visual field with complex head and hand movements interpretable as a defensive reaction. As another example, Bower, Broughton, and Moore (1970a; 1970b) found infants as young as 7 days of age sensitive to stereoscopic depth information. These infants were presented with a virtual image of an object by a stereoscopic display. They were upset when they failed to make contact with the object in reaching out for it. Bower (1973) and Yonas and Pick (1975) have a more complete analysis of these and related studies.

Thus, on the one hand, infants seem to be able to perceive an amazing amount about the world, more than had been imagined earlier. On the other hand, where there is evidence for perceptual development it seems to be very gradual over age without the interesting kinds of qualitative changes characteristic of other aspects of cognitive development. Yet, it seems obvious to even the naïve observer that there are marked differences in the perceptual based activity of children and adults. How is it possible to see these marked differences all around us, yet find them evaporate when subjected to careful experimental investigation?

In an earlier analysis (Pick, 1970), I suggested that one possibility for resolving this paradox is to examine more complex perceptual activities. The idea was that although relatively simple and primitive perceptual functions might show only slow continuous development with age, the integration of two or more of these functions into a more complex process might require a minimal level of development of the components. When these levels were reached, there might be discontinuous changes in the development of the more complex process. Other investigators have also recently suggested similar ideas. Addressing the development of hand—eye coordination in infants, Bruner (Bruner and Koslowski, 1972) suggests that this perceptual-motor activity is best examined as a skill. Like many skills, one of the major features is the perfecting of performance in the proper sequencing of the components. For example, prereaching infants showed differential responses to small graspable balls as opposed to balls whose size precluded holding. These responses to the graspable objects included such actions as adduction to the midline and proximal midline activity and to the larger objects breaking from the midline and forward swiping. These actions would have been appropriate if they had occurred in proper sequence with additional components and would, for example, have resulted in attaining the graspable object.

Within quite a different domain, Pollack (1969) has also focused on perceptual integration. He has observed that some perceptual tasks involve integration of information over time and that performance in these is related to mental age. In contrast, other tasks do not involve temporal integration, and performance in these is a function of chronological age. The Müller–Lyer illusion ($\overleftarrow{a}\rightarrow \overset{b}{\underset{}{\diagdown}}$, the fact that *a* is typically seen as shorter than *b*) is the prototype example for Pollack's distinction. When the illusion segments are presented simultaneously, the arrow tail segment is perceived as longer, an effect that diminishes with age. On the other hand, when the segments are presented successively, the arrow tail segment is perceived as shorter and the effect increases with age. Moreover, in this latter form, susceptibility is related to IQ (Pollack, 1964). While these effects do not show discontinuities in perceptual development, the differential directions of change and differential relations to intelligence may indicate qualitatively different processes in perceptual development. In any event, the present thesis, like those of Bruner and Pollack, argues for the examination of complex perceptual and perceptual motor activities that include a large component of integration of information.

With the young infant, one major problem concerning complex perceptual activities involves the question of meaning. Is it possible to speak of perception without meaning? This, of course, is a problem that has been argued for ages by philosophers and involves the distinction between sensation and perception. That debate will not be reviewed here. Rather, I want to state the thesis that it is an empirical question whether infants' perception has meaning. To illustrate, consider the issue of three-dimensional space. It might be possible to show that infants can see the difference between the shallow and deep side of a visual cliff using some sort of operant conditioning procedure. It is another question, given that they can discriminate between these two sides, whether they would respond appropriately by choosing to crawl off onto the shallow side. Such an experiment is difficult to perform because young infants (below 6 months of age) don't typically crawl. However, adults distinguish between "interesting" and "alarming" situations by making different heart rate responses to the two (Graham and Jackson, 1970). Heart rate deceleration is typically the response to interesting stimuli, and heart rate acceleration is typically the response to very intense, possibly alarming stimuli. Campos and his colleagues (Campos, Langer, and Krowitz, 1970; Schwartz, Campos, and Baisel, unpublished manuscript) based an investigation of depth perception on the possibility of obtaining such discriminative responses. They recorded the heart rate of infants between 2 and 9 months of age who were placed face down on the deep or shallow sides of a visual cliff. With the younger infants, heart rate deceleration occurred on both sides but it was greater on the deep side. By the age of 9 months, heart rate acceleration occurred to the deep side while heart rate deceleration continued to be the response to the shallow side. Such a pattern of results is consistent with a hypothesis that the younger infants perceive the difference between deep and shallow, but their perception does not involve "meaning." The older infants, on the other hand, respond to the depth with an appropriate change of response, implying they know the meaning of depth.

A similar result was obtained by Yonas and Hruska in a situation investigating sensitivity to stimulation specifying approach or recession of objects. A shadow expanding on a screen can very convincingly specify the approach of an object as, for example, a railroad engine in a moving picture. Similarly, a contracting shadow can specify a receding object. Hruska and Yonas (1971) showed that infants between the ages of 2 and 6 months responded with a heart rate deceleration to both the expansion and contraction of such a shadow. Again older infants responded to the possibly alarming expansion with a heart rate acceleration while continuing to respond with a deceleration to the contracting shadow. Again the older infants appear to have the appropriate meaning of this particular stimulus change.

It is important to note in both these examples that discrimination is not enough to infer meaning. Rather, what is sought is a qualitatively different response to qualitatively different stimulus situations. The fact that older infants show this suggests that they are making a richer distinction than at least Campos's younger infants. That is, they have integrated more information in their perception.

One way to test whether infants are indeed integrating information from different sources is to see whether they are disturbed by disruption in normally integrated information. One example demonstrating the development of such integration occurs in a study of reaching carried out by Lasky (1973). He examined the behavior of infants between the ages of 3 and 6 months as they reached for objects presented in front of them. Sometimes the objects were viewed directly and the infants could see the object and their hands as they reached. At other times the objects were presented optically in the same place by means of a mirror, but the mirror occluded vision by the infant of his own hand as it reached for the object. The younger infants (3 to 4 months) reached equally well with and without vision of their own hand. However, the older infants (5 to 6 months) were very much disturbed when their hand did not come into view. This was true even though their hand could make contact under the mirror with a dummy object that was in the appropriate location. That is, they were receiving appropriate proprioceptive and tactual stimulation. Apparently, by this age the infants were sensitive to normal integration of visual and proprioceptive information. (But cf. earlier note about the study of Bower *et al.*, on stereoscopic vision of very young infants.)

One of the more powerful paradigms for examining perceptual integration in older infants and young children is to examine the context with reference to which they make perceptual judgments. Are there developmental trends in the reference systems that determine children's perceptual judgments? A rather interesting example of this paradigm involves the study of sensitivity of 3-year-old children to shadow cues specifying depth. (Shadow or shading cues for depth are due to the fact that protuberances from, or indentations in, a surface have different shading dependent on the direction of illumination. Thus, for example, a protuberance on a vertical surface illuminated by the sun from above will be bright at its top and have a shadow on the bottom, whereas the indentation in the surface will have a shadow at its top and be bright on the bottom. That these shadow cues can be very effective is attested to by photographs (e.g., Gibson, 1950, p. 97) in which protuberances are seen as indentations when the photograph is turned upside down. Benson and Yonas (1973) taught 3-year-olds, in a discrimination learning paradigm, to choose consistently either an actual protuberance or an indentation in a vertical surface on the basis of tactual cues alone (i.e. without vision). After learning had reached criterion, the children were tested for transfer to photographs of the original stimuli—still presented in a vertical plane. In the case of the photographs, the only information for distinguishing between a protuberance or indentation was based on the shading cues described above. The 3-year-old children showed complete transfer, demonstrating first of all a kind of cross modal transfer. Moreover, this transfer showed that the children were taking into account the direction of illumination (from above) in their perception of shading information. When these photographs were placed on a horizontal plane such as they might be if viewed on a table, there was no transfer from the original tactual discrimination. Performance was at chance level. Such a pattern of results seems reasonable when one considers that illumination from above does not provide shading information about depth for objects on a horizontal plane. However, adults tested in the same situation respond as if the illumination is coming from the top of the picture; that is, that point of the picture farther away from them. The adults somehow (perhaps through experience) have come to make the identification of *up* in a picture plane as being equivalent to *far* in a horizontal plane. This identification is not made by the children. When and how it is made is a question for future research.

The argument being made here is that the use of reference systems by children reflects a kind of perceptual integration. It certainly implies that the perception of a particular stimulus takes into account the context stimulation. Most of the studies of the reference systems children use have focused on the perception of spatial layout. Here too there appear to be interesting developmental trends.

One of the classical problems in the study of children's perception is investigation of the ability to discriminate the orientation of stimuli. This may be motivated by the observation that young children are often quite happy to look at picture books upside down, and moreover, don't seem to have any particular difficulty identifying the pictured objects. This common observation has been verified in many experimental investigations. Typically in these investigations, children are given the task of discriminating between two lines, e.g., | vs. — or \ vs. ∕. The diagonals are invariably found more difficult to discriminate than the vertical and horizontal. In a recent series of studies of this problem, Berman (1973) examined the effect of different background shapes on this task. In particular she compared children's ability to make such discriminations when the lines were presented on large square or circular cards. (Thus, when a square card is used, the lines to be discriminated could be parallel or oblique with respect to the outline of the card.) The children were presented with a series of pairs of lines and had to select consistently a line of a particular orientation from the pair. When the square background was used, there was a significant developmental trend. Older children (five years) found discriminating between a horizontal and oblique, or a vertical and an oblique, easier than discriminating between a horizontal and a vertical. Younger children (four years) did not display this difference. With a circular background, the discrimination between horizontal and vertical was easier than between oblique and either rectilinear line. Thus, it would appear that type of background or reference system available markedly affects the relative difficulty of different orientation discriminations, and at least for the square backgrounds there is a developmental trend in the relative difficulty of the different orientation discriminations. Why should there be such a pattern of results? It would seem that square backgrounds are most likely to provide reference information for the discrimination, and older children use this to a greater degree than the younger children. With the circular backgrounds, there is no informative reference system, so discrimination is simply a function of amount of discrepancy (in degrees) between members of a pair, horizontal versus vertical being easier than horizontal or vertical versus oblique.

In Berman's study the effect of reference system was inferred on the basis of different behavior in different background contexts. However, psychologists have systematically studied the role of different reference systems determining how Ss judge up-down orientation of themselves and other objects. It is possible to distinguish three general strategies for investigating the use of frames of reference that might be referred to as deletion, conflict, and instruction. In the deletion technique, some frames of reference are removed and S's ability to continue to make orientation judgments is examined. In the conflict technique, different frames of reference are put in opposition to each other to see which ones are dominant in determining S's response. In the instruction paradigm, Ss are instructed to utilize one or another frame of reference in the presence of several, and their ability to do this is evaluated in a transfer test.

The use of reference systems for spaces that people look down upon such as Berman's (and e.g., Piaget's three mountain problem) may be quite different from their use for spaces in which people are actually behaving. Very little work has been done examining which reference system children use to orient themselves in spaces in which they actually are. Recently Acredolo (1974) completed a study examining just this question. In one experiment she used a conflict technique and pitted three possible reference systems against each other to see which ones children of various ages would use to orient themselves. In a small room one might distinguish the following three frames of reference: an egocentric frame defined in terms of the child's own body, an object-related frame of reference defined in terms of the objects in the room, and a "container" frame of reference defined in terms of the walls of the room. To make the situation more concrete, the small room that was used had a door at one end and a large window at the other end. The room was bare of furniture except for a table against one wall. The child was led to a corner of the table and blindfolded. He was then taken for a walk to one end of the room. The blindfold was removed and he was asked to go back to the place where the blindfold was put on. (The particular instructions used could have affected what the child did. In the study, the child was asked a number of probing questions after he made his choice. The answers indicated that the child was not biased by the particular wording of the instructions.) Where was the conflict between reference systems? Unknown to the child while he was blindfolded, the table was moved to the other side of the room. Would the child go back to the table or to the side of the room where the table had been? In terms of reference systems, would he be responding to an object reference system or to a container reference system? Seventy-four percent of the older children (4 to 5 years) and 62% of the younger children (3 to 4 years) went to the table. These results suggest that children of both ages use object rather than container reference systems. But consider a further breakdown of the data. Half the children were taken while blindfolded to the door-end of the room and asked to return to where they were when the blindfold was put on. If they made the same response as they did when they entered the room, e.g., turning to the right, they would tend to go to the same wall as initially. In other words, an egocentric frame of reference would work with the container frame of reference. The other children were taken to the window-end of the room, thus reversing their original view, in which case an egocentric response would work with an object frame of reference against a container frame of reference. Consider first the children taken to the window-end of the room. Eighty-three percent of the older children went to the table, and 87% of the younger children went to the table. That is, when an egocentric frame of reference works with an object frame of reference, response in terms of the container reference system is essentially nil. However, when the children were taken to the door-end of the room, 64% of the older children still went to the table but only 37% of the younger children went to the table. It would appear that the object reference system is strongest for both ages but its

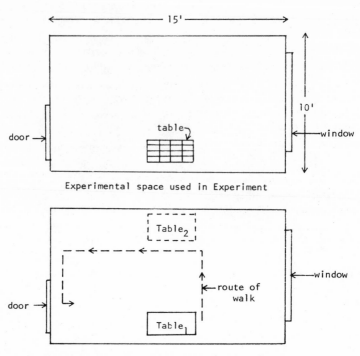

Experimental space used in Experiment

Condition I: Egocentric and Container versus Object

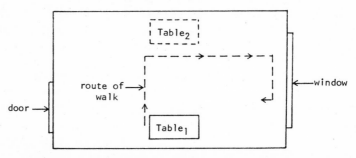

Condition II: Egocentric and Object versus Container

Figure 1. Situation used by Acredolo (1974) in Reference System Study.

influence is attenuated slightly by an egocentric reference system for the older subjects and more severely for the younger subjects. In a replication and extension of this experiment using a smaller room, Acredolo found older children responding very strongly to the container reference system, while the younger children could be influenced to go to the object when it and the egocentric reference system were both working against the container reference system.

These results, taken together with those of Berman, suggest that older children are more influenced by the more external reference systems than younger children. Speculating, one might hypothesize that there is a developmental trend toward using more and more external reference systems for perceptual judgments (cf. the difference found by Acredolo in her first study and in her replication with a smaller room). However, the fact that older children seem to be more influenced at all by external reference systems would seem to run counter to positions stressing decreasing field dependence as a function of age (e.g., Witkin *et al.*, 1954). Of course, perception of spatial layout as is being discussed here may have quite different bases from perception of verticality upon which Witkin's original hypothesis was based.

So far it has been argued that the traditional sensory functions are a poor place to seek interesting perceptual developmental changes. Rather, one needs to examine more complex perceptual activities for such changes. Two methods have been suggested as likely candidates: perceptual activities of infants that seem to imply meaning, and perceptual activities of older children that are concerned with spatial orientation and involve the use of frames of reference. It was also suggested that both these kinds of perceptual activities involve integration of information in perception. There is one type of classical perceptual problem, however, which does seem to involve a high degree of perceptual integration, but which only shows the slow gradual age change more characteristic of basic sensory functions. This is the problem of size constancy referred to earlier. As characterized by empiricist-minded psychologists, size constancy involves somehow integrating one's registration of the size of the retinal image of a target with one's information of target distance and then computing a real size. The fact that size constancy does not seem to be related to intelligence (animals exhibit it and correlations between size constancy and CA are higher than between constancy and MA) suggests that the characterization of size constancy as a computation problem may be wrong. Perhaps the size constancy effect should be interpreted more the way Gibson (1966) suggests, as direct perception of an invariant specifying constant size. For the case of size constancy such an invariant might be the relation of size of texture element in target to size of texture element in the ground plane.

Accepting for argument's sake the present thesis about interesting changes occurring in complex perceptual activities, does that thesis have any implications for the effect of experience on perception? Let me address this question by considering two examples of areas in which experience is considered to influence perception: sensory deficits and cultural experience.

For the area of sensory deficit, the effects of blindness on perception will be considered. Obviously, blindness has profound effects on visual experience but these are so self-evident that they do not merit discussion. What is less self-evident are the possible effects blindness has on nonvisual perception. A few studies of blind and sighted Ss find blind Ss superior to sighted in haptic perception, e.g., of form (Hatwell, 1959; Ebihara, 1958). However, by far the majority of such studies have either found no difference, or sighted Ss as superior. For example, Worchel (1951) compared a group of totally blind Ss (8 to 20 years in age) in the Texas State School for the Blind with a group of sighted Ss matched in age and sex. He gave them a haptic form perception task in which they had to draw the shape of objects, describe them verbally, and recognize a standard shape from a set of comparison shapes. The sighted Ss were considerably better in their drawings, slightly better in their verbal descriptions, but no better than the blind Ss in recognition. In another part of the experiment, the Ss were presented two forms and were asked to select from an array the composite form that would result if the two were put together. The sighted Ss performed considerably better than the blind Ss on this task, and the adventitiously blind performed better than the congenitally blind. Some of the introspective reports of the blind Ss suggested that the later blinded Ss who had had more visual experience used visual imagery in performing the tasks. The literature on this general topic has been recently carefully reviewed by Warren, Anooshian, and Bollinger (1973). They come to the conclusion that particularly for tasks involving perception of objects and position in near space, sighted Ss perform better than blind Ss and later blinded Ss typically perform better than early blinded Ss and congenitally blind Ss.

What could account for the typical finding of sighted superiority in haptic perception? One possibility is simply an overall advantage of skills and knowledge from the added visual experience. However, the fact that in many cases the IQs of the blind Ss are equivalent to the sighted, and the fact that blind Ss have obviously had more experience with haptic tasks than the sighted make such an explanation unlikely. Another possibility that has been suggested is that sighted Ss utilized visual imagery in their haptic perception. "The sighted invariably translated their tactile-kinesthetic impressions into visual imagery. Many of them stated that they got a picture of the form as they felt it" (Worchel, 1951, p. 12).

An objective definition of imagery is less troublesome now than it seemed to be in the height of the behaviorist era. The implication of imagery simply is that sighted Ss' processing of haptic information has some of the characteristics of their processing of visual information. One could suggest several such characteristics. One of the more interesting is the construction of an integrated simultaneously available "cognitive map." Thus, if one object is explored tactually and, as often happens with such exploration information, is received sequentially, one can ask to what degree does an S form an integrated map or picture of the object? For example, if S explores an object with seven distinctive points in the order 1, 2, 3, 4, 5, 6, 7, to what extent could he then go from point

1 directly to point 5; to what extent could he retrace part of the path; to what extent does he know alternate routes between points if he is blocked? All these things are possible if S has organized the information in what we typically think of as a visual image.

To my knowlege, no study fitting just this formulation has been carried out. A study by McKinney (1964), however, suggests a similar conclusion. Children with closed eyes were asked to point to the finger on the hand that had been touched by E. During the interval between being touched and pointing, each S either held his hand stationary or turned over his hand. The children who held their hands stationary made very few errors; those who turned them over made significantly more errors and these tended to be of a mirror-image type, i.e., responding to the finger opposite the one that was stimulated. The increase in errors was apparently not due to an intervening haptic activity, since a control group who turned their hands over and back before pointing to the stimulated fingers again made few errors. In contrast, a group of congenitally blind Ss made increasing numbers of errors as the amount of interpolated motor activity increased. The results seem reasonably interpretable in terms of the sighted Ss encoding the tactual information about position in a visual reference system and responding to this with their pointing while, of course, the blind Ss did not.

In the area of the effects of cultural experience on perception, popular topics for research have included the study of stimulus dimension preference in children, scanning tendencies in perception of briefly exposed stimuli, susceptibility to illusions, and pictorial perception. The present discussion will focus on susceptibility to illusions and picture perception. Since the early part of the present century, it has been known that different groups of people differ in their susceptibility to optical illusions. One recurrent and popular interpretation of that difference is an ecological hypothesis that implies that exposure to a particular type of environment modifies a person's susceptibility to such illusions. The most recent and dramatic application of this hypothesis is by Segall, Campbell, and Herskovitz (1966). These researchers examined susceptibility to such geometric illusions as the Müller–Lyer and horizontal-vertical illusions. In the case of the Müller–Lyer illusion, they suggested that the illusion might arise from Ss inappropriately interpreting the angles between the line segments and arrow heads and tails as oblique representations of right angles. This would be the case if, for example, S saw *a* as representing a sawhorse with legs extending away from him and *b* as a sawhorse with legs extending toward him. In that case, line segment *a* might be registered as closer than line segment *b*. If *a* is closer than *b* but projects the same size retinal image, it must be smaller. This train of inference results possibly in the typical perception of *a* as smaller than *b*.

But why should Ss perceive figures *a* and *b* as representing something like sawhorses? The ecological hypothesis suggests that among western literate observers there are two tendencies that would facilitate this. The first is that the environment is full of man-made right angles, and often oblique or obtuse images projected to the retina of the eye are merely due to perspective viewing of right-angled objects. Secondly, westernized *S*s are often exposed to two-dimensional drawings that present perspective views of three-dimensional objects. Again there may be a tendency to interpret any drawing as representing a solid object. The correctness of this aspect of the ecological hypothesis could be investigated by testing the susceptibility of the illusion with peoples who differ markedly in the degree of right-angle carpentering in their environment. (A similar ecological argument was made for susceptibility to the horizontal-vertical illusion.) Segall, Campbell, and Herskovitz tested susceptibility to such illusions in 15 cultures that differed widely in degree of carpentering and other possibly important variables. In general their results supported the ecological hypothesis. However, some of their own data and subsequent evidence again cast doubt on the ecological hypothesis. Briefly, developmental data from their own study do not conform to what might be expected from an ecological hypothesis. In most cultures, older *S*s were found to be less susceptible than younger *S*s. Secondly, additional studies (e.g., Jahoda, 1966) found results inconsistent with the original hypothesis. Finally, data on the Müller–Lyer illusion itself within our culture calls into question the original distance-related explanation.

Shifting now to picture perception, there are a number of cross-cultural studies that suggest that uneducated Africans in comparison with educated westerners have difficulty in perception of pictures (Hudson, 1960, 1967; Deregowski, 1968; Leibowitz, Brislin, Perlmuth, and Hennessy, 1969; Mundy–Castle, 1966; Kilbride and Robbins, 1968). On closer examination, however, it seems that the difficulty in picture perception is not difficulty in object recognition, but rather in perception of pictorial depth information. Indeed there is other reason to believe that naïve viewers with no prior experience can recognize photographs of familiar objects (Hochberg and Brooks, 1962). In order to perceive depth in pictures, one must be able to inhibit the information present that indicates that there is no depth such as binocular and motion parallax; then one can respond to the pictorial depth information. Perhaps this is what westerners learn by exposure to pictures in school and in their culture. It may also be the case that once having learned to respond this way to lines on paper, such subjects cannot turn off their inhibition and are compelled to interpret, in some sense, all drawings including illusion figures as being three-dimensional. This would explain the greater susceptibility of westerners to some of the illusions as well. (For a more detailed analysis of this and related issues, cf. A. D. Pick, 1973.) Thus, this hypothesis to explain cultural differences in susceptibility to illusions and picture perception implies an attentional mechanism involving selective inhibition. It also implies that perhaps this mechanism works to put one into a general mode of perceiving. For example, while in this mode two-dimensional information is generally inhibited. Some implications of this hypothesis are testable within a single culture.

In summary, what has been suggested in this paper is that interesting developmental changes in perception are likely to occur in those aspects of perception that are complex and involve integration of information. Such integration of information may be affected by rather massive differences in experience such as lack of visual experience or large and probably pervasive cultural experiences. When such differences in experience are present, the effect on perception may be in very general dispositions of information processing such as how information is organized or what mode of perceiving is adopted. Lesser differences in experience may affect more local mechanisms of perception, perhaps also attentional in nature. For example, experience may affect what aspects of stimulation are selected for processing and/or are inhibited from being processed. The way such selective mechanisms interact with processes of perceptual integration are a likely place for fruitful investigation.

Where might perception go wrong? It seems unlikely that slight differences in sensory function will make much difference in overall perceptual functioning. There are rather large differences in thresholds among children and adults who all function exceedingly well in normal perceptual and perceptual-motor activity. In fact, in the early history of mental testing, efforts to find relations between basic sensory and motor functions and intellectual behavior turned out to be markedly unsuccessful. It seems likely that the places where perception might go wrong are just those places where interesting developmental changes take place in perception, in complex perceptual activities, especially those involving integration of information.

ACKNOWLEDGMENTS

The present study was supported in part by the Program Project Grant (HD-03082) from the National Institute of Health to the Institute of Child Development of the University of Minnesota and by the Center for Advanced Study in the Behavioral Sciences, Stanford, California. It was written while the author held a National Institute of Health Career Development Fellowship (1-K3-HD12,396).

REFERENCES

Acredolo, L. P. Frames of referenced used by children for orientation in unfamiliar spaces. Unpublished doctoral dissertation, University of Minnesota, 1974.

Ball, W., and Tronick, E. Infant responses to impending collision: Optical and real. *Science,* 1971, *171,* 818–820.

Bartoshuk, A. K. Human neonatal cardiac responses to sound: A power function. *Psychonomic Science,* 1964, *1,* 151–152.

Benson, K., and Yonas, A. Development of sensitivity to static pictorial depth information. *Perception and Psychophysics,* 1973, *13,* 361–366.

Berman, P. W. How a child finds his way in two-dimensional space. Colloquium presented at Pennsylvania State University. 1973, and personal communication.

Bower, T. G. R. The development of reaching in infants. Unpublished monograph, University of Edinburgh, 1973.

Bower, T. G. R., Broughton, J. M., and Moore, M. K. Infant responses to approaching objects: An indicator of response to distal variables. *Perception and Psychophysics,* 1970, *9,* 193–196. (a)

Bower, T. G. R., Broughton, J. M., and Moore, M. K. Demonstration of intention in the reaching behavior of neonate humans. *Nature,* 1970, *228* (no. 5272), 697–681. (b)

Bruner, J. S., and Koslowski, B. Visually preadapted constituents of manipulatory action. *Perception,* 1972, *1,* 3–14.

Campos, J. J., Langer, A., and Krowitz, A. Cardiac responses on the visual cliff in prelocomotor human infants. *Science,* 1970, *170,* 196–197.

Dayton, G. O. Jr., Jones, M. H., Aiu, P., Rawson, R. H., Steele, B., and Rose, M. Developmental study of coordinated eye movements in the human infant I: Visual acuity in the newborn human: A study based on induced optokinetic nystagmus recorded by electro-oculography. *Archives of Ophthalmology,* 1964, *71,* 865–870.

Deregowski, J. B. Difficulties in pictorial depth perception in Africa. *British Journal of Psychology,* 1968, *59,* 195–204.

Eagles, F. L. Wishik, S. M., Doerfler, L. G., Melnick, W., and Levine, H. S. Hearing sensitivity and related factors in children. Published by Laryngoscope, 650 S. Kingshighway, St. Louis, Mo., 63110. 1963, Vol. XI, 220.

Ebihara, T. Moji ni okeru katachi no shigekiiki ni tsuite. (Stimulus thresholds of shapes for blind children.) *Journal of Psychology of the Blind,* 1958, *4,* 27–31.

Fantz, R. L., Ordy, J. M., and Udelf, M. S. Maturation of pattern vision in infants during first six months. *Journal of Comparative and Physiological Psychology,* 1962, *55,* 907–917.

Gibson, J. J. *The perception of the visual world.* Cambridge, Mass.: Riverside Press, 1950.

Gibson, J. J. *The senses considered as perceptual systems.* New York: Houghton Mifflin, 1966.

Gorman, J. J., Cogan, D. G., and Gillis, S. S. An apparatus for grading visual acuity of infants on the basis of opticokinetic nystagmus. *Pediatrics,* 1957, *19,* 1088–1092.

Graham, F. K., and Jackson, J. C. Arousal systems and infant heart rate responses. In H. W. Reese and L. P. Lipsitt, (Eds.), *Advances in Child Development and Behavior* (Vol. 5). New York: Academic Press, 1970.

Hatwell, Y. Perception tactile desformes et organisations spatial tactile. (Tactile form perception in the organization of tactile space.) *Journal de Psychologie Normale et Pathologique,* 1959, *56* (no. 2), 187–204.

Hochberg, J., and Brooks, V. Pictorial recognition as an unlearned ability: A study of one child's performance. *American Journal of Psychology,* 1962, *75,* 624–628.

Hruska, K., and Yonas, A. Developmental changes in cardiac responses to the optical stimulus of impending collision. Paper presented at the Meeting of the Society for Psychophysiological Research. St. Louis, Mo., 1971.

Hudson, W. Pictorial depth perception in sub-cultural groups in Africa. *Journal of Social Psychology,* 1960, *52,* 183–208.

Hudson, W. The study of the problem of pictorial perception among unacculturated groups. *International Journal of Psychology,* 1967, *2,* 89–107.

Jahoda, G. Geometric illusions and environment: A study in Ghana. *British Journal of Psychology,* 1966, *57,* 193–199.

Kilbride, P. C., and Robbins, M. C. Linear perspective, pictorial depth perception and education among the Baganda. *Perceptual and Motor Skills,* 1968, *27,* 601–602.

Lasky, R. E. The effect of visual feedback on the reaching of young infants. Unpublished doctoral dissertation, University of Minnesota, 1973.

Leibowitz, H. W., Brislin, R., Perlmutter, L., and Hennessy, R. Ponzo perspective illusion as a manifestation of space perception. *Science,* 1969, *166,* 1174–1176.

McKinney, J. P. Hand schema in children. *Psychonomic Science,* 1964, *1,* 99–100.

Mundy–Castle, A. C. Pictorial depth perception in Ghanaian children. *International Journal of Psychology,* 1966, *1,* 289–300.

Pick, A. D. Games experimenters play! Review of cross-cultural studies on cognition. Unpublished manuscript, University of Minnesota, 1973.

Pick, H. L. Jr. Systems of perceptual and perceptual-motor development. In J. Hill (Ed.), Minnesota symposia on child psychology (Vol. 4). Minneapolis: University of Minnesota Press, 1970.

Pick, H. L. Jr., and Pick, A. D. Sensory and perceptual development. In P. Mussen (Ed.), *Carmichael's manual of child psychology.* New York: Wiley, 1970.

Pollack, R. H. Simultaneous and successive presentation of elements of the Müller–Lyer figure and chronological age. *Perceptual Motor Skills,* 1964, *19,* 303–310.

Pollack, R. H. Some implications of ontogenetic changes in perception. In J. Flavell and D. Elkind (Eds.), *Studies in cognitive development: Essays in honor of Jean Piaget.* New York: Oxford University Press, 1969.

Schwartz, A. N., Campos, J. J., and Baisel, E. J. The visual cliff: Cardiac and behavioral responses on the deep and shallow sides at five and nine months of age. Unpublished manuscript, Psychology Department, University of Denver.

Segall, M. H., Campbell, D. T., and Herskovits, M. J. *The influence of culture on visual perception.* Indianapolis: Bobbs–Merrill, 1966.

Steinschneider, A., Lipton, E. L., and Richmond, J. B. Auditory sensitivity in the infant: Effect of intensity on cardiac and motor responsivity. *Child Development,* 1966, *37,* 233–252.

Warren, D., Anooshian, L. J., and Bollinger, J. G. Early vs. late blindness: The role of early vision in spatial behavior. *The American Foundation for the Blind Research Bulletin,* 1973, *26,* 151–170.

Weymouth, F. W. Visual acuity of children. In M. J. Hirsch and R. E. Wick (Eds.), *Vision of children.* Philadelphia, Penn.: Chilton, 1963.

Witkin, H. A., Lewis, H. B., Hartzman, M., Machover, K., Meissner, P. B., and Wapner, S. *Personality through perception.* New York: Harper, 1954.

Worchel, P. Space perception and orientation in the blind. *Psychological Monographs,* 1951, *65,* (Whole No. 332).

Yonas, A., and Pick, H. L. Jr. Infant space perception in L. Cohen and P. Salapatek (Eds.), *Perception in infants.* New York: Academic Press, 1975.

Zeigler, H. P., and Leibowitz, H. Apparent visual size as a function of distance for children and adults. *American Journal of Psychology,* 1957, *70,* 106–109.

5

The Nature of
the Neuropsychological Disability
in Autistic Children

MARIAN K. DeMYER

INTRODUCTION

Background

After Kanner (1943) first described infantile autism, the basic biological intelligence of these children was regarded as potentially normal in most cases. The reasons for this belief were the presence of splinter skills, "intelligent" faces, few reports of motor dysfunction, and "refusal" to perform when age-appropriate items from intelligence tests were presented to them. One widely held theory advanced to explain these "facts" was that most if not all autistic (Aut) children had anatomically normal brains, and that relatively high splinter skills were a "true" reflection of their potential intelligence. If the right treatment key could be found, then the seriously delayed verbal intelligence would advance in an accelerated fashion to catch up with the splinter skills and with the norms for the child's chronological age. Our research shows:

1. That the intelligence of Aut children can be measured reliably and validly.
2. That the IQ has good predictive power about the child's eventual functioning.

MARIAN K. DEMYER · Institute for Psychiatric Research, Indiana University Medical Center, Indianapolis, Indiana 46202.

3. That most Aut children have subnormal intelligence.

4. That in only a few children does the Verbal (Vb) IQ reach normal levels, no matter how intense the treatment and education.

Evidence for these assertions comes from a series of intelligence quotient studies by the staff of the Clinical Research Center for Early Childhood Schizophrenia located at Carter Hospital, Indiana University Medical Center. Clinical observations (DeMyer, Norton, and Barton, 1971) and formal experiment (Alpern, 1967) revealed that the nonperformance of Aut children on standard intelligence tests was related to task difficulty. Aut children could perform tasks designed for infants and showed high test–retest reliability in performing infant items. A survey of 155 Aut children, mean age 65 months, showed that the overwhelming number of Aut children (94%) had IQs of 67 or below (DeMyer, Barton, Alpern, Kimberlin, Allen, Yang, and Steele, 1974). Furthermore, 75% of Aut children had IQs below 51. Low Vb IQs accounted most heavily for this skew to the moderately to severely retarded end of the spectrum. Mean Vb IQ was 35, and mean Performance (Pf) IQ was 54. In contrast, a control group of 47 nonpsychotic subnormal (SNr) children, mean age 60 months, had significantly higher IQs, mean Pf IQ 70, and mean Vb IQ 55 (see Table 1). The IQ study was empirical and each referral child who was diagnosed as Aut or SNr was included.*

In testing the Aut and SNr children a mean of six years later, we found high correlations with the original IQs. The original General (Gen) IQs correlated with the Follow-up (FU) Gen IQs .700, Pf IQs correlated .577, and Vb IQs .630 (p < .001 all three correlations) (DeMyer *et al.* 1974). These correlation coefficients are similar to the .76 correlation found in normal children of similar ages using the Stanford–Binet.

Is the IQ of the Aut child useful for predicting other things besides itself? Does it relate to any other important features of the child's illness? We found:

1. The higher the child's measured IQ at initial evaluation, the better he did in work/school functioning at follow-up.

2. The higher the IQ, the less severe the emotional withdrawal and the less severe the speech symptoms.

3. Treated Aut children with initial IQs over 50 showed a greater increase in IQ over time than did untreated children in the same IQ range. Those children whose IQs were initially under 40 showed no differential IQ effect with treatment (DeMyer *et al.* 1974). The higher functioning the child was at initial

---

*For description of these diagnostic groups see Table 2. The SNr comparison group was selected from two sources: (1) centers in the city that trained preschool children with a general or specific learning deficit and who had the use of all four extremities (Down's syndrome children were excluded); and (2) referrals directly to the Research Center for evaluation of speech and emotional problems who were diagnosed as subnormal in a specific or general way but not psychotic.

Table 1

*Comparison of Evaluation IQ Scores of All
Consecutive Referrals*

Diagnostic group	No. *S*s	Mean age in years	Mean general IQ	Mean initial Pf. IQ	Mean initial Vb IQ
SNr	47	4.95	65.4	70.3	55.7
High Aut	26	6.62	61.0	67.0	51.1
Mid Aut	63	4.67	43.7	57.1	28.1
Low Aut	66	5.03	29.7	37.4	19.7
All Aut	155	5.44	44.8	53.8	34.9

Note: All group means differ significantly, $p < .01$, except for SNr and High Aut groups.

evaluation, the more likely he was to improve IQ-wise by follow-up time six years later.

While these IQ studies of large numbers of Aut children revealed that their IQs were related to important features of their illness, they told us little about the reason for the low measured IQ of 94% of the children. While the most socially withdrawn Aut children had the lowest IQs (DeMyer *et al.* 1974), we did not learn if the withdrawal caused the low IQs or if the low IQs were the cause of the withdrawal. We must look at the results of other studies to answer this question. Evidence from our neurological studies showed that Aut children had significantly more signs of neurological dysfunction than the Nr control group and nearly as many as the SNr group. (DeMyer *et al.* 1974). In studying the progress of the children through a process of diagnostic therapy, we found that even with high levels of motivation developed through operant conditioning techniques, Aut children demonstrated insurmountable blocks to learning. While the type of learning block varied from child to child, it was remarkably stable over time in the same child. Whatever neurological modalities were involved, there was a profound language dysfunction in each Aut child (Hingtgen and Churchill, 1969). This language dysfunction was manifest in symbolic aspects even if the mechanics of speech were present (Churchill, 1972). No amount of training or therapy seemed to help the child surmount his perceptual deficiencies, although improvement was possible for many children. Another bit of corollary evidence that implicated the nervous system as being disordered in Aut children came from a study of parental child-rearing practices in the infancy of these children. While we had to rely on the parental memories of this period, we

Table 2

DeMyer–Churchill Diagnostic Criteria

	Relations with adults	Speech and nonverbal communication	Use of toys and body	Intelligence test performance
Subnormal (nonpsychotic), general or specific learning disorder.	Overly dependent or negative but not consistently withdrawn. Like younger child.	Speech may be absent; if present, used for communication; if can't speak, can pantomime consistent with mental age.	Commensurate with mental age. Repetitive uses minimal.	Variable.
High autistic (symptoms appear before age 3).	Withdrawn. Islets of response to affectionate gestures and can give affection at times.	Some communicative speech, echolalia, disordered rhythm, emphasis tone, pronominal reversal repeat a question to ask a question. Only simple signaling for nonverbal communication.	Repetitive, nonfunctional toy use; or repetitive ritualistic body use. Pretend play minimal.	Various peaks and valleys on performance and verbal curves but generally does best with fitting and assembly tasks. May have a splinter skill such as "reading." Abstraction low.

Mid autistic (symptoms appear before age 3).	Withdrawn most of time, May cling physically to mo. or laugh when chased. Little response to affection. Does not initiate affectionate gestures.	No speech for communication beyond an occasional word. May have echolalia, immediate or delayed. Only simple nonverbal signaling.	As in High Aut. Pretend play absent.	As in High Aut, except performance mental age above verbal mental age, which is quite low. Has at least one splinter skill.
Low autistic (symptoms appear before age 3).	As in Mid Aut.	As in Mid Aut.	As in Mid Aut.	Verbal and performance low. No splinter skills. Gross motor often only peak on performance curve.

could find no important differences in how Aut parents and matched Normal (Nr) parents related to their infants. We found that SNr parents were less social and less warm than Aut parents. Most important, we found that parents of Aut and SNr infants had noted less mental alertness and slower motor development than sibs in 36% and 44% of the cases respectively (DeMyer, Pontius, Norton, Barton, Allen, and Steele, 1972).

All our evidence, indirect as much of it must be, points to a biological dysfunction of the central nervous system, particularly the language center, in the overwhelming majority of cases of infantile autism. Churchill (1972) argued persuasively that the chief difference between nonpsychotic SNr children such as aphasics must be in the greater degree of central language disturbance in Aut children. This argument is persuasive for those Aut children of low verbal intelligence, but not for the High Aut children whose Vb IQs are just as high as the SNr children (see Table 2 for diagnostic criteria of autism and its subcategories). Both SNr and High Aut children have equal numbers of signs of neurological dysfunction from the neurological examination and similar percentages of gross EEG abnormalities (DeMyer, Barton, DeMyer, Norton, Allen, and Steele, 1973).

Current Study

In view of the neurological and intellectual similarities, we had to attempt to explain why the clinical behavioral symptoms of the High Aut differ from those of the SNr. Given a group of children alike in intellect and signs of neurological dysfunction, how can we explain that some called "autistic" are withdrawn and noncommunicative, while others called SNr relate warmly, even being overly dependent, and use such speech as they have for communication?

There are two possible answers to this question:

1. The environment of the Aut children provided by the parents in the first years of life was less supportive of close emotional relationships.

2. There is a difference in the type of neurological modalities affected in Aut children. Again there is no evidence that High Aut children have any different early life experiences from the SNr group (DeMyer *et al.* 1973). Because the nervous system is nearly impossible to examine directly, we sought evidence that the performance of Aut and SNr children may be different in nonverbal as well as verbal test items. Psychological test items from the standardized test literature provided some clues for what these differences may be and have suggested future research questions. Our studies to date show that in addition to language deficiencies, many Aut children have more severe problems than SNr children in visual-motor imitation akin to a dyspraxia (DeMyer,

Alpern, Barton, DeMyer, Churchill, Hingtgen, Bryson, Pontius, and Kimberlin, 1972). Reported in the remainder of this paper will be results of testing of Aut and SNr children, using items gleaned from the standardized test literature, which suggest differential visual-motor and language features in the two groups of children.

The main questions to be answered with test data are:

1. Given similar IQs and neurological status between SNr and High Aut groups, are there some specific intelligence test items that differentiate the two groups? Specifically, (a) "Do High Aut children in comparison to SNr children have lower scores on verbal abstraction items and higher scores on rote verbal items such as digit span and word repetition?" (b) "Do High Aut children obtain lower scores than SNr children on certain visual motor items such as hand-finger imitation?"

2. In the case of Mid Aut and Low Aut children, are lower verbal IQs the only differentiating feature between them and SNr and High Aut? By definition, we subdivided the Mid and Low Aut groups on the basis of splinter skills present in the Mid Aut and absent in Low Aut. We had observed clinically and in experiment on a small number of children that these splinter skills were often in fitting and assembly tasks, and that splinter disabilities often involved verbal abstraction and motor imitation. The questions we wished to help answer by examination of IQ items in this regard were: (a) Do Mid Aut children generally have splinter skills in fitting and assembly tasks (i.e., object remains in visual field at all times) and splinter disabilities in motor imitation or in tasks that must be remembered visually, conceptualized visually, or related to the child's own body? (b) What kinds of verbal items account for most of the verbal disability in Mid and Low Aut children?

3. Of course, the ultimate question about which we wished to gain more insight concerned the nature of infantile autism: (a) Why are Aut children so withdrawn and noncommunicative in comparison to SNr children? (b) What accounts for the differences in degree of symptomatology among the three groups of Aut children? (See Table 2 for review of symptomatic difference in these four groups of children.)

At an initial evaluation, verbal and performance profiles (derivation of the test items and procedures are described fully in DeMyer *et al.,* 1972) were obtained for 66 Aut and 29 SNr children, referred consecutively to the Clinical Research Center for Early Childhood Schizophrenia. Mean age of the Aut was 5 years and of the SNr children, 6 years (see Table 3).

These children were selected by diagnostic criteria detailed in an earlier study (DeMyer, Churchill, Pontius, and Gilkey, 1971). These included severe and sustained emotional withdrawal, reduced communicative speech, and nonfunctional object use. We subdivided autism into three categories based on severity of

Table 3

Description of Subjects for Verbal and Performance Profile

Dx group	Total (N)	Mean CA (mos.)	Mean BDI*	%Abn EEG	Mean gen. IQ**	Mean Vine
Subnormal	(29)	71.8	58.8	75%	70.3	63.8
High A	(11)	93.8	51.1	82%	58.5	56.5
Mid A	(20)	56.4	30.8	75%	47.2	54.8
Low A	(35)	59.2	55.4	79%	28.9	37.9

*Brain dysfunction index.
**Cattell–Binet.

symptoms:

1. High autism (High Aut) was characterized by a mixture of communicative and uncommunicative speech and some islets of emotional relatedness in a background of withdrawal.

2. Middle Autism (Mid Aut) children showed severe withdrawal, no communicative speech, and some adaptive performance that approximated age level.

3. Low Autism (Low Aut) children showed the same features as Mid Aut with the exception that all verbal and adaptive behaviors were below that expected for chronological age.

In addition, there was a fourth group consisting of subnormal (SNr) children who demonstrated active emotional relationships on an immature level, fully communicative speech or adequate nonverbal communication, and appropriate use of objects.

VERBAL PROFILES

Method

For this section four types of verbal tests will be reported:

1. Verbal memory as tested by word and digit repetition.

2. Number concepts from Bayley (1969), Gesell and Amatruda (1965); Gesell, Halverson, and Amatruda (1940); Gesell and Ilg (1946).

3. Comprehension as tested by age-graded items from the Denver (Frankenburg and Dodds, 1967), Stanford–Binet (Terman and Merrill, 1960), and WISC (Wechsler, 1949).

4. Word recognition as tested by the Peabody Picture Vocabulary Test

(Dunn, 1965). Because many of the basement* mental ages were beyond the abilities of many children, performance cannot be reported for all children. The percentage of nonperformance is given in the results. All scores are mental ages (MA) corrected for chronological age (CA).

Results

Verbal Memory

The SNr children were superior to all Aut groups in word and digit repetition, a finding counter to our original expectation (see Table 4). The SNr were in the mildly retarded range, while most of the Aut were severely to profoundly retarded. A few Aut children tested in the normal range. This test had a basement mental age of 12 months. Since many of the Low Aut children were mute, this test was too difficult for about 87%.

Number Concepts

The SNr and High Aut achieved a number concept score of 71 and 77 respectively, which did not differ significantly. The basement mental age (i.e., the lowest possible mental age of number concept items) was 30 months and about half of the Mid Aut and 65% of Low Aut children could not pass this basement item, which demonstrated the concept of "one."

Receptive Language

Again the SNr and High Aut children had similar scores of 62 and 56 respectively. Mid and Low Aut were severely retarded in the recognition of the Peabody pictures, achieving scores of 37 and 22.

Comprehension (Abstraction) and Expressive Speech

Since most comprehension items required expressive speech, these two abilities are discussed together. They were tested by comprehension questions

---

*The term "basement" mental age as used here and in the following refers to the lowest possible mental age for that particular series of items. For example, no test item in the standardized psychological test literature contains a number concept item that is mental-age graded below 30 months. The lowest mental-age graded visual memory item (searching for a disappearing spoon) is by contrast 8 months. Other types of items have other basement mental ages. Item ceiling MAs also differ. These varying characteristics point up the roughness of our measures and the need for more specific experimentally designed test items to answer some of our questions. Also, new tests should be devised and standardized to test specific modalities as they progress in complexity as the normal child advances in chronological age, because there are serious gaps in our tests especially between infancy and early childhood.

Table 4

Comparison of Verbal Profiles in Four Diagnostic Groups

Tests from which items were derived	Rep. of words, digit span, Stanford–Binet, and WISC	Bayley, Gesell, and WISC	Peabody Picture Vocabulary and Bayley	Comprehension questions from Stanford–Binet, WISC, and Denver (for SNr and High Aut)
Basement mental age of items	12 months	30 months	6 months	30 months
Modality[a] / Diagnostic group	Verbal memory	Number concept	Receptive word skills	Abstract/creative language
SNr	63.9	70.5	62.2	53.0
High Aut	33.0	76.8	55.6	45.7
Mid Aut	46.0	57.6	37.0	29.5[b]
Low Aut	24.6		21.8	14.3[b]
Results of T-Tests				
SNr × HA	**			
SNr × MA			**	**
SNr × LA	**		**	**
HA × MA				*
HA × LA			**	**
MA × LA	*		**	**

[a]Displayed are mean group quotient scores.
[b]Mid and Low Aut groups were tested chiefly by means of sentence length and number of words spoken since they did not reach the basement abstraction mental age of 30 months. Thus, for most of the Mid and Low Aut children, these means do not reflect abstraction levels. The n of Low Aut children passing basement number-concept items was too small to compute a meaningful mean.
*$p < .05$.
**$p < .01$.

from the Stanford–Binet, WISC, and Denver Developmental Screening Test. The basement item was about 30 months. For those children with skills lower than 30 months, which included over 95% of the Low Aut children, we judged their verbal expressive age by determining the number of spoken words in their vocabulary and mean sentence length. The SNr children with a score of 53 were not significantly higher in comprehension (abstraction) than the High Aut with a score of 46. The expressive verbal quotient of the Mid Aut was 30 and that of Low Aut, 14.

In summary, SNr children and High Aut children were about equal in number concepts, word recognition, and language comprehension items, although there was a trend for the High Aut to be lower. The SNr were superior in digit and word repetition. Many Mid and Low Aut children, even though their chronological ages surpassed the mental-age level required for the basement items, could not be scored on verbal memory, arithmetic, verbal abstraction, and comprehension. Most Aut children could be tested for word-comprehension items from Bayley or the Peabody Picture Vocabulary Test, which demanded no expressive speech. Word comprehension IQs were about 10 points higher than abstraction IQs for each group.

The inability of so many of these low functioning preschool children to pass basement verbal abstraction test items at initial evaluation made it necessary to study the problem when the children were older and more speech had developed. We retested 46 children when they were in latency and teen-age by the WISC, which measures both the rote and more abstract aspects of language. Of these 46 subjects, 33 had been originally diagnosed as Aut and 13 had been diagnosed as SNr. Sixteen originally diagnosed Aut children, mean CA 11 years, were no longer emotionally withdrawn and could no longer be considered psychotic. All of the 13 children (mean CA 10 years) originally diagnosed as SNr remained nonpsychotic and all but one were still SNr in one or more ways. Of the 17 Aut children (mean CA 13½ years) who remained autistic, 10 had some useful, communicative speech and 7 were either mute or used only a few words (see Table 5).

The results of the verbal subtests are given in Table 6 by three diagnostic change groups:

1. SNr to SNr.
2. Aut to nonpsychotic (NP).
3. Aut to Aut.

Those children remaining Aut achieved the lowest scores (see Table 6 above) with their poorest verbal score in comprehension (mean IQ equivalent 29) and their best verbal score in digit span (IQ equivalent 59). Those children originally

Table 5

Subject Description for Follow-Up WISC Profiles by Change Diagnosis Groups

Change diagnosis	Total (N)	F-Up mean CA (mos.)	Mean BDI	Mean eval. IQ		
				Perf.	Verb.	Gen.
SNr → SNr	13	119	56.2	71	52	63
Aut → Nonpsychotic	16	133	40.7	67	50	61
Aut → Aut	17	162	40.9	65	33	47

Table 6

WISC Scores at Follow-Up Testing

Change diagnostic groups	Mean IQ equivalents for scaled scores WISC Verbal Subtests											
	Info.	S.D.	Compr.	S.D.	Arith.	S.D.	Simil.	S.D.	Vocab.	S.D.	Digits	S.D.
(1) SNr - to> SNr N=13	73	±20	68	±24	67	±17	74	±21	60	±18	65	±17
(2) Aut - to> SNr N=16	90	±36	71	±26	87	±39	85	±35	77	±27	93	±25
(3) Aut - to> Aut N=17	51	±22	29	±16	54	±29	48	±25	39	±14	59	±28
Significant difference:												
1 × 2	*										**	
1 × 3			**				*		*			
2 × 3	**		**		*		**		**		**	

*p < .05.
**p < .01.

Aut but whose clinical picture was no longer psychotic at follow-up also had their lowest verbal score in comprehension (mean IQ equivalent 71) and their highest score in digit span (IQ equivalent 93). In contrast, the lowest SNr score was vocabulary, 60, and the highest similarities, 74. Comprehension was about midway of the verbal scores, 68. Thus, the (Aut to NP) and the (Aut to Aut) WISC verbal profiles were nearly the same in configuration (see Figure 1), except that the scores were all about 30 to 40 IQ points apart.

The verbal profile of the (SNr to SNr) was different in that comprehension was not the lowest score. In fact the comprehension scores of the (SNr to SNr) and the (Aut to NP) were quite similar (67 and 71 respectively). The other WISC scales that might be expected to test thinking ability, namely, arithmetic and

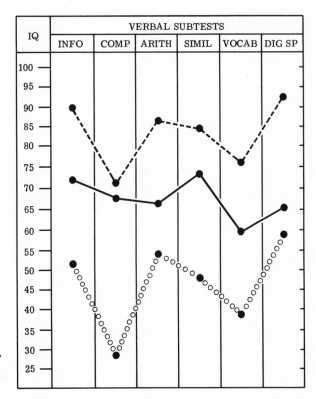

Figure 1. Profiles of WISC IQ equivalent scores at follow-up.

similarities, were little different from those scales that tested the more rote aspects of language such as digit span and information.

The one interesting finding that seemed to point to lesser abstracting ability in the Aut children who improved socially to the point that they were no longer psychotic was that comprehension scores were 15 IQ points lower than other subtest scores with the exception of vocabulary, which differed only 7 IQ points. The vocabulary subtest, of course, tests expressive speech as well as verbal-abstraction capacity.

We looked at the comprehension mental ages of the nonpsychotic children and found the lowest were in the range of 40 to 50 months. However, there were five children remaining autistic whose comprehension mental ages ranged from 40 to 77 months. Thus, if low comprehension age, i.e., below 40 months, was characteristic of most Aut children, there was also a sizable proportion (about one-fourth) whose comprehension age was equal to the comprehension mental age of the SNr. Also, at this point a question intrudes: Why aren't all children psychotic until 40-months mental age? The reason for the intrusion of the question was that one of the chief suspects for the cause of severe withdrawal in the autistic child was the inability to think or use speech symbolically or at least to be inferior in this regard to SNr children.

This critical comprehension mental age of 40 months for risk of psychosis must be taken with caution and regarded as a speculative level. Not only were the groups small, but we modified the handling of the scaled scores. Because several of the lower-functioning children obtained zero or less-than-zero scaled scores, all scaled scores were converted to IQ equivalents and extrapolated downward when necessary in order to score all children (DeMyer, Alpern, and Barton, 1973). However, this finding pointed to some potentially useful research in regard to an important modality to be measured while following the progress of Aut children. The principal abilities measured by the WISC Comprehension scale should be defined, and new tests for low mental-age children devised and carefully followed in Aut, SNr, and Nr children. Such a study would not only define more precisely the nature of the abstraction disturbance but also the comprehension mental age most likely to be associated with a change from psychotic withdrawal to nonpsychotic interpersonal relationships.

PERFORMANCE PROFILE

Method

For many autistic children, their low verbal abstraction abilities may be sufficient to explain in large measure their emotional withdrawal, their noncommunicative speech, and their nonsymbolic use of objects (Churchill, 1972). However, it is clear that children with an abstraction or comprehension age of even 42 months should be able to relate well emotionally, especially if the persons in their environment understand their limitations yet push sufficiently for intellectual and emotional growth. When a subnormal child is in the region of about 40 to 66 months in terms of speech comprehension (abstraction) ability, other special disabilities may complicate the child's understanding of communication aspects of his environment and tip the child into serious emotional withdrawal.

In an experiment (DeMyer, Alpern, Barton, DeMyer, Churchill, Hingtgen, Bryson, Pontius, and Kimberlin, 1972), the Aut children's imitation of body motion was more deficient than object imitation, which was in turn more deficient than their ability to assemble objects that suggested their own solutions. The body-imitation skills of Aut children were less mature than those of SNr children. Body imitation requires that the child remember a quickly disappearing motion or perceive that his body is like that of the demonstrator, and transfer the remembered motion to his own motor system. Experiments by Bryson (1972) suggest that some Aut children have a poor visual memory. Other autistic children may have relatively good visual memories but cannot transfer visual percepts to the motor system. Either deficit may result in visual-motor nonperformance that borders on dyspraxia. The low-level abstraction abilities and the motor-imitation difficulties can be used to explain the autistic child's emotional withdrawal. The child would have neither verbal nor nonverbal communication pathways open to other people. If the SNr child is particularly low in abstraction capacity, he may still have sufficient visual-motor skills to participate in nonverbal communication with others and thus would not likely be emotionally detached.

We have examined various aspects of the nonverbal (or performance) intelligence to seek some clues indicating that autistic children have some special perceptual-motor disabilities in addition to their severe verbal comprehension disabilities.

The same 66 Aut and 29 SNr children for whom verbal profile scores were determined at evaluation were tested for visual-motor skills involving both upper and lower extremities (see Figure 2).

Results

The results are listed in Table 7. All mean quotient scores (expressed as CA corrected mental ages) for the four diagnostic groups fell within the borderline to retarded levels in all types of tasks, meaning that most Aut and SNr children's perceptual-motor intelligence was borderline to subnormal. Except for stair

I. Upper extremities tests
   A. Motor skill required remains constant at 12 to 15 months.
      1. Model present during whole of task completion.
         (a) Matching colored discs to colored discs.
         (b) Placing geometric forms in formboard.
      2. Partial visual cues present.
         (a) Problem-solving (manikin and object assembly puzzles)—shapes and lines are the visual cues.
         (b) Ring Stack set (Fisher—Price)—size is the visual cue.
   B. Motor skill required advances with task complexity.
      1. Model present during whole of task completion.
         (a) Geometric drawing—exact model present.
         (b) Imitation of object use—use of object leaves some "permanent" environmental change (e.g., stringing beads, cutting with scissors).
      2. Model disappears and no "permanent" environmental change results.
         (a) Imitation of hand finger movements.
II. Lower extremities tests
   A. Motor skill required advances with task complexity.
      1. Model disappears and no "permanent" environmental change results.
         (a) Imitation of standing on one foot, jump, hop, skip, run.
      2. Partial visual cue available.
         (a) Use of object in stair climbing and descent.
III. Integration test
   A. Motor skill required advances with task complexity.
      1. Partial visual cue available.
         (a) Ball play—coordination of arms, hands, trunk, lower extremities, and vision.

Figure 2. Visual-motor profile test.

climbing and hop/skip/run/jump, the Low Aut group was significantly lower than the other three groups. The SNr and High Aut groups were alike except that the SNr were more adequate in ball play and stair climbing. The Mid Aut group was like the SNr and High Aut group, except that hand/finger imitation was significantly lower, falling into the severely retarded range (IQ equivalent 38). Hand/finger imitation was the lowest score of the Mid and Low Aut groups.

The influence of the type of task on scores is shown in Figure 3. If the children had before them at all times an exact replica of the visual component and the motor level required to complete the task was low (12 to 15 months), then all four diagnostic groups performed at the highest level. Color/shape matching was in the 75 to 85 IQ equivalent range for SNr, High, and Mid Auts, and 46 to 50 in Low Auts. When partial or more abstract visual cues were available at all times as in the Merrill—Palmer Manikin (Stutsman, 1948), WISC Object Assembly (Wechsler, 1949), and Fisher—Price Ring Stack set (standardization data unpublished) but the motor component remained at 12 months, the

Table 7

Profiles of Visual-Motor Skills in SNr and Aut Children[a]

Diagnostic group	Upper extremity							Lower extremity		Integration
	Color match	Form-board	Problem-solving	Ring stack	Geom. draw.	Fine motor w/obj.	Fine motor imit.	Gross motor imit.	Gross motor w/obj.	Complex motor ball play.
SNr (21)	79	78	77	65	61	50	56	54	58	72
High Aut (11)	63	75	63	62	55	60	54	42	41	47
Mid Aut (20)	83	85	64	63	51	55	38	50	65	48
Low Aut (35)	50	46	35	39	29	31	28	45	52	35
	Exact model available		Partial visual cue available		Exact model available		No visual cue remains		Partial visual cue available	
	Motor skill required remains constant at 12–15 months						Motor skill required advances with task complexity			

[a]Displayed are mean age corrected (quotient) scores.

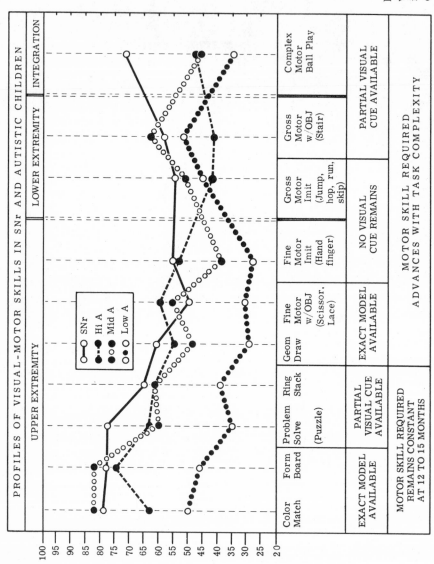

Figure 3. Profiles of visual–motor skills in SNr and autistic children.

effect was to decrease performance in all groups. If the motor skill required increased with the visual skill required, as in drawing of progressively more complex geometric figures, the effect was to decrease the level of performance still more. When object imitation was required, which left some "permanent" effect on the environment, e.g., stringing beads, lacing shoes, and scissoring, the effect was the same as in geometric drawing. The motor skills required increased with task complexity. When the imitation task required the children to copy a hand or finger motion that offered a quickly disappearing visual cue, then the effect was to decrease performance in the Mid and Low Aut groups only.

Lower extremity tasks, e.g., stair climbing and hop/skip/run/jump, further decreased the performance of High Aut only and this was the lowest visual-motor performance of High Aut children. In contrast, gross motor performance was as high as color/shape matching tasks for Low Aut children (IQ equivalent 45 to 52). A complex body-coordination task, ball play, which involved integrated use of vision, arms, hands, trunk, and legs was done best by SNr children (IQ equivalent 72), in the moderately retarded ranges (IQ equivalent 48) by High and Mid Aut children, and in the severely retarded range by Low Aut children (IQ equivalent 35).

COMMENTS

Nearly all types of tested perceptual-motor skills of most Aut and SNr children were borderline through subnormal. Two groups of Aut children performed hand/finger imitation tasks more poorly than SNr children. The SNr children performed the complex visual, arm, hand, body integration task of ball play better than High Aut children.

The type of visual-motor task affected the scores. If the exact visual cue remained in the sight of the children at all times (matching color and shape), performance in all diagnostic groups was top or nearly top. If either the visual or motor component of the task was made more difficult, then adequacy of performance dropped. Mid and Low Aut children had particular difficulties when memory of a motor cue was required in the upper extremity performance only. The High Aut children had particular difficulty in imitating movement of the lower extremities only.

The implications of these findings for the understanding of what "makes" one subnormal child psychotic and another subnormal child nonpsychotic were not firm, but some clues were available and should be followed in future research. The mixed findings with regard to body-imitation abilities are difficult to interpret, but all groups of Aut children were inferior to the SNr children in either upper- or lower-extremity imitation. In addition, the SNr children were superior to all Aut, even the High Aut children, in ball play. Since ball play involves integrating several parts of the body with each other and with vision, we have a tempting speculation about disabilities critical to the production of psychosis. It is possible that the complex visual-motor integration skills involved in ball play, if not important in their own right, are akin to some more important integrational skills involved in verbal abstraction and reasoning that we cannot yet conceive and, thus, have not measured.

If we look at the reasons for psychosis in the Low Aut group, it is clear that their verbal skills of all kinds, even word comprehension, are severely retarded, and that abstraction skills are so low as to be nontestable by current items. Their visual-motor skills are so low that taking away an exact visual cue or increasing the motor skill required above 12 months, makes the task almost impossible to do. Even with an exact visual cue and only infancy motor skill required, the visual-motor performance of Low Aut children is 50% retarded. No amount of treatment or education seems to enable the Low Aut child to advance in an accelerated fashion, although the passage of time, as the nervous system my-elenates and nerve cells branch, enables the low Aut child to acquire some increase in mental age—but not IQ. The Low Aut child may learn to recognize a few more words and draw a circle (where previously there was just muteness and scribbling), but his mental age line does not advance any faster than his chrono-logical age line. Only in gross motor skills does the Low Aut group approach the SNr group in adequacy of performance, and such relative adequacy (Mean IQ equivalent 57) seems unrelated to speech adequacy in this group of children.

We can see that Low Aut children can surpass infants only in matching like objects and in handling their lower extremities. They have virtually no splinter skills where thinking and fine perceptual-motor coordination is concerned. They could not be expected to handle their environment in any but the most simplistic ways or to understand anything but simple gestalts.

The Mid Aut children are higher in every way than the Low Aut except in use of the lower extremities. They equal both the Low Aut and SNr in this. Their splinter skills, however, are generally in doing matching tasks that require only infantile motor skill and either full or partial visual cues that stay in the child's field of vision at all times. Having to remember a quickly disappearing visual cue elicits the Mid Aut child's lowest performance, except for abstract language comprehension, which is generally so low that only word-comprehen-sion skills can be tested. These children also have severe difficulties in compre-hending complex aspects of the environment but can often handle visual stimuli, even complex ones, if they do not leave the field of vision. However, these splinter skills are not indicative of ability to think symbolically, using language, or to understand or use body language. The reason for emotional withdrawal and nonfunctional object use is not difficult to see.

The psychotic withdrawal of the High Aut children, which in our series comprised the fewest number of Aut children (16.8%), would appear to be the most difficult to explain. Our data suggests that while verbal comprehension is not normal, it is also not substantially different from that of nonpsychotic SNr children. Low ball-play scores and integration difficulty of their lower extremities in High Aut children suggest that more severe visual motor disabilities akin to a dyspraxia may tip a child who is only moderately retarded in verbal-comprehension skills into emotional withdrawal.

The higher-functioning children appear to benefit the most from treatment and education (DeMyer *et al.*, 1974). Some Aut children, about 8%, advance from subnormal measured intelligence to have either a verbal or performance IQ in the normal range. However, most children retain their particular pattern of learning dysfunction and generally low intelligence despite intensive treatment and education (Hingtgen and Churchill, 1969; DeMyer *et al.*, 1973).

REFERENCES

Alpern, G. D. Measurement of "untestable" autistic children. *Journal of Abnormal Psychology*, 1967, *72*, 478–486.

Bayley, N. *Bayley scales of infant development.* New York: The Psychological Corporation, 1969.

Beery, K. E. *Development test of visual-motor integration: Administration and scoring manual.* Chicago: Follett Educational Corp., 1967.

Bryson, C. Q. Short-term memory and cross-modal information processing in autistic children. *The Journal of Learning Disabilities*, 1972, *5*, 81–91.

Churchill, D. W. The relation of infantile autism and early childhood schizophrenia to developmental language disorders of childhood. *Journal of Autism and Childhood Schizophrenia*, 1972, *2*, 182–197.

DeMyer, M. K., Alpern, G. D., Barton, S., DeMyer, W. E., Churchill, D. W., Hingtgen, J. N., Bryson, C. Q., Pontius, W., and Kimberlin, C. Imitation in autistic, early schizophrenic, and nonpsychotic subnormal children. *Journal of Autism and Childhood Schizophrenia*, 1972, *2*, 264–287.

DeMyer, M. K., Alpern, G. D., and Barton, S. *A method for assigning IQ equivalents from WISC Performances of low functioning children.* Research Report No. 12. Indianapolis: Clinical Research Center for Early Childhood Schizophrenia, 1973.

DeMyer, M. K., Barton, S., DeMyer, W. E., Norton, J. A., Allen, J., and Steele, R. Prognosis in Autism: A follow-up study. *Journal of Autism and Childhood Schizophrenia*, 1973, *3*, 199–246.

DeMyer, M. K., Barton, S., Alpern, G. D., Kimberlin, C., Allen, J., Yang, E., and Steele, R. The measured intelligence of autistic children. *Journal of Autism and Childhood Schizophrenia*, 1974, *4*, 42–60.

DeMyer, M. K., Barton, S., and Norton, J. A. A comparison of adaptive, verbal, and motor profiles of psychotic and nonpsychotic subnormal children. *Journal of Autism and Childhood Schizophrenia*, 1972, *2*, 359–377.

DeMyer, M. K., Churchill, D. W., Pontius, W., and Gilkey, K. M. A comparison of five diagnostic systems for childhood schizophrenia and infantile autism. *Journal of Autism and Childhood Schizophrenia*, 1971, *1*, 175–189.

DeMyer, M. K., Norton, J. A., and Barton, S. Social and adaptive behaviors of autistic children as measured in a structured psychiatric interview. In D. W. Churchill, G. D. Alpern, and M. K. DeMyer (Eds.), *Infantile Autism: Proceedings of the Indiana University Colloquium.* Springfield, Ill.: Charles C. Thomas, 1971.

DeMyer, M. K., Pontius, W., Norton, J. A., Barton, S., Allen, J., and Steele, R. Parental practices and innate activity in normal, autistic, and brain-damaged infants. *Journal of Autism and Childhood Schizophrenia,* 1972, *2,* 49–66.

Dunn, L. M. *Expanded manual, Peabody picture vocabulary test.* Minneapolis: American Guidance Service, 1965.

Frankenburg, W. K., and Dodds, J. B. The Denver Development Screening Test. *Journal of Pediatrics,* 1967, *71,* 181–191.

Gesell, A., and Amatruda, C. S. *Developmental diagnosis: Normal and abnormal child development, clinical methods and pediatric applications* (2nd ed.). New York: Harper & Row, 1965.

Gesell, A. L., Halverson, M. M., and Amatruda, C. *The first five years of life.* New York: Harper & Bros., 1940.

Gesell, A., and Ilg, F. L. The child from five to ten. New York: Harper & Row, 1946.

Hingtgen, J. N., and Churchill, D. W. Identification of perceptual limitations in mute autistic children. *Archives of General Psychiatry,* 1969, *21,* 68–71.

Kanner, L. Autistic disturbances of affective contact. *Nervous child,* 1943, *2,* 217–250.

Stutsman, R. *Mental measurement of preschool children with a guide for administering the Merrill–Palmer scale of mental tests.* New York: Harcourt, Brace & World, 1948.

Terman, L. M., and Merrill, M. A. *Stanford–Binet intelligence scale, manual for the third revision, form L-M.* Boston: Houghton Mifflin, 1960.

Wechsler, D. *Wechsler intelligence scale for children: manual.* New York: The Psychological Corp., 1949.

6

The Modulation of Sensory Input and Motor Output in Autistic Children

EDWARD M. ORNITZ

Disordered perceptual processes in autistic children have been noted by many clinicians who have studied this developmental syndrome. The disturbances of perception in autistic children involve a distortion of the normal hierarchy of receptor preferences (Goldfarb, 1956), an impaired ability to use sensory input to make discriminations in the absence of feedback from motor responses (Hermelin and O'Connor, 1970), and a faulty modulation of sensory input (Ornitz and Ritvo, 1968a; Bender, 1947; Goldfarb, 1961; Ornitz, 1969; Bergman and Escalona, 1949; Anthony, 1958; Stroh and Buick, 1964).

Autistic children do not show the same preference in the use of the various sensory modalities as do normal children or nonautistic mentally retarded children. They have been described as preferring to use *proximal* receptors (touch, smell, and taste) rather than *distal* receptors (audition and vision; Goldfarb, 1956; Schopler, 1965, 1966). Both autistic and nonautistic children tend to respond to light in preference to sound, but nonautistic children can readily be conditioned to respond preferentially to a sound source, whereas this is not possible with autistic children (O'Connor, 1971). This apparent dominance of visual over auditory stimuli may actually be due to an inability to respond to two or more stimulus modalities in a complex stimulus presentation. Autistic children are overselective in responding to only one component of a stimulus complex consisting of, e.g., auditory, visual, and tactile components (Lovaas,

EDWARD M. ORNITZ · The Center for the Health Sciences, University of California, Los Angeles, California 90024.

Schreibman, Koegel, and Rehm, 1971; Lovaas and Schreibman, 1971). They also limit their attention to only one of two stimulus dimensions in a visual discrimination (Hermelin and O'Connor, 1970). Visual stimulation itself seems less meaningful to autistic than to nonautistic children in that autistic children show fewer eye movements in response to and spend less time regarding visual displays than do nonautistic children (Hermelin and O'Connor, 1970; O'Connor, 1971). While autistic children may have normal or even advanced form perception (Ritvo and Provence, 1953), they make poor use of visual discrimination in learning (O'Connor, 1971; Ottinger, Sweeny, and Lowe, 1965). They seem to be dependent on feedback from their own motor responses toward sensory stimuli in order to make sense out of perceptions (Hermelin and O'Connor, 1970; Frith and Hermelin, 1969). We will return to this theme after reviewing the symptoms of inadequate modulation of both sensory input and motor output.

SYMPTOMS OF INADEQUATE MODULATION OF SENSORY INPUT

The inability to adequately modulate sensory input constitutes a striking aspect of autistic symptomatology (Ornitz and Ritvo, 1968a; Goldfarb, 1961, 1963; Ornitz, 1971; Bergman and Escalona, 1949). All sensory modalities are affected and the faulty modulation of sensory input may be manifest as either a lack of responsiveness or an exaggerated reaction to sensory stimuli (Goldfarb, 1961, 1963). Both types of abnormal reactivity to sensory stimuli can occur in the same child (Goldfarb, 1963).

Hyporeactivity to auditory stimuli is apparent in the disregard of both verbal commands and loud sounds. Sudden sounds that would elicit an impressive startle reaction in normal children may elicit no response whatsoever in some autistic children (Anthony, 1958). Visually, the children may ignore new persons or features in their environment and they may walk into objects as if they did not see them. A similar response to tactile stimuli may occur during the first two years of life; objects placed in the hand may be allowed to fall away as if they had no tactile representation. Painful stimuli are often ignored; the children may not notice painful bumps, bruises, cuts, or injections.

Contrasting starkly to the hyporeactivity to sensory stimuli are markedly exaggerated reactions to the same stimuli. The children may show both heightened sensitivity to sensory stimuli and heightened awareness of sensory stimuli (Goldfarb, 1963).

The unusual sensitivity to sensory stimuli is manifest in many ways. The children may become agitated by the sound of sirens, vacuum cleaners, or barking dogs, and they may cup their hands over their ears in an attempt to shut out both these intense sounds and also mild novel sounds such as the crinkle of paper (Goldfarb, 1963; Bergman and Escalona, 1949). Sudden changes in illumination or confrontation with an unexpected object may elicit the same fearful reactions to visual stimuli. In the tactile modality, there may be severe intolerance for certain fabrics; the children are often disturbed by wool blankets or clothing and seem to prefer smooth surfaces. During the first year of life, the introduction of the rough-textured table foods may evoke distress. The children may show a marked aversion to the vestibular stimulation induced by roughhouse, antigravity play, or even riding in an elavator.

The heightened awareness of sensation is often associated with a tendency to seek it out and induce it. Some of the motor behaviors of autistic children seem to provide intense sensory stimulation. The children tend to induce sounds by scratching surfaces and putting their ears down close to the surface. They may be distracted by background stimuli of marginal intensity. They may rub, bang, or flick at their ears or grind their teeth, all of which activities induce intense auditory input. Visually, they regard their own writhing hand and finger movements or their more vigorous hand-flapping, and they scrutinize the fine detail of surfaces. There are also belief episodes of intense staring. The children may rub surfaces of furniture or fabric in response to fine textural differences. Many of the behaviors of autistic children also suggest that they are actively seeking out vestibular and proprioceptive stimulation (Bender, 1947, 1956). They whirl themselves around and around, repetitively rock and sway back and forth, or roll their heads from side to side. The repetitive hand-flapping also provides proprioceptive input.

SYMPTOMS OF INADEQUATE MODULATION OF MOTOR OUTPUT

The motor behaviors of autistic children do not necessarily provide sensory input. They are often such a predominant part of the syndrome as to merit attention in their own right. To a great extent, the strange and bizarre appearance of autistic children is due to their peculiar mannerisms and motility patterns. The deviant motility may involve the hands, the lower extremities, or the trunk and entire body. While the mannerisms are often complex and ritualistic and clearly do not have the appearance of either involuntary movements or seizure discharge patterns, they are stereotyped, strikingly similar in general pattern and form in most autistic children, and do not seem to be entirely voluntary. The severity of this aspect of the syndrome varies markedly from one autistic child to another. The deviant motility may appear intermittently or infrequently in some autistic children and may occur continuously in others (Sorosky, Ornitz, Brown, and Ritvo, 1968; Hutt, Hutt, Lee, and Ounsted, 1965).

Some of the most characteristic and striking motor behaviors involve the hands (Ornitz and Ritvo, 1968a; Sorosky *et al.*, 1968; Aug and Ables, 1971; Ornitz, 1971; Ritvo, Ornitz, and LaFranchi, 1968; Ornitz, Brown, Sorosky, Ritvo, and Dietrich, 1970). The autistic child may hold his hands in front of his eyes and writhe or twist the fingers and palms. This type of activity often merges into a repetitive, stereotyped wiggling of the fingers or the entire hand. This hand-flapping involves a rapid and untiring alternating flexion and extension of the fingers or hands or an alternating pronation and supination of the forearm. Similar flapping movements of the lower extremities may occur, but the most striking involvement of the lower extremities is toe-walking (Colbert and Koegler, 1958). This may occur transiently during states of excitement or while the child is running in circles. However, it is often the only mode of walking and may persist on occasion into adolescence.

Disturbances involving the trunk or entire body include staccato lunging and darting movements, terminated by sudden stops. The children also engage in an unusual amount of body-rocking and swaying, often accompanied by head-rolling or head-banging. A history of severe infantile hand-banging is often associated with the later development of self-mutilation (Green, 1967). The children also whirl themselves around the longitudinal body axis. In spite of all this gross motor activity, autistic children are not necessarily hyperactive. These children are not constantly in motion nor is there necessarily a restless, irritable quality to their activity. In fact, the various behaviors just described may be interrupted by sudden brief episodes of immobility, often associated with bizarre posturing of the trunk or extremities. Very young autistic children tend to arch the back and hyperextend the neck, maintaining this uncomfortable position for brief periods of time. Some or all of these motility patterns can at times be elicited by rapidly spinning a child's top in front of the patient.

EXPLANATORY HYPOTHESES

Several different hypotheses have been put forth to explain the relationship between the disturbance of perception and the disturbance of motility observed in autistic children.

Physiologic Overarousal

A plausible explanation of the apparent tendency toward a specific and peculiar type of motor discharge that seems to provide and at times to be triggered by sensory input is that autistic children are in a chronic state of physiologic overarousal. Hutt *et al.* (1965) found that autistic children show more frequent gesturing in more complex environments, suggesting that they are in a more aroused state and therefore more ready to respond to increased stimulation. However, investigations that focused on those motor behaviors that are very specific to the autistic syndrome, e.g., hand-flapping, demonstrated that the motor output persisted through long periods of reduced sensory input (Sorosky *et al.*, 1968) and did not increase significantly in the presence of increasing environmental complexity (Ornitz *et al.*, 1970; Hermelin and O'Connor, 1970). Furthermore, electroencephalographic studies have not consistently supported the notion that autistic children are in a chronic state of hyperarousal. Two reports of unusually low voltage EEGs suggestive of hyperarousal (Kolvin *et al.*, 1971; Hutt *et al.*, 1965) were not confirmed in two other studies (Creak and Pampiglione, 1969; Hermelin and O'Connor, 1968) when stimulus conditions were controlled. The evidence indicates that excessive motor activity by the autistic child is not necessarily caused by a chronic state of physiologic overarousal.

Insufficient Sensory Stimulation

Since many of the autistic motor behaviors seem to provide sensory input (see above), it seems natural to assume that autistic children have been in or are in a state of sensory deprivation for which they are trying to compensate by self-generated input. Maternal deprivation is a condition that may occur in institutionally reared (Provence and Lipton, 1962) or home-reared (Coleman and Provence, 1957) infants and results in severe sensory deprivation during the critical early months of life. However, comparison of the clinical syndrome of childhood autism with that resulting from maternal deprivation has shown that the two conditions are diagnostically distinct and that childhood autism does not result from earlier sensory deprivation (Ornitz, 1971, 1973). It still remains possible that autistic children are in a functional state of sensory deprivation, perhaps due to a neurophysiologic dysfunction that results in a tendency to gate out too much sensory input. This seems unlikely since clinical observation shows that the children react as if they are receiving too much sensory input as often as too little (Goldfarb, 1963; Bergman and Escalona, 1949; Ornitz, 1973). Although the motor behaviors appear to provide sensory input, a quantitative study of the amount of hand-flapping showed that it was not reduced when autistic children attended to a spinning object. This finding suggested that the hand-flapping was not compensating for lack of sufficient sensory input (Ornitz *et al.*, 1970). In the same experiment, however, restriction of visual input caused one autistic child to modify his hand-flapping by brushing his fingers against his body with each hand movement, apparently substituting tactile input for the reduced visual input. Thus, the possibility remains open that autistic motor behaviors may provide sensory input.

Inadequate Modulation of Sensory Input

Closely related to the notion that autistic children may excessively gate out sensory input is the more general concept of the breakdown or failure to develop of the neurophysiologic mechanisms that regulate the level of sensory bombardment (Ornitz, 1969). In this concept, the fact that autistic children both underreact and overreact to sensory stimuli (Goldfarb, 1963; Bergman and Escalona, 1949; Ornitz, 1973; Anthony, 1958) is taken into account. It has been presented in terms of a defective stimulus barrier or filtering function (Anthony, 1958; Bergman and Escalona, 1949), or as a basic state of perceptual inconstancy related to an imbalance between neurophysiologic excitation and inhibition (Ornitz and Ritvo, 1968a, 1968b). Those who have accepted these notions have either ignored the strange motility of autistic children or have treated the motility disturbance as an independent consequence of the postulated uncoupling of excitatory and inhibitory mechanisms (Ornitz and Ritvo, 1968a, 1968b). This failure to take into account the possible interaction of the modulation of sensory input and the strange motor output was a consequence of not paying sufficient attention to certain interesting behavioral sequences that can be observed clinically. In young autistic children, it is at times observed that certain types of sensory input, particularly sudden or intense auditory stimuli and visual stimulation with spinning objects, will induce excitatory motor behavior such as stereotyped repetitive flapping or oscillating of the extremities. At other times, such stimuli will cause transient catatonic-like arrests of motion, often with unusual posturing. These behavior sequences are similar in form to the subjective experience of adult schizophrenics, and have been discussed in relation to a postulated control of both sensory input and motor output by central vestibular mechanisms (Ornitz, 1970). The concept of failure of regulation of both sensory input and motor output due to a dysfunction of a common neurophysiologic mechanism has been elaborated in terms of the effect of sensory input on motor output and of motor output on sensory input (Ornitz, 1971). This concept of childhood autism as a disorder of sensorimotor integration (Ornitz, 1971) will now be developed in relation to two types of experimental investigation.

Disordered Sensorimotor Integration

Two convergent lines of investigation, one clinical and neurophysiologic (Ornitz, 1969, 1970, 1971), the other psychologic (Hermelin and O'Connor,

1970), have pointed toward a disturbance of sensorimotor integration in autistic children. I will first consider the careful psychological experiments of Hermelin and O'Connor (1970). In the process of confirming the dominant use of "proximal" receptors such as touch over "distal" receptors such as sound (Goldfarb, 1956; Schopler, 1965, 1966), they noted that a tactile stimulus, a light tug on a string around the child's ankle, was associated with induced movement of the child's leg. Thus, the apparent dominance of the tactile sense may have actually been due to a kinesthetic stimulus, i.e., sensory feedback from the child's own motor response. This was confirmed in a subsequent experiment in which it was found that autistic children were able to make discriminations on the basis of the position of a sound and light stimulus that determined the child's motor response to reach the reward rather than on the intensity-modality combination of the stimulus complex. The autistic children discriminated not according to, e.g., visual cues, but to their own hand movements, e.g., an upward versus a straight-ahead reach. In a related experiment, it was shown that both older autistic children (6 to 15 years old) and younger normal children (3 to 5 years old) learned to make a position discrimination more readily than a visual discrimination. Since the position discrimination involved the learning of a motor habit, i.e., reaching in the same direction, this result indicated that the defect in responding to sensory cues and the need for kinesthetic feedback from motor responses in the older autistic children represented a developmental disturbance. Thus the "maturational lag" that has been observed both clinically (Bender and Freedman, 1952) and in experimental sleep studies (Ornitz, 1972) of autistic children is also manifest in the need of the immature organism to receive feedback from self-generated motor responses in order to learn. In a final series of experiments, Hermelin and O'Connor (1970) and Frith and Hermelin (1969) used both a tracking and a card-arrangement task to show that autistic children learned through cues that were primarily manipulative, i.e., involving motor feedback, and benefited little from additional visual information. Thus, autistic children "seem to rely more on perceptual activity than on perceptual analysis," a tendency that is also seen in very young normal children and therefore represents, in part, a developmental delay.

HOW DOES THE AUTISTIC CHILD MAKE *SENSE* OUT OF *SENSATION?*

Can the impaired ability of autistic children to use sensory input to make perceptual discriminations in the absence of feedback from their own motor responses (Hermelin and O'Connor, 1970) help us to understand the significance of their strange motility patterns, e.g., hand-flapping? I have suggested that the bizarre and repetitive motor output may actually be a compensatory activity that helps the autistic child to make *sense* out of *sensation* (Ornitz, 1973). This notion follows from clinical observations that parallel the careful experimental work of Hermelin and O'Connor. In the task-oriented experiments, the autistic children utilized either manipulation or positioning of their extremities to make discriminations. In their spontaneous activity, autistic children are continually spinning, twirling, flicking, tapping, or rubbing objects. Furthermore, they repetitively flap, writhe, wiggle, or oscillate their extremities while regarding them intently. Analogous to the experimental learning situations, could autistic children in their spontaneous "play" be getting the *sense* of objects in their environment, including their own bodies and their parts, through kinesthetic (sensorimotor) feedback in lieu of normal perceptual processes?

OBSERVATIONS OF MOTOR INHIBITION IN RESPONSE TO SENSORY STIMULATION

Indirect support for this clinical inference comes from clinical neurophysiologic studies of sensorimotor dysfunction in autistic children. In these studies, the response of the oculo*motor* system to sensory stimulation during both wakefulness and sleep is presented as a possible model of more general sensorimotor function.

Experimental Findings

In the alert normal subject, the oculomotor response (nystagmus) to vestibular stimulation of the horizontal semicircular canals (provided by acceleration in a rotating chair) is consistently suppressed when optic fixation is permitted (Wendt, 1951; Collins, 1968). Studies of nystagmus in figure skaters (Collins, 1966) and ballet dancers (Dix and Hood, 1969) strongly suggest that the suppression of vestibularly induced nystagmus by optic fixation is an adaptive response that serves to prevent the disorientation, staggering, and loss of balance that would otherwise occur. This suggests that the modulation of the oculomotor output not only facilitates the stability of the peripheral vision but also in some way influences the processing of intense sensory input from the vestibular system so as to modify and improve the entire organismic response. Three studies of vestibular nystagmus in autistic children have shown that when visual fixation is permitted, the suppression of nystagmus it significantly greater in autistic children than in age-matched normal children (Pollack and Krieger, 1958; Colbert, Koegler, and Markham, 1959; Ritvo, Ornitz, Eviatar, Markham, Brown, and Mason, 1969). Recently completed studies in our laboratory (Ornitz, Brown, Mason, and Putnam, 1974a, 1974b) have also shown that vestibular nystagmus is more severely suppressed by autistic children than by normal children, not only when ocular fixation is permitted but also when the retina is stimulated by light while fixation is precluded. Therefore, excessive damping of the oculomotor response to vestibular stimulation in alert autistic children is dependent on at least two mechanisms, one that is oculomotor and does utilize ocular fixation, and another that is oculosensory and does *not* utilize ocular fixation. Thus, the suppression of postrotatory nystagmus in autistic children does not depend only on the occurrence of ocular fixation. Instead, a more pervasive interaction of the visual system and the vestibular system is involved. Furthermore, it now seems less likely that the greater suppression of vestibular nystagmus in the presence of ocular fixation in autistic children represents a learned response. Autistic children probably are not reacting to the vestibular stimulus by fixating in the sense that this reaction occurs in figure skaters (Collins, 1966) and ballet dancers (Dix and Hood, 1969). The present findings are more compatible with the hypothesis that in the presence of visual stimulation (either light or a fixation point), the excessive damping of the response to vestibular input reflects a basic neurophysiologic dysfunction.

A similar phenomenon has been demonstrated in a small group of sleeping autistic children who showed a damping of the phasic ocular activity of REM sleep in response to vestibular stimulation (Ornitz, Forsythe, and de la Peña, 1973a, 1973b). In these experiments a very mild sinusoidal oscillation was applied to a special bed in which the children slept throughout the night. Quantitative measures of the duration and organization of the rapid-eye-movement bursts significantly increased during the course of the night in the normal children in response to the vestibular stimulation and showed no response during the course of the night in the autistic children. The induced changes can be interpreted as manifestations of a specific effect on the phasic ocular activity of REM sleep, since no changes in the percent of REM sleep time or the nocturnal sleep cycle occurred. Since it is known that there is an enhanced activity of the visual system (increased neuronal discharge in the occipital cortex and the lateral geniculate nuclei) synchronous with the eye-movement bursts (Bizzi, 1966b), this relatively deficient oculomotor response to vestibular stimulation during REM sleep at the time of endogenous oculosensory stimulation may tentatively be attributed to defects in the same pathways that are involved in the deficient vestibular nystagmus response in the presence of visual input in the waking state.

Clinical Observations

Before indulging in speculations as to which neural pathways might be involved, it is necessary to return briefly to clinical observations of autistic children, in order to document the suggestion that the *deficient* oculo*motor* response to combined vestibular and visual *sensory* stimulation is a model of a more general sensorimotor dysfunction. Attention has already been directed to the hypermotility of autistic children in connection with the suggestion that they are *comprehending* their environment through sensorimotor feedback (see above). However, the deficient vestibularly initiated oculomotor responses in the presence of visual sensory input are more closely related to another aspect of the clinical syndrome—the hypomotility of autistic children. These children frequently respond to visual, auditory, or painful stimuli with a hypoactive startle response, catatonic arrests of motion, or general lack of *emotional* reaction. In general, a reduced motor response to sensory stimulation is a significant aspect of autistic symptomatology: Autistic children often "underreact" to visual, auditory, or painful stimuli. Minimal motor and emotional responses are characteristic symptoms of autism.

SENSORIMOTOR INCONSTANCY

Autistic children show both inhibited and facilitated motor responses to sensory stimuli. This unpredictability or inconstancy of behavior in response to stimulation had earlier been referred to as a state of *perceptual inconstancy* in autistic children (Ornitz and Ritvo, 1968a, 1968b). In the context of both the clinical and experimental data under consideration, this aspect of autistic behavior is better described as a state of *sensorimotor inconstancy*. Returning to the experimental data, we find that this facet of the clinical material—the combination of hyperreactive and hyporeactive motor responses to sensory stimulation— also has a parallel in the oculomotor response to vestibular stimulation. Greater within-subject trial-to-trial variability of the nystagmus duration in response to caloric vestibular stimulation has been demonstrated in autistic than in normal children under conditions of visual input (Colbert *et al.*, 1959). Recently we have obtained a similar result for the nystagmus response to an abrupt braking deceleration (Ornitz *et al.*, 1974b). In darkness the slope of nystagmus frequency as a function of postrotatory time is significantly more variable in autistic children than in normal children. Thus, under conditions of no visual input, the time course of the response of an autistic child to vestibular input is also less predictable from trial to trial than is the response of a normal child. Both inhibited and exaggerated motor responses to sensory stimuli are typical of autistic children. Thus, it is not surprising that, in nystagmus studies conducted both with visual input and in darkness, the variation of responses of the same subject is greater in autistic than in normal children.

THE IMPORTANCE OF THE CENTRAL CONNECTIONS
OF THE VESTIBULAR SYSTEM

In the preceding discussion, the deviant oculo*motor* responses to vestibulo-*sensory* stimulation have been used as an experimental model for the more generalized sensorimotor dysfunction observed clinically in autistic children. There is evidence, however, that the central connections of the vestibular system play a significant role in the mutual regulation of sensory input and motor output in normal development. This role will now be discussed as a background to our speculations concerning the pathways that may be involved in the deficient nystagmus response in autistic children. It will also be suggested that central vestibular dysfunction may be responsible for much of the general sensorimotor dysfunction observed in autistic children.

Schilder (1933) was one of the first to emphasize that "the vestibular nerve occupies a special position among the senses. Its sensations do not form a part of our conscious knowledge of the world. . . . Whenever we perceive an object we have already the basic knowledge about our body and about the attitude of our body . . . the vestibular apparatus with its influence on the muscle tone plays a part in every perception. . . . We may also expect that every change in the vestibular apparatus must have an immediate effect on all our senses. . . ." Bender (1956) noted that "gravity is the first sensory experience and responsed to long before birth. After birth the earliest relationship with the mother in which the child responds is in the setting and adjusting of body tone due to contact with the mother's body, or being lifted by the mother or in anticipation of such contact."

In general, if the individual is to correctly and consistently receive information through auditory, visual, and tactile sensory modalities, then these perceptions must take place in relation to the simultaneous perception of the individual's own position in the space from which these sensory inputs are derived. Thus, the other senses do have a functional dependence on and interaction with the vestibular sense. Both von Holst (1954) and Dijkgraaf (1955) pointed out that all animals must discriminate between externally generated sensory stimuli and those stimuli evoked by movement of the animal itself, since the same tactile receptors, muscle spindles, labyrinthine receptors, and retinal receptors are active both when at rest and while in motion. In order to receive reliable information about externally generated stimuli, self-generated stimuli must be "neutralized in some way within the central nervous system" (Dijkgraaf, 1955). Central vestibular mechanisms suppress sensory volleys elicited during movements and thus may fulfill this function (Cook, Cangiano, and Pompeiano, 1968). Vestibular output influences motility in respect to postural adjustment.

It seems reasonable that mechanisms may have evolved to regulate the complex interrelationships between general sensory input, vestibular input and output, and motility.

THE INFLUENCE OF VESTIBULAR INPUT
ON SENSORIMOTOR INTEGRATION

How might vestibular input influence sensorimotor integration? In addition to the impact of descending volleys from the lateral vestibular nucleus via the vestibulospinal tract to the alpha motoneurones, motility is readily effected through excitation of fusimotor neurons by stimulation of vestibular components of the eighth cranial nerve (Diete–Spiff, Carli, and Pompeiano, 1967). Information from the contracting spindles may be fed back into the central nervous system and possibly partake in the adjustment of sensory perception (Eldred, 1960), since muscle afferents project to sensory cortex (Gardner and Morin, 1953). At the same time that spinal motoneurons are excited by stimulation of the vestibular components of the eighth cranial nerve, the vestibular system actively inhibits segmental afferent input to these motoneurons, thereby preventing "instabilities . . . which might occur when somatic sensory volleys elicited during movements are fed back into the spinal cord and interact with the discharging motoneurons" (Cook *et al.,* 1968). Also, responses to eighth cranial nerve stimulation recorded in the medical longitudinal fasciculus are depressed during phasic excitation accompanying the eye-movement bursts of REM sleep and during orienting reactions to arousing stimuli (Lenzi, Pompeiano, and Satoh, 1968). As the medial longitudinal fasciculus carries fibers of the medial vestibular nucleus to motoneurons, a depression of the influence of vestibular input on motor output occurs just at the time of internally generated excitation during both REM sleep and externally induced excitation during waking.

In addition to these descending effects upon the modulation of sensation, motility, and sensorimotor integration, low-intensity stimulation of the vestibular nerve results in ascending activity, evoking slow wave potentials from the orbital surface of the feline cerebral cortex (Megirian and Manning, 1967). Slow wave potentials in this same area have also been evoked by somatosensory, visual, and auditory stimulation, while electrical stimulation of this area affects spinal motoneuron excitability. Studies of single neurons also demonstrate the convergence of vestibular responses with responses in other sensory modalities throughout the cortex and in the lateral geniculate nucleus (Kornhuber and da Fonseca, 1964).

Stimulation of the eighth cranial nerve augments the antidromic response in the optic tract to lateral geniculate stimulation, suggesting presynaptic inhibition of visual input (Marchiafava and Pompeiano, 1966). The same presynaptic inhibition occuring during the rapid eye movements of REM sleep has been demonstrated by: (1) augmentation of the optic tract antidromic response and reduction of the optic tract orthodromic response to electrical stimulation of the lateral geniculate and the optic tract; and (2) reduction of flash evoked responses in the lateral geniculate and in the visual cortex (Bizzi, 1966a). The pathway for this vestibularly induced inhibition of visual input is through the medial and descending vestibular nuclei that activate the spontaneous neuronal activity of the lateral geniculate nucleus during the eye movement bursts of REM sleep (Morrison and Pompeiano, 1966). It has also been suggested that since natural labyrinthine stimulation induces eye movement, vestibularly induced inhibition of visual input at the lateral geniculate level might control the strong retinal barrage accompanying postrotational nystagmus elicited in light (Marchiafava and Pompeiano, 1966).

THE INFLUENCE OF THE CENTRAL NERVOUS SYSTEM ON THE VESTIBULAR SYSTEM

Thus, vestibular input seems to interact with and may modulate both other forms of afferent input and motor excitability at spinal, subcortical, and cortical levels. A central dysfunction of this vestibular control of sensory input-motor output interaction could explain much of the sensorimotor dysfunction observed clinically in autistic children.

The experimental observations relevant to vestibular dysfunction have demonstrated: (1) a reduced oculomotor response (nystagmus) to vestibular stimulation in the presence of exogenous visual input in the waking autistic child; and (2) a reduced oculomotor response (rapid eye movement bursts) to vestibular stimulation in the presence of endogenous visual stimulation in the sleeping autistic child. Thus, our attention must now turn to consideration of those central nervous system mechanisms that can influence the vestibular system and thus modify its effect on sensorimotor interactions. Just as the vestibular nuclei effect sensorimotor integration at spinal, midbrain, and cortical levels (see above), so do these regions both facilitate and inhibit the vestibular system (Markham, 1972), thereby completing a feedback loop with broad implications for sensorimotor control. The final common pathway of this descending control over the vestibular nuclei may be an efferent vestibular system that modifies the impact of vestibular stimuli at the level of the peripheral receptors (Sala, 1965). Since the experimental data have been in the direction of a reduced nystagmus in response to vestibular stimulation of autistic children, the continuing discussion will focus on those neural pathways that inhibit the response of the vestibular system. The vestibular nuclei affect sensorimotor integration at spinal, midbrain, and cortical levels. At the same time these regions both facilitate and restrain the vestibular system, completing a feedback loop vital to sensorimotor control.

Since all subjects were studied with eyes open in a nonsleepy state of relaxed attention, the basal experimental conditions facilitated the production of nystagmus in both the normal and autistic children (see Tjernström, 1973). Only the experimental variables, oculomotor (visual fixation) and oculosensory (diffuse light) stimulation, inhibited the nystagmus; and both forms of visual stimulation induced a significantly greater degree of inhibition in the autistic children (Ornitz *et al.*, 1974a, 1974b). Several possible pathways could be involved in this type of excessive inhibition. At the cortical level, experimental ablations of either occipital lobes or frontal lobe areas 4 and 6 enhanced nystagmus to the side of the lesion, indicating a release from cortical inhibition (Wycis and Spiegel, 1953). Also, stimulation of cortifugal fibers in the cerebral peduncles and internal capsule inhibited vestibular nystagmus (Scheibel, Markham, and Koegler, 1961). The cerebellum has also been implicated in inhibitory control over vestibular afferents from both the otolith system (Llinás and Precht, 1972) and the semicircular canals (Baker, Precht, and Llinás, 1972). Cerebellar inhibition of vestibular nystagmus is particularly relevant to the experimental finding of increased suppression of nystagmus during visual fixation in autistic children, since stimulation of the cerebellar roof nuclei induce centering of the eyes and complete inhibition of nystagmus in the cat (Wolfe, 1969). Several studies have suggested that the efferent vestibular system may receive impulses directly from brain-stem regions. Alterations in the DC resting potential of one labyrinth after electrical stimulation of the reticular substance or caloric stimulation of the other labyrinth in precollicularly decerebrated and decerebellated preparations suggested a bulbopontine reticular origin of the efferent vestibular system (Sala, 1965). This system has inhibitory components that are probably located in part within and between the vestibular nuclei and work through a cholinergic mechanism (Pompeiano, 1972). Scheibel *et al.* (1961) were able to consistently inhibit vestibular nystagmus by stimulating the brain-stem reticular core, although they point out that the suppression of nystagmus amplitude was associated with a very great increase in nystagmus frequency; the later observation suggests that an excitatory effect may be associated with the manifest inhibition of the vestibulo-ocular reflex arc. Markham (1972) has discussed the complex pathways by which two specific midbrain centers may inhibit the vestibulo-oculomotor arc: The mechanism by which the nucleus of Darkschewitsch inhibits vestibularly induced eye movements is unclear (Scheibel *et al.*, 1961), while stimulation of the interstitial nucleus of Cajal inhibits type-I vestibular cells of the horizontal semicircular canals (Markham, Precht, and Shimazu, 1966). Another midbrain inhibitory circuit may take its origin in supranuclear oculomotor centers. Observation of frequency modulation in the vestibular nerve in relation to vestibularly induced eye movements demonstrated the possible existence of vestibular afferent modulation by oculomotor impulses mediated by efferent fibers (Dichgans, Schmidt, and Wist, 1972). These impulses may also be the source of monophasic wave activity in the lateral geniculate nuclei (LGN), since monophasic waves recorded in both LGN and visual cortex are preceded by monophasic waves in the oculomotor nuclei (Costin and Hafemann, 1970). Tonic retinal inhibition of the vestibulo-ocular reflex arc by retinal stimulation (Markham, 1972) can be inferred from the enhancement of postrotational nystagmus following lesions of the LGN (Spiegel and Scala, 1945) or the superior quadrigeminal bodies (Spiegel and Scala, 1946). Finally, light-evoked discharges from the LGN may be enhanced or depressed by labyrinthine stimulation (Papaioannou, 1973). Thus, a complex brain-stem circuitry may involve the mutual regulation of visuosensory input (retina, LGN, superior colliculus), oculomotor output (oculomotor nuclei, vestibular nuclei), and vestibular input (labyrinth, vestibular nuclei). Dysfunction of such a system could be the neurophysiologic basis of the excessive inhibition of postrotatory nystagmus in autistic children that was found in the presence of retinal stimulation (Ornitz *et al.,* 1974a, 1974b).

SUMMARY AND CONCLUSIONS

This paper explores the possible pathophysiologic mechanisms that might underlie the unusual motility distrubances that occur in autistic children. The strange motility patterns of autistic children are characterized by both hypomotility and hypermotility and cannot readily be explained by either postulated states of overarousal or insufficient sensory stimulation. This dysfunction of the modulation of motor output is in some way related to the faulty modulation of sensory input, which is also a significant feature of the autistic syndrome because the children frequently show underreactive or overreactive motor responses to sensory stimuli. Psychologic experiments have revealed that autistic children learn through manipulation and position cues rather than through normal perceptual processes. It is therefore suggested that the spontaneous spinning and flicking of objects, the flapping and oscillating of their extremities, and the whirling and rocking of their bodies may be the autistic children's way of making sense out of the sensations in their environment, including their own bodies and their parts, through kinesthetic (sensorimotor) feedback. Clinical neurophysiologic studies of the oculomotor response to vestibulosensory stimulation in the presence of visuosensory stimulation have demonstrated that there is a significantly greater inhibition of postrotatory nystagmus in autistic children than there is in normal children. During sleep the vestibularly mediated phasic eye movement bursts of REM sleep are also diminished in autistic children in response to vestibular stimulation. These experimental demonstrations of a deficient oculomotor response to vestibular or vestibular-and-visual stimulation parallel clinical observations of the hypomotility also seen in response to sensory stimulation. While the oculomotor responses to vestibulosensory stimulation serve as an experimental model for the more generalized sensorimotor dysfunction observed in autistic children, there is reason to suspect that a dysfunction of the central vestibular system might be fundamental to this facet of the autistic syndrome. Review of the neurophysiology of the vestibular system reveals that the vestibular nuclei either directly modulate or transmit modulating influences over motor output at the time of sensory input and over sensory input at the time of motor output. While cortical centers may inhibit vestibular function, the experimental findings of depressed oculomotor response to vestibular stimulation in the presence of either visual fixation or visuosensory stimulation are more compatible with a dysfunction of cerebellar or brain-stem influence. To conclude, a dysfunction of a complex circuitry involving the central connections of the vestibular system with the cerebellum and the brain stem may be responsible for the strange sensorimotor behavior observed in autistic children. This postulated dysfunction of subcortical neural mechanisms may also have implications for understanding the manner in which autistic children learn about their environment and develop their body image, since clinical studies point toward a strong motor component to their perceptual processes.

REFERENCES

Anthony, J. An experimental approach to the psychopathology of childhood autism. *British Journal of Medical Psychology*, 1958, *31*, 211–225.

Aug, R. G., and Ables, B. S. A clinician's guide to childhood psychosis. *Pediatrics,* 1971, *47*, 327–338.

Baker, R., Precht, W., and Llinás, R. Mossy and climbing fiber projections of extraocular muscle afferents to the cerebellum. *Brain Research,* 1972, *38*, 440–445.

Bender, L. Childhood schizophrenia: Clinical study of one hundred schizophrenic children. *American Journal of Orthopsychiatry,* 1947, *17*, 40–56.

Bender, L. Schizophrenia in childhood—its recognition, description and treatment. *American Journal of Orthopsychiatry,* 1956, *26*, 499–506.

Bender, L., and Freedman, A. M. A study of the first three years in the maturation of schizophrenic children. *Quarterly Journal of Child Behavior,* 1952, *4*, 245–272.

Bergman, P., and Escalona, S. K. Unusual sensitivities in very young children. *Psychoanalytic Study of the Child,* 1949, *3–4*, 333–353.

Bizzi, E. Changes in the orthodromic and antidromic response of optic tract during the eye movements of sleep. *Journal of Neurophysiology,* 1966, *29*, 861–870 (a).

Bizzi, E. Discharge patterns of single geniculate neurons during the rapid eye movements of sleep. *Journal of Neurophysiology,* 1966, *29*, 1087–1095 (b).

Colbert, E., and Koegler, R. Toe walking in childhood schizophrenia. *Journal of Pediatrics,* 1958, *53*, 219–220.

Colbert, E. G., Koegler, R. R., and Markham, C. H. Vestibular dysfunction in childhood schizophrenia. *Archives of General Psychiatry,* 1959, *1*, 600–617.

Coleman, R. W., and Provence, S. Environmental retardation (hospitalism) in infants living in families. *Pediatrics,* 1957, *19,* 285–292.

Collins, W. E. Vestibular responses from figure skaters. *Aerospace Medicine,* 1966, *37,* 1098–1104.

Collins, W. E. Special effects of brief periods of visual fixation on nystagmus and sensations of turning. *Aerospace Medicine,* 1968, *39,* 257–266.

Cook, W. S., Jr., Cangiano, A., and Pompeiano, O. Vestibular influences on primary afferents in the spinal cord. *Pflugers Archiv.,* 1968, *299,* 334–338.

Costin, A., and Hafemann, D. R. Relationship between oculomotor nucleus and lateral geniculate body monophasic waves. *Experientia,* 1970, *26,* 972.

Creak, M., and Pampiglione, G. Clinical and EEG studies on a group of 35 psychotic children. *Developmental Medicine and Child Neurology,* 1969, *11,* 218–227.

Dichgans, J., Schmidt, C. L., and Wist, E. R. Frequency modulation of afferent and efferent unit activity in the vestibular nerve by oculomotor impulses. *Progress in Brain Research,* 1972, *37,* 449–456.

Diete-Spiff, K., Carli, G., and Pompeiano, O. Comparison of the effects of stimulation of the VIIIth cranial nerve, and vestibular nuclei or the reticular formation on the gastrocenemius muscle and its spindles. *Archives Italiennes de Biologie,* 1967, *105,* 243–272.

Dijkgraaf, S. The physiological significance of the so-called proprioceptors. *Acta Physiologica et Pharmacologica Neerlandica,* 1955, *4,* 123–126.

Dix, M. R., and Hood, J. D. Observations upon the nervous mechanism of vestibular habituation. *Acta Oto-Laryngologica,* 1969, *67,* 310–318.

Eldred, E. Posture and locomotion. In H. W. Magoun (Ed.), *Handbook of physiology* (Vol. 2). *Neurophysiology.* Washington, D.C.: American Physiological Society, 1960.

Frith, U., and Hermelin, B. The role of visual and motor cues for normal, subnormal, and autistic children. *Journal of Child Psychology and Psychiatry,* 1969, *10,* 153–163.

Gardner, E. D., and Morin, F. Spinal pathways for projection of cutaneous and muscular afferents to the sensory and motor cortex of the monkey. *American Journal of Physiology,* 1953, *174,* 149–152.

Goldfarb, W. Receptor preferences in schizophrenic children. *Archives of Neurology and Psychiatry,* 1956, *76,* 643–652.

Goldfarb, W. *Childhood schizophrenia.* Cambridge, Massachusetts: Harvard University Press, 1961.

Goldfarb, W. Self-awareness in schizophrenic children. *Archives of General Psychiatry,* 1963, *8,* 47–60.

Green, A. H. Self-mutilation in schizophrenic children. *Archives of General Psychiatry,* 1967, *17,* 234–244.

Hermelin, B., and O'Connor, N. Measures of the occipital alpha rhythm in normal, subnormal and autistic children. *British Journal of Psychiatry,* 1968, *114,* 603–610.

Hermelin, B., and O'Connor, N. *Psychological experiments with autistic children.* Elmsford, New York: Pergamon Press, 1970.

Hutt, C., Hutt, S. J., Lee, D., and Ounsted, C. A behavioral and electroencephalographic study of autistic children. *Journal of Psychiatric Research,* 1965, *3,* 181–197.

Kolvin, I., Ounsted, C., Humphrey, M., McNay, A., Richardson, L. M., Garside, R. F., Kidd, J. S. H., and Roth, M. Six studies in the childhood psychoses. *British Journal of Psychiatry,* 1971, *118,* 381–419.

Kornhuber, H. H., and da Fonseca, J. S. Optovestibular integration in the cat's cortex: A study of sensory convergence on cortical neurons. In M. B. Bender (Ed.), *The oculomotor system.* New York: Harper & Row, 1964.

Lenzi, G. L., Pompeiano, O., and Satoh, T. Input-output relation of the vestibular system during sleep and wakefulness. *Pfluegers Archiv.,* 1968, *299,* 326–333.

Llinás, R., and Precht, W. Vestibulocerebellar input: Physiology. *Progress in Brain Research,* 1972, *37,* 341–359.

Lovaas, O. I., and Schreibman, L. Stimulus overselectivity of autistic children in a two stimulus situation. *Behavior Research and Therapy,* 1971, *9,* 305–310.

Lovaas, O. I., Schreibman, L., Koegel, R., and Rehm, R. Selective responding by autistic children to multiple sensory input. *Journal of Abnormal Psychology,* 1971, *77,* 211–222.

Marchiafava, P. L., and Pompeiano, O. Enhanced excitability of intrageniculate optic tract endings produced by vestibular volleys. *Archives Italiennes de Biologie,* 1966, *104,* 459–479.

Markham, C. H. Descending control of the vestibular nuclei: Physiology. *Progress in Brain Research,* 1972, *37,* 589–600.

Markham, C. H., Precht, W., and Shimazu, H. Effect of stimulation in interstitial nucleus of Cajal on vestibular unit activity in the cat. *Journal of Neurophysiology,* 1966, *29,* 493–507.

Megirian, D., and Manning, J. W. Input-output relations of the vestibular system. *Archives Italiennes de Biologie,* 1967, *105,* 15–30.

Morrison, A. R., and Pompeiano, O. Vestibular influences during sleep. IV. Functional relations between vestibular nuclei and lateral geniculate nucleus during desynchronized sleep. *Archives Italiennes de Biologie,* 1966, *104,* 425–458.

O'Connor, N. Visual perception in autistic children. In M. Rutter (Ed.), *Infantile autism: Concepts, characteristics and treatment.* London: Churchill Livingstone, 1971.

Ornitz, E. M. Disorders of perception common to early infantile autism and schizophrenia. *Comprehensive Psychiatry,* 1969, *10,* 259–274.

Ornitz, E. M. Vestibular dysfunction in schizophrenia and childhood autism. *Comprehensive Psychiatry,* 1970, *11,* 159–173.

Ornitz, E. M. Childhood autism: A disorder of sensorimotor integration. In M. Rutter (Ed.), *Infantile autism: Concepts, characteristics and treatment.* London: Churchill Livingstone, 1971.

Ornitz, E. M. Development of sleep patterns in autistic children. In C. D. Clemente, D. Purpura, and F. Mayer (Eds.), *Sleep and the maturing nervous system.* New York: Academic Press, 1972.

Ornitz, E. M. Childhood autism: A review of the clinical and experimental literature. *California Medicine,* 1973, *118,* 21–47.

Ornitz, E. M., Brown, M. B., Mason, A., and Putnam, N. H. The effect of visual input on postrotatory nystagmus in normal children. *Acta Oto-Laryngologica (Stockholm),* 1974, *77,* 418–425. (a)

Ornitz, E. M., Brown, M. B., Mason, A., and Putnam, N. H. The effect of visual input on vestibular nystagmus in autistic children. *Archives of General Psychiatry,* 1974, *31,* 369–375. (b)

Ornitz, E. M., Brown, M. B., Sorosky, A. D., Ritvo, E. R., and Dietrich, L. Environmental modification of autistic behavior. *Archives of General Psychiatry,* 1970, *22,* 560–565.

Ornitz, E. M., Forsythe, A. B., and de la Peña, A. The effect of vestibular and auditory stimulation on the rapid eye movements of REM sleep in normal children. *Electroencephalography and Clinical Neurophysiology,* 1973, *34,* 379–390. (a)

Ornitz, E. M., Forsythe, A. B., and de la Peña, A. The effect of vestibular and auditory stimulation on the REMs of REM sleep in autistic children. *Archives of General Psychiatry,* 1973, *29,* 786–791. (b).

Ornitz, E. M., and Ritvo, E. R. Perceptual inconstancy in early infantile autism. *Archives of General Psychiatry,* 1968, *18,* 76–98. (a)

Ornitz, E. M., and Ritvo, E. R. Neurophysiologic mechanisms underlying perceptual inconstancy in autistic and schizophrenic children. *Archives of General Psychiatry*, 1968, *19*, 22–27. (b)

Ottinger, D. R., Sweeny, N., and Lowe, L. H. Visual discrimination learning in schizophrenic and normal children. *Journal of Clinical Psychology*, 1965, *21*, 251–253.

Papaioannou, J. N. Changes in the light-evoked discharges from lateral geniculate nucleus neurones in the cat, induced by caloric labyrinthine stimulation. *Experimental Brain Research*, 1973, *17*, 10–17.

Pollack, M., and Krieger, H. P. Oculomotor and postural patterns in schizophrenic children. *Archives of Neurology and Psychiatry*, 1958, *79*, 720–726.

Pompeiano, O. Reticular control of the vestibular nuclei: Physiology and pharmacology. *Progress in Brain Research*, 1972, *37*, 601–618.

Provence, S., and Lipton, R. C. *Infants in institutions*. New York: Inter-University Press, 1962.

Ritvo, E. R., Ornitz, E. M., Eviatar, A., Markham, C. H., Brown, M. B., and Mason, A. Decreased post-rotatory nystagmus in early infantile autism. *Neurology*, 1969, *19*, 653–658.

Ritvo, E. R., Ornitz, E. M., and LaFranchi, S. Frequency of repetitive behaviors in early infantile autism and its variants. *Archives of General Psychiatry*, 1968, *19*, 341–347.

Ritvo, S., and Provence, S. Form perception and imitation in some autistic children: Diagnostic findings and their contextual interpertation. *Psychoanalytic Study of the Child*, 1953, *8*, 155–161.

Sala, O. The efferent vestibular system. Electrophysiological research. *Acta Oto-Laryngologica*, 1965 (Suppl. 197), pp. 1–34.

Scheibel, A., Markham, C., and Koegler, R. Neural correlates of the vestibulo-ocular reflex. *Neurology*, 1961, *11*, 1055–1065.

Schilder, P. The vestibular apparatus in neurosis and psychosis. *Journal of Nervous and Mental Disease*, 1933, *78*, 1–23, 137–164.

Schopler, E. Early infantile autism and receptor processes. *Archives of General Psychiatry*, 1965, *13*, 327–335.

Schopler, E. Visual versus tactile receptor preferences in normal and schizophrenic children. *Journal of Abnormal Psychology*, 1966, *71*, 108–114.

Sorosky, A. D., Ornitz, E. M., Brown, M. B., and Ritvo, E. R. Systematic observations of autistic behavior. *Archives of General Psychiatry*, 1968, *18*, 439–449.

Spiegel, E. A., and Scala, N. P. Changes of labyrinthine excitability in lesions of optic tract or external geniculate body. *Archives of Ophthalmology*, 1945, *34*, 408–410.

Spiegel, E. A., and Scala, N. P. Effects of quadrigeminal lesions upon labyrinthine nystagmus. *Confinia Neurologica*, 1946, *7*, 68–76.

Stroh, G., and Buick, D. Perceptual development of childhood psychosis. *British Journal of Medical Psychology*, 1964, *34*, 291–299.

Tjernström, O. Nystagmus inhibition as an effect of eye-closure. *Acta Oto-Laryngologica*, 1973, *75*, 408–418.

von Holst, E. Relations between the central nervous system and the peripheral organs. *Animal Behaviour*, 1954, *2*, 89–94.

Wendt, G. R. Vestibular functions. In S. S. Stevens (Ed.), *Handbook of experimental psychology*. New York: Wiley, 1951.

Wolfe, J. W. Mesodiencephalic and cerebellar influences on optokinetic and vestibular nystagmus. *Experimental Neurology*, 1969, *25*, 24–34.

Wycis, H. T., and Spiegel, E. A. Effect of cortical lesions and elimination of retinal impulses on labyrinthine nystagmus. *Acta Oto-Laryngologica*, 1953, *57*, 1–11.

Discussion of Biological Section

The papers in this section were included to give some perspective on the biological structures and processes underlying both normal development and behavioral disturbances, as in autism. This is not to revive the obsolete nature—nurture controversy. It is now widely conceded, although often more in word than in action, that the dichotomization of biological versus experiential factors allows for neither the most interesting research hypotheses nor the most useful clinical questions. It is, however, important to attempt to understand the changing biological matrices in which experiential effects are embedded, and the mutual effects and limits biological and psychological processes impose on each other through a continuous interaction. Most of the biological data, inferences, and concerns discussed here are very much involved with effects of psychological experience.

In order to examine adaptive responses to disturbances of neurotransmission and neurointegration, such as might be produced by drugs, extreme nutritional conditions, or radical environments, human subjects are of only limited use. Ethical considerations preclude human studies except for inferences from naturally occurring events or extrapolation from more moderate experimental conditions. In addition, the human situation is always complex and lends itself less readily to control of multiple parameters. It is not surprising that the body of research informing both the Mandell and Rosenzweig chapters is primarily based on experiments with rodents and other animals.

The difficulty of inferring applications of such results to the human species is pointed out by Rosenzweig. Despite such inherent limitations, important hypotheses may be generated from such available data, and significant implications arise for the developmental and clinical investigator that condition the paradigms and interpretations used in human studies.

This discussion will examine the specific models and mechanisms presented in the studies in this section, discuss differences and similarities between models,

135

and identify significant sources of limitations from the experimental models used. Finally, it will propose some potential implications and interpretations of the data.

Mandell presents studies of a number of macromolecular adaptive changes in adrenergic and serotonergic neurons in the brain. He indicates that in the adrenergic system norepinephrine is thought to be related to states of arousal, attention, and perhaps mood; and that serotonin has been implicated in involuntary vascular functions, emotional memory, and moods of sexuality and rage. Both transmitters have been implicated in models of adult disorders of mood (depression and mania) derived from psychopharmacological studies. Focusing on responses to drug administration, primarily in rodents, Mandell identifies a series of interesting processes. These range from alterations in receptor sensitivity, biosynthetic enzyme activity in nerve endings, and the uptake, degradation, and flow rate by which enzymes synthesized in the nucleus are transported to the nerve ending where they function. He derives a model of a homeostatic mechanism that produces a defensive, compensatory response to state deviations in the adult organism. The mature organism has the capacity to maintain its baseline state in response to deviations of the external or internal environment. When the irregularity or change in the condition is removed, the neuronal system returns to the baseline condition. His data suggest that the developing organism is susceptible to more lasting changes in response to experienced perturbations. The baseline state that controls such a homeostatic mechanism would, in the developing organism, become a function of the "disturbed" environment, and a return to a "normal" environment would be responded to as if it were a deviation from "reality."

The baseline of the developing homeostatic mechanism may be established in a "critical period," during which it is sensitive to direct effects (e.g., drugs, hormones) and experiential conditions (e.g., stimulus deprivation). Chronicity of conditions as well as the critical timing apparently affect the reversibility of such changes.

Rosenzweig's paper summarizes what has become a classical series of studies. He demonstrates a predictable differential effect on the brain chemistry and structure of genetically identical littermates according to whether they are exposed to an enriched or impoverished environment. The Rosenzweig data demonstrate several significant, specific effects of environmental variations. For example, under conditions of enriched environmental stimulation, he finds an increase in cholinesterase (BChE), an increase in number of glial cells, increased cortical thickness, an increase in cerebral weight, differences in synaptic function dimensions with an increase in dendritic spines. All of these changes have been associated with increase in activity and complexity of cortical function (Valverde and Ruiz–Marcos, 1968) and improved learning responses in animals. In regard to questions of the specificity of these responses, Rosenzweig points out that they are quite specific and not due to artifactual effects of increased motor activity nor to increased water content of the brain tissue. The enzymatic effects are specific, showing a decrease in neuronal cell acetylcholinesterase (AChE) while glial cholinesterase (BChE) increases. Differences in RNA/DNA ratio and changes of various biogenic amines have also been demonstrated. The brain changes observed are limited to the cortex, chiefly in the occipital area.

The model which evolves from Rosenzweig's data is of an open, responsive system without critical periods during the interval studied involving relatively mature rats. The differences observed in rats raised under impoverished conditions (IC) are readily overcome by exposure to an enriched environment (EC). The effects of enrichment are relatively stable, at least for 47 days follow-up after exposure to EC for 80 days.

Cortical effects seen due to an impoverished environment are similar to those seen in malnourished animals and humans. Studies of interaction between nutritional states and environmental conditions in animals suggest similar directional effects on behavior of malnutrition and restricted environments; interestingly, a restricted environment in nutritionally adequate animals appears to have more severe effects than nutritional deficiency in an adequate environment. Both conditions act synergistically when present. The suggestion has been made that an enriched environment may partially compensate for the effects of malnutrition (Frankova, 1974).

Rosenzweig briefly identifies another neurodevelopmental model that is modality-specific. In kittens and young monkeys, stimulation in a sensory modality, at least in the visual system, appears to be required during a critical period in development in order to "confirm" innate but labile neural connections. Similar effects are known for the human visual system, but the dimensions of the critical period are not known. Children who have congenital cataracts removed in early adolescence are unable to visually identify shapes of objects although they can correctly discriminate haptically. Intense training only partially overcomes this deficit (Weill and Pfersdorff, 1935).

Apparent inconsistencies between the closed, critical period, compensatory model generated by Mandell and the open, continuously developing, active responding system explicated by Rosenzweig may be resolved by examination of the characteristics of the brain sites of their investigations. Mandell's model derives from analysis of subcortical systems, essentially midbrain, which primarily serve affective-motivational functions. The Rosenzweig model, on the other hand, applies to the cortex, which apparently functions as the major locus for continued learning, processing, and integration of new information. These systems are largely served by different chemical mechanisms, and have different phylogenetic and ontogenetic histories. At least a third system is suggested by the data on critical periods for sensory systems. Yet a fourth system is suggested by the later development and maturation of the cerebellum (Chase, 1973).

Unfortunately, data on the relative development of these different systems and their mutual interactive effects on each other are largely unavailable. Investigators studying various effects on one system generally have not shown an interest in seeking the effects on the other mechanisms. Further, experimental paradigms devised to examine a particular mechanism dictate animal models, developmental stages, and conditions that optimize the probability of discovering an effect on the model under investigation, and often obscure effects on other systems that might be apparent if younger (or older) animals were studied under other conditions. Clearly, some sequential studies are needed that investigate very young animals under a variety of conditions and follow these effects through later stages of development under conditions that vary in parameters significant for later development. The possibility for such interactive effects is suggested, for instance, by Rosenzweig's report of potentiation of enrichment effects by use of the psychotropic drug Ritalin.

Although the interaction between biological structure and experience has been increasingly accepted as a conceptual statement for studying development, it is a generalization, not much more meaningful than dichotomizing nature and nurture. Both Kaye and Pick provide eloquent illustrations of the complexities involved in identifying the specific processes, which are even greater when human children are used for experimental studies. Kaye points out that it is deceptively simple to measure the learned effects of certain stimuli on the infant's behavior; especially since the behavioral base itself is changing in the developing infant. These changes in the infant's neurobiological and physiological processes, which may in various ways also be responding to various experimental stimuli, are not known specifically. Accordingly, the study of any particular developmental sequence must be defined by the investigators' theoretical and procedural constraints. From a series of sophisticated studies of infant sucking response, Kaye illustrates how the built-in reflex may be separated from the learned response. By varying the nipple shape, the infant's sucking response can be shaped. However, his jaw movements may be regarded as the built-in response. This knowledge may be used for treating an infant's inadequate feeding response. Nevertheless, it is also possible that with another set of theories and procedures, the jaw movement response itself may be further broken down into built-in and learned components. Clearly, the interaction between experience and environment becomes meaningful only relative to the particular structures studied.

This is illustrated in Pick's remarkably clear discussion of the relatively obscure relationship between perception and cognition. He avoids this philosophic controversy by supplying experimental evidence. For example, the young infant's ability to discriminate visually the edge of a cliff had been demonstrated, and heart rate was used for distinguishing a curiosity response from an alarming fear response. Infants did not show accelerated heart-rate (alarm) response to the cliff until they reached 9 months of age. Prior to that age they responded to their perception of the change in depth only with decelerated heart rate (interest). Through such tiny glimpses of the complex developing relationship between perception and meaning, Pick shows that with increasing perceptual complexity it becomes increasingly difficult to separate integration of information from perception. Massive cultural experience can affect the organization of perception, while lesser experiential differences may affect attention, what aspects of stimulation are selected for processing and which are inhibited. This aspect of attention and selection may relate to Mandell's neural mechanism, while the continuous effects of learning and complex perceptual integration are likely served by the cortical mechanisms identified by Rosenzweig. Pick suggests that differences in sensory functions of children and adults have not been shown to involve any substantial differences in normal perceptual-motor activity. On the contrary, the places where perception seems most likely to go wrong is in those places where developmental changes are taking place, especially those involving integration of new information. Here again is the suggestion of a critical period, or at least a vulnerable period during which experience can affect the neurobiology of the developing organism in a more pronounced way than will be the case at maturity. This kind of sensitivity has been referred to by each of the investigators reporting on biological changes in early development.

The problem of translating data derived from particular species of animals to the human species has serious limitations. However, even with human subjects, for example, autistic children, the controversy over subject selection continues. Thanks to careful observations documented in the pioneer work of Leo Kanner, some consensus on the behavioral description of these children persists today. Nevertheless, diagnostic differences also continue, depending on whether the investigator is concerned with autism and retardation, autism and vestibular function, autism and metabolic disorders, autism and rubella, or combined with any number of other handicaps.

Often the controversy over the "correct" identification becomes heated, especially when research funding agencies stress the need for diagnostic "accuracy." This issue is clearly illustrated by research focused on different biological processes in both the DeMyer and Ornitz presentations. DeMyer, studying mental function, groups her autistic subjects into high, medium, and low autistic depending on the severity of the impairment on the child's intellectual level. This grouping is dependent on the obtaining of meaningful intellectual assessment, with procedures successfully developed by DeMyer's group. For Ornitz, on the other hand, studies of vestibular dysfunction are limited to the motor peculiarities such as peculiar spinning and hand-flapping found in autistic children. Although both investigators are agreed on the behavioral description of autism, Ornitz's groupings focus on perceptual motor peculiarities. As these two research interests focus on different biological systems, their differences in diagnostic groupings follow appropriately.

The Ornitz chapter suggests a parallel between certain clinical and experimental data. Experimentally, a deficient oculomotor response to vestibular and visual stimulation has been demonstrated, as has hypomotility in response to sensory stimulation. Dysfunction of the central vestibular system is suggested with involvement of defective cerebellar and brain-stem influence. DeMyer, on the other hand, has studied the performance of autistic children on various intelligence test functions. On comparing the performance of autistic children with subnormal children without autism, she observes that the subnormal group was superior to all autistic groups in ball play. Perhaps the complex visual motor integration skills involved with ball play are akin to integrational skills of higher verbal and mental functions, the latter deficiency being obvious in autistic children. By studying test behavior and mental skills, DeMyer's current research focus appears to converge with Ornitz's, who implicates visual motor deficiencies from direct neurophysiological experiments.

The difficulty in relating complex disorders such as autism to the more discrete animal studies in part rests on the convergence of such studies; there is difficulty in differentiating the primary deficit from secondary and tertiary effects and the inadequate understanding of interactions between different systems. For instance, if the primary dysfunction is cerebellar, this is a late developing system and should suggest relative adequacy of other functions if cerebellar inadequacy can be compensated. If complex visual motor integration is the area of primary disturbance, it may be responsive to appropriate experiential conditions provided at appropriate periods of development as suggested by the Rosenzweig model. If, on the other hand, the basic disturbance is in the homeostatic mechanisms described by Mandell, the condition is relatively fixed at an early stage of development and may be most readily amenable to specific chemical interventions. Whichever the primary locus of deficit may be, the potential for improved function in one system to compensate for deficiencies in the other systems is implied but largely unexplored in current investigations.

The difficulty in the translation of results from animal experiments to the human species becomes apparent. Not only are there species-specific differences in morphology, physiology, and biochemical processes; but there are even more significant differences in developmental and maturational rates and patterns, and in behavioral repertoires. Differences in maturational patterns affect the equivalence of developmental stages studies, the susceptibility to specific conditions, and the duration of exposure to such conditions. The different rates of development of different systems in different animals, and the consequent accessibility to specific environmental events (as discussed by Pick) and the emergence of specific behaviors may all have interactive effects on the response to noxious environmental conditions. Whether these effects increase or compensate for the vulnerability of an organism may vary from one species to another. Each of these factors may affect the appearance of a critical period. Similarly, there may be specificity to the ability of various conditions to affect various species in specific ways.

Further problems are presented by species-specific behaviors (e.g., language) and methodological limitations of various studies as to what are considered CNS effects, what behaviors are studied, and what criterion are used to assess differences.

Despite these limitations of specific application of findings in animal investigations to the human species, several implications for studies of human development and disorders emerge:

1. There are several relatively distinct neurological systems that contribute in various degrees and have interactional effects on behavior in a fundamentally unknown manner. Each system has its own neurophysiological and biochemical structures. These are governed by their own maturational and developmental sequencing and involve differential sensitivities, responses to stimulus specificity, and varying degrees of plasticity.

Therefore, individual behaviors must be understood as the expression of a final common pathway of behavior and interpreted with caution, especially vis-à-vis particular biological substrata.

2. Accepted behavioral units may be composed of unidentified subcomponents, which may be independently responsive to different events or conditions, i.e., simple behaviors are more complex than they appear (Kaye). Likewise, differences in expressed behavior may reflect the interaction of different integrative components (Pick).

In developmental and clinical research, behavioral units must be carefully defined in terms of the particular paradigm used. Within such a system, the varying contribution of each behavioral unit under study must be carefully controlled for or accounted for in the analysis and interpretation of the data.

3. Behaviors under study may be primary or derivative effects of the underlying biological processes under investigation. Selection of specific behaviors for study may therefore lead to subject populations with disparate biological structures and processes, producing a final common pathway of behaviors.

Clearly, specific results from one system of research do not equally apply to another system. Instead of searching for this kind of equation, more complicated mental operations are involved. These include the understanding of research findings on their own terms and the flexibility to make general adaptations from one's own system to those of others.

R. J. R. and E. S.

Part II
Developmental:
Development of Social Behavior
and Deviations

7

The Bases of Language Acquisition: Some Questions

PAULA MENYUK

The history of explanatory theories of language acquisition is largely a story of the changing views of the nature of man and his physiological and psychological capacities. As views of these capacities changed or varied, so did explanations of language acquisition. Since a great deal of the theorizing took place in the absence of detailed description of the process, differing theories were based on prejudices toward accepting theories that predicted what was known about stages in the acquisition of language or theories that explained behavioral changes that occurred under certain conditions of teaching language. This has led to two contrasting kinds of theories (Slobin, 1971): those that suggest a linguistic or cognitive predisposition on the part of the human child to acquire language, and those that suggest that language acquisition, like all other learning tasks, can be explained by the principles of S–R learning. In the past decade, language acquisition has been examined in much greater detail than in previous years and with children from varying cultural backgrounds and of varying sensory–motor and cognitive capacities. Although a great deal of the data are still missing, these studies indicate that the way to determine the bases for language acquisition is to observe the child, examine the context in which language is acquired, and then probe for experimental validation of the descriptions obtained.

In this paper, the findings of available studies of the early development of language (from birth to approximately school age) will be outlined. The effects

PAULA MENYUK · School of Education, Boston University, Boston, Massachusetts 02215.

of known physiological, cognitive, and social changes during this developmental period on the structure of the language understood and produced at various stages are examined. These findings are compared to those of studies of the language development of children who deviate from the norm in various aspects of physiological and cognitive development. The differences in language development under various conditions of deviancy will be examined to determine what these differences can tell us about the bases for the language acquisition process.

PATTERNS OF NORMAL LANGUAGE ACQUISITION

Those who have studied the perception, production, and use of language at various stages of development have usually looked at one aspect of development. They have concerned themselves with either the child's phonological knowledge, his syntactic knowledge, his semantic knowledge, or his communication knowledge, in an attempt to evaluate the child's understanding of the function of the language that he hears or produces. The discussion that follows is an effort to integrate information on all the above aspects of language acquisition. The discussion is necessarily an oversimplification, but it should allow us to compare patterns of development in the normally developing child and in the child with developmental problems. These studies indicate that with normally developing children there are both universal stages and individual variations in the acquisition of language behaviors.

The First Stage: before Babbling

During the first stage of development, both cry and noncry vocalizations are produced by the child. All vocalizations are not cry vocalizations. Indeed, Bateson (1971) has observed what she terms "conversational" patterns between a mother and her infant beginning in the second month of life under certain conditions. In addition, studies of the speech sound discrimination of infants 1 to 2 months of age indicate that at this early age infants can discriminate between speech stimuli that mark differences in speech sound categorization (for example /pa/ versus /ba/), but can't discriminate between stimuli that are only acoustically different—for example, two acoustically different /pa/s or /ba/s (Morse, 1974). They also discriminate between rising and falling intonational contours (Morse, 1974) and between friendly and unfriendly voices (Kaplan and Kaplan, 1970).

A study of the developmental pattern of infant cry in terms of amount and duration of cry and mother's responses to cry during the first year of life indicated the possible importance of mother's responses to vocalizations on the development of the child's concepts of the communicative functions of these vocalizations (Bell and Ainsworth, 1972). Although there was no relation between the frequency of cry and mother's ignoring cry during the first quarter of the first year, there was a significant correlation between these factors in the third and fourth quarters of the year. Infants whose mothers responded more to cry not only cried less in the last half of this year, but also used a variety of ways to communicate. Infants whose mothers responded less not only cried more, but seemed to lack other modes of communication.

In summary then, there is some indication that during this first stage of development infants can discriminate between certain acoustic parameters that are important markers in speech perception; they produce both cry and noncry vocalizations; they can engage in noncry communicative interaction; and their cry behavior and other communicative behaviors are significantly affected by their mothers' responsiveness to their vocalizations. Although infants may be able to discriminate between some speech sounds and make intonational distinctions and may engage in vocal communicative interactions, not all infants necessarily use these abilities during this stage of development. They do, however, engage in noncry as well as cry vocalizations and they respond differentially to the suprasegmental aspects (intonational aspects) of the voices they hear. These might be termed the *universal linguistic behaviors* during this period. There is also evidence that during this period infants vary in the frequency with which they engage in cry vocalization. This frequency may be dependent on the degree to which their mothers ignore this cry.

There are, then, individual differences in linguistic behavior (proportion of cry to noncry behavior) and possibly the beginning of differences in children's concepts of the function of vocalization behavior. Some infants may conceive of this behavior as relatively nonfunctional, and other infants may conceive of it as serving the social function of establishing communication and as a way of manipulating their environment.

The Second Stage: Babbling

Studies of language behavior during the babbling period, the second stage of development, have largely been concerned with what the infant produces rather than what he perceives. It is during this period that the infant's repertoire of speech sounds grows and that the frequency of his utterances increases. Now, as compared to the previous period, repetitive consonant as well as vowel sounds can be found in his productions. Obviously, he continues to cry. As indicated by spectrographic analyses, however, he achieves much greater control of his cry utterances, and, as indicated in the Bell and Ainsworth (1972) study cited previously, the frequency of the cry utterances decreases markedly for some infants and less so for others. During this period the infant responds differentially to male and female voices and to the voice of his mother as compared to that of a female stranger (Kagan and Lewis, 1965). It is also during this period that the prosodic features (intonation and stress) of his babbled utterances begin to be differentiated (Tonkova–Yampolskaya, 1969). Behaviorally he differentiates (cardiac rate changes and motor responses) between sentences read with statement intonation and those with question intonation, but does not differentiate between sentences read with steadily rising or steadily falling intonation (Kaplan, 1969). This period of speech soundmaking has been termed a *play period* (Nakazima, 1970); that is, the infant does not seem to relate the speech sounds he hears or the sounds he produces with the objects or actions he observes. On the other hand, the prosody of the utterances he hears appears to convey to him differential meaning, and he appears to communicate differential meaning to his caretakers by his use of varying prosodic features. Thus, although he does not relate particular phonological sequences to categorizations of environmental phenomena during this period, he does appear to relate the prosody of utterances to what I will term *the purpose of communication:* to establish contact, to state, to demand, to request, etc.

Irwin (1957), in examining the effect of socioeconomic status of infants' families, has found that there is a relationship between socioeconomic status and the patterns of growth in type and frequency of speech–sound use. A similar kind of examination of the effect of socioeconomic status on the development of prosody has yet to be carried out. Lewis and Freedle (1972) have observed the communicative interactions between mothers at five levels of socioeconomic status and their 4-month-old infants. They found that the most frequent interaction that occurred was vocalization to vocalization. There were considerable individual differences in the frequency of vocalizations by infants regardless of socioeconomic status or sex, although both these factors did have an effect on the vocal interactions between mother and infant. The experimenters suggest that these differences are related to language use at a later stage of development. Follow-up data on only three children appear in the report. The rank order of these infants at 12 weeks in amount of vocalizations, amount of quiet play, amount of maternal play, and the degree to which they differentiated between themselves and others as being the object of mothers' vocalizations was correlated with their rank order at age 2 years in knowledge of preposition and adjective contrasts, performance on the Peabody Picture Vocabulary Test, expression of semantic relations in sentences (Subject–Verb, Verb–Object), and the mean length of utterances in spontaneous speech.

All infants during this period expand their speech–sound repertoire, increase the frequency of their utterances, generate utterances with differing prosody, and engage in vocalization interaction with their mothers. The rate at which these changes occur, however, and the frequency with which infants use some of these differential features seems to be dependent on individual differences, socioeconomic status, and sex.

The Third Stage: One Word

The next stage of development, the one-word stage, marks the beginning of what has been termed *true language* (Jakobson, 1968). At the beginning of this stage a definitive change occurs in the production of language; there is some slight evidence to indicate that such a change also occurs in perception. Infants begin to notice word-length utterances and to produce word-length utterances, whereas previously they seemed to notice the prosody of utterances and to produce strings of consonant–vowel or vowel–consonant syllables that are marked by prosodic features (Menyuk, 1974). The first phase of this stage of development is the acquisition of the concept that any phonological sequence can stand for or represent an object or action in the environment. Earlier, vocalizations were used to express needs and feelings and to manipulate the environment. This concept of the communicative function of vocalizations persists into the one-word period and beyond, but added to this is the concept that phonological sequences can be used to represent. Once having acquired this concept, the infant begins to relate the phonology of what he hears to particular objects and events. Finally, he begins to relate what he hears to what he produces. This latter process is lengthy and reflects both the infant's physiological maturation (what he can do with his articulatory mechanism) and the development of different kinds of hypotheses about how best to represent what he hears at various stages of development. A very strong argument has been presented by Piaget (1970) and others that this process has at its source the imitative behavior of human infants. Studies on the communicative interactions of mothers and infants during this period indicate, however, that different mothers use different styles. Some mothers preponderantly use the technique of pointing and naming and others spend more time attempting to elicit imitation from their infants. Some lexical items are produced only after comprehension is exhibited and others are imitated before comprehension is exhibited (Menyuk, 1971, Chapter 6). The evidence for the development of representation by language as an outgrowth of simply imitative behavior is, therefore, questionable. Its source may have more to do with the biological nature of human infants than with their tendency to imitate (Geschwind, 1965), but this is, of course, purely speculative, as are notions about language use having its roots in imitation.

There are at least three theoretical descriptions of these early one-word utterances. The first is that they can be described as names for concepts (Nelson, 1973). Concepts are described as a structural set of features that the child uses to organize his experience. These concepts may be more general than those of adults or more specific, and may match those of the adult or be a total mismatch. As the word for the concept is stored in memory a reorganization of the child's cognitive system takes place. It is suggested that as the child matures and gains experience those concepts that are more general, more specific, and totally incorrect are abandoned rather than added to or refined. The second description of these one-word utterances is that they represent basic and primitive percepts of categorizations of visual, auditory, tactile, gustatory, and olfactory events that are innate to the human organism. First, the unmarked properties of these percepts and then their marked properties are represented in the words used (Clark, 1973). A third description of these one-word utterances is that they are not only representations of objects and events but that they are in addition representations of relations that the child observes first between himself and other objects and events and then between other humans, animate objects, inanimate objects (in that order) and other objects and events (Greenfield *et al.*, 1972).

A study of the development of the first 50 one-word utterances of 18 children (Nelson, 1973) indicates that children at this stage vary in rates of acquisition from the first 10 to the last 10 of these 50 one-word utterances, vary in the primary function of their one-word utterances, and also vary in the proportional semantic content of their utterances (for example, proportion used to name objects or events) in general and during the time of acquisition. The 50-word level was reached by ages 15 to 24 months. Some children acquired lexical items at a slow rate during the first part of this period and then, during the later part, at a very rapid rate; other children acquired items at a steady rate. The experimenter described two groups of children. One group used language proportionately more to "refer" and the other group used language proportionately more to "express." Finally, although the experimenter stated that all grammatical categories appeared to be represented in these early utterances, a large proportion of these words were what the experimenter termed *nominals* for general objects that is, names for substances, people, animals, letters, numbers, and pronominalizations. These words made up 51% of the sampled vocabulary. Although the composition of the vocabulary shifted from the first to the last 10 of the 50 words used, use of general nominals remained high throughout the period (from 41% at the beginning to 62% at the end). However, the experimenter was presumably able to distinguish two groups of children: those who were thing oriented (the referrers) and those who were socially oriented (the expressers).

As the experimenter stated, and as may appear obvious, the particular words a child uses are in part determined by his particular experiences. The principal function of these first words must also be determined by his particular experiences in part. Another experimenter (Dore, 1973) also found two types of children at this one-word stage of development: those who use language primarily to categorize environmental phenomena and those who use language primarily to express and manipulate. The first type of child acquires a proportionately more extensive vocabulary during the one-word period but does not develop much differentiation in the prosodic features of these utterances. The second type of child does not develop such an extensive vocabulary, but does develop the prosody of the utterances he has. This experimenter suggested that one factor in the differential development of these children is that children who are not allowed by their mothers to manipulate the situation but are instead manipulated themselves show the first kind of development, whereas children who are permitted to manipulate the situation show the second kind of development. Nelson (1973) suggests a somewhat different process. Mothers' feedback, both positive and negative, facilitates object-oriented language since in these situations the mother is not directing the child but, rather, responding to his utterances. Minimal responses from mothers therefore may lead to proportionately greater use of language to express needs and feelings.

What of the correlation between intelligence and language acquisition at this stage? The correlations found by Nelson between tests of intelligence (the Bayley Motor and Mental Scales; the Concept Familiarity Index; the Peabody Picture Vocabulary Test) and measures of language acquisition (age at 10 words and 50 words; rate of acquisition; age at 10 phrases; mean length of utterances and vocabulary at 24 months; and mean length of utterances and vocabulary at 30 months) indicate some strong correlations between the intelligence scales and language measures up to 24 months, but weak correlations at 30 months. One might infer that only at a very early stage are language and measured intelligence strongly related, or that the assessment measures of language and intelligence used were inadequate, or that the relation is only evident at the extremes and therefore that no linear correlation exists. This question of measured intelligence and language acquisition will be reexamined in the continuing discussion of normal language development and in the discussion of deviant language development.

Particular experiences apparently lead to different patterns of development. In each of these descriptions of the one-word utterance stage, however, the child is not simply a passive acquirer of certain words or prosodic features, but rather an active searcher for those aspects of the language that will represent both his needs and feelings and his cognitive constructs. What is suggested in the studies cited is that there is a tendency for children to use a particular linguistic style more frequently, not that only one style is used by particular children. Measured intelligence and rate of language acquisition seem to be related at a very early stage of development; thus, there are individual differences in proportional usage of linguistic features and rate of acquisition of numbers of lexical items. The overall functions and possibly the structure of these one-word utterances appear to be universal.

The Fourth Stage: Two Words

The next stage of development, the two-word stage, has been described as one during which semantic relations are expressed and the development of syntax begins. Some researchers hypothesize that only semantic relations are expressed; others hypothesize that syntactic relations are expressed as well. It should be kept in mind that interpretations and descriptions of two-word utterances as well as one-word utterances are based on the contexts in which these utterances are produced and the nonverbal aspects (gesture, expression, looking) and suprasegmental aspects (prosodic features) of these utterances. For those who assume the expression of semantic relations at the one-word stage, the transition from the one- to two-word stage is continuous (Greenfield *et al.*, 1972); that is, the relations already exist in one-word utterances and are fully realized in two-word utterances. For those who hypothesize that syntactic categorizations and relations are being expressed in these two-word utterances, a reorganization of knowledge is postulated (Bloom, 1973). The utterances themselves have been described as having the underlying structure of Subject—Verb—Object (McNeill, 1970) or of having the structure of semantic relations that can be described by a case grammer (Brown, 1973; Schlesinger, 1974) such as Actor—Object or Action—Object.

Some examples of the varying positions follow. If one assumes that one-word utterances express a relation, then an utterance such as "chair" may be interpreted as expressing the relation agent and location, depending on the context, gesture, and prosody used. Later, at the two-word stage, the relation is fully expressed by labeling the agent as in "daddy chair." If one assumes that one-word utterances only categorize an object or attributes of objects, then at the one-word stage the utterance "milk" denotes the object milk and the utterance "more" denotes an attribute of objects (they can appear again or in greater quantity). Not until the two-word stage, however, is the relation expressed as in the utterance "more milk." Still another position is that the one-word utterance can be described as the topic or aspect that the child is focusing upon in communication. These utterances function as sentences because of the use of prosodic features and context (Menyuk, 1969). At state one the utterance "doggie" can mean, That's a doggie; Is that a doggie?; or I want the doggie!, depending on the prosody of the utterance and the context in which it is produced. Later, at the two-word stage, the topic is modified by the use of an adverbial or adjectival word as in "That doggie," "Big doggie," or "Doggie up." Only the predicate and not the subject and predicate relation is expressed in these sentences, because the subject is always the speaker.

Clarification of what indeed the child knows about language at these stages would provide some insights into the bases of language acquisition. An important question is: Do we see in the language used by the child at this stage only a reflection of what he perceives in the world around him, or has he acquired some abstract linguistic categorizations? Clearly, the use of words is a perceptual generalization in that words do not merely stand for a specific object but represent a class of objects. Is the use of words, however, merely a reflection of perceptual categorizations or must there be, in conjunction with this, the ability to determine how this class should be represented in the language as a speech–sound sequence? The intent of the speaker to state, question, negate, and demand can be communicated by gesture and context. Is the ability of the child to isolate and use the linguistic features of prosody to communicate differential meaning a specific linguistic ability? The expression of relations between objects and events may merely reflect how things happen in the world. For example, animate objects act upon inanimate objects and therefore it is understandable that two-word utterances reflect this order of events, i.e., actor and action, or actor and object, or action and object and not object and action. There is some indication that order may be a function of the frequency with which mothers use certain orders to describe events (Bowerman, 1973), and there is some indication that although there is universality in the relations expressed at this stage, children will use the ordering of their particular language although it does not reflect the perceived order of events (Ervin–Tripp, 1971). Is appropriate word-ordering a specific linguistic ability, a reflection of cognitive development, or a result of experience? These are not only important questions to resolve in understanding the language acquisition of normally developing children, but are also crucially important in understanding this development in children with special problems.

The Fifth Stage: Acquisition of the Grammar of the Language

The next stages of development are subsumed under a very general heading in this discussion. The title is indicative, however, of two important changes that occur during these stages. The first is that the language used by the child can be increasingly understood, independent of the context in which it is used and the gestures that accompany it. Complete (Actor and Action and Object) rather than partial relations (Actor and Object, for example) are expressed in sentences. Both the development of sentence types to more clearly represent intent and the development of morphological markers to indicate tense and number begin at this stage. Modification of the noun phrase and of the verb phrase in a sentence begins at this stage. These factors interact in directing the child toward the solution of the problem of determining the rules used in his language to generate sentences. For example, in the development of the negative sentence type, the child begins by generating negative sentences through adding the negative word to the topic of the sentence ("no go"). The child then specifies in each utterance who is not going ("me no go" or "daddy no go"). He then specifies the time or mode of action ("daddy no can go"; "daddy no going"). He finally applies the negative attachment rule in the appropriate way (auxilary/modal + negative + verb) and generates the complete negative ("Daddy isn't going"; "Daddy can't go").

The second important change that occurs during this period is that children acquire rules for expressing relations between sentences as well as within sentences. These relations may be conjunctive or dependent in nature. Once the child learns to conjoin sentences and to embed sentences he has, theoretically, the ability to create infinitely long sentences. Outside of this theoretical accomplishment, the ability to conjoin and embed allows him to express logical relationships (*and, and not, but, or, if—then, because*); time relationships (*when, and then*); and spatial relationships (*where*) between predications.

The sequence of acquisition of the structures described above seems to be dependent on three factors. Those structures that are functionally important, eliminate possible ambiguities, and are less complex in the operations required to generate them are acquired first (Menyuk, 1971). Although negative and question utterances appear almost at the same time in their simple form (i.e., "no go" and "where go?"), they do not appear in their complete form at the same time. In those small populations that have been observed, the negative structure is complete before the question structure. Since questions are marked either by question word or intonation or both and are thus unambiguous as to structure, and because questions require a permutation operation ("Where the baby is?" to "Where is the baby?"), the question structure is completed after the negative structure. In like fashion, the ability to understand and produce conjoined sentences precedes the ability to understand and produce embedded sentences. The ability to understand and produce right-embedded sentences precedes the ability to understand and produce center-embedded sentences (i.e., "I see the boy who took my hat" emerges before "The boy who took my hat ran away").

The same sequence of development has been observed in the acquisition of these sentence types by groups of children. What seems to vary among children is the rate at which these structures are acquired, and this variation may be due to experience, cognitive development (perceptual strategies used), and/or physiological development (cerebral dominance establishment) (Bever, 1970). The particular relations that are suggested between any or all of these factors to any or all aspects of this structural development are at the moment hypothetical, however.

By the time the child reaches school age, he produces utterances that are for the most part grammatical and semantically appropriate. It has been found, however, that although a child may use a set of words appropriately in a context, his understanding of the meaning of these words varies from that of the adult and changes in time (Werner and Kaplan, 1950). In addition, certain sets of words in particular semantic fields are distinguished from each other earlier and their adult meanings are acquired earlier than are others. It has been hypothesized that the child's distinction between these words and the acquisition of their meanings is directly dependent on the child's perceptual development. Thus, for example, location terms are distinguished from each other and their full meanings acquired before time terms, which in turn are acquired before kinship terms (Clark, 1974). Children conjoin and embed sentences, but the relations understood and expressed in these sentences are limited. Thus, for example, causal relations are understood and expressed before conditional relations; that is, those relations that are perceivable are understood and expressed before those that must be inferred. Cognitive development is the factor that is considered to be causal in this sequence of development. The sequence of development observed in the acquisition of meanings of words and relations expressed in conjoined and embedded sentences appears to be similar for groups of children, but the rate at which the acquisitions occur varies among children. The frequency with which they use conjoined and embedded sentences also varies, and this seems to be a reflection of experience. That is, the communicative situations in which the child ordinarily engages obviously affects both the content and structure of the kinds of utterances he uses most frequently.

This is a brief summary of the research findings of studies in which the language development of children who are developing normally has been examined. The first and early stages of development were dwelt upon because these stages seem to be the most germane to possible studies of deviant language development. Most of the reports of the language development of children who are not developing language normally have indicated that they are functioning at these early levels for very long periods of time. I felt it was necessary, however, to discuss stages of language development up to school age since most studies of the language development of developmentally deviant children usually have as their sample populations children of at least this age.

PATTERNS OF DELAYED AND DEVIANT LANGUAGE DEVELOPMENT

Children with developmental problems are usually categorized in terms of diagnostic labels such as blind, deaf, aphasic, autistic, mentally retarded, learning disabled, or multiply handicapped. An examination of the literature on the language development of these children can quickly lead us to the conclusion that these labels do not define the language behavior that has been observed within these populations. Varieties of language behavior, and, perhaps, language competence appear within each diagnostic category. In addition, one can also quickly observe that, unlike studies with normally developing children, most of the research with this population has been done with school-aged children and often with children who have been institutionalized. Further, these studies have most frequently only measured the language performance of these children on tests of language development and compared the results with those found in normally developing children. It is obviously difficult to compare the findings of descriptive and experimental studies with those measuring test performances. All of these factors make the task of comparing the language development of children with and without developmental disorders a difficult one.

Despite these difficulties I will attempt to summarize the few descriptive findings that are available and to compare patterns of language development in the two populations. I will then see if any conclusions can be drawn from these comparisons about the bases of language acquisition. I have arbitrarily selected to organize the discussion around children with sensory deficits (the deaf and the blind) and children with cognitive deficits and/or known or suspected central nervous system deficits (the mentally retarded, the aphasic, and the autistic).

Sensory Developmental Disorders

Current findings of studies of the language development of deaf and blind children give us some indication that in both instances language development may be normal in sequence if not in rate. When we discuss deaf children, we of course have to consider the development of their sign language. The little research that has been done in the development of sign indicates that: (1) the child appears to capture the same semantic relations in his early signed messages as those that are expressed by the hearing child (genitives, attribution, Agent–Action–Object, affected person, locations, and datives); and (2) the development of the negative structure is similar to that of the hearing child (Bellugi and Klima, 1972). There have been few studies of the deaf child's oral language development or of his development of written language. These few studies, again, indicate a normal sequence of development but a delayed rate of development. For example, in the comprehension and production of written symbols, it has been found that the 17- or 18-year-old deaf child appears to perform like the 8- to 11-year-old hearing child (Schmitt, 1968) and that the deaf child of 17 has not yet acquired some rules used by the 10-year-old hearing child (Quigley, Smith, and Wilbur, 1974). What is quite interesting in the language performance of these children is the finding that some of them who have been exposed to sign may be bilingual. Thus, when testing their oral- or written-language behavior, one can observe instances in which alternation of rules from sign to standard English may be occurring. Studies of the cognitive development of deaf children have indicated that in some instances they perform commensurately with hearing children (for example, Furth, 1964) and in other instances they do not. Differences have been ascribed to different amounts of cognitive and social experience.

The literature on the language development of the blind child is not only limited and spotty but also appears to be contradictory. For example, one experimenter found that blind children lagged behind sighted children in their ability to name meaningful nonverbal sounds and concluded that previously acquired visual naming facilitates naming for corresponding sounds (Bartholomews, 1971). Another experimenter found that there was great similarity in the way blind, severely visually impaired, and normally sighted children ascribed affective meanings to concepts when they were asked to judge the meaning of words on the semantic differential scale and concluded that this equality in "knowledge" is due to the fact that meaning is derived from within the language rather than from visual experience (Demott, 1972).

Presumably, the onset of language for these children is somewhat delayed (Telford and Sawrey, 1967), but no study of the structure of the language perceived and produced by these children at various stages of development has been carried out. In a study of the performance of blind and sighted children on a cognitive task calling for recognition and recall of 3-dimensional figures that are familiar objects, geometric shapes, and that differ topologically (open and closed ring, for example), the blind and sighted children performed equally well, and developmental changes in performance occurred at the same ages (Gottesman, 1971). It has been hypothesized that haptic development occurs through vision and thus blind children should be retarded cognitively. In this experiment, at least, the position was not upheld.

In summary, the cognitive development of blind and deaf children appears to be the same as that of sighted and hearing children in some aspects that have been measured and different in other aspects. Furthermore, in those aspects of language that have been measured, the sequence of language development seems to be similar for blind and deaf children and normally developing children, although possibly delayed in onset and delayed in age of development. Clearly, many questions about these children's language development remain to be answered.

Cognitive and/or Central Nervous System Developmental Disorders

Studies of the language behavior of mentally retarded children have led to two conflicting hypotheses: (1) these children develop language in the same sequence as normally developing children but at a much slower rate; (2) the sequence of development differs because of differences in language-processing strategies. Of course, theoretically, delay per se may lead to deviance as well. Piaget (1970, p. 713) has suggested that ". . . the stability and even fruitfulness of a new organization (or structurization) depends on connections which cannot be instantaneous, but cannot be indefinitely postponed either since they would lose their power of internal combination." If we take this rather loose statement and attempt to apply it to language development, an appropriate analogy might be that a surface behavior that looks like a normal development, may finally be obtained, given enough time, but that this behavior may be dependent on an exact replicative encoding rather than being based on a knowledge of the rules that underlie this behavior and that can then be applied in other instances.

A very interesting study carried out by Cromer (1974) sheds some light on this possibility. Cromer examined the development of children's ability to determine the subject of sentences that contained the subject ("The horse is willing to bite") and those that contained only the object ("The horse is fun to bite"). The children were asked to identify the subject: either the animal named or another animal. Three stages of development were observed: primitive (the noun named is always the subject), intermediate (inconsistent behavior but increasing use of an "object" strategy), and mature (consistent identification of subject as being either within or outside the sentence). In a similar study of mentally retarded children, Cromer found that these children used the primitive rule until about chronological age 14 to 16 when they began to use the mature rule. This same linguistic rule was tested with nonsense words. Normally developing children in the primitive stage (age 6–7) used the subject strategy. In the intermediate stage (age 9–10), one-half of them used the subject strategy and the other half the object strategy. In the mature stage (age 10 +), those who used a set strategy used the object strategy. Adults, who were also tested, never made use of the object strategy, and neither did the mature (age 14 to 16) mentally retarded children. The experimenter hypothesizes that delay in language development may result in the use of different processing strategies during the language acquisition period, and thus different bases for the structures used by older mentally retarded children as compared to children developing normally.

In general many conflicting statements about the language development of these children appear in the literature. These statements are made by those experimenters who claim that language development takes place in a normal sequence but at a much slower rate, and that when no further development is observed the mentally retarded child "has" less than the normally developing child "has" at a very much younger age. How much the retarded child "has" depends on his degree of retardation as indicated by his measured intelligence (Lenneberg, 1966). It is not clear, however, that measured intelligence accurately predicts the linguistic performance of these children. Studies in which the correlation between linguistic performance of these children and their performance on intelligence tests was examined showed that, depending on the aspect of language measured, there was a high correlation or a low correlation (Yoder and Miller, 1972); e.g., the correlation between vocabulary and IQ was .72, but the correlation between type/token ratio in spontaneous speech and IQ was .04. Similar discrepancies exist even when, presumably, the same aspect of linguistic performance is being measured. The correlations between mean length of sentence and IQ have been found to be .17, .42, and .68 in different studies (Yoder and Miller, 1972).

In a developmental descriptive study by Lackner (1968), the grammatical development of a group of mentally retarded children was found to follow similar developmental trends as those found with normally developing children. On the other hand, Semmel, Barritt, and Bennett (1970) found that mentally retarded children acquire specific instances of structures in language rather than rules for sentence generation; he stated that this is because they use a sequential or chaining strategy in processing sentences rather than a chunking strategy to derive rules of relations. These conflicting findings may be because of the nature of the question each study asked (what aspect of language was being assessed in each instance); the manner in which it was asked (use of spontaneous language, specific task, or test to evaluate language); and to whom the questions were being addressed (that is, mentally retarded children may differ from each other as much as they differ from normally developing children).

In like fashion the aphasic child's language has been described (indeed, by the same experimenters) as being similar to that of the normally developing child, but much slower; it has also been described as being different. In a series of studies of the spontaneous language of these children, the experimenters found that acquisition of basic syntactic relations and of some transformational rules was delayed, but appeared in the same order as was found with normally developing children. Aphasic children presumably differ, however, in semantic development. They do not use major linguistic categories in as many different contexts or syntactic frames as do normally developing children. They also acquire grammatical markers of tense and pluralization earlier in the sequence of development than do normally developing children. This may either reflect learning of apparent structures before learning structures that require a deeper analysis of the language, or the fact that particular aspects of the language were emphasized in the teaching of these children and were reproduced in some rote manner. In addition, these children developed deviant phonological rules, rather than simply reflecting normal development at an older age. Finally, both their auditory processing of speech material and their short-term storage capacities were described as being different (Institute for Childhood Aphasia, 1972).

Again, these similarities and differences may be due to the particular aspect of language development being examined and also to difference within the group of children being examined. In a study of sentence and speech repetition abilities of a group of children with a specific language disorder, it was found that different levels of comprehension and recoding abilities existed within the group. Some of the children appeared to have acquired unique phonological rules, while others reproduced phonological sequences in accordance with rules used by younger, normally developing children. Age played no role in the level of performance within the group; the oldest children did no better in the task than the youngest children. Differences were also found in the syntactic repetition abilities of these children, but all of them preserved the basic semantic relations expressed in the sentence (Actor—Action—Object) and also the modality (assertion, negation, question, and imperative) by the use of simple markers— prosody, negative morpheme, etc. (Menyuk and Looney, 1972a). It was also found that those children who used unique rules in reproducing phonological sequences were also those children at the most primitive level in sentence reproduction (Menyuk and Looney, 1972b).

Finally, we come to descriptions of the language behavior of autistic children and again we find that there appear to be great individual differences among these children. However, the differences between them and normally developing children in language behavior and other behaviors are most marked, and *delay* is a nondescriptive term. Rutter (1968) states that autistic children have a defect of language in particular and of symbolization in general. This symbolization defect is most marked in language. He further observes that social withdrawal occurs in children with more widespread perceptual defects. He hypothesizes that the asocial behavior of these children is a product of their perceptual defects rather than a cause for their bizarre behaviors. Many of these children appear to be limited to nonlinguistic vocalizations, whereas others engage in what has been termed *echolalic language.* Interestingly, this echolalic behavior is not restricted to language alone but can be found in other symbolic behaviors as well. Premack and Premack (1974) engaged these children in a picture completion task and found that they would "echo" the parts presented rather than complete the figures. Other experimenters have found that some of these children do not display a memory deficit per se but rather an organizational deficit. That is, whereas normally developing children's memory for sentences is better than their memory for unorganized lists, autistic children treat both types of material equally (Hermelin and O'Connor, 1970).

Wing (1969) carried out a study comparing the behaviors of autistic, receptive and executive aphasic, Down's syndrome, partially blind—deaf, and normal children. Their present states and past histories were examined. Unfortunately, the data on past histories of these children were based on schedules of development completed by parents retrospectively. The study is instructive, however, in that comparisons may at least lead to the development of important research questions, if not to understanding. The autistic child as described by Wing displays some of the behaviors found in all other groups of children. For example, comprehension and use of speech, pronunciation, and voice control is like that of the aphasic and deaf child. One might add that none of the descriptions of these children indicates that they develop the rich gesture language used by deaf children who have not been exposed to sign language. Their difficulty in understanding gestures, their abnormal body movements, and their preference for use of the proximal senses is like that of the partially deaf–blind child. Wing concluded that autistic behavior reflects abnormal brain function in dealing with linguistic and other input stimuli.

IS LANGUAGE ACQUISITION SPECIAL?

Normal language development has been studied in a variety of ways. Descriptions of observable behavior covering certain periods of development abound in the literature. Other periods have received much less attention. Descriptions vary in terms of their detail and what they have selected to describe in the child's language behavior, the language behavior of those who are communicating with him, and the situations in which this communication takes place. As these descriptions have accumulated, explanations for the onset of language and for the changes that occur in the child's knowledge and use of language have been sought. Sometimes these explanations are based on theoretical assumptions concerning these descriptions alone, or are derived from these descriptions in correlation with other developmental data. Other explanations are based on experimental interventions. Testing of the child's knowledge and use of language at various stages of development from infancy on has been attempted. Over the years, techniques have been developed that can more effectively elicit information about the infant and young child's handling of linguistic input and the structure of his output, and thus our understanding of the earliest periods of development has grown.

Language development is clearly dependent on physiological development and is a part of cognitive and social development in that, at various stages of development, different relations between phonological sequences and objects and events in the environment are observed. Thus, at various stages of development, both the form and function of the language understood and produced change. At the earliest stages of development, some aspects of the surface structure of utterances are observed. The constraints on these observations are because of what the infant conceives of as the function of language—to communicate his needs and feelings and to establish contact—and the limitations of his competence in memory, observations of regularities, and so on. As the child matures, his concept of the functions of language changes. Language is now not only used to communicate his needs and feelings and to establish contact, but also to codify environmental objects and events for himself and to communicate these codifications to others for description and verification. What he codifies is dependent on his neurophysiological and cognitive development. His concepts of the functions of language are dependent on his social experience; thus, the speed with which language maturation occurs for a given child is dependent on his neurophysiological and cognitive development, but how he uses language for himself and to others is dependent on his social experience. I would add that the ability to initially observe the relation between phonological sequences (or signs) and objects and events in the environment, under the conditions with which this occurs for the normally developing child, and to specify the relation is a special function of the human infant and child. One experimenter has stated that "It is quite apparent then, that the child must have great skill in detecting the syntactic regularities of his language whether or not they can be tied in some way to meaning." (MacNamara, 1972, p. 6). As we study and compare the language development of children who display developmental variations, we may be able to more clearly define what this special function is. This can only be accomplished, however, if we study the language development of these children with the intensity and care with which normal language development is being studied. What we know thus far is extremely limited.

Research has indicated that various groups of children with language disorders all display difficulty in phonological processing either in terms of input of information or output or both. This appears to be true even of blind children (Telford and Sawrey, 1967). Why this should be the case is not clear unless one hypothesizes that the course of language development is at first dependent on establishing relations between phonological language events and environmental events. (Morse, 1974, hypothesizes just this.) Later, as semantic and syntactic structures are acquired, understanding of relations between phonological sequences and environmental events is dependent on these structures.

Research has also indicated that various groups of children display differences in the amount of time needed to move from one developmental linguistic stage to another. Some linguistic problems seem to be more difficult to solve than others for different children, and the degree of difficulty encountered is not wholly dependent on the diagnostic classification of these children but rather on individual differences.

Some children display great difficulty in moving from vocalization to babbling or from babbling to one-word utterances. Other children display great difficulties in moving from the expression of basic relations to the development of transformational rules. As was stated, these differences are not defined by diagnostic categorizations. For example, we have found children who do not move from one-word utterances to the expression of basic relations for long periods of time, and others who do express these basic relations but who have not moved to the development of transformational structures during a period of over three years. All these children are within a population that has been diagnostically categorized as being homogeneous. The basis for the long period of time that is spent at any particular level of development may be the differences in their ability either to initially observe relations between language structure and communicative needs, to observe relations between language structure and coding of environmental phenomena, or to deal with the amounts of material or structure of the material that is required in any instance of linguistic categorization. The important point is that these children do differ in their capacities and therefore in their needs as far as educational programs are concerned.

Comparative research has shown that damage to one of the peripheral sensory mechanisms and delay in cognitive and social development make the task of language acquisition difficult and may alter it, because delay itself may lead to different processing strategies. Central nervous system damage may not only make the task difficult, but may alter it in specific ways that may be due to the nature of the damage; it may affect the ways in which these children organize both linguistic and nonlinguistic information. These are obviously gross descriptions. Both explanations of behavior and methods for remediation should become clearer as we study the behavior of these children over developmental periods, and use experimental techniques for study that go beyond the tests currently used to evaluate development.

REFERENCES

Bartholomews, B. Naming of meaningful nonverbal sounds by blind children. *Perceptual and Motor Skills,* 1971, *33,* 1289–1290.

Bateson, M. C. The interpersonal context of infant vocalization. *Quarterly Progress Report, Research Laboratory of Electronics, Massachusetts Institute of Technology,* 1971, No. 100, 170–176.

Bell, S. M., and Ainsworth, M. D. S. Infant crying and maternal responsiveness. *Child Development,* 1972, *43,* 1171–1190.

Bellugi, U., and Klima, E. S. Roots of language in the sign talk of the deaf. *Psychology Today,* 1972, *6*(1).

Bever, T. The integrated study of language behavior. In J. Morton (Ed.), *Biological and social factors in psycholinguistics.* Urbana: University of Illinois Press, 1970.

Bloom, L. *One word at a time: The use of single-word utterances before syntax.* The Hague: Mouton, 1973.

Bowerman, M. *Early syntactic development: A cross-linguistic study with special reference to Finnish.* Cambridge, England: W. Heffers, 1973.

Brown, R. *First language: the early stages.* Cambridge: Harvard University Press, 1973.

Clark, E. What's in a word? On the child's acquisition of semantics in his first language. In T. E. Moore (Ed.), *Cognitive development and the acquisition of language.* New York: Academic Press, 1973.

Clark, E. Some aspects of the conceptual basis for first language acquisition. In R. Schiefelbusch, and L. Lloyd (Eds.), *Language perspectives: acquisition, retardation and intervention.* Baltimore: University Park Press, 1974.

Cromer, R. Receptive language in the mentally retarded: Processes and diagnostic distinctions. In R. Schiefelbusch, and L. Lloyd (Eds.), *Language perspectives.* Baltimore: University Park Press, 1974.

Demott, R. M. Verbalism and affective meaning for blind, severely visually impaired and normally sighted children. *The New Outlook for the Blind,* 1972, *16*(1).

Dore, J. The development of speech acts. Unpublished doctoral dissertation, Baruch College, New York, N.Y., 1973.

Ervin-Tripp, S. An overview of theories of grammatical development. In D. I. Slobin (Ed.), *The ontogenesis of grammar.* New York: Academic Press, 1971.

Furth, Hans. Conservation of weight in deaf and hearing children. *Child Development,* 1964, *35*, 143–160.

Geschwind, N. Disconnection syndromes in animal and man. *Brain,* 1965, *88* (Part II), 237–294.

Gottesman, M. A comparative study of Piaget's developmental schema of sighted children with that of a group of blind children. *Child Development,* 1971, *42*, 573–580.

Greenfield, P. M., Smith, J. H., and Laufer, B. *Communication and the beginning of language: the development of semantic structure in one-word speech and beyond.* Unpublished manuscript, Harvard University, 1972.

Hermelin, B., and O'Conner, N. *Psychological experiments with autistic children.* Oxford: Pergamon Press, 1970.

Institute for Childhood Aphasia, *Papers and reports on child language development.* No. 4. Stanford, Calif.: Stanford University, June 1972.

Irwin, O. C. Phonetical descriptions of speech development in childhood. In *Kaiser's manual of phonetics.* Amsterdam: North Holland Publishing Co., 1957.

Jakobson, R. *Child language, aphasia and phonological universals.* The Hague: Mouton, 1968.

Kagan, J., and Lewis, M. Studies of attention. *Merrill-Palmer Quarterly of Behavior and Development,* 1965, *4*, 95–127.

Kaplan, E. L. The role of intonation in the acquisition of language. Unpublished doctoral dissertation, Cornell University, 1969.

Kaplan, E. L., and Kaplan, G. N. The prelinguistic child. In J. Eliot (Ed.), *Human development and cognitive processes.* New York: Holt, Rinehart & Winston, 1970.

Lackner, J. R. A developmental study of the language behavior in retarded children. *Neuropsychologia,* 1968, *6*, 301–320.

Lenneberg, E. Natural history of language. In F. Smith and G. A. Miller (Eds.), *Genesis of language.* Cambridge, Mass.: M.I.T. Press, 1966.

Lewis, M., and Freedle, R. *Mother–infant dyad: the cradle of meaning.* Princeton, N.J.: Educational Testing Service, 1972.

MacNamara, J. Cognitive bases of language learning in infants. *Psychological Review,* 1972, *79*, 1–13.

McNeill, D. The development of language. In P. H. Mussen (Ed.), *Carmichael's manual of child psychology.* New York: Wiley, 1970.

Menyuk, P. *Sentences children use.* Cambridge, Mass.: M.I.T. Press, 1969.

Menyuk, P. *The acquisition and development of language.* Englewood Cliffs, N.J.: Prentice-Hall, 1971.

Menyuk, P. Early development of receptive language: from babbling to words. In R. L. Scheifelbusch and L. L. Lloyd (Eds.), *Language perspectives: Acquisition, retardation and intervention.* Baltimore: University Park Press, 1974.

Menyuk, P., and Looney, P. A problem of language disorder: length versus structure. *Journal of Speech and Hearing Research,* 1972, *15,* 264–279. (a)

Menyuk, P., and Looney, P. Relationships among components of the grammar. *Journal of Speech and Hearing Research,* 1972, *15,* 395–406. (b)

Morse, P. Infant speech: a preliminary model. In R. Schiefelbusch and L. Lloyd (Eds.), *Language perspectives: acquisition, retardation and intervention.* Baltimore: University Park Press, 1974.

Nakazima, S. A comparative study of speech development of Japanese and American English in childhood. *Studia Phonologica,* 1970, *5,* 20–35.

Nelson, K. Structure and strategy in learning to talk. *Monograph of the Society for Research in Child Development,* 1973, *38,* Nos. 1 & 2.

Piaget, J. Piaget's theory. In P. H. Mussen (Ed.), *Carmichael's manual of child psychology.* Vol. I. New York: Wiley, 1970.

Premack, D., and Premack, A. J. Teaching visual language to apes and language-deficient persons. In R. Schiefelbusch, and L. Lloyd (Eds.), *Language perspectives: acquisition, retardation and intervention.* Baltimore: University Park Press, 1974.

Quigley, S. P., Smith, N. L., and Wilbur, R. B. Comprehension of relativized sentences by deaf students. *Journal of Speech and Hearing Research,* 1974, *17,* 325–341.

Rutter, M. Concepts of autism: a review of research. *Journal of Child Psychology and Psychiatry,* 1968, *9,* 1–25.

Schlesinger, I. M. Relational concepts underlying language. In R. Schiefelbusch and L. Lloyd (Eds.), *Language perspectives: acquisition, retardation and intervention.* Baltimore: University Park Press, 1974.

Schmitt, P. Deaf children's comprehension and production of sentence transformations. Unpublished doctoral dissertation, University of Illinois, 1968.

Semmel, M. I., Barritt, L. S., and Bennett, S. W. Performance of EMR and nonretarded children on modified cloze task. *American Journal of Mental Deficiency,* 1970, *74,* 681–688.

Slobin, D. I. (Ed.). *The ontogenesis of grammar.* New York: Academic Press, 1971.

Telford, C. W., and Sawrey, J. M. *The exceptional individual.* Englewood Cliffs, N.J.: Prentice-Hall, 1967.

Tonkova-Yampolskaya, R. V. Development of speech intonation in infants during the first two years of life. Translated in *Soviet Psychology,* 1969, *7,* 48–54.

Werner, H., and Kaplan, E. Development of word meaning through verbal context. *Journal of Psychology,* 1950, *29,* 251–257.

Wing, L. The handicap of autistic children—a comparative study. *Journal of Child Psychology and Psychiatry,* 1969, *10,* 1–40.

Yoder, D. E., and Miller, J. F. What we may know and what we can do: input toward a system. In J. E. McLean, D. E. Yoder, and R. Schiefelbusch (Eds.), *Developing strategies for language intervention.* New York: Holt, Rinehart & Winston, 1972.

8

Cognitive Development and Psychopathology: Observations on Egocentrism and Ego Defense

DAVID ELKIND

Over the past decade and a half, American research on the cognitive development of children has received its greatest impetus from the work of Jean Piaget (e.g., Piaget, 1963). Most of this research started from Piaget's later studies and theorizing concerned with the evolution of rational thought. Much less attention was paid to Piaget's early work (e.g., Piaget, 1929) on egocentrism. But the work on egocentrism seems most closely related to psychopathology and thus seems to warrant more study than it has heretofore received. The intent of the present paper is to provide a brief example of one of the directions such a study might take. The paper is divided into four sections. The first section reviews some of the history of the study of egocentric thought. In the second section, some of my own conceptions of the evolution of egocentric structures in children and adolescents will be described. The third section of the paper deals with the relation between egocentric structures and ego defenses at three age levels. Then, in the final section, some clinical and research implications of the discussion will be briefly presented.

DAVID ELKIND · Department of Psychology, University of Rochester, Rochester, New York 14627.

THE STUDY OF EGOCENTRISM
BRIEF HISTORY AND INTRODUCTION

The study of egocentrism in children grew out of the interest in nonrational thought that was one of the preoccupations of the new disciplines of psychology, cultural anthropology, and psychoanalysis that emerged at around the turn of the century. Much of this work, with the exception of Freud's, was carried out within a Darwinian framework, which suggested that rational thought evolved from nonrational thought much as man evolved from the apes. Cultural anthropologists sought and found evidence of primitive thinking among esoteric peoples living in remote and isolated places. Cultural historians likewise found evidence for primitive ideas in earlier eras of western society. Freud noted primitive "primary process" thinking in the dreams, fantasies, and free associations of normal as well as disturbed adults. Any early developmental psychologists found evidence of nonrational thought among children.

The early work on nonrational thought was primarily descriptive and contrasted these modes of thought with those of rational discursive thought. In a series of classic studies, Jean Piaget (1929, 1948, 1951) dealt with nonrational thought from a perspective that was at once empirical and philosophical. Piaget was cognizant of the epistemological questions raised by the discovery of primitive thought and tried to answer some of these questions with his early investigations. Basically the epistemological question can be phrased, How is primitive, nonrational thought possible?

The discovery of primitive thought challenged in nontrivial ways traditional theories of knowing. If esoteric peoples, children, and even normal people could entertain false notions about the world, then experience could not be the sole source of knowledge. Experience could not be the source of both true and of false pictures of the world. Where then do such erroneous notions as animism come from? The appeal to the innateness of these ideas is also unsuccessful. Young children have primitive ideas but give them up as they grow older. But innate ideas are, by definition, fixed and unchanging so that they cannot be the source of developmentally malleable primitive ideas.

Spurred on by such questions and by the results of his researches, Piaget was led to a constructivist epistemology. Basically, this epistemology insists that the child constructs reality out of his experiences with the environment. We can never know the environment directly, but only indirectly, through our intellectual constructions, which approximate the environment but are never identical to it. As children grow older and their intellectual abilities mature, they progressively construct a series of realities that move ever closer to the reality of adults. But the reality of adults is also only an approximation and continues to change and be modified with the accumulation of new knowledge and new reconstructions of reality.

From this point of view, the designation of a particular mode of thought as primitive is necessarily relative. Primitive or egocentric thought is unshared and unsocialized thought; it lacks what Sullivan (1953) called consensual validation. In this sense, the animism of primitives was not egocentric because it was a mode of thought that was consciously shared by a given society. In the same way, the heliocentric theory was not egocentric at the time it was held because it was socially shared and agreed upon. In contrast, the animistic ideas of the preschool child are implicit and unconscious in his thinking and are not agreed upon or shared by adults within the society. In short, egocentric thought and concepts are those that lack social articulation and consensus.

In Piaget's view, egocentric thought progressively declines in importance as children grow older and their intellectual abilities mature. Rational, discursive thought gradually predominates in the thinking of older children and adults. After his initial concern with egocentric thought, Piaget turned to his major opus, the mechanisms by which the child constructs progressively more socialized realities. This is not the place to review the stages Piaget delineated in the child's conquest of objective socialized reality, for our concern is with the fate of egocentric thought.

Although Piaget soon lost interest in egocentric thought as he began to deal with the evolution of logical thought, other investigators did not. The gifted Russian psychologist, Vygotsky (1962) for example, took issue with Piaget regarding the fate of egocentric thinking. For Vygotsky, egocentric thought did not disappear but rather became successively internalized and transformed into private, inner speech and thought. These two interpretations have continued to interest investigators who have tried to devise investigations to decide between them. The research as of this date (cf., e.g., Kohlberg, Yaeger, and Hjertholm, 1968) remains ambiguous as to the fate of egocentric thought in general.

Other investigators have looked at egocentrism with respect to its relation to communication (Flavell, 1968) or to pathology (Anthony, 1956) or to delinquency (Chandler, 1973). In all of these approaches, egocentric thought is regarded as a stage of mental development that can be overcome by movement to the next higher level of development. In particular, movement to concrete operations and the ability to take another person's point of view, required for the socialization of thought, are regarded as crucial to overcoming the egocentric stage of thought. By helping children take the point of view of others, it is hoped that children will move out of their egocentricity.

The perspective of the present paper is somewhat different. From this perspective, egocentrism is not limited to a particular stage of development but is present at each stage, though in different degrees and in different forms. At each stage of development, the child's new forms of thinking enable him to overcome early forms of egocentrism, but also ensnare him in new more complex varieties of unsocialized thought. In general the sphere of egocentric thought diminishes with age and pertains to more specific and more abstract aspects of the physical and social world. These more advanced forms of egocentric thinking are less well known than those of the preschool period but are equally important. Indeed, the last section of the paper will argue that many defenses and symptoms can be described in terms of the egocentric structures characteristic of childhood and adolescence.

Before turning to a discussion of the egocentric structures at three stages of development, something has to be said about egocentric concept formation. Basically, egocentric concepts are formed because there is a lag between the development of ability to form concepts and the ability to check or test their social validity. Hence the preschool child has the ability to form causal concepts such as animism before he has the logical abilities (the concrete operations that appear at 6 and 7) that are necessary to test them. In fact, most veridical concept formation at a particular stage is the correction of erroneous concepts formed at the previous stage.

That is to say, much of the concept-formation activity of a particular stage of development is directed not so much at realizing the potentials of the abilities of that stage as at correcting the erroneous conceptions formed at previous stages. In fact, this is why egocentrism declines in extent with age. As the child is more and more concerned with reconstructing his previous erroneous conceptions of space, time, causality, and so on, he has less time to form totally new concepts that would bring his egocentrism into play. But when he does use his conceptual powers in new situations, egocentrism is likely to emerge, at least temporally.

EGOCENTRIC STRUCTURES IN CHILDHOOD
AND ADOLESCENCE

At each stage of development, egocentric structures reflect the child's cognitive abilities of the moment and his attempts to make sense out of his world. Egocentric concepts are, in essence, assumptions about some aspects of the environment that the child takes as given, because he lacks the ability to challenge or test them. Egocentric ideas are given up as the child attains the prerequisite mental abilities to test them, and as his ideas are challenged by social interactions. The kinds of assumptions made at each major stage of development and characteristic aspects of egocentric thought will now be described.

Egocentric Structures at the Preoperational Stage

Between the ages of 3 and 6, children acquire the symbolic function, the ability to create symbols and to learn signs that can represent their experience and their concepts. But the young child's ability to create symbols and to learn signs far outstrips his ability to comprehend them in socially accepted ways. Because this discrepancy pervades the young child's thinking, egocentrism is rampant during this stage. His egocentrism covers his attempts to discover all aspects of his world and justifies referring to this stage as one in which the child behaves according to *assumptive philosophies,* a global set of beliefs as to how the physical and social worlds operate.

Many assumptions of young children's philosophies are by now well known. One assumption is that the world is *purposive,* that everything has a purpose or cause and that there is no possibility of chance or arbitrary events. Another assumption is that of *artificialism,* that everything in the world is made by and for man. Still another assumptive philosophy is *nominal realism,* the belief that names are essential components of the objects they designate and cannot be separated from them or changed. Finally, although it does not exhaust the list, there is the assumption of *animism,* the belief that nonbiological objects are alive.

What is typical of the egocentric concepts of this and later stages is a fundamental confusion between what comes from within and what from without the child. Such confusion is to be expected if reality is truly constructed and is neither copied from some fixed and separate world, nor simply remembered as if it were an innate idea. But this epistemological confusion takes different forms at different age levels, and reflects the level of conceptualization at those age levels.

At the preschool level, the confusion is between what the child knows concretely of himself, feelings, intentions, sensory experiences, and what he knows concretely of the world, namely, its tangibility, and its objectivity. In effect, what the young child does is construct his psychic world on the model of the physical world and construct the physical world on the model of his psychic reality. Hence the young child believes that his dreams come in through the window at night, that other people can feel his toothache, and that the wind, moon, and sun are alive. Again these ideas are egocentric, not in and of themselves, but in the context of a society where they are not acceptable to the adult mind.

Egocentric Structures in Childhood

At about the age of 6 or 7, in Piaget's view, new mental abilities emerge that take the child far beyond what he was capable of doing at the preschool level.

These new mental abilities, concrete operations, resemble the operations of arithmetic in their mode of activity, and function as a system rather than in isolation. Thus, if a child knows that the class of children minus the class of boys equals the class of girls $(C - B = G)$, one can infer, with reasonable certainty, that he also knows that the class of children minus the class of girls equals the class of boys $(C - G = B)$. These operations also enable the child to grasp the notion of a unit that is at once like every other unit in being a unit and different in order of enumeration or seriation.

Concrete operations thus enable the school-age child to progressively comprehend many of the verbal representations he acquired but understood only egocentrically at the preschool level. He begins to grasp, for example, that "right" and "left" are relations and not absolute properties of things. And he comes to appreciate that changes in the appearance of quantities does not mean a change in their amounts. The concrete operations of middle childhood thus progressively overcome the egocentric notions found at the preschool level.

But concrete operations also engender new egocentric concepts in their own right. With his new mental abilities, the school-age child can now mentally represent various possible courses of action. The preschool child, in contrast, was able to represent only properties and things. The new ability to represent possible courses of action appears in many different ways. For example, when a preschool child is presented with a finger maze, he proceeds by immediately putting his finger to the maze and succeeds, if he does, by trial and error efforts. A school-age child will, in contrast, survey the maze and mentally represent various paths until he discovers the right one. Only at that point will he put his finger to the maze.

In the maze situation, the ability to internally represent actions works quite well because there is immediate and inequivocal feedback as to the correctness of the representation. But in many other situations, there is no mental way to test which of several possible courses of action will succeed. In such circumstances an experimental frame of mind is required that permits one to hold several hypotheses in mind while testing each in succession. The ability to do this is, however, only made possible by the formal operations of adolescent intelligence. Consequently the school-age child is in the position of being able to conceptualize alternate paths of action, but of not being able to test these alternate paths in systematic ways.

The school-age child is thus in the same position with respect to understanding possible courses of action that the preschool child was with respect to representing classes, relations, and units. In both cases, there is a lag between the ability to represent experience and the ability to test out the social validity of the representations. In the school-age child, as in the preschool child, the result is the formation of egocentric conceptions. Again at this stage these egocentric conceptions deal with assumptions about the world, but at this stage the assumptions have to do with possible courses of action in the real world and might be called *assumptive realities.*

As in the case of the assumptive philosophies of the preschool child, the assumptive realities of the school-age child reflect a confusion between the mental and the physical, between the reality of mind and the reality of matter. When the school-age child arrives at a possible course of action, a hypothesis, or strategy that cannot be immediately tested he often mistakes this *conceptual possibility* for a *material necessity.* Once he has adopted this egocentric position, he proceeds to make any disparate facts fit the hypotheses rather than the reverse. This mode of egocentric thought is not unfamiliar at the adult level and is epitomized in folk sayings such as "Love is blind" or "No mother has a homely child."

To make the operation of assumptive realities concrete, consider some of the following examples. In one study, Peel (1960) gave children and adolescents a passage describing the rock formations at Stonehenge but without revealing their supposed function. The subjects were asked to decide whether the formations were used as a fort or as a religious shrine. The children (9 years old) made their decision on the basis of a few facts and, if given contrary information, rationalized this to fit in with their hypothesis. Adolescents, in contrast, based their hypotheses upon multiple facts and, if given sufficient contrary information, changed their hypotheses.

In another experiment Weir (1964) had 5- to 17-year-old children work on a probability task. The apparatus was a box with three knobs and a pay-off chute. One knob was programmed to pay off (in M&Ms or tokens) 0% of the time, another was programmed to pay off 33% of the time, and a third was programmed to pay off 66% of the time. Subjects were instructed to find a pattern of response (knob pressing) that would produce the most rewards. The solution was to press only the 66% knob inasmuch as it "paid off" more times in any hundred pressings than any other knob.

The results, plotted as number of trials to a successful solution, showed an inverted U curve with respect to age. Young children, who were getting M&Ms, did not waste time and quickly learned which button gave them the most candy. Adolescents approached the task with many complex hypotheses and tried out multiple complex patterns. In the process they discovered the fruitfulness of the 66% knob and eventually stuck to pressing it. But the 7–9 age children had great trouble. They adapted a "win stick, lose shift" strategy that they assumed was correct and blamed the machine for being wrong. This is a good example of the assumptive realities of the school-age child.

Other examples could be given (e.g., Elkind, 1966) but these few may suffice to illustrate the character of egocentric thought at the elementary school level. Whenever children are in a position where they can form possible courses of action in their heads, without immediate and unequivocal evidence of their correctness, the stage is set for assumptive realities. The child mistakes his hypothesized course of action for the real or necessary course of action and attributes more weight to it than to contrary bits of evidence. Such assumptive realities are egocentric because the child lacks the means to check them against the facts.

Clearly, if the child is given the correct solution to these problems or to those that may arise in other situations, then the assumptive reality is given up. This happens because the child can then see the relation between the correct course of action and the result. The preschool child too can be shown that a particular object like a stone does not have feelings. But these specific discoveries do not abolish the egocentric mode of thought, but only an egocentric concept in a particular situation. Egocentric concepts will emerge again when the child is in a situation where he can represent more than he can comprehend.

Egocentric Structures in Adolescence

Roughly coincident with the onset of puberty, is the appearance of new mental structures that Piaget calls "formal operations." Like concrete operations, formal operations function as a system but extend the young person's intellectual powers far beyond what they were in childhood. This is true because formal operations allow the preadolescent to set forth his own representations. Formal operations are to concrete operations as algebra is to arithmetic, a second order, higher level symbol system. While concrete operations make it possible for the child to conceive possible courses of action in the real world, formal operations make it possible for the adolescent to conceive of possible representations. Possible representations include theories, ideals, metaphors, and so on. Formal operations also enable the young person to hold many hypotheses in mind while testing each one systematically. In a word, formal operations make possible experimental thinking.

Formal operations enable the child to be aware of his hypotheses as hypotheses, as mental constructions, and permit him to test these against the evidence. In this way, formal operations enable the child to overcome his egocentric assumptive realities. But these operations also make it possible for the adolescent to represent his own and other persons' feelings and thoughts. Although he has the mental ability to test out these assumptions, the young adolescent lacks the motivation to do so. He is so preoccupied with the changes in his physical appearance and his new feelings and emotions, that he has little interest in checking out his assumptions about what other people think and feel. For a few years, therefore, the young adolescent operates on the basis of *assumptive psychologies* about himself and other people.

As in the case of assumptive philosophies of preschool children and assumptive realities of elementary school children, the assumptive psychologies of the young adolescent represent a confusion between the child and his world but now on a psychological plane. What happens is that the young adolescent takes what is unique to himself as being universal to mankind, but also believes that what is universal to mankind is unique to himself. Such assumptive psychologies are sometimes gratifying and sometimes painful, and it is often the painful assumptions that eventually cause young people to test out their assumptions about how other people think and feel.

To illustrate some assumptive psychologies, consider the attractive young woman with a minor facial blemish. At this stage, early adolescence, she is convinced: (a) that everyone notices and thinks about it; (b) that everyone regards it as horribly ugly and detestable; and (c) that it is the sole criterion on which people judge her as a person. Hence she concludes, "Everybody thinks I am ugly. I must be ugly." In this instance, which is so familiar as to be commonplace, the young person mistakes a personal, idiosyncratic appraisal of herself for one that is a uniform, consistent appraisal of mankind.

The reverse is also true and young people also mistake what is universal, or nearly so, as being unique to themselves. A young man who has been saving up to buy a new car feels that no boy in the world has ever wanted a car as much as he. But boys growing up all over the world want horses, boats, or even bows and arrows as signs of their maturity. Far from being unique, the desire for a symbol of adult male status is probably universal to male adolescents. In the same way, the young woman who is in love for the first time feels that her feelings are unique and that no one has ever experienced the exquisite pain she is enduring. "Oh, Mommy, you don't know how it feels," she says, and yet every woman at one time or another has felt the same way.

These are but a few of the assumptive psychologies of adolescence, the egocentric ideas that permeate this age period. Again, these ideas are egocentric only because the individual assumes they are shared by others when in fact they are not, or that they are not shared by others when in fact they are. Many of the interpersonal interactions among young adolescents are governed by assumptive psychologies, and this accounts, in part at least, for the self-centeredness of these interactions.

EGOCENTRIC STRUCTURES AND EGO DEFENSES

The delineation of the defense mechanisms of the ego evolved primarily out of the clinical work of Freud (1957) and his followers who, for the most part, worked with adults. When the developmental aspect of ego defenses was discussed, as in the work of Anna Freud (1946), it was primarily in connection with the psychosexual stages of development. These stages, the oral, anal, oedipal, latency, and adolescent periods (together with their substages) were defined primarily in terms of the vicissitudes of the child's developing sexual orientation. In Freudian theory, therefore, structural changes in cognitive functioning are derived from "geographical" changes in sexual orientation.

With the advent of psychoanalytic ego psychology (cf. Rapaport, 1960, for a historical summary) and the postulation of autonomous ego functions, a path was opened between psychoanalytic and cognitive theories of development. Much of the work on cognitive styles (e.g., Klein, 1958) was an attempt to show how autonomous ego functions could be related to personality dynamics. But the work on cognitive styles has been, for the most part, nondevelopmental. That is to say, styles such as "field independence—dependence" (Witkin, Dyk, Faterson, Goodenough, and Karp, 1962) and "impulsivity/reflectivity" (Kagan, 1966) are present at all age levels, although perhaps to different extents. Cognitive styles appear to be more closely related to long-standing affective orientations than to changing cognitive structures.

The work on cognitive styles evolved before much was known about cognitive development, and was based on the assumption that thought did not change qualitatively with age once secondary, rational thinking came into appearance. But the work of Jean Piaget (1963) has demonstrated that rational thought is not of one piece, but rather evolves in a series of stages that are related to age. These stages were briefly described in the preceding section of this paper. Piaget's work thus forces a reconsideration of cognitive styles generally and of ego defenses in particular. The present discussion attempts such a reconsideration of ego defenses within a cognitive development framework.

Because ego defenses were derived from dynamic considerations, and without regard to cognitive development, they do not always make sense from a Piagetian standpoint. Rather than try to reinterpret ego defenses from the standpoint of cognitive growth, I propose to describe cognitive structures available for defensive purposes at successive age levels. Traditional ego defenses, such as denial, can then be defined in terms of cognitive structures at a particular age level and in this way lose some of their ambiguity. This is clearly an ambitious project and only a brief introduction to what might be accomplished in this domain will be presented here.

Egocentric Structures and Defenses at the Preschool Level

In the earlier discussion, it was suggested that the egocentric structures of the preschool period have to do with assumptive philosophies. One of these assumptive philosophies is *phenomenalistical causality*, the belief that events that happen together cause one another. Such thinking is evidenced when a child who sees the sun appear when the window shade is raised believes that raising the shade causes the sun to rise. Phenomenalistic causality is tied up with animism and with artificialism, all of which reflect a confusion between the psychic or the physical.

Although phenomenalistic causality is a general characteristic of young peoples' thinking, it can be used for defensive purposes. To illustrate, the work on father absence (Herzog and Sudia, 1973) suggests that such absence or separation is most detrimental when it occurs before the age of 6 or 7. Clearly, this is an important period of identification, particularly for the boy. In addition, however, it is also the period of phenomenalistic causality thinking. Boys who may fantasy the father gone may find that he has gone in fact. The association of fantasy and fact leads the child to believe that one "caused" the other. That is, of course, what is usually called "magical thinking." But magical thinking is merely a special case of phenomenalistic causal thinking that is derived from the preoperational period.

Phenomenalistic or precausal thinking does not disappear as children mature and continues to appear even at the adult level. A salesman who makes an unexpected sale after crossing his fingers may cross his fingers prior to the next sale in hopes it will "work" again. The popularity of the TV show "Bewitched" for both adults and children suggests the ease with which both children and adolescents can fall back into the "magical thinking" mode.

A very common example of phenomenalistic causality thinking occurs in the children of divorced couples. Such children, particularly at the early elementary school level, are likely to believe that some misbehavior on their part brought about the separation. The magical thought, which grows out of guilt feelings, further aggravates guilt feelings and hence leads to the perpetuation of the magical thought. Since such children are capable of more mature thought, their difficulty is primarily emotional rather than rational. A therapeutic approach aimed at their feelings, rather than at their magical thinking, would thus seem to be most efficacious.

Egocentric Structures and Ego Defenses in Childhood

During childhood, the egocentric structures that are in prominence derive from concrete operations and amount to *assumptive realities*. The characteristic of assumptive realities is that the child mistakes a possible course of action, a mental construction, for the real or actual course of action or events. As a consequence, the child views his mental construction as necessary and defensible against contrary evidence. While such assumptive realities are normal to most children at one or another time, they can become defenses when strong emotions are involved.

Elsewhere (Elkind, 1973) I have described some of the defensive egocentric structures in latency and I will briefly review some of those structures here. One of these structures I have called "cognitive conceit." During the preschool years the child believes his parents are all-powerful and all-knowing. With the advent of concrete operations and elementary reasoning abilities, the child has the intellectual wherewithal to detect the fallacies in parental logic and the gaps in their knowledge. Once a child has the revelation that a parent, a grownup, can be in error, he jumps to the conclusion that he knows more than the adult and that the adult is stupid. This belief that he is clever and that adults are stupid is the cognitive conceit of the school-age child.

Cognitive conceit is common to children in greater or lesser degrees. It is embodied in their language and lore and is exemplified in jokes and riddles wherein adults are made to look stupid. That is one reason children at this age prefer stories in which children outwit adults (Shlager, 1974). When children play games with adults, cognitive conceit becomes apparent in their boasting when they win and in their rationalizations when they lose. Children seek evidence to bolster their cognitive conceit and often delight in tripping up adults when they can catch them in error.

Another assumptive reality common to the elementary school period is the "tall tale." Children often make assumptions about the world that add to their sense of adventure. They may assume that there is buried treasure in the backyard and proceed to dig up a flower bed in search of it. Or, they may skulk about following a "suspicious"-looking stranger who, they are sure, is some spy or gangster. Although at some level children understand that the "tall tale" is just that, they also maintain it cognitively and rationalize a good deal of information to maintain such assumptive realities intact.

From an ego-defense point of view, assumptive realities and their maintenance relate to what has been called *denial* and *rationalization*. Denial is seldom, if ever, a passive nay saying. Rather, it is a reconstruction of reality for defensive purposes. It is a hypothesis about reality that the subject mistakes for reality itself. A common example of assumptive reality as denial occurs when a child is accused of stealing or lying. In this situation the child may, even though aware of having taken something or told an untruth, reconstruct his memory of the event in such a way that he appears innocent and uninvolved. He then treats his memory reconstruction as a veridical memory and asserts his innocence, to his parents' great consternation.

Rationalization goes hand in hand with assumptive realities and is the use of reason to defend an assumptive reality. It is the modification of facts to fit the hypothesis rather than a modification of hypothesis to fit the facts. When a child denies his guilt by memory reconstruction, he must also rationalize a good deal of evidence that is in conflict with that reconstruction. Accordingly, from a developmental point of view, denial—in the sense of memory reconstruction—

and rationalization—in the sense of reasoning so as to make the facts fit the hypotheses—are ego defenses that make their appearance during childhood and in connection with the egocentric assumptive realities that mark this period.

Egocentric Structures and Ego Defenses in Adolescence

At about the age of puberty, the gradual emergence of formal operations makes possible the conceptualization of thought and of other peoples' thinking. The egocentric structures of this age period amount to assumptive psychologies, beliefs about other peoples' thoughts and feelings. As indicated earlier, the young adolescent confuses the universal with the unique and the unique with the universal. The assumptive psychologies of the early adolescent period give rise to some characteristic structures described below.

One of these structures is an *imaginary audience,* an assumption that other people are as interested in the young person as he is himself. The imaginary audience derives from a confusion between what is important in the young person and what he believes is important to others. The young adolescent believes that other people are observing and evaluating his appearance and his clothing because he mistakes his unique concern for himself, engendered by all the many and sundry changes of adolescence, for a concern that is common to everyone. The imaginary audience grows naturally out of the characteristic self—other confusion of this age period.

Coupled with the imaginary audience is a complementary egocentric structure, the *personal fable.* Just as the young person mistakes what is unique to himself for what is common to everyone, so too does he mistake what is common to everyone as unique to himself. Most adolescents find it hard to conceptualize their own death and believe that while everyone else in the world may die, they will live on forever. While this notion is well nigh universal among young people (and among many older ones as well), each adolescent feels that the belief is unique to himself. The personal fable is the story each individual tells himself about his own immortality and specialness, which happens not to be true. While each individual is indeed unique and special, it is not in the ways that are embodied in each individual's personal fable.

If we look now at these egocentric structures from the standpoint of ego defense, they appear to be comparable to what is usually called projection. Dynamically *projection* is defined as the attribution to others of one's own feelings, impulses, and thoughts. But such attribution must, of necessity, wait upon the child's ability to conceptualize the thoughts, feelings, and impulses of others. This does not appear until adolescence. Projection is, therefore, another name for assumptive psychologies (or vice versa).

But assumptive psychologies, such as the imaginary audience and the personal fable, move in two directions. One direction is the attribution as common to others of what is unique to the self, and the other is the attribution as unique to the self of what is common to others. In the latter case the individual fails to attribute to others what is characteristic of them. This latter process is a form of *rejection*, a refusal to accept that what is true of the self might also be true of others: "Oh, Mommy, you just don't know how it feels to be in love." Projection and rejection are, in the sense defined here, characteristic of the adolescent period and of the formal operations that generally emerge with the advent of puberty.

SOME CLINICAL IMPLICATIONS

The foregoing discussion is an attempt to relate cognitive development to the construction of ego defenses. The analysis offered here suggests that magical thinking derives from the preschool period, that denial and rationalization derive from the elementary school period, and that projection and rejection (in the sense defined here) are the outcomes of the formal operations of adolescence. In view of the preliminary nature of this discussion, it would not be in order to advance a detailed presentation of clinical implications. It does seem appropriate, however, to mention a few issues that appear to warrant further research exploration.

First of all, it might be possible to relate traditional clinical syndromes to the age when the cognitive component of their characteristic defenses emerge. While the dynamic underpinnings for the use of these defenses may well appear earlier in development, the defensive pattern itself will not appear until the appropriate structures are available. This type of analysis would suggest that more consideration must be paid to the ages when the cognitive structures of various syndromes emerge in development.

The obsessive–compulsive neurosis, for example, is often traced to fixations at the anal stage of development, namely at the age of 1 to 2 years of age. But what characterizes the obsessive–compulsive is the prevalence of a few assumptive realities about the danger inherent in loss of control and environmental disorder. As in the case of all assumptive realities, evidence to the contrary is no way to combat them. But the point is that assumptive realities are the product of concrete operations that do not appear until after the age of 6 or 7. According to this analysis, obsessive–compulsive symptomatology should not appear until middle childhood except in intellectually precocious children. This is a hypothesis that might be tested.

A similar case could be made for paranoia not appearing, in symptomatic form, until adolescence. At the cognitive level, paranoia involves projection of feelings and thoughts onto others. Such projection, however, cannot, in theory, occur until the advent of formal operations. Indeed, the imaginary audience and the personal fable could be the normal analogs to delusions of persecution and of megalomania. The fact that paranoia does not usually appear until adolescence, and that it generally occurs in individuals of better than average intelligence, would support the argument that formal operations are required for the realization of this syndrome. Again, this is a matter that could be put to test.

A final example may help to further support the value of the approach suggested here. Although some forms of mild depressive states are observed in children, true depression is not usually observed until adolescence. It is generally recognized that the central dynamic of depression is the loss or separation from a loved object. When separation occurs early in life, when no defenses are possible, the infant shows anaclitic depression. But when the separation or loss occurs during childhood, the young person can use assumptive realities, denial, and rationalization to deal with the separation. The assumptive reality of the "good parent" regardless of the parents' real qualities is often employed to deal with separation during the latency period.

With the emergence of adolescence and formal operations, however, separation and loss are experienced with full cognitive force. The young person can no longer cling to assumptive realities that deny the facts. Moreover, once the young person can conceive how other people think about him, a new kind of loss or separation becomes possible, namely, the loss of "face" or of "reputation," the good will toward us held in the minds of others. Many serious depressions and suicides are the direct result of such "social" losses or separations, which are only possible to individuals who can conceptualize the way others think about them.

The cognitive dimension of depression is seen most dramatically and tragically in the case of young people who have suffered from a physical defect or handicap. During childhood, thanks to assumptive realities such as "I will get better," they often appear as happy children. When adolescence and formal operations arrive, however, these children sometimes experience severe depressions. The assumptive realities must be given up. Moreover, the young person can now conceive the thoughts of others and believe they reject his defect as he does. Such children no sooner gain a sense of the esteem of others, than they lose it, in imagination, due to their defect. In such instances, cognitive development is the precipitating factor in the depression.

These few examples of the relation between egocentric structures, ego defenses, and psychopathology are merely suggestive. Much more theoretical, clinical, and research work needs to be done before we can be more sure about the tentative ideas presented here. I do hope, however, that the material presented suggests the potential fruitfulness of cognitive developmental theory for the study of psychopathology.

SUMMARY

The study of cognitive development has, for the most part, been concerned with the evolution of rational, socialized thought. The evolution of egocentric, nonrational thought has, on the other hand, been neglected. The present paper concerns itself with the development of egocentric thought and its relation to ego defenses. The first section of the paper traces the history of the study of egocentric thought to the early anthropological studies of primitive thinking in esoteric peoples and to psychological studies of primitive thinking in children and adults. The advent of ego psychology in some ways blocked further study of the development of egocentric thinking.

The second section of the paper describes the evolution of egocentric thinking from the perspective of Piagetian theory. Egocentric thinking occurs because there is a discrepancy between the growing individual's ability to form hypotheses and his ability to test them. Egocentric concepts are those that, at any level of development, the child can form but not test. These concepts amount to assumptions about the self and the world that take different forms at different age levels. At the preschool level the child forms assumptive *philosophies,* at the school-age level he forms assumptive *realities,* while at the adolescent level he forms assumptive *psychologies.*

A third section of the paper details some of the particular egocentric structures at each age level and relates them to familiar ego defenses. At the preschool level the assumptive reality of phenomenalistic causality was related to the defense of magical thinking. Among the egocentric structures of the school-age child are the notions of "cognitive conceit" and "tall tales." The ego defenses most closely related to the egocentric structures at this age period are denial and rationalization. From the standpoint of cognition, denial is an active reconstruction of past events with rationalization brought in to support it. At the adolescent level, the egocentric structures of the imaginary audience and the personal fable resemble ego defenses of projection and rejection.

In the concluding section of the paper, some possible implications of the discussion for research and practice are suggested. It was hypothesized that the obsessive—compulsive neurosis should not appear until childhood and the emergence of assumptive realities. In addition, it was suggested that paranoia and depression must wait upon the assumptive psychologies of adolescence for their emergence. These suggestions do not presuppose that the dynamic "anlage" of those syndromes could not be laid down earlier in development. It does suggest that a certain level of cognitive development must be present before certain psychopathological syndromes can become manifest.

REFERENCES

Anthony, E. J. The significance of Jean Piaget for child psychiatry. *British Journal of Medical Psychology,* 1956, *29,* 20–34.

Chandler, M. J. Egocentrism and antisocial behavior: The assessment and training of social perspective-taking skills. *Developmental Psychology,* 1973, *9,* 326–332.

Elkind, D. Conceptual orientation shifts in children and adolescents. *Child Development,* 1966, *37,* 493–498.

Elkind, D. Cognitive structure in latency behavior. In J. C. Westman (Ed.), *Individual differences in children.* New York: John Wiley & Sons, 1973, 105–117.

Flavell, J. *The development of role-taking and communication skills in children.* New York: John Wiley & Sons, 1968.

Freud, A. *The ego and the mechanisms of defense.* New York: International Universities Press, 1946.

Freud, S. *The ego and the id.* London: The Hogarth Press, 1957 (originally published in 1923).

Herzog, E., and Sudia, C. E. Children in fatherless families. In B. M. Caldwell and H. N. Ricciuti (Eds.), *Review of Child Development Research.* Chicago: The University of Chicago Press, 1973, 141–232.

Kagan, J. Reflection-impulsivity: The generality and dynamics of conceptual tempo. *Journal of Abnormal Psychology,* 1966, *71,* 17–24.

Klein, G. S. Cognitive control and motivation. In G. Lindzey (Ed.), *Assessment of human motives.* New York: Rinehart, 1958, 87–118.

Kohlberg, L., Yaeger, J., and Hjertholm, E. Private speech: Four studies and a review of theories. *Child Development,* 1968, *39,* 691–736.

Peel, E. A. *The pupil's thinking.* London: Oldhourne Press, 1960.

Piaget, J. *The child's conception of the world.* New York: Harcourt Brace, 1929.

Piaget, J. *The moral judgment of the child.* Glencoe, Illinois: The Free Press, 1948.

Piaget, J. *The child's conception of physical causality.* New York: The Humanities Press, Inc., 1951.

Piaget, J. *The psychology of intelligence.* New Jersey: Littlefield, Adams & Co., 1963.

Rapaport, D. Psychoanalysis as a developmental psychology. In B. Kaplan and S. Wapner (Eds.), *Perspectives in psychological theory.* New York: International Universities Press, 1960, 209–255.

Shlager, N. *Cognitive development and reading preferences.* Unpublished doctoral dissertation, Claremont College, Claremont, California, 1974.

Sullivan, H. S. *The interpersonal theory of psychiatry.* New York: W. W. Norton, 1953.

Vygotsky, L. S. *Thought and speech.* Cambridge: M.I.T. Press, 1962.

Weir, M. W. Development changes in problem-solving strategies. *Psychological Review,* 1964, *71,* 473–490.

Witkin, H. A., Dyk, R. B., Faterson, H. F., Goodenough, D. R., and Karp, S. A. *Psychological differentiation.* New York: John Wiley & Sons, 1962.

9

The Socialization of the Individual

BOYD R. McCANDLESS

SOCIALIZATION: A DEFINITION

Socialization is a behavioral term that refers, first, to the way children, youth, and adults behave with reference to other children, youth, and adults; and, second, how they function in the several social roles that are specified in families and communities.

For example, people (or cultures) are variously described as friendly, gregarious, outgoing, generous, selfish, withdrawn, larcenous, cooperative, aggressive, suspicious, honest, dependable, and so on. These adjectives are summaries of types of social behavior that we think of, in a somewhat magical, unrealistic, and thus often not very useful way, as traits that are reasonably consistent in an individual or a culture, across many situations. Thus summarized, we use the terms to predict our own behavior and the behavior of others. In short, such adjectives are meant to summarize social behavior as a *product,* a characteristic and dependable way in which an individual or a culture does things. Autistic is one such "trait term," it seems.

All societies that are known to this author also create role expectations for their members. These are classifications of behavior for which standards are set. They exist in many dimensions, such as sex role, citizen role, worker role, father or mother role, or son and daughter role, and so on. These role expectations change with the age of an individual in most cases. For example, almost no one expects 10-year-olds to be very knowledgeable about politics, or to vote; but

BOYD R. McCANDLESS · Psychology Department, Emory University, Atlanta, Georgia 30322.

such expectations are held for those of 18 and older. A son or daughter, aged 8 years, one is looked after by his parents, and honors his mother and father, especially by obeying them and adopting their behavior standards. A son or daughter 50 years old, one is quite likely to be looking after his father or mother rather than being looked after by them and, while honoring and loving them, one is expected to make his own decisions about his social and personal behavior, rather than model his parents.

Role expectations, thus, are behavior classifications that are commonly considered as traits: One is a lawbreaker, a heterosexual, normal or psychotic, or an informed voter, for example. Social roles, like personal characteristics, are examples of socialization as *product*.

Every parent and every teacher (this includes psychiatrists, psychologists, social workers, and so on) is faced with conflicts in deciding about what socialization *product* to strive for in the children to whom he/she gives care and training. Most of us want children to be creative, but few of us want children who extend creativity to bizarre extremes. Dali must have been a difficult child. Autistic children are certainly different—thus "creative"—but very ill. Almost all of us want trusting children, but we do not want our children to be gullible "patsies." We want thrifty children in our American culture, but we do not want misers. A list of conflicts in the choice of socialization goals for children, youth, and adults could be extended indefinitely, but these illustrations will suffice.

Once having formulated a goal or goals for socialization as a product, how does one carry out the process? Today, as far as the product socialization is concerned, most agree that a product results from learning in social and private contexts, but few discount organism (biological) variables and the culture within which we live.

Culture is a term that refers to the common ways in which problems are approached and solved by circumscribed, definable groups of people. Families are shaped by cultures, and transmit cultural values, usually somewhat modified, to the children in the family as they grow up. For example, *extended families* consist of fathers, mothers, children, uncles, aunts, cousins, and grandparents who live close together spatially and psychologically, and they are still common in many parts of the world, such as India and Pakistan. A *nuclear family* includes the father, mother, and one or more children living in self-contained units that are often far from any relative and, in today's mobile society, the site of residence changes often. The pattern in the United States is one almost exclusively of nuclear families. *Culture* is a term that implies a public, social learning context in which one or another type of learning process and product is encouraged or discouraged. Certain processes in learning are thought to be used in different cultures, for example, so that different socialization products emerge. For example, Mexican village children have been found to be more cooperative than U.S. children (Madsen and Shapira, 1970); and those from

Sierra Leone have been found to test as more suggestible and conforming than those from Scotland, who in turn are more suggestible and conforming than Eskimos (Berry, 1967).

To illustrate further, in our rather sexist society, a quite high activity level may be an advantage for a boy, a disadvantage for a girl. Boys are "supposed to be" vigorous, athletic, on-the-go; girls are "supposed to be" quiet, gentle, and retiring. Thus, in conventional circles, highly active boys may be met with positive learning contingencies, highly active girls with a pattern of negative reinforcements ("Isn't he all boy! What a rowdy tomboy *she* is!").

Across cultures, mesomorphy (an athletic build) seems to be an advantage (see McCandless and Evans, 1973). The mesomorphic boy or girl is viewed more favorably, is granted more positive learning contingencies, in terms of fitting the roles of friend, attractive, a leader, than the "string bean" ectomorph, who in turn is more favorably viewed by his peers (across a wide range of ages, races, and both sexes, in several different types of culture) than the stout endomorph (the "butterball"). Those who are judged to be attractive in appearance (see Cavior and Dokecki, 1973) are more popular than those judged to be less attractive.

Methods of care-giving (the circumstances under which one learns, the types and schedules of reinforcement one is given, and how they are administered) make profound differences in the history and outcome of the human organism. Skinner (1972, pp. 107–108) puts the matter well:

> We are likely to appeal to some inner virtue . . . to explain why a person behaves well with respect to his fellow man, but he does so not because his fellow-men have endowed him with a sense of responsibility or obligation or with loyalty or respect for others but because they have arranged effective social contingencies.

Just as parents and teachers experience conflicts in defining their aims for socialization *products,* so they experience conflicts in defining and applying the *processes* they employ in trying to achieve the products in their children that they have decided upon. In the United States, we remain a rather Puritan culture in the way in which we regard ourselves and give care to our children. The standard pattern is one in which virtue is considered to be its own reward, but deviations in behavior are punished. We are more a punishment- than a reward-oriented culture.

From behavior theory have come studies that demonstrate that punishment-oriented management is not the most effective way to achieve the product for which a teacher or parent aims. Baumrind (1971), for example, demonstrates that the most autonomous and socially responsible of the many 4-year-olds she studied came from homes where parents were authoritative, but not authoritarian and not permissive. By authoritative, Baumrind means that the parents regard themselves as people of considerable worth, that they formulate their goals for their children clearly, but have great respect for the integrity and ingenuity of their children in achieving these goals, and that they guide their children as loving and reasoning experts while at the same time giving the children much leeway in behavior. Hoffman (1970) reviews child-rearing research, and concludes that the parent who uses mild, inductive techniques rather than love withdrawal or punishment produces children who attain a higher level of moral development. Rollins, McCandless, Thompson, and Brassell (1974) find that benign behavior management techniques (ignoring the negative, rewarding the positive behavior) socialize poor inner-city black and white children from kindergarten through eighth grade more effectively than conventional restriction and punishment-oriented techniques of classroom management.

Socialization, then, is both product (e.g., altruistic) and process (e.g., benign, variable schedule patterns of reinforcement are used rather than aversive, consistent patterns). Whatever the *product* desired, some *processes* are more likely than others to achieve the desired goal. Major tasks for sciences of human behavior are to formulate clear, socially useful definitions of product, and to investigate further to find out which processes result in which products, and which work the most effectively to achieve *any* product. In other and simpler words, *how* does one proceed to produce a child who, as an adult, is curious, creative, and stress resistant; or, on the other hand, who is delinquent or emotionally disturbed, or both.

Deciding on the product (what are the values we hold in common in a society about socialization?) has commonly been considered to be outside the realm of science, and has been implicitly or explicitly left to philosophers, the religious, the lawmakers, and such. It is probably a mistake for behavioral scientists to abjure decisions about values. It seems to the present author that, at least in the United States, behavioral scientists have done well enough as far as agreeing about products is concerned. Most will say that we should rear children so that they function well in a democratic society, and that they are kind, realistically altruistic, quite cooperative and considerate of others, are effective problem-solvers, are independent and self-sufficient, and yet able to enter into close personal relations. However, there are many disputes about products. See, for example, the long-standing arguments among educators over the advantages of the open, free classroom as opposed to the structured, traditional classroom as related to the end result for pupils. The recommendations about child-rearing made by behavioral experts in 1920 are very different from those being made today (but so is our society, and values are always a reflection of the structure and change of a society).

Nonetheless, the track record of behavioral scientists, as far as value specification (choice of product) is concerned, compares well with the track records of those to whom the choices of values have commonly been left.

A value, as Skinner says, is essentially a choice of reinforcers and rules for their administration. In a democratic society, quite good agreement about reinforcers can be reached. Most of us agree that positive contingencies are more humane, and the evidence suggests that for normal children, at least, they work better than negative contingencies. Most of us agree that we cannot obtain our own reinforcers at the cost of cutting off an undue share of the reinforcers given to other people. Most of us agree that knowing what we are doing is more efficient than proceeding blindly. Most of us agree that a certain number of rules—a rule is an abstraction of contingencies, as Skinner (1972, pp. 96–120) points out convincingly—are necessary. Rules define consensual contingencies in a culture: *Thou shalt not steal,* for example, indicates that society expects one to work for his own contingencies rather than take the reinforcers someone else has amassed for himself. *Thou shalt not kill* recognizes the fact that one's life is his most important avenue for reinforcement, and that it must not be taken away. Negative contingencies for stealing and killing in one's own group are clearly prescribed in all cultures known to the present author.

The processes for achieving the products of socialization are more commonly granted to be matters of science than are the choices of products, although there is no reason that is clear why this should be the case. In any event, answers to questions such as, How does one rear children to be happy, normal, and well socialized (however defined); and, when the process breaks down, what do we do to mend it? are commonly granted to be functions of behavioral scientists.

THEORIES OF SOCIALIZATION

For the purpose of this paper, there are five major theories about socialization. Some of them include hypotheses about both the process and the products of socialization, some are concentrated on process, some on product. Some are concentrated on the normal, some on the abnormal, others on both. The most influential of the theories seem to have been humanism, cognitive-developmentalism, psychoanalysis, self-theory, and behaviorist theory.

Some of these theories are addressed more to developmental psychology, normal or abnormal, than are others, as will be evident in the following section. Humanists have little to say about deviant behavior, much to say about prosocial behavior; little to say that is specific about process, much about product. Cognitive developmentalists have contributions to make about disorders of thinking (for example, magical, preoperational thought in schizophrenia), but do not much consider affect. They neglect learning and change. Psychoanalysts have postulated theories about both socialization process and product, as have behaviorists; and both address themselves to normal and deviating behavior and life outcomes. Self-theorists are difficult to classify; typically, they are more concerned with outcomes (products) than with processes, although learning theories close to behaviorism, have been tied in with self-theory (see Rotter, 1954, for example).

Humanistic psychologists have not often been involved in the study of human development, although there have been many implications drawn from or suggested by this school about how children should be reared and educated, and about what the results of this rearing should be. Humanists have been influential in moving behavioral scientists in the direction of studying prosocial behavior, such as altruism and cooperation. Their contribution seems to the present writer to be more that they have contributed a point of view—a philosophy—than that they have provided methods of studying human behavior. They have not been much preoccupied with deviating children or adults, although today humanists are active in certain types of therapeutic endeavors (but usually with "bright normals").

The five theories are summarized very briefly below.

Humanism

Humanists typically stress the psychology of normality and excellence more than that of abnormality and pathology. Humanists are self-actualizers who emphasize positive growth and prosocial rather than antisocial behavior. Phenomena (traits?) of curiosity, creativity, imagination, and subjective experience intrigue humanists. They are also likely to be social activists who apologize to no one about their choices of the valued goals within socialization, in the product sense. They typically show a lively aversion to social and cultural forces that debase human beings and prevent people from realizing their fullest potentials. Allport summarizes humanist philosophy nicely (1955, p. 18):

> Some theories of becoming but are based largely upon the behavior of sick and anxious people or upon the antics of captive and desperate rats. Fewer theories have derived from the study of healthy human beings, those who strive not to preserve life as to make it worth living. Thus we find today many studies of criminals, few of law-abiders; many of fear, few of courage; more on hostility than on affiliation; much on the blindness in man; little on his vision; much on his past, little on his outreaching into the future.

In humanism, there is no id, no original sin. People of all ages are viewed optimistically. There are no immutable stages of growth. People can learn and grow positively at any time within the developmental span. The proper subject of psychology is man, the prosocial man is more interesting than antisocial man, happy and curious man more interesting than depressed and apathetic man.

Humanists are vague about the processes through which the products of socialization can be achieved. Not for them (or at least for very few of them) the tedious study of such concepts as rule-dependent contrasted with contingency-dependent shaping of behavior. They imply that, if one is free and loved, then he will become well socialized, but they typically do not specify the conditions of freedom and lovingness: When does my freedom become your restriction? When does my love help you to evade reality, and thus escape from what may be a constructive growth process? But, despite their casual scientific approach, a healthy infiltration of humanism makes psychology and people more fun than it would otherwise be.

Cognitive-Developmentalism

Cognitive-developmentalists have some of the same historic roots as humanists, although they are more businesslike and, to inject frivolity, often not so much fun to be around. They have concentrated more on how knowledge is organized and used than they have on what is the good life, although they have made important contributions to the study of moral development. Moral development may be the most important core of social development, construed as product. Rousseau has influenced both humanism and cognitive-developmental psychology powerfully. Like humanists, cognitive-developmentalists pay little attention to process and concentrate mainly on product, which they typically classify into stages, such as sensorimotor (cognitive) or Level III (morality of self-accepted moral principles); Stage 6 (morality of individual principles of conscience [Kohlberg, 1963]).

Like most stage theorists, cognitive-developmental people are likely to test and to classify rather than to work at understanding how an individual got to be the way he is and how, if it is to his or society's advantage, he can be changed. Nor do cognitive-developmentalists seem to be very strong on arranged or planned experiences such as delight, baffle, and preoccupy Americans. Experience, they say, should be free: The child actively engaged with the things in his natural environment will develop in good shape, although there is considerable scope for active teaching after children (sometime near the age of puberty) reach the cognitive stage of formal operations.

Psychodynamics

Psychodynamics, the third theory, has its roots in the writings and teachings of Sigmund Freud. The classical psychodynamic theorists take a gloomy, pathology-based view of human development. None of us is really happy or well adjusted—some are simply better compensated than others. Basic to socialization are the *defense* (not *approach*) mechanisms. Man is engaged in a lifelong struggle to fit the pleasure with the reality principle. None of us ever really knows himself. If something happens to us at an early stage of our development, we never quite get over it, or at least not without a process of therapy that the average American cannot afford. Men and women are profoundly different psychologically, and the implication from psychodynamic theory seems to me clearly to be that women are less good, less moral, less creative, and so on. Some neopsychodynamic theorists have been influenced by sociological and learning research, and are not well characterized by the statements above, which, because of restrictions in length, are perhaps oversimplified in this paper.

Psychodynamic theorists pay a good bit of attention to socialization both as process and product, and they have given us good and testable ideas. Certainly, they have previously and still do influence our thinking about human development. Essentially, unlike the humanists, their preoccupation (except perhaps in matters clerical and sexual) is to adjust man to life as it is, rather than to change the culture so that it is a more humane setting for man to live in.

While this author believes that psychodynamic psychology is of more historic than contemporary importance, no student or practitioner of socialization phenomena should be without a working knowledge of it (see, for a beginning, Freud, 1950; Erikson, 1963; and Sullivan, 1953).

Self-Theory

Self-theory, the fourth theory, is in some disarray at present, and has been for some time (for example, see Wylie, 1974). However, there is much to be learned from it, and interesting ideas and research still spring from it (for example, see McCandless and Evans, 1973, pp. 387–425). Like humanists and cognitive developmentalists, self-theorists pay relatively little attention to how people came to be the way they are. Like cognitive-developmentalists, self-theorists are more interested in measuring, categorizing, scaling, and describing people than they are in explaining how these people arrived at some spot in or on their scores, categories, and scales.

However, the notion of "self" is here to stay. It has face validity for each and every one of us. All of us have fitted ourselves into categories as neatly as the most measurement-inclined self-theorist could do it: We think of ourselves as handsome or pretty, old or young, knowledgeable of the literature in our field or behind in our reading, good or poor at gadgeteering around the house, and so on. No one who takes professional therapeutic-counseling contact with an individual seriously can fail to inquire about how that individual regards himself, what his self-concept is. There are many dimensions of the self-concept. The one most commonly used is self-esteem: Does an individual think well or ill of himself? Other dimensions are self-acceptance: Regardless of whether he thinks well or ill of himself, can he live comfortably with himself? Complexity of self-concept is another dimension, congruence still another: Is one's self-concept appropriate for his/her age–sex status, for example?

In behavioral terms, people with poor self-esteem will not be positively reinforcing of their own behavior. Also, they may be blind to reinforcements that others give them: "That is what he/she thinks, but I did not really deserve this reward." People with simple self-concepts are likely to respond only to a narrow band of reinforcements (for example, only that which is role appropriate for a 9-year-old boy or girl living in the inner city, and who is black, will be reinforcing). Those with unrealistic self-concepts are likely to respond to reinforcements in such a way as to minimize later reinforcements: The 14-year-old boy or girl who looks older than 14 may respond to reinforcement about how mature he/she looks by getting into social/personal situations that are more complex than the adolescent has learned to deal with, and encounter later negative contingencies as a result.

However, in practical dealings with people, we must consider self-theory, if for no other reason than it can give us a useful definition of what an individual's reinforcers—his contingencies—are. Knowing the dimensions of these reinforcers, we will understand and predict a person better, and may be useful to him. In short, self-theories and learning (behaviorist and psychodynamic) theories can be meshed potentially profitably.

Most self-theorists are also sociological and learning theorists. One's feelings about himself (whether he regards himself as positively or negatively reinforcing, or takes his own reinforcements seriously; i.e., is a person of internal or external locus of control) have resulted from the family and culture within which he has lived (see Cooley, 1902; Mead, 1934; and Rotter, 1954, 1966, for examples of the way this thought has developed). However, self-theorists have seldom studied in detail the way in which families and cultures have applied reinforcements so as to produce positive or negative self-esteem, simple or complex, or realistic or unrealistic self-concepts. Coopersmith (1967) is an exception. His results in a major study of self-esteem among preadolescent boys fit well with Baumrind's (1971) results for 4-year-old boys and girls. For 10-year-old boys, Coopersmith finds that authoritative child rearing is associated with high self-esteem.

Behaviorism

The fifth of the theories that can be applied to socialization is behavioral theory. Many behavioral theorists have modeled themselves on pre-atom-bomb theorists in the field of physics: They deal only with the *facts,* and values are outside their ken. Skinner (e.g., 1972) is one of the first of the behaviorists to say flatly that a concern with values is as much his business as is his interest in variable or fixed ratios of reinforcement. Skinner, thus, is one of the earlier behaviorists who is willing to talk about products as well as processes of socialization.

Behaviorists consider that psychology is a hard science, and thus all its concepts and processes must be public, not private. Lundin (1963, p. 258) gives a reasonable definition of behaviorism. One is a behaviorist "if he believes psychology to be the study of observable behavior and that the methods employed are the methods of science, namely, controlled systematic observation including experimentation. . . . The behaviorist identifies himself with carefully controlled and executed experiments in which the stimulus variables are appropriately manipulated, exact controls are executed, and the resulting behavior can be accurately observed and measured."

Those who have lived for a long time with psychiatric and clinical psychological work think of behaviorists as men and women who isolate themselves in laboratories and who confine most of their endeavors to white rats, although they occasionally venture into timid and well-controlled dealings with college sophomores. Many behaviorists still do just that, and their patient, precise, and humorless dealings with white rats and college sophomores are beginning to have many practical consequences in such settings as inner city schools, institutions for the emotionally disturbed and the retarded, and practical matters of parent-child relations, such as reducing chaos at the dinner table. To demonstrate the practical *and public* virtues of behaviorism, one needs only look at an issue or so of the *Journal of Applied Behavior Analysis.*

The quantitative, public nature of behaviorism has much to recommend it. If a behaviorist mates himself, psychologically speaking, with a humanist, it is likely that the psychology of human socialization will make dramatic and constructive steps forward. There are virtues to the behaviorist position of being very cautious about prescribing values for other people; there are values in the precise, often timid approaches to reaching conclusions; and it is good to have psychology as a public matter (thus, knowable and not mysterious, rather than unknowable and mysterious). Impersonal though it may be, the quantified and sterile lab and its treatment spinoff do, for example, more for venereal disease than is otherwise possible. In other words, precise, communicable methods are necessary in the study of all phenomena, social or physical or personal.

To summarize this section, it seems that the best bet in the study of human socialization, product and process, is an infusion of unabashed humanistic value (product) studies and judgment, with the methods of behavioral psychology.

MEASURES OF SOCIALIZATION

As was mentioned earlier in this paper, socialization as a product or products smacks of trait theory. Developmental, social, and personality psychologists have typically tried to measure "traits" or characteristic ways of behaving that they have called honesty, creativity, curiosity, or sex-role adoption and identification. Trait theory has not fared well scientifically (see Feshbach, 1970; Harris, 1973; Hoffman, 1970; and Mischel, 1970, for examples). Human behavior is remarkably situation specific, we are beginning to learn. Of course, we should have known this for many years. In the late twenties and early thirties of this century, Hartshorne and May (1928–1930) told us so. However, some of our attempts to predict by trait-theory types of measurement are by no means idle (see, for example, the voluminous and constantly expanding literature in which internal and external locus of control is considered).

However, there are those who argue that the trait-theory approach to socialization products (another word, really, for personality) has been remarkably inefficient. Few, for example, have any deep regard for the Rorshach Test these days. Harris (1973) documents the failure of a massive trait-theory testing approach to evaluating staying power of Peace Corps personnel. A reasonably sophisticated "old-fashioned" rating approach worked much better.

However, to cast out trait theory entirely is rather like eliminating the baby with the bath at this stage in psychology. As has been mentioned above, ideas about the tests for such trait concepts as internal and external locus of control (Rotter, 1966; Rollins, *et al.* 1974), interpersonal trust (Katz and Rotter, 1969), or high/low self-esteem (Coopersmith, 1967; Reschly and Mittman, 1973), impulsivity/reflectivity (Kagan, Rosman, Day, Albert, and Philips, 1964), or task orientation/social orientation/self-assurance (Nakamura and Finck, 1973) have proved quite useful in describing and predicting the behavior of human beings of a wide range in age and in many situations.

From a behaviorist point of view, a trait may be thought of as a classification of reinforcers, or behavior contingencies, that maintains a rather consistent behavior pattern. For instance, one who is high in internal locus of control has learned that he can generate his own contingencies, positive or negative, and applies this learning across a wide range of situations and people.

In her classic *Patterns of Culture,* Benedict (1953) talked of Apollonian and Dionysian cultures. One can pull from her ideas a simple two-dimensional description of human behavior—one that is not unduly Procrustean when applied to people in a western society. The Dionysian in each of us is his lovable (or possibly hateful), human, sweaty, biological side. The Apollonian in us is more refined. It includes our dimensions of social, technical competence—our unique, it is to be hoped, refined, and thoughtful, set of attributes of the species, homo sapiens. If you will, Apollonianism is our civilized, achieving self.

Each of us likes to be loved and to love, to be comfortable, relaxed, and intimate. These are our Dionysian reinforcements. Each of us also likes to be thought competent and to be respected. These are our Apollonian reinforcements.

It is suggested here that we employ such concepts in measurements of socialization as a product. It also seems that, used with full ethical considerations, the buddy rating or peer judgment of socialization is the best one we have available (Moreno, 1953).

Two types of buddy ratings (sociometrics) can be easily devised to fit Dionysian and Apollonian classes of reinforcers. The first type is the standard friendship or intimacy sociometric, in which others make judgments about how well they like us. Typically, they do this by naming their three to five best friends, or rating us on a scale from "1. Like very much," to "5. Not one of my friends." From the literature, we know that those who receive many friendship nominations are likely to give many positive reinforcements to others, and to be comfortable, warm people—Dionysian, in other words. However, it is obvious that such people can also be amiable slobs who administer and receive much comfort, but accomplish little that is concrete for themselves or others. Thus, a second type of sociometric, the Apollonian or competence sociometric, is advocated: "Whom will you choose as the most effective president for the class?" "With whom in your class would you most prefer to study for the algebra examination?" "Who will make the most effective new president of the firm?" From such a sociometric—obviously, it must consist of more than three questions and must be appropriate to the setting within which it is administered—we learn who are the competent ones, the doers.

In western society, it is important to know about both dimensions, the persons with whom it is comfortable to be, and the persons who will get things done, in other words, the types of people who will provide us with the maximum gains of positive contingencies. If we build a simple X^2 table (Figure 1), it seems safe to say that those who are entered in Cell 1 (High/High) for both friendship/intimacy and competence can almost always be said to be well socialized *according to the values of the culture within which they live.* Careful note of this point is made a bit later.

Those who are low in friendship/intimacy but high in competence are likely (to simplify) to get things done, but at a cost in terms of the reinforcers they offer their fellow-man. They may be low in interpersonal warmth and social sensitivity, or even callous to the rights of others in the interest of getting on with the task at hand, and Dyonisian reinforcers that are offered to them affect

	High competence	Low competence
High friendship/intimacy	1	2
Low friendship/intimacy	3	4

Figure 1. Representative figure for those who are high and low in friendship/intimacy, and competency ratings, as given to them by their peers.

their behavior little or not at all. Those who are entered in Cell 2, high friendship/intimacy, low competence, may be the amiable slobs mentioned a bit earlier: "Everyone loves her, but she is no damned good." Finally, in our culture, those who fit into Cell 4, low friendship/intimacy, low competence, are society's losers: They provide few positive contingencies for anyone on any dimension, and they receive few. (For at least two research documentations that bear on these points, see Hartup and Coates, 1967; and Hartup, Glazer, and Charlesworth, 1967). It is suggested that our population of the unhappy and socially ill-adjusted is composed heavily of those who would be entered into Cell 4 of Figure 1 if one were entering them in cells (in a different sense of the word, one suspects that a disproportionate number of them *are* placed quite literally into cells).

Implications for treatment are clear: Behavior therapy (or any therapy) can be arranged so that Cell 2 people, high in friendship, low in competence, can in most cases learn with profit to be more competent and to appreciate and reward competence in others; Cell 3 people, low friendship/high competence, can come to be modifiable in their behavior by Dionysian reinforcers, and can learn to increase their rate of dispensing them. Finally, treatments can and have been devised to upgrade Cell 4 people in both their own competence and in the Dionysian and Apollonian reinforcers they provide for others (see, for example, Shore, Massimo, and Ricks, 1965).

Some cautions must be made about proposals for measurement and treatment such as have been made above. First, sociometrics are not practical for groups whose members do not know each other well, i.e., who have been in interaction for very short periods of time, or who interact in impersonal settings such as, say, an assembly line. Second, they are not practical for large groups. There must be a chance to interact with some frequency with every member of one's group over a period of time before anything resembling an accurate judgment of that person's likability or competence can be made. Third, some "soft sell" members of the group may be underjudged for both the dimensions of friendship/intimacy and competence. "It takes a long time to know him, but he grows on you" is a social cliché about this type of person. Finally, and probably most important, sociometrics must be interpreted within the context of the culture within which they are administered. One who was entered into Cell 1 (high friendship/intimacy, high competence) by his colleagues in a Hitler *Jugend* group would almost certainly have been different from a similarly entered child or youth in a democratic society, although the difference may well be more related to the dimension of competence as defined in different settings than to the dimension of friendship/intimacy.

However, a virtue of the sociometric method of judging the product, socialization, is that it reflects the situation-specificity of socialization, and gives us useful information about predicting behavior when we know the situations in which the behavior will occur. We need to conduct research about the generalizability of sociometric information: Is a high-school senior who is ranked as a high/high, who is strong in both his friendship/intimacy and his competence dimensions, likely to do well in a college setting, an industrial setting, a political setting?

We do not know for sure, although we have some indications that quite successful predictions can be made (see, for example, Roff, 1961; and Willems, 1967).

To summarize this section: Predictions made from trait theory to date have worked only fairly well with people of any age. It seems sensible to move to a more behavior-based set of techniques, by means of which we assess the reinforcements individuals are able to give their peers in given situations, and the types of reinforcers received from others that in turn affect their own behavior; then go on to see if these assessments generalize to situations that are different from the ones in which we made them.

COURSE OF SOCIALIZATION

The last time the present author wrote formally about the course of socialization, his colleague and he (McCandless and Evans, 1973) devoted nearly 270 printed pages to the topic. It is obvious that not much can be done with the details of socialization in this short paper. It is important to note that in one's life span, if one is appropriately socialized (in the product sense), he has moved from a point as an infant where his reinforcements are tangible in nature (i.e., he reacts to that which makes him more comfortable, such as having a full stomach or a dry bottom) to where they are social or intangible in nature. This is to say that the well-socialized person will change his/her behavior more for people's approval or disapproval than for their feeding or helping with toileting, but it is not to say that in our maturity tangible, physical reinforcers are not important. Our pay check comes close to being a primary reinforcer. It is only a step or so between it and consummation in terms of food, shelter, warmth, and other physical comforts. The prestige of the physician is closely related to his fundamental reinforcing potential: He can stop us from hurting, can keep us well, can delay death.

The literature contains all-too-preliminary suggestions about methods of child rearing or other treatment conditions that move people in the direction of responding to socially desirable reinforcers, and themselves emitting socially desirable reinforcers with greater frequency. Hoffman (1970) summarizes literature to the effect that high power assertion by parents is related to lower stages of moral development. Baumrind (1971) shows that authoritative parents, those who are self-confident and sure of their goals and values, but allow their children much leeway in reaching these goals, and provide them with many Dionysian and Apollonian reinforcers (much love and warmth, much respect for individuality), generally produce children who are competent and socially responsible at age 4. Shore, Massimo, and Ricks (1965) show that therapeutically administered skills training improves the academic performance of delinquent and adolescent boys who, then and only then, change positively in self-concept, then in attitudes toward authority, and finally, improve in behavior (react to available socially desirable reinforcers and then emit such reinforcers with greater frequency). As mentioned earlier, Rollins, *et al.* (1974) demonstrated that large numbers of first-through-eighth-grade public school inner-city (disadvantaged) Afro-American children, through the use of behavior-modification-derived techniques of benign behavior management in classrooms, can be moved, when compared with matched control classes, in the direction of higher internal locus of control, less disruptive and more on-task behavior, higher IQs, and greater skill in reading and arithmetic.

Each of these authors advances workable and testable ideas for child rearing, teaching, and treatment of children and youth, and other such suggestions exist in the literature. Such authors provide guidelines for (1) how the course of desirable socialization can be charted, and (2) how those who have deviated from it can be reshaped in their behavior.

In the main, the course of social development from babyhood through adulthood is from the more to the less obvious reinforcers. For an adult whom we call well socialized, we must look hard, long, and cleverly to determine the contingencies for which he is working. As Skinner (1972) says, we give the most credit to the man whose reinforcers are the least obvious—he is the "truly moral man." Not only are many of the reinforcers for which youth and adults work more concealed, complex, and subtle than those that influence the infant and young child, but it is certain that there are more and more types of them. It may be that in late middle age and old age, the subtlety, complexity, variety, and types of reinforcers again become fewer.

For infants and young children, reinforcers are tangible and physical. Very early, at least in model, middle-class American families, the nature of reinforcers is changed toward a social, more intangible direction, typically by attaching labels and implicit promises such as "good" and "bad" or smiles and frowns to behavior. From about 18 months or so, one's peers increasingly become reinforcers; they help us learn to guide our behavior so it is more efficient in getting what we want, as well as reinforce us directly. We learn to use similar techniques with them.

Peers become increasingly important in shaping behavior for several reasons, among them: (1) From about 18 months, parents reinforce their children for social interactions with other children of about the same age. (2) Language and the beginnings of thought have progressed to the degree that a child sees others of about his age as being similar to himself. Such perception seems to be reinforcing (e.g., see Byrne and Griffitt, 1966). (3) Competition for contingencies occurs when a child begins to interact with his peers. Thus, he must learn to provide his peers with contingencies that enable him/her to gain particular contingencies that are reinforcing to him.

By adulthood, human beings should have learned to administer much of their own reinforcement, and this reinforcement must be of a socially desirable or at least socially tolerated nature. Otherwise, a person is likely to be classed as psychotic or emotionally disturbed, a criminal, or a psychopath.

The terms, intrinsic motivation and internal locus of control, subsume self-reinforcement without outside help. However, the intrinsically motivated person, or one with high internal locus of control, has *learned* such a manner of behaving. It can be suggested from research that has been mentioned above that he/she has been treated by parents and teachers as a worthwhile person (i.e., day-to-day behavior has been more often positively than negatively reinforced, usually on an unplanned schedule). He has learned that responses generated "on his own" have been rewarded by labels such as "What a big boy" or "What a big girl," and associated rewards. Developmental guidelines have been reasonably clear and consistent. It is understood that if one type of behavior occurs, positive contingencies will result; if another type occurs, either nothing will result, or there will be aversive consequences. In other words, for many behaviors, there is a *planned* schedule of reinforcement. Responsible adults have been present, their own goals and values have been clear to them and have been made clear to the child; and the child's behavior that is in line with the goals has been systematically noted and rewarded.

If a child is organically vulnerable, for instance, or possesses a specific learning disability, help is sought or made available so that the child learns to cope.

Thus, it may be said, the well-socialized adult has learned not only to administer a large share of his own reinforcement (although he continues to want to be loved, comforted, and fed), but has learned to regard his reinforcements in the light of how they are related to the welfare of his fellow-man.

Perhaps this is what John Donne meant when he wrote, "Ask not for whom the bell tolls. . . ."

REFERENCES

Allport, G. W. *Becoming: Basic considerations for a psychology of personality.* New Haven: Yale University Press, 1955.

Baumrind, D. Current patterns of parental authority. *Developmental Psychology,* 1971, *4,* No. 1, Part 2. Pp. 103.

Benedict, R. *Patterns of culture.* New York: New American Library of World Literature, 1953.

Berry, J. W. Independence and conformity in subsistence-level societies. *Journal of Personality and Social Psychology,* 1967, *7,* 415–418.

Byrne, D., and Griffitt, W. B. A developmental investigation of the law of attraction. *Journal of Personality and Social Psychology,* 1966, *4,* 699–702.

Cavior, N., and Dokecki, P. R. Physical attractiveness, perceived attitude similarity, and academic achievement as contributors to interpersonal attractiveness among adolescents. *Developmental Psychology,* 1973, *9,* 44–54.

Cooley, C. H. *Human nature and the social order.* New York: Scribner, 1902.

Coopersmith, S. *The antecedents of self-esteem.* San Francisco: W. H. Freeman, 1967.

Erikson, E. H. *Childhood and society* (2nd ed.). New York: Norton, 1963.

Feshbach, S. Aggression. In P. H. Mussen (Ed.), *Carmichael's manual of child psychology* (Vol. II). New York: Wiley, 1970. Pp. 159–260.

Freud, S. *Collected papers.* London: Hogarth, 1950.

Harris, J. G., Jr. A science of the South Pacific: Analysis of the character structure of the Peace Corps volunteers. *American Psychologist,* 1973, *28,* 232–248.

Hartshorne, H., and May, M. A. *Studies in the nature of character:* Vol. I: *Studies in deceit; studies in self control;* Vol. III: *Studies in the organization of character.* New York: Macmillan, 1928–1930.

Hartup, W. W., and Coates, B. Imitation of a peer as a function of reinforcement from the peer group and rewardingness of the model. *Child Development,* 1967, *38,* 1003–1016.

Hartup, W. W., Glazer, J. A., and Charlesworth, R. Peer reinforcement and sociemetric status. *Child Development,* 1967, *38,* 1017–1024.

Hoffman, M. L. Moral development. In P. H. Mussen (Ed.), *Carmichael's manual of child psychology* (Vol. II). New York: Wiley, 1970. Pp. 261–360.

Kagan, J., Rosman, B. L., Day, D., Albert, J., and Philips, W. Information processing in the child: Significance of analytic and reflective attitudes. *Psychological Monographs,* 1964, *78* (Whole No. 578).

Katz, H. A., and Rotter, J. B. Interpersonal trust scores of college students and their parents. *Child Development,* 1969, *40,* 657–661.

Kohlberg, L. The development of children's orientations toward a moral order. I: Sequence in the development of moral thought. *Vita Humana,* 1963, *6,* 11–33.

Lundin, R. W. Personality theory in behavioristic psychology. In J. M. Wepman and R. W. Heine (Eds.), *Concepts of personality.* Chicago: Aldine, 1963. Pp. 257–290.

McCandless, B. R., and Evans, E. D. *Children and adolescents: Psychosocial development.* Hinsdale, Ill.: Dryden Press, 1973.

Madsen, M. C., and Shapira, A. Cooperative and competitive behavior of urban Afro-American, Anglo-American, Mexican-American, and Mexican village children. *Developmental Psychology,* 1970, *3,* 16–20.

Mead, G. H. *Mind, self and society: From the standpoint of a social behaviorist.* Chicago: University of Chicago Press, 1934.

Mischel, W. Sex-typing and socialization. In P. H. Mussen (Ed.), *Carmichael's manual of child psychology* (Vol. II). New York: Wiley, 1970. Pp. 3–72.

Moreno, J. L. *Who shall survive?* Beacon, New York: Beacon House, 1953.

Nakamura, C. Y., and Finck, D. Effect of social or task orientation and evaluative or nonevaluative situations on performance. *Child Development,* 1973, *44,* 83–93.

Reschly, D. J., and Mittman, A. The relationship of self-esteem status and task ambiguity to the self-reinforcement behavior of children. *Developmental Psychology,* 1973, *9,* 16–19.

Roff, M. Childhood social interactions and young adult bad conduct. *Journal of Abnormal and Social Psychology,* 1961, *63,* 333–337.

Rollins, H. A., McCandless, B. R., Thompson, M., and Brassell, W. A. Project Success Environment: An extended application of contingency management in inner-city schools. *Journal of Educational Psychology.* 1974, *66,* 167–178.

Rotter, J. B. *Social learning and clinical psychology.* Englewood Cliffs, N.J.: Prentice–Hall, 1954.

Rotter, J. B. Generalized expectancies for internal versus external control of reinforcement. *Psychological Monographs,* 1966, *80* (Whole No. 609).

Shore, M. F., Massimo, J. L., and Ricks, D. F. A factor analytic study of psychotherapeutic change in delinquent boys. *Journal of Clinical Psychology,* 1965, *21,* 208–212.

Skinner, B. F. *Beyond freedom and dignity.* New York: Bantam/Vintage, 1972.

Sullivan, H. S. *The collected works of Harry Stack Sullivan.* New York: Norton, 1953.

Willems, E. P. Sense of obligation to high school activities as related to school size and marginality of student. *Child Development,* 1967, *38,* 1247–1260.

Wylie, R. *The self-concept.* Vol. 1. Rev. Ed. Lincoln: University of Nebraska Press, 1974. Pp. xviii + 433.

10
Peer Interaction and the Behavioral Development of the Individual Child

WILLARD W. HARTUP

Experience with peers is commonly assumed to make numerous contributions to child development. Such experiences are believed to provide a context for sex-role learning, the internalization of moral values, the socialization of aggression, and the development of cognitive skills. The research literature, however, contains relatively little hard data concerning the functional contributions of peer interaction to the development of the individual child. There is little evidence that the give-and-take occurring during peer interaction actually determines the moral structuring that occurs in middle childhood, as Piaget (1932) suggested; there is no direct evidence that rough-and-tumble play contributes to the effectiveness with which the human child copes with aggressive affect (Harlow, 1969); and the contributions of peer attachments to social and intellectual development are largely unspecified.

Nevertheless, the purpose of this paper is to argue that peer interaction is an essential component of the individual child's development. Experience with peers is not a superficial luxury to be enjoyed by some children and not by others, but is a necessity in childhood socialization. And among the most sensitive indicators of difficulties in development are failure by the child to engage in the activities of the peer culture and failure to occupy a relatively comfortable place within it.

WILLARD W. HARTUP · Institute of Child Development, University of Minnesota, Minneapolis, Minnesota 55455.

Two issues provide the basis for this discussion: (a) the thesis that peer interactions are essential to the normal development of children; and (b) the contention that intervention in children's peer relations can appropriately alter the general course of behavioral development.

PEER RELATIONS AND THE INDIVIDUAL CHILD'S DEVELOPMENT

Attachment and Sociability

Recent research confirms that during the third and fourth years of life there is a decrease in the frequency with which the child seeks proximity with the mother (Maccoby and Feldman, 1972), an increase in the frequency of attention-seeking and the seeking of approval relative to the frequency with which the child seeks affection (Heathers, 1955), and a change in the objects toward whom social overtures are made; specifically, there is an increase in the frequency of contact with peers (Heathers, 1955). Peer attachments become even more characteristic of the child's social life during middle childhood. The bonds that children establish with agemates are dissimilar to the earlier bonds that are forged between mother and child (Maccoby and Masters, 1970). First, children employ different behaviors to express affection to agemates and to adults. They follow one another around, giving attention and help to each other, but rarely express verbal affection to agemates, hug one another, or cling to each other. Moreover, children do not seem to be disturbed by the absence of a specific child even though the absence of specific adults may give rise to anxiety and distress.[1] Second, the conditions that elicit attachment activity differ according to whether the available attachment object is an adult or another child. For example, fear tends to elicit running to the teacher rather than fleeing to one's peers. Third, the behavior of adults toward children differs qualitatively from the behavior of one child toward another. Adults do not engage in sustained periods of playful behavior with children; rather, they assume roles as onlookers or supervisors of children's playful activities. In fact, play appears to emerge in the human repertoire almost completely within the context of peer interaction.[2]

---

[1] A possible exception to this statement is the mild depression that is sometimes reported when younger children are separated from their siblings.

[2] Just why adults do not engage in long periods of play with their children is something of a mystery. From a psychological viewpoint, it is probably not possible for an adult to regress cognitively to a degree sufficient to permit sustained, childlike play. From an evolutionary viewpoint, it is probably not conducive to species survival for adult members of a troupe to spend large blocks of time playing with their offspring instead of hunting and gathering. The fact remains, however, that play occurs primarily in the context of peer interaction rather than in interaction with adults.

This fact casts further doubt on the assumption that the parent–child and child–child social systems are manifestations of a unitary "attachment" orientation.

What developmental benefits does the child derive from peer attachments? What are the correlates and/or consequences of sociability with agemates? What attitudes and orientations typify the child who is *not* involved in easygoing social activities with peers? To my mind, the best evidence (although not the only evidence) bearing on this problem is to be found in Bronson's (1966) analysis of the data from the Berkeley Guidance Study. Among three "central" behavioral orientations emerging in her analysis, the clearest was a bipolar dimension labeled *reserved-somber-shy/expressive-gay-socially easy*. Across each of four age periods, covering the ages from 5 through 16 years, this orientation (social reservedness) in boys was associated with: (a) an inward-looking social orientation, (b) high anxiety, and (c) low activity. In later childhood, the correlates of reservedness also came to include: (a) vulnerability, (b) lack of dominance, (c) nonadventuresomeness, and (d) instability. In other words, lack of sociability in boys was correlated with discomfort, anxiety, and a general unwillingness to engage the environment.

The correlates of social reservedness among girls were not substantially different. The associations between sociability and vulnerability, level of activity, and caution were significant across all four age periods, and a correlation with passivity tended to increase over time. Note that the cluster of traits that surrounds low sociability may be indicative of behavior that is in greater accord with social stereotypes among the girls than among the boys. In general, though, the findings suggest that failure to be involved with one's peers is accompanied by a lower level of instrumental competence (Baumrind, 1972) and higher anxiety than is the condition of high peer involvement. Other research provides a composite picture of the socially *rejected* child that is very much like the composite picture of the socially *inactive* child: He is neither outgoing nor friendly; he is either very high or very low in self-esteem; he is particularly dependent on adults for emotional support; he is anxious and inappropriately aggressive (Hartup, 1970).

Although the foregoing findings are relatively firm, interpretation of them is difficult. Everything we know concerning the developmental consequences of peer involvement is based on correlational data. It is not clear, therefore, that peer involvement is instrumental in producing an outgoing, active, nonanxious, assertive posture toward the world, or whether a reverse interpretation is to be preferred. More than likely, some set of external influences is responsible for this whole configuration of traits, i.e., for both sociability and its correlates. But what might such external influences be? Clearly, biological factors may be operative as well as social influences. Individual differences in sociability stabilize early, such differences are not closely associated with child-rearing practices (Bronson, 1966), and these characteristics possess moderate heritabilities (Scarr,

1969). Thus, the origins of the linkage between general personal–social effective-ness and the presence or absence of effective peer relations remain obscure. It is important, however, for both theoreticians and practitioners to know that this linkage exists, and to know that it characterizes child behavior across a variety of samples, times, and circumstances.

Aggression

Scattered evidence suggests that children master their aggressive impulses within the context of the peer culture rather than within the context of the family, the milieu of television, or the culture of the school. Nonhuman primate studies demonstrate rather convincingly that peer contact during late infancy and the juvenile stage produces two effects on the individual: (a) he acquires a repertoire of effective aggressive behaviors; and (b) he acquires mechanisms for coping with the affective outcomes of aggressive interaction (Harlow, 1969). In fact, socialization seems to require both rough-and-tumble play and experiences in which rough play escalates into aggression, and de-escalates into playful interaction (Hamburg and Van Lawick-Goodall, 1974). Field studies suggest that such experiences are readily available to the young in all primate species, including homo sapiens, although opportunities are greater for males than for females (Jay, 1968; Hartup, 1974).

Whether parents can produce such a marked impact on the development of aggression is doubtful. The rough-and-tumble experiences necessary for aggres-sive socialization seem to be incompatible with the demands of maternal bond-ing because, for all primate species, some tie to the mother must be maintained after the time when socialization of aggression is begun. Fathers may contribute significantly to aggression learning, both because they provide frequent and effective displays of aggressive behavior with their children and because bonding to the father is "looser," more "secondary," and less constraining than is bonding with the mother. Selected studies support this: Research on father absence shows that boys from such homes are less aggressive than boys in father-present homes (Hetherington and Deur, 1972). Nevertheless, whether fathers alone could effectively socialize their children's aggression– even their male children–remains doubtful. The father's social role in western culture requires him to spend most of his time outside the family and, even in close-knit family cultures, paternal contacts with the young child are insufficient to produce all of the learning required for the successful modulation of aggressive behavior.

Thus, Nature seems to have prepared for human socialization in such a way that child–child relations are more important contributors to the successful control of aggressive motivation than parent–child relations. Patterson and his associates (Patterson, Littman, and Bricker, 1967; Patterson and Cobb, 1971) have confirmed convincingly the various ways in which reinforcement for both aggression and yielding to aggression are provided within the context of peer interactions.

According to this line of reasoning, children who show generalized hostility and unusual modes of aggressive behavior, or children who are unusually timid in the presence of aggressive attack, may be lacking exposure to certain kinds of contacts with peers, i.e., rough-and-tumble play. In other words, peer contacts that never allow for aggressive display or that allow only for successful aggression (never for unsuccessful aggression) may be precursors of malfunctioning in the aggression system. Clearly, this hypothesis is plausible when applied to boys, although it is more tenuous for girls. Traditional socialization produces women who are ineffectively prepared for exposure to aggressive instigating events (except, perhaps, for threats to their children). Women are notably more anxious and passive than men when exposed to aggressive instigation, and this sex difference may be greater than is good for the future of the species. In any event, if women are to assume social roles more like those of men, and men are to assume roles more like those of women, some manipulation of early peer experiences is necessary. Opportunities for early exposure to rough-and-tumble play must be as equal for males and for females as opportunities for exposure to other normative behaviors.

Sex

If parents were to be given sole responsibility for the socialization of sexuality, homo sapiens would not survive. With due respect to the efforts of modern sex educators, we must recognize that the parent–child relationship is no better suited to the task of socializing sex than to the task of socializing aggression. Evolution has established the incest taboo (Lindzey, 1967), a taboo that is so pervasive that interaction with agemates is virtually the only opportunity available to the child in which he may engage in the trial and error, the modeling, and the information-gathering that ultimately produce his sexual life style.

There can be little doubt that sexual attitudes and the basic sexual repertoire are shaped primarily by contacts with other children. Kinsey (1948) said:

> Children are the most frequent agents for the transmission of the sexual mores. Adults serve in that capacity only to a smaller extent. This will not surprise sociologists and anthropologists, for they are aware of the great amount of imitative adult activity which enters into the play of children, the world around. In this activity, play though it may be, children are severe, highly critical, and vindictive in their punishment of a child who does not do it "this way," or "that way." Even before there has been any attempt at overt sex play, the child may have acquired a considerable schooling on matters of sex. Much of this comes so early that the adult has no memory of where his attitudes were acquired (p. 445).

These comments are repeated, nearly word for word, in the records of those many investigators who have observed the various nonhuman primate species in the field (Jay, 1968).

Of course, the child's earliest identification of itself as male or female and the earliest manifestations of sex-typed behavior patterns derive from interactions with its parents. Parents are known to respond differentially to boys and to girls from infancy onward (Rothbart and Maccoby, 1966), and the sex-typed outcomes of parent–child interaction have been discussed extensively in the child development literature (e.g., Lynn, 1969). Nevertheless, there is strong evidence that the peer culture supports and extends the process of sex-typing beginning in the earliest preschool years. Sex is the overriding polarizer in peer group formation in all primate species from the point of earliest contact (Hartup, in press). Sex is a more powerful determinant of "who plays with whom" than age, race, social class, intelligence, or any other demographic factor with the possible exception of propinquity. And, clearly, this sex cleavage is instrumental in transmitting normative sex-role standards to the child. How else to account for the vast number of sex differences that have been observed in the social activities of children (e.g., aggression) beginning with the preschool years?

Another vivid demonstration of the power of the peer culture in early sex-typing is contained in a series of experiments by Kobasigawa (1968). With kindergarten children, Kobasigawa found that: (a) exposure to peer models who inhibited playing with inappropriate-sex toys enhanced the observer's self-control over inappropriate responses; (b) exposure to models demonstrating alternative activities to sex-inappropriate responses also reduced inappropriate sex-typed activity; (c) exposure to peer models who displayed sex-inappropriate behavior had disinhibitory effects on the observer, although the amount of the disinhibition depended on the sex of the model in relation to the sex of the child—that is, boys disinhibited inappropriate sex behavior only when the model was a boy, while the sex of the model made relatively little difference in amount of disinhibition for girls. Similar results have been found in other modeling work: For example, aggressive peer models enhance aggression in young children, but more effectively if the model is a boy than if the model is a girl (Hicks, 1965).

Do these findings imply that aberrant and inadequate sexual behaviors derive from aberrant and/or inadequate contacts with the peer culture? My knowledge of life-history research in sexual pathology is very limited, but my impression is that most such pathologies derive from some combination of early hangups with parents and hangups with peers. Peer modeling, in other words, seldom accounts for all of the variance in criminally violent or aberrant sexual behavior. Even so, Roff (1966) has shown that a history of poor peer relations is more characteristic of certain kinds of homosexual males than comparison groups of heterosexual males; case studies show with considerable frequency that persons committing crimes of sexual assault have histories of peer rejection and social isolation.

Moral Development

According to Piaget (1932), both the quantity and the quality of social participation are related to the child's moral development. Moral understanding is assumed to derive partly from the amount of social interaction in which the child participates and partly from his centrality in the peer group. During early childhood, the child's behavior reflects an "objective" moral orientation (i.e., he believes that rules are immutable and the power of adults is absolute). Adoption of a "subjective" moral orientation requires some opportunity to view moral rules as changeable products of group consensus. For this purpose, social give-and-take is required. Such opportunity is not common in the child's experiences with his parents and teachers, because social systems such as the family and the school are structured in authoritarian terms. Only in rare instances is there sufficient reciprocity in adult–child interaction to facilitate the disequilibration that is necessary to form a mature moral orientation. The peer group, on the other hand, is seldom organized along authoritarian dimensions and possesses the inherent characteristics for furthering moral development.

Precious little data exist to support the thesis that the *amount* of agemate contact is associated with advanced moral development. Keasey (1971) has recently published a study, however, based on 144 preadolescents, in which he found that children who belonged to relatively many clubs and social organizations had higher moral judgment scores than children belonging to few organized groups. These results, which were somewhat stronger for boys than for girls, stand alone in revealing a correlation between amount of social participation with peers and advances in moral functioning.

Evidence is more profuse concerning the association between the *quality* of a child's peer contacts and the level of his moral reasoning. Keasey (1971) also reported that self-reports of leadership functions, peer ratings of leadership and friendship nominations, and teacher ratings of leadership and popularity were all positively related to level of moral judgment as assessed by Kohlberg's (1958) techniques. Irwin (1967) was unable to demonstrate consistent relations between popularity and measures of moral understanding within several groups of nursery school children, either because the samples were too homogeneous, or because the period in question is too early for the relation between acceptance and morality to be reflected in a systematic manner. Other data, though, support Keasey's findings: Gold (1962) reported that peer leaders have "more socially integrative" ideologies than nonleaders; Porteus and Johnson (1965) showed that acceptance was related to good moral judgment as perceived by peers; Campbell and Yarrow (1961) found that popular children, as compared to less popular children, made more extensive use of subtle inferences concerning the causes of other children's behavior; and Klaus (1959) found that accepted children tend to emphasize being neat and tidy, being a good sport, and being able to take a joke in their descriptions of classmates. Each of these diverse findings suggests that popularity is linked with effectively internalized social norms. Studies of peer group leaders also show them to be actively and appropriately sociable.

Once again, there is difficulty in interpreting the findings. Existence of a significant correlation between the extent of social participation and level of moral functioning does not prove that the latter derives from the former. Membership in clubs may facilitate change in the structuring of moral understanding, but higher levels of moral understanding may also be prerequisite to membership in large numbers of social clubs. Children may choose friends, and teachers may nominate children as popular who can demonstrate advanced levels of moral understanding; on the other hand, popularity itself may enhance the child's level of moral reasoning. Another possibility is that the linkages cited here exist partly because estimates of moral understanding and estimates of popularity are both modestly related to intelligence.

Thus, the basic hypothesis that peer interaction contributes to advances in moral development remains unproven. The available evidence is consistent with this hypothesis, to be sure, but only controlled manipulation of the child's social experiences with agemates can provide adequate causal evidence. Needless to say, such manipulations are very hard to produce.

Are children who have successful peer relations more overtly honest and upright than children who are loners and/or who are rejected by their peers? Some of the previously cited evidence is suggestive of such a state of affairs, although additional evidence is not extensive. In one early investigation, Roff (1961) found that in a sample of servicemen, all of whom were former patients in a child-guidance clinic, those receiving bad conduct discharges were significantly more likely to have been rated by their childhood counselors as having poor peer adjustment than those with successful service records. These data are important for two reasons: (a) They demonstrate a linkage between peer adjustment and moral behavior; and (b) The relation is a predictive one—childhood failure in peer relations was correlated with bad conduct discharge rates in adulthood. In a more recent study (Roff and Sells, 1968), a significant relation was demonstrated between peer acceptance–rejection during middle childhood and delinquency during early adolescence. Among upper lower-class and middle-class children, there was a dramatically higher delinquency rate among children who were not accepted by their peers than among those who were. Among the very lowest social class subjects, however, a different pattern held: Both highly accepted and highly rejected boys had higher delinquency rates than those who were moderately accepted by their peers. Examination of individual case records indicated that the nature of the delinquency and the adequacy of the child's personality adjustment differed between the chosen and nonchosen lower class groups. In fact, there is every reason to expect that, among the subjects from the lowest social strata, ultimate adjustment of the peer-accepted delinquent group will be better than the nonaccepted delinquent subjects. Thus far, path analysis techniques have not been applied to Roff's data, so that some question still remains concerning the relative primacy of delinquent activity and the poor peer relations. But the data point to peer interaction as one source of the individual's willingness to live according to accepted social standards.

Other research, dealing with the problem in a different manner, suggests that peer pressures can move child behavior both in the direction of socially accepted and socially unaccepted norms. Such pressures are directly revealed in the studies of spontaneous peer groups published by the Sherifs (1964) and more indirectly in Kandel's (1973) study of peer influences in relation to drug use among adolescents.[3] Indirect peer influences on moral behavior are also shown in a set of studies by Shelton and Hill (1969) in which it was found that children were more likely to falsify their scores in a laboratory game, if they expected that their peers would be informed about their performance than if information about the subject's performance was to be kept secret.

Anxiety and Emotional Disturbance

Evidence can be found in at least 20 studies to show that a child's general emotional adjustment is related to his popularity (Hartup, 1970). Assessment of adjustment in these studies has been accomplished with devices as various as the TAT, on the one hand, and observations of school adjustment, on the other. The data consistently show that, in samples of children who are functioning within the normal range, degree of maladjustment is inversely related to degree of social acceptance. In addition to the studies with normal samples, work with institutionalized populations shows that popularity in disturbed groups is also inversely related to relative degree of maladjustment (Davids and Parenti, 1958). Sheer quantity of social participation has not been studied in relation to general personality adjustment, although one suspects that such a relation exists.

Some 15 years ago, a spate of studies was published concerning the relation between a more specific affective component, anxiety, and social acceptance. In general, there tends to be a low negative correlation between anxiety, as measured by the *Children's Manifest Anxiety Scale,* and sociometric status (e.g.,

---

[3] A significant concordance between friends in incidence of drug use does not, of course, reveal which comes first, the use of drugs or contact with drug-using friends.

McCandless, Castaneda, and Palermo, 1956) although, once again, we know very little about the relation between amount of social participation and anxiety.

The major predictive studies of the relation between childhood peer status and adult emotional adjustment have been completed by Roff (1963) within the context of his follow-up investigations of the adult status of boys who, as children, were seen in child guidance clinics. Within these samples, poor peer relations in childhood have been predictive of both neurotic disturbance and psychotic episodes of a variety of types.

Once again, the evidence relating affective disturbance and peer relations is correlational and invites an interpretation suggesting that rejection leads to anxiety, lowered self-esteem, and hostility, which in turn lead to further rejection. A simple unidirectional interpretation does not seem plausible. However, despite the fact that explanatory hypotheses do not receive clear support from this research, there is no evidence that contradicts the basic hypothesis that peer relations are of pivotal importance in personality development (Roff, Sells, and Golden, 1972).

Intellectual Development

The contributions of peer relations to intellectual development are difficult to specify. There seems to be no evidence that sociability is related to IQ, either in younger or older children. Parten (1932) found a small positive correlation between cooperative participation and IQ ($r = .33$) but an even larger correlation was obtained between parallel play and IQ ($r = .62$). On the other hand, amount of social participation appears to be neither markedly greater or less among gifted children than among children of average IQ (Terman and Oden, 1947), and moderately retarded children are not notably less sociable than children of greater intellectual ability. Brighter children occupy more central positions in the peer culture, being of higher sociometric status than less bright children (Roff, Sells, and Golden, 1972) and of higher social effectance (Hartup, 1970), but competence in social relations does not bear a consistent relation to IQ. At least one study (Lurie, Newberger, Rosenthal, and Outcalt, 1941) shows an inverse relation between measured intelligence and social maturity. Thus, it is difficult to make a case for the hypothesis that social participation is related to mental abilities (as measured by IQ tests) in any systematic way.

The evidence is also conflicting concerning the relation between sociability and achievement; much depends on the parameters of achievement and social behavior being measured. For example, Van den Munckhof (1970) reported a correlation of .42 between sociability and performance on the *Nijmegen School Achievement Test* for a sample of 454 Dutch school children, a finding that was replicated with a second sample, including 91 handicapped young girls. On the other hand, Crandall (1970) found that both men and women who spend large amounts of time in academic achievement efforts had early childhood histories of alienation from their peers.

Several studies indicate that peer affiliations can either reward or punish academic performance, depending on the values of the peer group. An inverse correlation has sometimes been found between studiousness and popularity (Coleman, 1961), but opposite findings have also been obtained (Hartup, 1970). Thus, at the moment, there is no strong evidence that either sheer amount of social participation or the centrality of the child's position in the peer group has a consistent bearing on achievement behavior.

The status of Piaget's (1926) hypothesis that peer interaction is the primary mechanism of overcoming childhood egocentrism is also uncertain. Most of the research based on this hypothesis has involved the study of correlations between measured popularity, on the one hand, and measures of role-taking ability or referential communication, on the other hand. Using this paradigm, Rubin (1972) found that popular kindergarten and second-grade children had low scores on a measure of communicative egocentrism as compared to their unpopular peers. Finley, French, and Cowan (1973), however, reported that they were unable to generate any significant relations between popularity and three different measures of egocentrism in two different samples of elementary school children. And, finally, Rardin and Moan (1971) reported very, very weak relations between popularity and classification and conservation abilities among kindergarten and first-grade children.

Thus, the evidence does not support the Piagetian thesis that the peer group is the primary locus of social "decentration." Of course, certain questions may be raised concerning the adequacy of the research strategies that have been used to explore the interface between peer relations and cognitive development. Covariation of individual differences within age groups should not be expected to reveal the functional contribution of social experience to the restructuring of mental abilities. Also, popularity may not be the most appropriate index of social participation for studying this problem. Although popular children are more sociable than unpopular children (McCandless and Marshall, 1957), the relation between amount of social experience and cognitive change should be explored more directly.

Thus, the contribution of peer relations to intellectual development is unclear. Neither general nor specific cognitive abilities appear to be consistently related to either the quantity or quality of a child's contact with the peer culture. Whether such social experiences represent unimportant contributions to mental development, or whether our research strategies have been defective, remains an open question. But no claim can be made, on the basis of present data, to the effect that large portions of variance in children's intellectual competencies derive from their commerce with agemates.

IMPROVING CHILDREN'S PEER RELATIONS

Calculated attempts to improve children's peer relations have been successful since the first behavior modification experiments (Jack, 1934; Page, 1936; Chittenden, 1942). These early studies included the invention of protocols that utilized out-of-class training experiences in modifying assertive and dominance behaviors. The protocols, which made liberal use of contingent social reinforcement, modeling, and verbal instructions, represent excellent examples of efficient supplemental socialization experiences for young children. The procedures were clearly explicated, and the outcomes were documented with respect to both short-term and somewhat longer-term effects. More recent studies, such as those by Harris, Wolf, and Baer (1967), demonstrate how contingencies of adult attention can be used within the classroom itself to bring about increased peer contacts from isolated, socially incompetent children. Although most of these studies have included follow-up checks that were conducted weeks or months later and that demonstrate the relative permanence of the induced effects, long-term follow-up studies are rare. This deficit can be cited as a critical gap in this literature.

Other ways of modifying children's social competencies consist of manipulating the context in which peer interaction occurs. One contextual element that can be used to modify the individual child's behavior is feedback from the peer group itself. Thus, Wahler (1967) picked five nursery-school children, established baseline rates for a number of different response classes (e.g., cooperation, social overtures, and social speech), and then instructed the peer group to behave toward the target children with different contingencies than were ordinarily used. Two outcomes of this experiment should be mentioned: (a) The children's peers were able to use attention selectively, thus demonstrating the feasibility of programming peer interaction; and (b) behavior change in the selected response class occurred during the experimental phase for each of the five subjects. Other studies (e.g., Patterson and Brodsky, 1966) have described instances in which the peer group has been used to modify more deviant behaviors than in the Wahler experiment.

Group leaders can manipulate the context of peer interaction in a variety of other ways. The classic studies of group atmosphere, in which social behavior was determined by leadership style, are pertinent to this discussion (e.g., Lewin, Lippitt, and White, 1938). So are the studies of the effects of superordinate goals of intergroup conflict and cooperation (Sherif, Harvey, White, Hood, and Sherif, 1961).

Simply manipulating the composition of the peer group apparently has therapeutic potential. For example, there is the possibility that interaction with nonagemates provides a more sanguine context for the development of social competence by low competent children than does interaction with children who are similar in age. Suomi and Harlow (1972) reported that the untoward effects of prolonged isolation on the social development of rhesus monkeys is effectively reversed by a carefully managed program of contact between the isolated monkey and other monkeys who are appreciably *younger* in age. The data indicate that such a program of social rehabilitation is more effective than contact with agemates. Similarly, human children who are not especially competent in social situations may be assisted by opportunities to interact with younger children. Indeed, this idea seems implicit in the strategies commonly employed by nursery-school and kindergarten teachers. Two practices are typical: (a) At the beginning of the school year, socially incompetent children are frequently assigned to classes of younger rather than older children; and (b) subgroups are used within a classroom in which less skilled children are placed in contact with younger (but not inept) peers. These procedures undoubtedly maximize the less competent child's chances of obtaining positive feedback for prosocial activity while, at the same time, chances of social punishment are minimized.

CONCLUSION

Access to agemates, acceptance by them, and constructive interactions with them are among the necessities of child development. There is a relation between the child's personal–social effectance and his sociability with peers, and opportunities for early peer contact appear to enhance the socialization of aggression. At later stages of development, peer contacts provide essential inputs into sexual socialization, although present research does not clearly establish a relation between peer contact and either moral or intellectual development. Major predictive studies, however, have shown that the adequacy of adjustment to the peer group is a good predictor of adolescent and adult emotional status. Thus, no evidence contradicts the notion that peer relations are crucial to a child's development and much evidence supports this contention.

Recent studies also demonstrate that the sensitive student of child behavior has a variety of avenues available through which to maximize the input of peer relations to the development of the individual child. Ensuring each child the opportunity for productive commerce with peers is not an easy task, but such experiences would seem essential to normal social development.

ACKNOWLEDGMENTS

This paper was completed with assistance from Grant No. 5-PO1-05027, National Institute of Child Health and Human Development.

REFERENCES

Baumrind, D. Socialization and instrumental competence in young children. In W. W. Hartup (Ed.), *The young child: Reviews of research* (Vol. 2). Washington, D.C.: National Association for the Education of Young Children, 1972. Pp. 202–224.

Bronson, W. C. Central orientations: A study of behavior organization from childhood to adolescence. *Child Development,* 1966, *37,* 125–155.

Campbell, J. D., and Yarrow, M. R. Perceptual and behavioral correlates of social effectiveness. *Sociometry,* 1961, *24,* 1–20.

Chittenden, G. E. An experimental study in measuring and modifying assertive behavior in young children. *Monographs for the Society for Research in Child Development,* 1942, *7,* No. 1.

Coleman, J. S. *The adolescent society.* Glencoe, Ill.: Free Press, 1961.

Crandall, V. C., and Battle, E. S. The antecedents and adult correlates of academic and intellectual achievement effort. In J. P. Hill (Ed.), *Minnesota symposia on child psychology* (Vol. 4). Minneapolis: University of Minnesota Press, 1970. Pp. 36–93.

Davids, A., and Parenti, A. N. Time orientation and interpersonal relations of emotionally disturbed and normal children. *Journal of Abnormal and Social Psychology,* 1958, *57,* 299–305.

Finley, G. F., French, D., and Cowan, P. A. Egocentrism and popularity. XIVth Inter-American Congress of Psychology. São Paulo, Brazil, April, 1973.

Gold, H. A. The importance of ideology in sociometric evaluation of leadership. *Group Psychotherapy,* 1962, *15,* 224–230.

Hamburg, D. A., and Van Lawick-Goodall, J. Factors facilitating development of aggressive behavior in chimpanzees and humans. In J. de Wit and W. W. Hartup (Eds.), *Origins and determinants of aggressive behaviors.* The Hague: Mouton 1974. Pp. 59–86.

Harlow, H. F. Agemate or peer affectional system. In D. S. Lehrman, R. A. Hinde, and E. Shaw (Eds.), *Advances in the study of behavior* (Vol. 2). New York: Academic Press, 1969. Pp. 333–383.

Harris, F. R., Wolf, M. M., and Baer, D. M. Effects of adult social reinforcement on child behavior. In W. W. Hartup and N. L. Smothergill (Eds.), *The young child: Reviews of research.* Washington, D.C.: National Association for the Education of Young Children, 1967. Pp. 13–26.

Hartup, W. W. Peer interaction and social organization. In P. H. Mussen (Ed.), *Carmichael's manual of child psychology* (Vol. 2). New York: John Wiley, 1970. Pp. 361–456.

Hartup, W. W. Aggression in childhood: developmental perspectives. *American Psychologist,* 1974, *29,* 336–341.

Hartup, W. W. Cross-age vs. same-age peer interaction: Ethological and cross-cultural perspectives. In V. L. Allen (Ed.), *Children as teachers: Theory and research on tutoring.* Madison, Wisc.: University of Wisconsin Press, in press.

Heathers, G. Emotional dependence and independence in nursery school play. *Journal of Genetic Psychology,* 1955, *87,* 37–57.

Hetherington, M., and Deur, J. The effects of father absence on child development. In W. W. Hartup (Ed.), *The young child: Reviews of research* (Vol. 2). Washington, D.C.: National Association for the Education of Young Children, 1972. Pp. 303–319.

Hicks, D. J. Imitation and retention of film-mediated aggressive peer and adult models. *Journal of Personality and Social Psychology,* 1965, *2,* 97–100.

Irwin, D. M. Peer acceptance related to the young child's concept of justice. Unpublished bachelor's thesis, University of Minnesota, 1967.

Jack, L. M. An experimental study of ascendent behavior in preschool children. *University of Iowa Studies in Child Welfare*, 1934, *9*, No. 3.

Jay, P. (Ed.). *Primates: Studies in adaptation and variability*. New York: Holt, Rinehart, & Winston, 1968.

Kandel, D. Adolescent marihuana use: Role of parents and peers. *Science*, 1973, *181*, 1067–1070.

Keasey, C. B. Social participation as a factor in the moral development of preadolescents. *Developmental Psychology*, 1971, *5*, 216–220.

Kinsey, A. C., Pomeroy, W. B., and Martin, C. E. *Sexual behavior in the human male*. Philadelphia: W. B. Saunders, 1948.

Klaus, R. A. Interrelationships of attributes that accepted and rejected children ascribe to their peers. Unpublished doctoral dissertation, George Peabody College for Teachers, 1959.

Kobasigawa, A. Inhibitory and disinhibitory effects of models on sex-inappropriate behavior in children. *Psychologia*, 1968, *11*, 86–96.

Kohlberg, L. The development of modes of moral thinking and choice in the years ten to sixteen. Unpublished doctoral dissertation, University of Chicago, 1958.

Lewin, K., Lippitt, R., and White, R. K. Patterns of aggressive behavior in experimentally created "social climates." *Journal of Social Psychology*, 1938, *10*, 271–299.

Lindzey, G. Some remarks concerning incest, the incest taboo, and psychoanalytic theory. *American Psychologist*, 1967, *22*, 1051–1059.

Lurie, L. A., Newburger, M., Rosenthal, F. M., and Outcalt, L. C. Intelligence quotient and social quotient. *American Journal of Orthopsychiatry*, 1941, *11*, 111–117.

Lynn, D. B. *Parental and sex role identification: A theoretical formulation*. Berkeley: McCutchan, 1969.

Maccoby, E. E., and Feldman, S. S. Mother-attachment and stranger-reactions in the third year of life. *Monographs of the Society for Research in Child Development*, 1972, *37* (No. 146).

Maccoby, E. E., and Masters, J. C. Attachment and dependency. In P. H. Mussen (Ed.), *Carmichael's manual of child psychology* (Vol. 2). New York: Wiley, 1970. Pp. 73–157.

McCandless, B. R., Castaneda, A., and Palermo, D. S. Anxiety in children and social status. *Child Development*, 1956, *27*, 385–391.

McCandless, B. R., and Marshall, H. R. A picture sociometric technique for preschool children and its relation to teacher judgments of friendship. *Child Development*, 1957, *28*, 139–148.

Page, M. L. The modification of ascendant behavior in preschool children. *University of Iowa Studies in Child Welfare*, 1936, *12*, No. 3.

Parten, M. B. Social participation among preschool children. *Journal of Abnormal and Social Psychology*, 1932–1933, *27*, 243–269.

Patterson, G. R., and Brodsky, G. A behavior modification program for a child with multiple problem behaviors. *Journal of Child Psychology and Psychiatry*, 1966, *7*, 277–295.

Patterson, G. R., and Cobb, J. A. A dyadic analysis of "aggressive" behaviors. In J. P. Hill (Ed.), *Minnesota symposia on child psychology* (Vol. 5). Minneapolis: University of Minnesota Press, 1971.

Patterson, G. R., Littman, R. A., and Bricker, W. Assertive behavior in children: A step toward a theory of aggression. *Monographs of the Society for Research in Child Development*, 1967, *32*, No. 113.

Piaget, J. *The language and thought of the child.* New York: Harcourt, Brace, 1926.

Piaget, J. *The moral judgment of the child.* Glencoe, Ill.: Free Press, 1932.

Porteus, B. D., and Johnson, R. C. Children's responses to two measures of conscience development and their relation to sociometric nomination. *Child Development,* 1965, *36,* 703–711.

Rardin, D. R., and Moan, C. E. Peer interaction and cognitive development. *Child Development,* 1971, *42,* 1685–1699.

Roff, M. Childhood social interactions and young adult bad conduct. *Journal of Abnormal and Social Psychology,* 1961, *63,* 333–337.

Roff, M. Childhood social interaction and young adult psychosis. *Journal of Clinical Psychology,* 1963, *19,* 152–157.

Roff, M. Some childhood and adolescent characteristics of adult homosexuals. U. S. Army Medical Research and Development Command, Report No. 66–5, May, 1966.

Roff, M., and Sells, S. B. Juvenile delinquency in relation to peer acceptance–rejection and socioeconomic status. *Psychology in the Schools,* 1968, *5,* 3–18.

Roff, M., Sells, S. B., and Golden, M. M. *Social adjustment and personality development in children.* Minneapolis: University of Minnesota Press, 1972.

Rothbart, M. K., and Maccoby, E. E. Parents' differential reactions to sons and daughters. *Journal of Personality and Social Psychology,* 1966, *4,* 237–243.

Rubin, K. H. Relationship between egocentric communication and popularity among peers. *Developmental Psychology,* 1972, *7,* 364.

Scarr, S. Social introversion–extraversion as a heritable response. *Child Development,* 1969, *40,* 823–832.

Shelton, J., and Hill, J. P. Effects on cheating of achievement anxiety and knowledge of peer performance. *Developmental Psychology,* 1969, *1,* 449–455.

Sherif, M., Harvey, O. J., White, B. J., Hood, W. R., and Sherif, C. W. *Intergroup conflict and cooperation: The robbers cave experiment.* Norman: University of Oklahoma Press, 1961.

Sherif, M., and Sherif, C. W. *Reference groups.* New York: Harper & Row, 1964.

Suomi, S. J., and Harlow, H. F. Social rehabilitation of isolate-reared monkeys. *Developmental Psychology,* 1972, *6,* 487–496.

Terman, L. M., and Oden, M. H. *Genetic studies of genius, Vol. IV: The gifted child grows up: Twenty-five years' follow-up of a superior group.* Stanford, Calif.: Stanford University Press, 1947.

Van den Munckhof, H. C. P. Sociale interaktie en cognitieve ontwikkeling bij kleuters. Niet-gepubliceerde doctoraalscriptie ontwikkelingspsychologie, Universiteit Nijmegen, 1970.

Wahler, R. G. Child–child interactions in five field settings: Some experimental analyses. *Journal of Experimental Child Psychology,* 1967, *5,* 278–293.

11
Socializing the Severely Disturbed Child

CARL FENICHEL

Twenty years ago the League School for Seriously Disturbed Children was started for children diagnosed as autistic, schizophrenic, and/or psychotic who had been turned down as uneducable and untreatable by every school and agency in the community. Except for a few very costly and distant residential centers, there were no facilities but state hospitals that would accept these children.

When the League School started, the field was relatively unexplored with no substantial body of tested and recorded educational experiences to guide us. With rare exception, the few who had been working with disturbed children in child guidance clinics, residential treatment centers, or in private practice assumed that childhood mental illness was psychogenic in origin. Individual psychotherapy was the treatment favored and prescribed. At the time it was generally believed that education could do little or nothing for these children and that the psychiatric profession must assume responsibility for whatever treatment was possible.

From the start we decided that the teacher would play the key role in working with our children, but we weren't sure what that role should be. It began as an accepting, permissive, unstructured one—very much like that of the traditional therapist who permits and often encourages the patient to freely express impulses and ventilate feelings. We believed this was what a mentally ill child needed. At that time, most professionals believed that parents of disturbed

CARL FENICHEL · Founder of The League School, Brooklyn, New York 11203. Deceased.

children had denied them the expression and fulfillment of the basic needs and pleasures of infancy, and that these children should be permitted the freedom to release their repressed impulses and drives until basic emotional conflicts were "worked through" and resolved. Our children taught us otherwise.

We learned that disorganized children need someone to organize their world for them. Disturbed children fear their own loss of control and need protection against their own impulses. We began to see that what they needed was a highly organized program of education and training that could bring order, stability, and direction to minds that are disorganized, unstable, and unpredictable. Their lack of internal organization, integration, and self-control makes it difficult and often impossible for most disturbed children to learn, and to organize what they have learned into more mature patterns of socialized living and functioning.

After the first few years of close and intensive work with our children, we began to question and eventually to scrap the official dogma held by nearly every professional in the field, which attributed the mental and emotional disorders of these children to rejecting, refrigerated, and inadequate parents. We found increasing evidence of severe neurological, biochemical, and organic disorders that could better explain the disturbed behavior of these children than impaired relationships with their parents. We soon learned that what our parents needed was not the finger of blame put on them by professionals but a chance to work together with our day school staff in a joint effort to find ways of helping their children learn to live and thrive and grow within their home, school, and community. By working closely and intensively with these children and studying their early developmental histories, we accumulated evidence that their deep isolation and withdrawal from life, their problems in using and understanding language, their bizarre behavior and strange rituals, their anxieties often bordering on panic, are all closely related to serious disorders of perception, learning, and language. Their disorders not only interfere with formal learning but inevitably reduce or impair their ability to receive and interpret accurate impressions of social situations and to respond appropriately.

Relationships with other human beings require an understanding of how to act and react with social situations. The demands and complexities of these social processes, when they are beyond a child's capacities or comprehension, will usually result in continuous failure that leads to avoidance and withdrawal from people, preoccupation with self, and rigid, repetitive behavior.

THE CHILDREN

When they first come into the League School, most of our children are isolates who appear to be totally indifferent or oblivious to the presence and activities of the other children. Their failure to understand social stimuli and to pick up adequate clues for understanding social procedures and group situations makes it much too confusing or threatening for them to participate in group activities. The few who may try to initiate contact with others don't seem to know how or where to begin, and unless we can succeed in training our children to understand what the expressions in people's faces, voices, and gestures are saying, they will be unable to acquire appropriate patterns of social behavior.

It is an encouraging sign of emotional growth when our children begin to relate to their peers. It indicates that their highly individualized program within a group setting and their relationships with their teachers have succeeded in getting them to recognize the feelings and needs of others and in helping them develop socially appropriate responses.

Deficiencies in the ability to use and understand language and to make sense of what they see and hear make socialization difficult, often impossible, for most of our children when they first come to League School. Their lack of awareness of social requirements is reflected in their bizarre behavior in and outside the home. They may flap their arms, jump up and down, spin around, grab, kick, or bite the people around them. Their wild and strange behavior in public provokes critical reactions from the people who witness it in stores, on buses, in parks or playgrounds. To protect the children and themselves from the cold and hostile stares and comments of neighbors, many families hesitate to allow their children to leave the privacy of their home, and the children's withdrawal and isolation from the world deepen more and more. There are children admitted to League School whose behavior and intellectual functioning are so infantile, aimless, and chaotic that they need an intensive training program on an exclusively one-to-one basis before they can even begin to function meaningfully within a small group. They are the very withdrawn and lethargic or the extremely restless and hyperactive, many of whom need to be trained to sit in a chair, to make eye contact, to look, listen, and attend to a simple detail or respond to a simple directive.

HOME TRAINING

The preschool children (ages 3 to 7) are taken into our Home Training Program, which involves the parent as the chief therapeutic agent. The child has an individual weekly one-hour session with his teacher while his mother is in the room as a participating observer. This pioneering Home Training Program, funded by the National Institute of Mental Health in 1966, has proven to be highly effective in stimulating change and growth in the behavior of severely handicapped children. The major emphasis is on socializing the child, helping him become a self-managing member of his family, working toward interaction with his peers and the community through a program that emphasizes self-care, impulse control, language, and socializing skills. By observing and participating in the training and educational techniques used by the teacher, and by regularly scheduled discussions with the teacher, program director, social worker, and other parents, each mother learns how to cope with many of the overwhelming problems of living with her mentally disturbed child. At the same time, each child's home becomes a school and each mother a teacher who helps her child gain the skills and habits needed for emotional and social growth, family living, and eventual schooling.

Problems in communication are seen in all our children. With the preschooler in Home Training we help his mother to learn that the child does not understand social demands. It is not that he is stubborn and *won't* do what is asked, it is that he *can't* do what is asked because he does not tune in on the cues that would help him understand. Consequently, the parents are taught to use several modalities to get the message across to the child. If Johnny runs into the street, telling him to come back won't help. One must say "No" firmly, loudly, sharply, look angry, frown, and hold him physically. Thus, the verbal prohibition is reinforced by facial expression and by physical inhibition. Eye contact is essential for a child who is learning social cues. Mothers are taught to guide the child's face gently but firmly until he is looking at her before she uses words and facial expression to communicate her message.

Teachers as well as parents often assume that listening—like walking—comes naturally, and that if a child is able to hear he is able to listen. Listening is essential if a child is to learn, but first he must learn to listen. Listening is essential for socialization and yet even our more advanced children who have speech are often unable to listen to another child or engage in a dialogue with him. Some of our children with speech are completely unaware that conversation is a two-way process that involves listening as well as talking. Quite a few of them engage only in long or endless monologues and are indifferent to the reactions and replies of the people to whom they are talking. Activities that train a child in the art of listening are an essential part of every classroom program; they range from simple nursery games for our nonverbal children to conversation clinics for our more advanced talkers. Many of our Home Training children make sufficient progress within a year to be admitted to regular or special nursery school classes or kindergartens; some require further training and education at League School.

MINI-KINDERGARTENS

Once a child begins to recognize and accept some control by a teacher, we believe he can benefit more from a group than from an individual setting. With many isolated and withdrawn children, a one-to-one relationship serves only to feed their excessive need to cling to a dependency figure.

Even after a year some of our preschool children still need practice in a very small group before they can participate in a larger one. These children are placed in one of our mini-kingergarten classes, each of which has three children with two teachers, in a half-day program. The program aims to achieve the beginning of socialization through individual and group activities that help the child become aware of himself and others, develop language, control his impulses, and take care of himself. Nearly all these children are initially nonverbal. Some are totally withdrawn and respond only to self-stimulating activities. Others express themselves largely by screams and striking out at themselves, other children, or their teacher. These children often need the help of firm but gentle physical intervention before they can learn to sit, listen, or attend to a task. They are taught how to interact with other children in play activities and nursery games such as peek-a-boo, taking turns in manipulating toys for cause and effect, labeling and touching or pointing to objects, simple cooking, and washing dishes. Getting a helpless child to work at the daily tasks of self-care has many educational and therapeutic implications beyond helping him to take care of his needs and become self-managing. By involving a child in some of the essential demands and realities of daily living, we are taking him out of his preoccupation with self. We are helping him develop manipulative and other skills that will facilitate more advanced skills and activities. The child's mastery of any of these simple tasks is part of the socializing process, and it also increases his feelings of adequacy and self-control. Through carefully planned daily programs and through procedures with consistency of purpose and direction, many of these children begin to have some understanding of what is expected of them. Increased demands and expectations are made upon each child as he progresses. Gradually most of them are able to acquire self-managing and social skills and to perform other tasks and activities that bring their behavior under some control by the teacher. Many of our impulse-ridden children need a teacher's protection from drives that must be controlled and redirected into more meaningful, useful, and socially acceptable channels. Emphasis is on discipline that is neither punitively severe nor destructively permissive. Discipline means channeling a child's energies and drives toward constructive goals. It means reducing the child's confusion and disorganization by setting up clear and reasonable limits that help him understand what is expected of him. It means consistent routines and procedures that bring order and stability into disordered lives. It means supportive controls that help a child respond more effectively to the world by more appropriate and more adequate looking, listening, and attending. It means guidance and direction that facilitate learning and social functioning.

From the mini-kindergarten the children move on to regular or special classes in the public schools or into the full-day program at League School.

THE FULL-DAY PROGRAM

In this program each classroom has two teachers and five to seven children. We set up short- and long-range goals for each child based on an ongoing comprehensive assessment by the clinical team of his intellectual, linguistic, and social development as well as his specific problems of learning and behavior. Each child therefore has a highly individualized program. Priority is given to improving those skills and behaviors that are prerequisite for all learning and to filling in the gaps and discontinuities in the child's development that, if left unfilled, would hinder his future learning and hold back his mental, emotional, and social growth. The program must also reflect the long-range goals that have been projected for that child. These goals are based on an initial evaluation and periodic reevaluation and prognosis of each child's intellectual, educational, and vocational potential, made jointly by his teacher, supervisor, and the clinical staff. The curriculum and daily program will thus be used to attempt to translate the current prognosis by aiming to prepare each child adequately for eventual placement in a regular public school class, a special public or private school class, a vocational training school or a sheltered workshop, a residential center, state school, or mental institution.

We find that some of our children are not able to advance academically. For these children, who have acquired fragmented academic skills that they cannot use in a meaningful way, the program emphasis is on teaching them skills that will enable them to function more independently and appropriately in the daily situations and activities outside the classroom. Along with functional academic work, the program includes intensive training in self-care, shopping, preparing and serving food, traveling alone by public transportation, using the telephone, receptive and expressive language required for expressing needs and following directives, and appropriate verbal and nonverbal behavior in a variety of social situations.

STRUCTURE OF CLASSES

Much thoughtful planning goes into the process and criteria for grouping in all our classes. A child's impact on the group and the impact of the group on that child must be carefully considered. We try to avoid placing within the same group any two children whose problems and pathology might be intensified or contaminated by their mutual presence and interaction. In order to have effective group activities, we try not to have too wide a spread in the intellectual and social functioning of the individual children within a group. At the same time, we try to avoid placement of children with similar management problems within the same group: A group of *all* hyperactive, *all* withdrawn, or *all* nonverbal children would not make for balanced interaction. In teacher-planned and directed group activities and interaction, these children can and often do help each other develop the capacities to work and play and live together—something they must achieve if they are to remain and function within the community. This kind of learning can only take place in a group setting. Social relationships are lived, not taught.

In the group setting at meal time, rest time, play time, and work time our children learn that certain procedures and regulations are not only fair but essential for group living; they learn to wait their turn, to ask for and not grab, to share, to postpone, to comply as well as to assert. It is in the process of group living that many of our children begin to recognize and respect the presence, needs, and rights of others as well as of themselves.

The classroom curriculum, atmosphere, grouping, scheduling, regulations, and routines, and how they are handled by the teacher all have implications and potentials for positive learning and socializing experiences that can induce change, adjustment, and growth. The educational and therapeutic value of the daily program will depend on how effectively the teacher employs individual tutoring and remediation based on an ongoing assessment of each child's learning and behavioral problems and deficits, and on how well she can integrate each child's individual skills, interests, and needs into the programming and group processes of the classroom.

Disturbed children, like young infants, are generally oriented toward the here and now. They must learn to give up, postpone, or limit immediate desires and gratifications. Children at League School are slowly made aware that they must modify their impulsive behavior and conform to minimal social demands before they can participate in the many activities and privileges of the classroom. They learn that screaming, kicking, or biting will not get them what they want but that socially acceptable behavior will. A child must learn to wait his turn with other children on the slides or bicycles in the playground. He must learn to sit at table for snacks and lunch before his teacher will take him for a pizza treat in the neighborhood restaurant. He must learn to lower his voice and speak softly when he goes with his group to the public library. He must learn to remain quiet in a darkened room before he can watch a movie. He must learn to control his impulse to touch, grab, or throw the groceries before he can go shopping with his class at the supermarket.

GROUP ACTIVITIES

Throughout the school day much emphasis is placed on helping each child improve his self and social awareness. Carefully planned individual and group activities within and outside the classroom help our children learn to share their teacher with classmates and to work, play, and live together—something they must achieve if they are to remain, function, and mature within the community. This kind of learning can only take place in a group setting. Through carefully planned group experiences, our children are motivated to explore and interact with the world around them and with the people who live in it. The children are taken out of the building for community trips to the pet store, the supermarket, or to the park. Now they must look, listen, and interpret the simultaneous cues given by total strangers in unfamiliar surroundings. These trips must be repeated again and again to attempt to develop the automatic integration of all the social cues so that the response of the child is relevant to the situation. Parents are frequently included in the programming for our children who are learning these aspects of social living. We recommend that the child's weekends include similar experiences with the parents, such as shopping, park trips, ferry rides, and bus rides.

In our classrooms, as the children develop, part of the curriculum is a regular discussion of weekend experiences, planning for group activities, or oral book reports and assignments. Such classroom reports require the student to be alert to the expressions of the listener's face, the questions raised by the other students, the level of interest and involvement of his classmates in his subject. Long monologues are discouraged by calling the child's attention to his self-involvement, and to his bored, squirming audience.

Through planned group activities, children once detached and uncomfortable in a group are now discovering the pleasures of playing, learning, and working together. They have learned to function as a team, writing a class newspaper, painting a class mural, or playing a game of soccer. They go together to after-school "Y" programs where they join normal peers in activities, to weekend ice hockey or basketball games as well as to movies, concerts, theaters, and restaurants.

In the older group, cameras and tape recorders are used to mirror their behavior at the lunch table, in a classroom activity, or on a trip. The teacher then meets with them to review their individual and group behavior and to have an open, give-and-take discussion on the appropriateness of their social behavior.

For this group we have devised a conversation clinic that is a role-playing session monitored by the language therapists. In the clinic, the students are reminded of social cues. They sit in a relaxed casual group, learning how to begin a conversation; how to respond to conversation "openers" appropriately; how to sit, listen, and look. As they talk, the language therapist monitors the group and reminds them to look at each others' faces, to interpret the expressions, to vary the tone of voice, to change the subject, etc. Our goal is a fairly smooth interchange that makes use of the listening, looking, and talking skills that have been developed throughout their school years. Proficiency in our academic curriculum must go hand in hand with developing social skills or the child remains an isolate, "different" and alone.

Many of our adolescent boys are in a program of prevocational training to prepare them for gainful employment and community living. Nearly all of this group have been taught to travel to school by themselves on buses and subways. The daily program of work activities is integrated with academic work in functional reading, language, arithmetic, and other learning skills they will need for maintaining a job and for adequate functioning and daily living within the community. Through the many jobs they are being taught to perform at the school—working in the dining room and kitchen, helping to take inventory of supplies and equipment, taking care of our lawn and playground, collating office material, etc.—these boys are learning the skills, work habits, and discipline essential for holding a job, including the ability to work cooperatively with their peers in coordinating the tasks assigned to them. Every Friday they receive a small pay check for their work and begin to understand the value and meaning of money.

CONCLUSION

Over the years our program of special education has succeeded in rehabilitating many severely disturbed and disorganized children who might otherwise have had to spend and end their days vegetating in state institutions. The League School's staff and program have been able to reach and teach many children considered inaccessible and uneducable. They have furthered the mental and emotional growth of severely disordered children by helping them achieve varying degrees of impulse control, gross and fine motor coordination, self-discipline, language development, and cognitive competencies as well as the social skills and appropriate behavior necessary to play, work, and relate effectively with others. All this has made it possible for many of these children to move on to regular or special classes in the public schools, acquire vocational skills, hold down jobs, earn a livelihood, and lead fuller, more meaningful, and useful lives.

12

Factors Affecting the Development and Evaluation of Handicapped Children

STELLA CHESS

Part III of this volume presents two major intervention strategies for children with deviant development. Dr. Campbell has provided a lucid and organized summary of the current status of a range of biological agents that have been used in the treatment of psychotic children. The varied responses of patients with the same diagnosis tend to underscore the opinions that state that the types of childhood psychoses have yet to be clearly identified. The degree of responsiveness to specific medications can, in some degree, supply clues to biochemical imbalances that exist in such children. However, we are still unable to predict with certainty how such psychotic children will respond to a given pharmacological agent. Of necessity, drug-therapy research continues to be largely empirical, both in methodology and in our understanding of the effects of such drugs.

Drs. Mann and Goodman, in their consideration of perceptual and perceptual-motor training, complain of too little empiricism. They challenge the assumption that certain tests truly identify areas of weakness, and the validity of using such test scores as a basis for training programs with a developmental approach. Although reported results have not borne out the theory, training of perceptual modalities continues to consume major educational effort, which, they say, could be used to better advantage.

These two thoughtful discussions highlight one of the basic decisions that must be made in dealing with children whose development has been deviant: Will

STELLA CHESS · Department of Child Psychiatry, New York University Medical Center, New York, New York 10016.

there be a *spontaneous correction* of a given malfunction or is some *planned intervention* necessary for such correction?

It is a truism of child psychiatry that, when making an evaluation, one must think developmentally. New capacities become part of the young child's repertoire with great rapidity. Unless one keeps this clearly in mind, it becomes very difficult to determine whether or not a complaint is valid, and if so, whether the behavior in question represents an earlier normative stage that should no longer be in evidence, or whether it is a distortion that corresponds to no age-specific normal level. For every stage a range of normative behavior exists; inconvenient behavior is not necessarily abnormal. However, it is essential to distinguish between those deviations that have a promise of being self-limiting and those that require interventions.

Certain developmental milestones are used as reference points for identifying deviations. Developmental lags, such as a 1½-year-old's failure to walk, may represent an actual retardation or merely the slow end of a normal continuum. A 2-year-old whose tantrums are extreme may simply be demonstrating the high intensity characteristics of his overall temperament, or, in fact, some emotional or cerebral disorder may be present.

At still later ages, an awareness of age-appropriate conceptual abilities is essential. For instance, adult concepts of space and time develop gradually over the first 12 years. Words like "next week" or "in an hour" are only comprehended by age 6. Angularity and projective space are understood at a later age. By age 12 more sophisticated conceptual thinking makes it possible to hypothesize temporal and spatial cause and effect and verify them through deductive reasoning.

Concepts of morality also develop gradually over a similar time span. Until age 6 or 7, words are taken as literal truth; right and wrong are situationally determined. A 5-year-old can hardly be called a liar, because his comprehension of the difference between fantasy and reality is still limited. A 5-year-old "cheater" is unjustly accused. Though he may obey the rules in one set of circumstances, he is not yet experienced enough to make the transition from the specific to the general application of these rules. From age 7 to 12 the moral values of society are being actively internalized and concepts are being acquired as to which rules are inviolate, which are flexible, and under what circumstances. Only later will an *individual* moral code become possible.

In the case of the handicapped child, the problem is compounded. As the infant mortality rate decreases, more children are surviving with various physical and neurological defects, the child psychiatrists are increasingly aware of the need for adequate developmental scales for such children. These children experience, and are experienced by, their environments differently from normal children. In order to evaluate a child with a sensory or motor handicap, it is not enough to be knowledgeable about normal developmental expectations. It is also necessary to learn a second set of norms regarding motor milestones, speech acquisition, and affective responsiveness for each type of handicap in children whose other facilities are intact. Without such reference points, it is easy to assume intellectual retardation or other behavioral deviance, where none exists. Similarly, aberrant development may be overlooked because of a lack of knowledge of the child's developmental potential. When a child has multiple handicaps, an evaluation is manifestly more complicated.

In the hope of adding to our understanding of cognitive and affective development in both normal and handicapped children, my colleagues and I have undertaken a longitudinal study of 243 children with congenital rubella. These children, now 8 and 9 years old, were examined four years ago. Thus far, 125 have returned for reevaluation.

Only handicaps considered to have the greatest impact on development were selected for study. These were visual, auditory, neurological, and cardiac defects. To avoid contamination of the data, in the neurological area mental retardation is classifed as a behavioral finding, not as a physical defect.

In our reexamination of the children, certain trends are in evidence, though we can only draw tentative conclusions at the present time. For example, certain types of defect have a greater or lesser impact on the child's future. Cardiac malfunctions were for the most part correctable and have proved to be only a minor influence on behavior. On the other hand, sensory—and particularly auditory—defects have been of crucial importance in the child's overall development.

A number of investigators have noted that certain physical handicaps adversely influence other areas of development. Rutter, in his book *Maternal Deprivation Revised* (1972) argues that, where perceptual and linguistic stimulation is inadequate or disorganized, cognitive development is likely to be retarded. Sensorially handicapped children are frequently deprived of such stimulation, unless their caretakers compensate for the child's lack of initiative. Deafness, for example, may indirectly result in devastating cognitive and psychological effects for the child, should his parents fail to engage him actively in communication. A similar lack of stimulation may result in speech retardation for the motorically impaired child. And Fraiberg [Intervention in Infancy: A Program for Blind Infants" *Journal of the American Academy of Child Psychiatry 10:* 381–405, 1971] has found that blindness leads to impairment in the areas of human object relations, adaptive hand behavior, and gross motor development. She found that when verbal and tactile stimulation were increased, and when the hands were educated to understand "graspability" and to reach for sound on cue, defects in these other areas were minimized. In other words, early developmental retardation may be a function of understimulation, resulting indirectly from the sensory defect.

Thus far in our follow-up study we have not obtained clear evidence of such a cross-over effect. However, it is our impression that this is an operative element in many cases, though difficult to isolate where multiple handicaps are present.

It is our hope that a follow-up of the entire sample will enable us to pinpoint this factor more accurately.

A number of other factors appear to affect the child's development. Though a particular defect may remain unchanged, its handicapping *influence* may decrease or increase as the child grows older and a more complex social and cognitive level enables him to make progressively better use of other intact senses, with consequently greater feedback from his environment. One sense may compensate for another, as in the case of Rhoda, whose visual acuity appears to have positively influenced her ability to lip-read and communicate orally. The ability to read may also make up in part for experiential deprivations resulting from hearing and visual loss.

Unfortunately, the reverse may also be true, as we have found in the case of two children with auditory and motor defects. These children, and a number of others, appear to have an additional problem with sequencing, that is, the ability to arrange ideas and words in a logical, sequential order. This is manifested both verbally and nonverbally. Reading, and in the case of deaf children, lip-reading and speech, become much more difficult where a sequencing problem exists. Inevitably, this defect will have an increasing negative influence as more complex age-appropriate demands are made in such areas as mathematics and deductive reasoning.

This brings us to another problem in the accurate evaluation of the handicapped child. A defect may go undetected until a later stage, at which time an anticipated higher level of functioning fails to appear. For example, in the case of two children with severe hearing loss, additional related defects were not noticed until they were 8 years old. They were both experiencing great difficulty with oral communication, despite an otherwise good adaptation to their handicap. In the case of Eddie, whose Performance IQ was 132, a central language disorder was found to be present. Kenneth had difficulty with sequencing, and in addition, a genuine organic inability to control his tongue and other muscles involved in articulation. In view of their excellent facial and gestural ability to communicate, it was felt that they would both profit from learning sign language.

Temperament—that is, the way in which an individual characteristically reacts to a situation—also has an influence on the child's adaptation to his handicap. Elsewhere my colleagues and I have discussed our research on temperament in normal and mentally retarded children; we found that the so-called "difficult child"—one who scored high on irregularity, withdrawal response, negative mood, intensity, and slow adaptability to change—was the one most at risk in developing a behavior disorder. Obviously youngsters with the "difficult child" temperament are not very rewarding and frequently exceedingly frustrating, to their parents. We found that the mentally retarded "difficult child" was at greater risk for behavior disorder than the normal child, and we expected to find similar results in our study of the handicapped child. In fact we found that the "difficult child" syndrome was in evidence three times more often in handicapped rubella children than in the physically normal rubella population. Also, those who were classified as "difficult children" were three times as likely to develop behavior disorders as those with other temperamental styles.

I would like to make clear at this point that the "difficult child" syndrome is not directly responsible for psychiatric disorder; rather, it is the way in which the child is handled by his environment that gives rise to such difficulties. The so-called "easy" or "slow-to-warm-up" child may also develop behavioral problems, if there is too much dissonance between his temperament and his environment. For example, the "easy" child may be inadvertently infantilized by parents who are too willing to do things for him; the "slow-to-warm-up" child may be forced to adapt too rapidly and too often to new situations. However, in the case of the "difficult child," the risk of mishandling is greater. He requires unusually firm and consistent handling and an acceptance on the part of his parents and teachers of his particular behavioral style. The child who is easily distracted will learn more readily if external stimuli are reduced and work is divided into small components. The child with a high activity level (so distinct from the hyperactive child) will not respond well to repeated demands for motor restraint.

Let me give an example of the way temperament interacts with environment and handicap. Rhoda is an intellectually above-average child with severe hearing loss and a slow-to-warm-up temperament. The parents, initially overwhelmed by her handicap, were inconsistent and overly permissive; at 4 1/2 she was diagnosed as having a mild reactive behavior disorder. With parental counseling and good consistent handling at her school for the deaf, she made excellent progress and her behavior disorder disappeared. At present, the possibility of transferring her to a normal school is being considered. With a competent understanding of her intense, highly negative reaction to new situations, the difficulties of such a transfer should be greatly minimized.

One note of caution. There are certain hazards involved in obtaining correct test results from sensorially deprived children. What appears to be a cognitive lack may in fact be a functional lack arising from the difficulty of accurately communicating the task to the child, or understanding his response. There may also be an experiential lack, resulting from sensory privation. In testing these children, we made every effort to motivate and communicate accurately with the child, and where necessary, we judged intellect on the basis of performance tasks only.

Evaluating the handicapped child is indeed a complex task. Before suggesting any kind of intervention strategy, the psychiatrist must examine the interaction of a whole network of factors. It is insufficient merely to assess the *immediate* effects of a given handicap; the child must be viewed in the light of his handicap, its influence now and in the future, the potential rallying force in his intact resources, his temperament, his family and school environment. The psychiatrist, and others who work with him, must be aware of the child's increased vulnerability to behavior disorder, particularly in the case of the "difficult child"; to the discovery of heretofore unnoticed defects; and also to the dramatic developmental gains that may occur as new routes of stimulation open up. Only through such a dynamic approach to the child can the psychiatrist accurately assess the need, if any, the kind, and the optimum timing for intervention.

Discussion of Normal Development

The papers in this section were grouped for their relevance to the understanding of normal development, i.e., the study of regularities in change with which the normal infant grows up. Although the investigators are discussing data derived from different research methods, it is the only section in this volume in which the research subjects were primarily normal children.

The changing functions to be studied can be divided and subdivided into different categories such as motor behavior, speech, thought, number concepts, social behavior, moral judgment, and so on. A different age range may be involved, depending on the category studied.

Thus, speech development, as in Menyuk's presentation, is mainly studied in preschool children. Peer relations, in Hartup's work, is based mainly on the school-age child. Issues of moral thinking and the relatively undistorted ability to understand the other person's point of view as distinct from the egocentric, discussed by Elkind, reaches salience in the observation of adolescents. Each of these papers is concerned with some of the significant progress made in recent years in the understanding of normal developmental changes.

However, it is peculiar to the human species that children can be raised with a considerable variation in behavior, depending on the child-rearing and cultural experiences they are exposed to while growing up. The discovery of the regularities in developmental changes is further confounded by being responsive to the values, priorities, and theories held by the investigating social scientist. Some of these effects may be a predictable, socially desirable outcome of the research, while others are not. Some developmental researchers believe that their own values and theories should be controlled or kept out of the research as much as possible, while others believe that this is not possible and perhaps even their most important contribution. It is therefore not surprising that developmental change patterns are not uniformly established and are sometimes hopelessly obscured.

In his chapter on socialization of the individual, McCandless discusses five major theories or professional orientations affecting socialization. Some are mainly concerned with the process by which socialization occurs while others are mainly interested in the product.

The humanist's position is most clearly product oriented, and less interested in the study of human development. It is focused on prosocial behavior such as curiosity, creativity, and subjective experience, rather than abnormality and deviation. For problems of adjustment, an activistic position is taken against social and cultural inequities. Although humanists may be politically visible, they have little to offer for understanding the specific social interaction processes making for developmental changes.

The psychoanalytic orientation derives from clinical experience with people suffering from adjustment problems. Clinicians of this orientation tended to reconstruct developmental theory primarily from clinical experience with a small number of upper middle-class patients. This is illustrated by the Freudian personality theory in which normal development was conceptualized as a series of stages going from the oral, the anal, the oedipal or phallic, to the genital. These stages were only globally representative. They were not primarily based on significant behavioral changes observed in normal children. Instead, they were based on creative reconstructions of free associations overheard on the analytic couch. It is not surprising that these psychosexual stages of development do not offer much help for predicting specific developmental changes. Historically, they were often used for predicting global personality types such as anal and oral character. However, these were not based on empirical studies. Moreover, developmental data were scarcely available at the time. Perhaps the most direct effect of psychoanalytically oriented child rearing on normal development has been increased freedom of emotional expression and the movement away from theological traditions and values.

Behaviorists have been concerned with both normal and deviant children. While some have been interested in the product of socialization, their major contribution has been to process techniques for shaping problematic behavior of individuals in socially deprived or institutional environments. The behaviorists' training has its roots in the methods of experimental science, based on laboratory work with rats and other animals. They have tended to confine their research hypotheses to those questions answerable with existing research methodology. This has resulted in effective and publicly applicable behavior modification. However, this same scientifically narrow approach has offered less help with the more complex issues of socialization and developmental change. The behavioristic orientation can be applied in any of diverse cultural contexts. It does not have an equally unique contribution for assessing cultural or socializing values.

McCandless points out that both self-theory and the cognitive developmental orientation involve systematic measurement and categorization. Self-theory helps to explain traits like self-confidence, self-concept, and the complexities on which it is based. It has helped to identify and measure an important mental health concept based on the degree of congruence between ideal self and actual self. However, self theorists have not developed any special interest or handle for studying how culture and families have reinforced and shaped particular self-concepts. These five theoretical orientations have been reviewed to suggest how their direct effect on child rearing may influence some of the developmental change patterns in the growing child.

It is perhaps cognitive developmental orientation more than any of the other four that gives primary focus on the ways in which perception, cognition, language, and social behavior change. Such changes are formulated and measured as stages and age-graded functions. Clearly, these five orientations identified by McCandless are not independently worked out theoretical systems. They can overlap in various dimensions. However, from the view of understanding developmental changes in children, the chapter on language development is based on observation of the preschool child during the first five years of life.

Menyuk proposes five stages of language acquisition. They are identified as (1) prebabbling, (2) babbling, (3) one-word stage, (4) two-word stage, and (5) grammar acquisition stage. There is no doubt that language development could be grouped into different stages as well. For the purposes of this volume, it is important to bear in mind that the clinically useful distinction between the infant's receptive capacity to discriminate sound and his vocalizations is not used. Instead the attempt is made to conceptualize language development from the point of view of the growing child and the actual behavior marking the increasing complexity of his communication skills.

Hartup describes some of the changes in the child's social development, and the important part played by the peer group. While the mother and the nuclear family are the young child's main source of social experience, there is during the third and fourth year of life a decrease in the frequency with which the child seeks proximity with his mother, and an increase in his frequency of seeking contact with peers. The shift toward peer attachments becomes even more characteristic during the child's middle years. Hartup reviews the research demonstrating how this important developmental shift affects the child's socialization, such as coping with aggression, sex roles, and normal development. Although the child's social passivity or activity are shaped by biological factors and early experience, it is clear that peer-group learning makes a contribution to socialization that parent—child relations cannot. For example, the child's ties to his mother, and to a lesser degree, his father, must be maintained after socialization of aggression is begun. The rough-and-tumble play with peers in which rough play escalates into aggression and de-escalates into playful interaction cannot be adequately replicated in the parent—child relationship. The clinician's

traditional tendency to seek explanation for problems in a child's social development by focusing on his relationship with his parents may rule out some of the
most likely sources of difficulty in his peer relations.

In the discussion of his educational work with severely disturbed children,
Carl Fenichel points out how knowledge of normal changes in the social
development of children can be used in the socialization of severely deviant
children. When the child's disturbance is at a sufficient severity, Fenichel does
not try to use the peer group for socialization, but instead relies on the
one-to-one relationship with an adult. After the child has acquired the precursors
of socialization, he is considered ready to continue his socialization in the
classroom with peers. This procedure reflected the developmental change from
parents to peers mentioned by Hartup for the normal 3- to 4-year-old.

In addition to discussing developmental changes in language and socialization, this section also includes information on how children change in egocentricity as they grow older. David Elkind's discussion of egocentricity is based on
projection theory, and is actually about the structural changes in the child's
ability to think. Elkind defines egocentric thinking as the discrepancy between
the growing child's ability to form explanatory hypotheses about his life experience, and his ability to test them. At the preschool level, for example, when the
child sees the sun when the window shade is raised, he may believe that raising
the shade causes the sun to rise. This type of normal, preschool-age thinking
error is referred to as *phenomenalistic causality.*

During childhood another kind of thinking error tends to shape the egocentricity of this age group. Elkind refers to *assumptive reality* as the tendency of
the child to mistake a possible course of action (a thought) for the actual course
(or event). This can be seen in the confusion between a "tall tale" and reality.
For example, a child may assume there is a treasure in the backyard, and
proceed to dig up a flower bed, or he may tell a lie and then continue to believe
it.

The adolescent phase of egocentric thinking involves the characteristic of
assuming that other people are as interested in the adolescent as he is himself.
This confusion of the universal with the unique and vice versa makes for the
egocentric structures characteristic of adolescents. All the research bases for
these are not presented. Even if they were, there would probably be room also
for different interpretations.

Perhaps the most important distinction between cognitive developmental
data and clinical developmental data is in the study population from which they
were derived. The cognitive developmental information is generally derived from
research with normal children, while clinical developmental data are derived
from a deviant population. Developmental teachers call our attention to structural changes evolving from the interaction between the child's biological
changes and learning experiences. These changes need to be recognized and

understood in their own terms. They are easily confounded with the effects of so-called pathological family interactions. Moreover, even behavior defined by biologically deviant structures, as frequently occurs with autistic children, is frequently shaped by the child's age. For example, lack of human relatedness is often a complaint with the younger autistic child and replaced by mental retardation as he gets older. Indeed it is quite likely that the developmental processes in pathological behavior will be more clearly identified as the interaction between developmental and clinical research increases.

The scientific study of normal development in children and the discovery of regularities in developmental changes is beset by several sources of uncertainty. These include the variability of the underlying genetic composition, the physiological development, and experiential differences in what is taught and learned, and finally the variable effects of the research methods themselves. In short, given the multiply complex factors involved, we should not expect the same specificity in the study of human behavior that has characterized discoveries in the physical sciences. Conversely, if such laws of child development were to be found, they would require a degree of genetic and socializing homogeneity that would mitigate against the adaptational variability apparently needed in human social living. In the research papers of this section, results are often qualified as suggestive, and they sometimes appear to lack the certainty needed for making practical decisions with individual children.

How the knowledge of normal development and its variability may be used as guidelines for individual assessment and counseling is clearly presented in Stella Chess's discussion. She underscores the importance of distinguishing between normal variations in development and developmental malfunctioning. Developmental lags, such as a 1½-year-old's failure to walk may represent a critical retardation or merely the slow end of a normal range. If it is the latter, spontaneous correction may be anticipated, without the special planning of intervention. On the other hand, if a 2-year-old has extreme tantrums, they may derive from a cerebral or emotional disorder rather than intense temperament. Chess's work with rubella children suggests that a multiplicity of handicaps in a child makes him more vulnerable to emotionally disturbed and disturbing behavior. Therefore, the distinction between the range of normal individual variations in any developmental functions and specific deviations is necessary for the appropriate understanding and guidance of individual children.

E. S. and R. J. R.

Part III
Intervention: Interventions for Deviant Development

13

Biological Interventions in Psychoses of Childhood

MAGDA CAMPBELL

An up-to-date review of biological interventions in psychoses of childhood is presented here, together with occasional comments on efficacy based on the author's experience. After brief mention of earlier forms of biological–organic treatment (psychosurgery, insulin, and electroconvulsive therapies), the review focuses on drug therapy. Relative prominence is given to major tranquilizers, lithium, and the hormones. Suitable information is also presented on hypnotics, anticonvulsants, sedatives, stimulants, antidepressant drugs, minor tranquilizers, hallucinogens, L-dopa, and vitamins. It is suggested that no specific drug is available for the treatment of any diagnostic category. Currently available drugs are most effective in reducing such symptoms as insomnia, hyperactivity, impulsivity, irritability, disorganized behavior, psychotic thought disorder, and certain types of aggressivity. The need for uniformity in the classification of child psychoses is stressed in light of its potential value in predicting responses of children to specific drugs.

All psychiatric disturbances in early childhood can be viewed as delays, exaggerations, or distortions of development that yield fixations and regressions. The most severe distortions are seen in the childhood psychoses involving major behavioral disturbances and overall retardation.

A great need for classification in the area of infantile psychoses still persists. The same symptoms, including autism, may be caused by a variety of etiologic factors, which may affect the individual's response to treatment. It has not been settled whether early infantile autism is a separate entity from childhood

---

MAGDA CAMPBELL · Department of Psychiatry, New York University Medical Center, New York, New York 10016.

schizophrenia, or its earliest expression (Bender, 1967, 1973; Eisenberg, 1957, 1972; Goldfarb, 1961; Kanner, 1943; Piggott and Gottlieb, 1973; Rimland, 1964; Ruttenberg, 1974; Rutter, 1972). In addition, children who suffer from brain damage of a known etiologic factor (i.e., congenital rubella) and are mentally retarded and autistic, are often misdiagnosed as early infantile autistic. However, efforts have been made to establish certain descriptive diagnostic criteria (Creak, 1961).

The promotion of development and maturation constitutes the essence of psychiatric treatment of young children. Age is an important factor. The younger child is more globally affected by the psychosis and requires more intensive treatment. Total treatment comprising a well-structured clinical residential or day program with individual planning and highly individualized therapeutic objectives is essential for each psychotic child of preschool age. Thus, the promotion of development in psychotic children usually calls for a multidisciplinary approach intended to include special education, individual and speech therapy, and also work with parents. All such forms of treatment represent an attempt to manipulate the environment so as to evoke a therapeutic change in the child. Biological therapies, on the other hand, are in a more immediate manner directed toward the organism or the central nervous system.

Biological interventions in the treatment of psychotic conditions in childhood are largely confined to the use of a variety of drugs. Psychosurgery and convulsive therapies have been replaced by psychopharmacology, a rapidly developing specialization that appears to have made some inroads into the rather conservative field of child psychiatry. After a brief mention of earlier forms of biological—organic treatment, this presentation will focus on drug therapy. It is intended to provide an up-to-date review of principal drug agents with occasional comments on efficacy based on the author's experience in the treatment of psychotic children.

PHYSICAL THERAPIES

At present, in child psychiatry, all forms of physical therapies have practically disappeared from practice. The use of electroshock treatment in catatonic states in adolescence constitutes about the sole remaining exception.

Psychosurgery

Brain surgery in the form of lobotomy was developed by Egas Moniz (1936) and first performed by Almeida Lima. Modified in this country by Freeman, it was found unsatisfactory in operations involving children (Williams and Freeman, 1953; Freeman, 1959). Lobotomy and topectomy (excision of portions of the frontal cortex) were intended to eliminate symptoms of aggressiveness in children (Ajuriaguerra, 1971).

Insulin Shock Therapy

This form of treatment, introduced by Sakel (1938), has been applied to schizophrenic children in Europe (Annell, 1955; Heuyer, Lang, and Rivaille, 1956), reportedly with satisfactory results with respect to promotion of maturation.

Electroconvulsive Therapy

In this country, convulsive therapy, as first described by Cerletti and Bini in 1938 (Cerletti, 1950), was used extensively in the treatment of young schizophrenic children (without ill effects on development) by Lauretta Bender. The children were said to tolerate shock treatment better than adults. Although the schizophrenic process did not seem to be modified, certain symptoms decreased and the children were "better able to accept teaching or psychotherapy in groups or individually" (Bender, 1947). There was an indication that shock therapy prompted a reorganization, resulting in a more integrated body image (Bender and Keeler, 1952). Intellectual functioning also improved in some children, although not statistically significantly (Gurewitz and Helme, 1954).

Electroconvulsive therapy has also been used to treat manic-depressive and other depressive conditions (Campbell, 1955; Frommer, 1968). In this author's limited experience with two preschool schizophrenic children who failed to respond to other treatment modalities (including drug therapy), shock treatment yielded some positive though transient behavioral changes. Of note were gains in the children's weight and height.

Other Convulsive Agents

In adult schizophrenics, pharmacological convulsive agents were reported to be more effective than electroshock. Hexafluorodiethyl ether (Indoklon) was described by Krantz, Truitt, Spears, and Ling (1957). Indoklon was administered (i.v.) by this author to a 4-year-old schizophrenic child with resulting therapeutic changes such as decreases in irritability and certain compulsive mannerisms.

DRUG THERAPY

In addition to the almost chaotic state of diagnosis, research in children's psychopharmacology with the exception of "hyperkinetic syndrome" or minimal brain dysfunction is much less advanced than in the adult population of psychiatric patients. This is partly due to the fact that in its beginnings psychopharmacology in children was without methodology, such as was available to adults (Eisenberg, 1964; Fish, 1968). Reliable, standardized measures assessing the child's initial state and reflecting specific types of change due to different types of treatment were not available. Investigators had to develop their own measures, appropriate to the population of children and their status (inpatient or clinic). The diversity of the rating scales, even though used in diagnostically presumably identical populations, made communication between investigators very difficult. The rating scales for children that have recently become available were not developed specifically for autistics, but rather for a spectrum of behavioral disorders (National Institute of Mental Health, Psychopharmacology Research Branch, Early Clinical Drug Evaluation Unit, Assessment Battery for Pediatric Psychopharmacology). In addition, young psychotic children's responses to any available treatment, including pharmacotherapy, are rarely dramatic. Measures are often not sufficiently sensitive to reflect changes in this population produced by drugs, and this is only worsened by the fact that the psychotic child's behavior is often variable and unpredictable.

In the population under discussion, the elementary requirements for evaluating the efficacy of drug treatment in children, outlined by Eisenberg (1964),[*] were only infrequently met and the problems are challenging. More recently, these issues have been reviewed by Conners (1973), and Sprague and Werry, (1971).

The specification of the phenomenon to be studied in this population is not only psychosis but also the associated mental retardation. Currently available drugs may be effective in reducing symptoms, such as hyperactivity, irritability, etc., but they cannot create intelligence. In adult psychotics, functions are present but deviate, and administration of a drug such as chlorpromazine results, among other effects, in correction of mentation.

Even the mute, catatonic schizophrenic adult has once spoken, while in many young psychotic children functions such as language and adaptive skills have to be developed, and not merely returned to normal levels. Drugs with sedative effects might be even contraindicated, since they interfere with func-

---

[*]Specification of the phenomenon to be studied; accurate instruments to measure the phenomenon; control for subject variables likely to influence the outcome; random assignment to treatment groups; numbers sufficient to permit statistical analysis of findings; representative study population; and double blind conditions.

tioning. The effect of drugs on cognition is of utmost importance in children; reports are sparse and conflicting concerning this issue in psychotics treated with major tranquilizers, mainly phenothiazines, although there is some evidence that these drugs have a negative effect on cognitive behavior (Eisenberg and Conners, 1971; Freeman, 1966, 1970; Hartlage, 1965; Helper, Wilcott, and Garfield, 1963; Lipman, 1971; McAndrew, Case, and Treffert, 1972; Sprague and Werry, 1971; Werry, Weiss, Douglas, and Martin, 1966).

Knowledge is still limited concerning the late effects of pharmacotherapy, influencing growth, weight, endocrine systems and organs, as well as withdrawal phenomena (Crane, 1973; DiMascio, Soltys, and Shader, 1970; Martini and Ganong, 1971; McAndrew, Case, and Treffert, 1972; Polizos, Englehardt, Hoffman, and Waizer, 1973; Safer and Allen, 1973; Schaub, Soulairac, and Franchimont, 1971; Sherman, Kim, Benjamin, and Kolodny, 1971). However, normal growth patterns are seen in psychotic children who never received pharmacotherapy (Campbell *et al.* in preparation; Dutton, 1964; Simon and Gillies, 1964).

Drug side effects in children are not different from those seen in adults (DiMascio, Soltys, and Shader, 1970) although the young child appears to be biologically more sturdy. Extrapyramidal signs are less frequent in children than in mature adults. Behavioral side effects are frequently seen before other signs and symptoms of excess drug occur (Campbell and Shapiro, 1975).

The possible therapeutic effectiveness and hazards of drug treatment have to be carefully weighed in view of the poor prognosis and the severe limitations of all other available (often lengthy) therapeutic modalities.

Experience has shown that drug treatment is frequently a valuable component of the total treatment of the psychotic child. Certain psychoactive agents can make such a child more amenable to educational and play therapies. Even when a comprehensive treatment program is not available, drug induced therapeutic changes can make the psychotic child more manageable and easier to live with in the community.

Hypnotics, Anticonvulsants, and Antihistaminics

Hypnotics and anticonvulsants have been in use for a long time. However, because of the advent of major tranquilizers, they no longer have a place in the therapeutic arsenal. Actually, barbiturates may increase disorganization in the severely disturbed child.

Diphenhydramine (benadryl) was found effective even in some schizophrenic children, particularly in those with higher IQs (Effron and Freedman, 1953; Fish, 1963; Silver, 1955). It appears that benadryl has not been sufficiently explored in severe behavioral disorders of childhood and that the cause of such failure may be traced to doses, usually neither individualized nor sufficiently high. Prior to placing a schizophrenic child on a major tranquilizer, it is worthwhile to try benadryl as a first stage of drug therapy. It is a safe drug, easy to regulate, and potentially useful to merit exploration.

Stimulant and Antidepressant Drugs

The psychomotor stimulants, benzedrine and d-amphetamine (dexedrine), have been in use in child psychiatry since the 1930's (Bradley, 1937; Bradley and Bowen, 1941; Bender, and Cottington, 1942; Bender and Nichtern, 1956; Fish, 1971). Therapeutic results in psychotic children were minimal, absent, or more frequently poor. In our experience, nonpsychotic children tolerate higher doses of D-amphetamine than the schizophrenic and autistic, who often become more psychotic and disorganized, even on very low doses, regardless of hyperactivity (Campbell, Fish, David, Shapiro, Collins, and Koh, 1972a, Campbell, Fish, Shapiro, and Floyd, 1972c). The psychotic child who shows some overall improvement on D-amphetamine, with a decrease in hyperactivity and an increase in attention span, may at the same time become more withdrawn and less verbal.

More recently, L-amphetamine (cydril) has been found effective in some disturbed children, particularly in reference to decreasing hyperactivity and aggressiveness (Arnold, Wender, McCloskey, and Snyder, 1972; Arnold, Kirilcuk, Corson, and Corson, 1973). It was hypothesized that L-amphetamine "via dopaminergic mechanism, may equal dextroamphetamine in benefiting the subgroup of hyperkinetic children who could be diagnosed as unsocialized aggressive by Fish's criteria. If so, this might eventually make levo-amphetamine with its lower anorexogenic potency and lower potential for abuse, the drug of choice for this subgroup" (Arnold and Wender, 1975).

Since a great number of young psychotic children are not only hyperactive but also quite aggressive (aggressiveness manifested toward others or in the form of self-mutilating behavior), which interferes with social life and learning (Campbell and Hersh, 1971), we hoped that by controlling aggressiveness with L-amphetamine the child would be able to develop positive and adaptive social interactions that in turn would improve learning (Corson, Corson, Kirilcuk, Knopp, and Arnold, 1972). We also hoped that L-amphetamine, because its effects are mediated via dopaminergic neurons (Snyder, Taylor, Coyle, and Meyerhoff, 1970; Taylor and Snyder, 1970) may have less untoward effects on psychotic children than D-amphetamine, which, in our experience was a poor drug for both hyperkinetic and hypoactive patients.

Our experience with L-amphetamine in psychotic children is very limited (Campbell, Small, Collins, Friedman, David, and Genieser, 1976). Although increases in attention span were noted, the child frequently also became less verbal and more stereotyped, or stereotypies *de novo* were observed. In general, therapeutic changes were minor and few, and were usually outweighed by worsening of preexisting symptoms.

Both the tricyclic antidepressants (amitryptyline and imipramine) and the monoamine oxidase inhibitors (phenelzine and isocarboxazid) were used extensively by Frommer (1968) in an outpatient population of childhood depressives as young as 2½ years of age.

Kurtis (1966) treated 16 autistic children, 4 to 15 years of age, with nortriptyline, an imipraminelike antidepressant. These children were mute or had only psychotic speech. Their symptoms, quite difficult to manage, had been refractory to previously applied medication, particularly to tranquilizers. Among other symptoms, nortriptyline proved instrumental in influencing hyperactivity, aggressivity, and destructiveness.

In our pilot study of imipramine in 10 schizophrenic and autistic children, 2 to 6 years of age, the overall effect of the drug was infrequently therapeutic and usually outweighed by toxic effects, showing a mixture of stimulating, tranquilizing, and disorganizing actions. We suggested that imipramine merits further exploration in the most retarded, mute, anergic psychotics, and in children with only borderline or little psychotic symptomatology (Campbell, Fish, Shapiro, and Floyd, 1971b). Our findings were similar to those of Gershon, Holmberg, Mattson, and Marshall (1962), Klein, and Fink (1962) and also to Pollack, Klein, Willner, Blumberg, and Fink (1965), in relation to adult schizophrenics. Frommer (1968) also suggested that the "same contraindications as for adults apply" to the treatment of children with antidepressants, and that monoamine oxidase inhibitors may cause disorganization of behavior. One must conclude that well-controlled studies with homogeneous populations are needed in this area.

Major Tranquilizers

While the role of barbiturates and other sedatives was only to facilitate management of the agitated and acutely disturbed child, the advent of major tranquilizers created hope that these agents may also be of therapeutic value. It was anticipated that these agents would achieve (1) an antipsychotic effect so that the psychotic process would be arrested or decreased and the child, initially in a state of withdrawal and/or apathy, would become less resistant to educational and other therapies; and (2) a symptomatic effect to decrease anxiety, hyperactivity or aggressiveness, such as that expressed in the form of self-mutilation, that would permit the child to develop more adaptive and socially acceptable patterns of behavior that facilitate learning.

Phenothiazines

Both chlorpromazine (thorazine) and thioridazine (mellaril), the sedative type of this class of drugs, are widely used (Lipman, 1970). However, well-controlled studies and experimental findings are extremely sparse. Although chlorpromazine is of inestimable value for children with onset of psychosis at school age, and particularly for adolescents with acute symptomatology (where its effect and the results were similar to those in adults), the young psychotic child is often excessively sedated at doses that control certain psychotic symptoms, and thus are not amenable to educational therapy. In our experience many young psychotic children exhibit sleepiness and psychomotor retardation even at very low doses of chlorpromazine, irrespective of body weight and either presence or absence of hyperactivity and aggressiveness (Fish, Campbell, Shapiro, and Floyd, 1969a; Campbell, Fish, Korein, Shapiro, Collins, and Koh, 1972b; Campbell, Fish, Shapiro, and Floyd, 1972c). Thus, an extremely hyperactive and aggressive schizophrenic boy, 5 years and 8 months of age and weighing 57 pounds, was sleepy on 20 mg per day; a 3-year-old, retarded, hypoactive, and irritable girl, weighing 29 pounds, fell asleep on 10 mg per day within less than 20 minutes after administration.

Clincal experience prompted Fish to suggest that very young autistic children, often apathetic and anergic, resemble chronic adult schizophrenics in their responses to drugs (Fish, 1960, 1970). It was thus expected that they will respond better to the more potent and less sedative phenothiazines than chlorpromazine. Trifluoperazine (stelazine), a piperazine derivative, proved to be somewhat better than chlorpromazine (Fish, 1960; Fish, 1968; Fish, Shapiro, and Campbell, 1966). Even with the high doses, this drug only seldom produced dystonic reactions in this young age group, while in older children such extrapyramidal side effects often limit its use. Fluphenazine (prolixin, permitil), another compound with a piperazine sidechain, was found to be highly effective in prepubertal severely disturbed schizophrenic and autistic children (Engelhardt, Polizos, and Margolis, 1972; Engelhardt, Polizos, Waizer, and Hoffman, 1973).

Butyrophenones

This class of major tranquilizers proved to be particularly useful in chronic schizophrenic adults, whose predominant symptoms were autism, apathy, and inertia (Gallant, Bishop, Nesselhoff, and Sprehe, 1965; Fox, Gobble, Clos, and Denison, 1964).

The combination of excitatory psychomotor and antipsychotic properties of trifluperidol prompted us to explore its effects in preschool-age, retarded schizophrenic, and autistic children. It proved to be an antipsychotic agent with stimulating qualities, significantly more effective in the same subjects than chlorpromazine or trifluoperazine (Fish *et al.,* 1969a; Campbell *et al.,* 1972c). The most responsive symptoms were psychotic speech, underproductive speech, withdrawal, and apathy. However, the relatively narrow therapeutic index, with extrapyramidal symptoms at doses 1.3 and 2 times higher than the optimal, limited trifluperidol to investigational use and even resulted in its subsequent· withdrawal.

Haloperidol (haldol), also a butyrophenone, has been demonstrated as a potent antipsychotic agent in schizophrenic (Engelhardt *et al.,* 1973) and mentally retarded children with severe "emotional disturbance." According to Burk and Menolascino (1968) and also LeVann (1969), it was particularly effective in reducing or controlling hyperactivity, assaultiveness, and self-injury in both retarded and nonretarded children. Haloperidol is now on the market for patients whose age exceeds 12 years; for younger children it is still at the stage of investigational use.

Thioxanthenes

Thiothixene (navane) was found to have both stimulating and antipsychotic properties, not unlike trifluperidol, in adult schizophrenics (Gallant, Bishop, and Shelton, 1966; Gallant, Bishop, Timmons, and Gould, 1966; Simpson and Igbal, 1965; Sugerman, Stolberg, and Herrmann, 1965). Our group investigated the possible beneficial effects of this drug in retarded schizophrenic children of preschool age (Fish, Campbell, Shapiro, and Weinstein, 1969c; Campbell, Fish, Shapiro, and Floyd, 1970). Later, other investigators (Simeon, Saletu, Saletu, Itil, and DaSilva, 1973; Waizer, Polizos, Hoffman, Engelhardt, and Margolis, 1972) confirmed our findings that thiothixene proved in daily doses from 1 to 40 mg, with a wide therapeutic margin, an effective, safe therapeutic agent in psychotic children. Again, it is the combination of stimulating and antipsychotic properties that makes this drug superior to phenothiazines in young children. It appears that chlorprothixene (taractan) has a profile of action similar to that of thiothixene (Oettinger, 1962).

Indoles

Molindone hydrochloride was found to have antipsychotic and stimulant properties in chronic schizophrenic adults (Gallant and Bishop, 1968; Simpson and Krakov, 1968; Sugerman and Herrmann, 1967). The combination of these two properties prompted us to explore this drug in very young, severely disturbed patients, including some who were apathetic and anergic. Our pilot study involved 10 children (8 schizophrenic and 2 nonpsychotic), whose ages ranged from 3 to 5 years. Because molindone had occasionally stimulating as well as sedative therapeutic effects, it was felt that it should be further explored in a larger sample of patients (Campbell, Fish, Shapiro, and Floyd, 1971a). To the best of our knowledge, we were the only ones to study this compound in children.

Minor Tranquilizers

Chlordiazepoxide (librium) was reported to be helpful in reducing anxiety in inhibited phobic children. It seems to be less effective or even contraindicated in certain diagnostic categories or behavioral profiles. LaVeck and Buckley (1961) reported an increase in "undesirable behavior," and hyperactivity and decreased attention span in a group of 28 retarded and disturbed children. LeVann (1962), while treating 47 mentally retarded children with behavioral disorders, reported an acute paranoid reaction in an epileptic. Skynner (1961) also found a worsening of hyperactivity and aggressiveness in similar children who exhibited these symptoms prior to chlordiazepoxide treatment. Pilkington (1961a, 1961b) commented on worsening of symptomatology in retarded schizophrenics, while Kraft, Ardali, Duffy, Hart, and Pearce (1965) reported improvement in two schizophrenic children on this drug.

It appears that chlordiazepoxide with its stimulating (mood-elevating, euphoric) actions may worsen the psychosis or even cause a florid psychosis in children with borderline schizophrenic features.

Other minor tranquilizers are usually ineffective in the treatment of severely disturbed children.

Hallucinogens

The use of these psychoactive agents in the treatment of psychotic children was introduced by Lauretta Bender. She reported that LSD-25 (D-lysergic acid diethylamide) administered to 26 schizophrenic children, and methysergide—a methylated derivative of LSD (L-methyl-D-lysergic acid butanolamide bimaleate, sansert)—given to 28, for a period of up to one year, were effective stimulants leading to improvement in behavior (Bender, Goldschmidt, and Sankar, 1962; Bender, Faretra, and Cobrinik, 1963; Bender, Cobrinik, Faretra, and Sankar, 1966). Bender's patients were 6 to 12 years of age. Therapeutic changes included increases in motor initiation and alertness, and decreases in stereotypy and psychotic speech. However, there was an increase in anxiety and disorganization in some older, more verbal schizophrenic children exposed to these hallucinogens. Clinical trials with LSD-25 in autistic and schizophrenic children were also reported by Freedman, Ebin, and Wilson (1962), and Simmons, Leiken, Lovaas, Schaeffer, and Perloff (1966). The results reported by Rolo, Krinsky, Abramson, and Goldfarb (1965) were inconclusive.

Fish, Campbell, Shapiro, and Floyd (1969b) carried out a pilot study of methysergide on 11 retarded schizophrenic children, 2 to 5 years of age, over a period of 3 to 11 weeks. Most patients manifested a mixed reduction and worsening of symptoms, similar to those observed by Freedman *et al.* (1962) in the acute study of LSD-25 in older schizophrenic children. Only the two most retarded, mute psychotic children improved, exhibiting increased alertness, affective responsiveness and goal directedness.

Lithium

In adults, this ion has a well-established role in the treatment of the manic phase of recurrent manic-depressive illness, which probably does not exist under 10 years of age. It also appears to be of value as a prophylactic agent for recurrent manic-depressive illness and periodic endogenous depression. There are some indications in the literature that lithium maintenance may have "a stabilizing and normalizing action" in children and adolescents with "undulating or periodic disturbances of mood and behavior" (Schou, 1972).

Frommer (1968) treated hypomanic and depressed children, 4 to 14 years of age, with small doses of lithium (50 to 250 mg per day), either alone or together with antidepressants. Annell (1969a, 1969b) administered lithium to older children, in daily doses from 900 to 1800 mg (serum lithium level of 0.6 to 1.2 mEq/liter). The patients were reported to manifest typical manic conditions, periodic conditions other than mania (with a high incidence of periodic psychosis, and manic-depressive illness in relatives), and even schizophrenia. Most of Annell's patients responded favorably. Dyson and Barcai (1970) found lithium effective while treating two boys whose parents were lithium responders suffering from manic-depressive illness. However, the diagnoses of these young patients were unclear.

Whitehead and Clark (1970) found no difference between the effect of lithium and placebo on hyperactivity, while noting a slight decrease in this symptom on thioridazine. In this pilot study of 7 prepuberal children, one psychotic patient showed an overall improvement, while the condition of others remained unchanged. Gram and Rafaelsen (1972) in their controlled clinical trial of lithium in 18 psychotic subjects (8 to 22 years of age) reported a decrease in hyperactivity, aggressiveness, stereotypies, and psychotic speech.

The effects of lithium in counteracting aggression were established in animal work (Weischer, 1969; Sheard, 1970a, 1970b) and noted in adult human subjects (Sheard, 1971a, 1971b; Tupin and Smith, 1972). Dostal (1972) found that lithium had a significant "affect-damping and antiaggressive" effect in treating 14 mentally retarded, aggressive, and hyperactive phenothiazine-resistant boys. However, the antiaggressive effects of lithium were seen only when aggressiveness was associated with excitability and explosiveness.

The action of lithium on hyperexcitability suggested that we should investigate its possible therapeutic effects in hyperactive psychotic and nonpsychotic children and compare such effects with those of chlorpromazine (Campbell *et al.*, 1972b). The 10 children involved in this controlled crossover study were 3 to 6 years of age. While more individual symptoms diminished on chlorpromazine than on lithium, improvements were only slight on both drugs, except in one schizophrenic child whose self-mutilating behavior and explosiveness practically ceased on lithium.

A most interesting finding in that study was the role of the child's EEG as a predictor of "lithium responders"; if the drug accentuated the focal abnormality, behavior either deteriorated or remained unchanged. Behavioral improvement usually occurred when the focal abnormality was decreased by the drug, or when the drug caused increases in diffuse slow activity and a slowing of α in normal EEGs (rather than no changes in EEG). Such relationships between EEG and clinical responses applied to lithium as well as to chlorpromazine.

We believe that lithium merits further exploration in psychotic and retarded children whose aggressive or self-mutilating behavioral manifestations with excitability represent prominent symptoms, and when such symptoms prove to be refractory to standard drugs (Campbell, 1973).

L-*Dopa*

Psychiatry's interest in L-dopa can be traced to reports of many behavioral effects that this compound produced in patients with Parkinson's disease. Psychomotor activation, awakening–alerting effect, improvement in cognitive function, elation, and depression were reliably observed in Parkinsonian patients receiving L-dopa by various investigators (Arbit, Boshes, and Blonsky, 1970; Loranger, Goodell, Lee, and McDowell, 1972; O'Brien, DiGiacomo, Fahn, and Schwarz, 1971). The antidepressant effect of L-dopa was reported in some adults with retarded depression, and it was noted that this drug enhanced learning and memory in depressed patients (Goodwin, Murphy, Brodie, and Bunney, 1970; Murphy 1972b).

L-Dopa's biochemical effects on the brain include the elevation of dopamine, which may be related to its behavioral effects. In experimental mice it produces a marked decrease in brain serotonin (Everett and Borcherding, 1970); it may enter central serotonin terminals with ensuing displacement of the endogenous serotonin from vesicular stores (Butcher, Engel, and Fuxe, 1970; Ng, Chase, Colburn, and Kopin, 1970).

Since serotonin abnormalities were found in the blood of some autistic, schizophrenic, and other retarded children (Schain and Freedman, 1961; Ritvo, Yuwiler, Geller, Ornitz, Saeger, and Plotkin, 1970; Coleman, 1970, 1973) and in the platelets of children with a diagnosis of infantile autism (Boullin, Coleman, and O'Brien, 1970; Boullin, Coleman, O'Brien, and Rimland, 1971), Ritvo and his associates carried out a study in order to determine whether clinical and biochemical changes might occur in autistic children if their blood serotonin was lowered. Four autistic children were placed on L-dopa maintenance for 6 months. Although a significant decrease of blood serotonin concentrations was noted in 3 children, this was not accompanied by clinical changes (Ritvo, Yuwiler, Geller, Kales, Rashkis, Schicor, Plotkin, Axelrod, and Howard, 1971). Children who showed a lowering of blood serotonin were 3 to 9 years of age. The child who failed to follow the pattern was 13 years old. One can speculate that the patient's age or stage of illness was possibly the factor responsible for the failure to elicit a therapeutic response.

We initiated a study of L-dopa in severely disturbed preschool children (most were schizophrenic), even though we knew that L-dopa was reported to produce exacerbation of psychosis in schizophrenic adults (Angrist, Sathananthan, and Gershon, 1973). Our experience with some very young retarded schizophrenic and autistic children indicated that certain drugs that may produce excessive excitement and/or deterioration in acute schizophrenic adults proved to be therapeutic when administered to such children (Campbell *et al.*, 1971b, 1972b). On daily doses of 900 to 2250 mg, therapeutic changes such as gain in social initiation, verbal production and play, and decreases in withdrawal and psychotic speech were in evidence. Also, hypoactive and apathetic children demonstrated increases in motor initiation and affective responsiveness (Campbell *et al.*, 1976).

Hormones

Endocrine systems and psychoneuroendocrine interrelations in adult depressives as well as in schizophrenic adults and adolescents were studied for sometime (Anderson and Dawson, 1965; Brambilla and Penati, 1971; Durell, Libow, Kellam, and Shader, 1963; Gjessing, 1938, 1953; Hoskins, 1946; Persky, Zuckerman, and Curtis, 1968; Reiss, 1954, 1958; Prange and Lipton, 1972; Sachar, 1963; Sachar, Harmatz, Bergen, and Cohler, 1966; Sachar, Hellman, Roffwarg, Halpern, Fukushima, and Gallagher, 1973). The variations of behavioral and endocrine parameters with various biological treatments were also investigated, suggesting possible correlations between endocrine and behavioral characteristics, and implying that simultaneous treatment of both parameters may yield better and more lasting results (Brambilla and Penati, 1971; Reiss, 1954).

Although various endocrine anomalies were found in psychiatric patients, hormones were usually administered not as replacements but as drugs (Hoskins, 1946; Reiss, 1954, 1958, 1971). Long-term daily administration of human chorionic gonadotropin (HCG) to children from socially deprived homes with stunted longitudinal and mental growth and retarded gonadal development produced an increase in 17-ketosteroid excretion rate and also progress in the rate of growth. This was accompanied by behavioral and academic improvement with increased IQ. Increase in growth hormone content of the blood was found on the first day of treatment, and the increased growth rate did not cease even long after discontinuation of the treatment with HCG. Previously these children failed to improve in an enriched therapeutic environment (Reiss, 1971).

Thyroid anomalies were found by several investigators in some adult schizophrenics, especially in those with periodic manifestations of the psychosis (Durell *et al.*, 1963; Gjessing, 1938, 1953; Hoskins, 1946; Simpson, Cranswick, and Blair, 1963, 1964). Although behavioral improvements in schizophrenics (with or without thyroid dysfunction) treated with desiccated thyroid or triiodothyronine (T_3) were reported (Danziger, 1958; Danziger and Kindwall, 1953; Hoskins, 1946), the most impressive results with these hormones were obtained by Gjessing (1932, 1938, 1953), who managed to prevent the reccurrence of periodic psychosis.

T_3 was effective in the treatment of depressions in adults, either alone (Feldmesser–Reiss, 1958; Wilson, Prange, and Lara, 1972) or in conjunction with imipramine (Prange, Wilson, Rabon, and Lipton, 1969; Wilson, Prange, McClane, Rabon, and Lipton, 1970). To the best of our knowledge, thyroid hormones were not used in the treatment of depressive conditions in childhood.

Sherwin, Flach, and Stokes (1958) used T_3 in the treatment of two 6-year-old autistic "euthyroid" boys. Their encouraging results included increases in alertness, social and affective contact, and speech, as well as decreases in stereotypy on 50 μg or higher daily doses. The clinical trial was followed by our controlled study involving a relatively large number of preschool schizophrenic and other severely disturbed patients and intended to examine the parameters of thyroid functions in greater detail (Campbell *et al.*, 1972a; Campbell, Fish, David, Shapiro, Collins, and Koh, 1973).

Blind ratings on optimal daily doses ranging from 12.5 to 75 μg ($M = 46.25$) indicated statistically significant improvement in overall symptomatology. Due to its antipsychotic and stimulating effects, T_3 is viewed as an agent that is potentially effective in the treatment of childhood schizophrenia and autism.

It is difficult to explain the therapeutic effects of T_3 in the psychotic group, since hypo- and hyperactive children responded equally well, and since four of the improved schizophrenic children had somewhat elevated baseline T_4 levels (thyroxine iodine by column chromatography and "free" thyroxine). A review of pertinent literature shows that while many schizophrenic adults treated with thyroid hormone were euthyroid by ordinary standards, some were also found to be hypothyroid. However, in adults with periodic catatonia a shift from the euthyroid toward a relatively hyperthyroid state was said to have taken place immediately before, or roughly at the time of the psychotic episode (Gjessing, 1932, 1938, 1953; Durell *et al.*, 1963).

Gjessing, as well as some other investigators (Durell *et al.*, 1963; Hoskins, 1946) hypothesized that diencephalic (hypothalamic) mechanisms involved in schizophrenia result in a general lack of integration and that the same mechanisms are responsible for dysthyroidal states. The therapeutic effect of T_3 in a subgroup of our schizophrenic children (with somewhat elevated baseline T_4) might be related to its stabilizing effect on the hypothalamic-pituitary axis, and more immediate effects on its interaction with biogenic amines (serotonin and dopamine). Careful clinical studies with detailed workup are needed to evaluate the relevance of biochemical and neuroendocrine changes in response to T_3 and correlate such changes with behavioral manifestations and therapeutic response. Until the results of such studies are available, the use of T_3 should be limited to investigative objectives.

Monoamine neurotransmitters are said to control the secretion of hypothalmic releasing factors, including the thyrotropin releasing factor (TRH), and of anterior pituitary hormones (thyrotropin, TSH), which in turn control the secretion of thyroid hormones (Anton-Tay & Wurtman, 1971; McCann, 1971). Serotonin, one of such neurotransmitters implicated in affecting behavior, was found to be elevated in the blood of some retarded and psychotic children (Campbell, Friedman, DeVito, Greenspan, and Collins, 1974; Campbell, Friedman, Green, Collins, Small, and Breuer, 1975; Ritvo *et al.*, 1970; Schain and Freedman, 1961), and its efflux from platelets was reportedly increased in autistic children compared to normal (Boullin *et al.*, 1970, 1971). Thus, alterations in neuronal transmission of serotonergic and other neuronal systems (dopaminergic and noradrenergic) could lead to, or be associated with, thyroidal as well as behavioral changes. Central nervous system dysfunction responsible for a general lack of integration or adaptive inefficiency may be reflected at all levels.

The thyroid hormone plays an important role in the maturation and development of the CNS (Eayrs, 1968; Sokoloff and Roberts, 1971), and animal studies have demonstrated that the long-term effects of dysthyroidal states (both hypo- and hyperthyroid) are deleterious to cerebral development during the early stages of life (Balázs, Kovács, Cocks, Johnson, and Eayrs, 1971, Eayrs, 1968; Schapiro, 1971).

Some of the developmental lags or defects in childhood schizophrenia and other severe disturbances of early childhood (of unknown origin) might be altered or replaced by biological substances, including hormones (such as T_3) or even neurohormones (such as TRH). Our limited experience with T_3 supports this.

ORTHOMOLECULAR PSYCHIATRY

The concept of "orthomolecular" treatment in psychiatry was introduced by Linus Pauling in an article published in 1968. Pauling suggested that this method constituted the "treatment of mental disease by the provision of the optimum molecular environment for the mind, especially the optimum concentration of substances normally present in the human body." Deficiencies of certain vital substance(s) in the brain may lead to mental illness. These deficiencies may not exist in the peripheral blood and lymph; they may be "localized cerebral deficiency diseases." Pauling believes that the brain is probably more sensitive to changes in concentrations of these vital substances than any other organ, and that there could be a decreased permeability of the blood–brain barrier or an increased rate of metabolism of the vital substance(s) in the brain of certain individuals, including schizophrenic patients, on a genetic basis.

Ascorbic acid, thiamine, pyridoxine, folic acid, and other substances (normally present in the organism), such as L-(+)-glutamic acid, were investigated as a therapeutic substance in animal work and in psychiatric patients.

Successful treatment of adult stuporous psychiatric patients (most were elderly with arteriosclerosis) with moderately large doses of nicotinic acid was reported prior to World War II by Cleckley, Sydenstricker, and Geeslin (1939). Hoffer and Osmond, who used large doses of nicotinic acid or nicotinamide in the treatment of schizophrenia (Osmond and Hoffer, 1962; Hoffer, 1973; Osmond, 1973), reported good results. Some of these studies were controlled and the follow-ups reported. However, collaborative studies with large numbers of newly admitted as well as chronic schizophrenic adults did not substantiate Hoffer's and Osmond's findings. Clinical trials with nicotinic acid yielded either no therapeutic effect or even negative effects (Ban, 1971; Ban and Lehmann, 1970; McGrath, O'Brien, Power, and Shea, 1972; Mosher, 1970; Ramsey, Ban, Lehmann, Saxena, and Bennett, 1970; Wittenborn, Weber, and Brown, 1973).

While Hoffer reported that niacinamide and ascorbic acid proved superior to placebo in children (1970), Greenbaum (1970) could not confirm these findings in a double-blind study of 17 children receiving niacinamide and 24, a placebo. Even Rimland, a strong advocate of megavitamine therapy, calls the results of this treatment only "encouraging." In a preliminary report, he detailed the results of a study of 190 outpatient psychotic children receiving megadoses of vitamins over a period of 24 weeks with a month-long vitamin-free period at the end of that study (Rimland, 1973). The vitamin regime consisted of increasing doses of niacinamide, ascorbic acid, pyridoxine, and pantothenic acid, in addition to multiple B tablets, following a certain schedule. Parents were to record their observations semimonthly with the physicians each month rating behaviors such as "change in speech, alertness, irritability, understanding, eating, sleeping, social responsiveness, tantrums, and overall behavior." Criteria of vitamin efficacy were the reports of parents and physicians during the vitamin therapy period, during the nonvitamin treatment period, and also whether or not the vitamins were reordered. All data were subjected to statistical analysis. The subgroup of 37 children identified as having "classical infantile autism" showed the greatest improvement on the regime, particularly the 6 who were receiving dilantin together with vitamins. Among "specific" vitamin effects, increases in alertness, social awareness, and sociability were reported with vitamin C. Niacinamide "appeared" to have an antipsychotic effect, while pantothenic acid made some children more alert, calmer, and more accessible. The most obvious changes were attributed to vitamin B6, particularly in increasing the initiation of speech and verbal production. However, some children showed a worsening of behavior, including hyperactivity and irritability, among other side effects. According to the "overall improvement" ratings, 45.3% of the group showed definite improvement, 41.0% possible improvement, 10.5% no improvement, and only 3.1% of the children in the group manifested adverse effects. It is not clear how many children were on psychoactive drugs (other than dilantin and mellaril) concomitantly with vitamins, and whether any differential response to megavitamin treatment was in evidence. It is also not clear what diagnostic categories other than early infantile autism were involved in the study (although presumably some children were schizophrenic). One might also mention the absence of data pertaining to the age of children or treatment program (other than megavitamin therapy) to which some, if not most, must have been exposed.

An American Psychiatric Association (APA) task force, after an impressively thorough investigation, came to the conclusion that megavitamin therapy does not meet the "test of scientific validity" and has no value in the treatment of schizophrenia (Lipton, Ban, Kane, Levine, Mosher, and Wittenborn, 1973).

CONCLUDING NOTE

This presentation represents an attempt to outline various biological–organic interventions in childhood psychoses without due effort to evaluate the methodology employed by other investigators or consideration for the possible long-term hazards of drug therapy.

Therapeutic efforts and speculative attempts have been made for sometime to find more rational modes of treatment for the psychoses. Since the late 1920's, our libraries have been accumulating volumes devoted to research studies of biochemical, hormonal, and physiological deviations and their behavioral correlates in adults. During the past decade, many interesting hypotheses have implicated biogenic amines in depression and schizophrenia in adults, suggesting that clinical distinctions could be correlated with various biochemical criteria. It is believed that neuropharmacology of effective psychoactive drugs may facilitate insight not only into the biochemical mechanisms that serve in conjunction with certain drugs to decrease the symptoms, but also into the biology of the mental illness itself (Himwich, Kety, and Smythies, 1967; Lapin and Oxenkrug,

1969; Kety, 1972; Murphy, 1972a; Schildkraut and Kety, 1967). More recently, such investigations have also been directed toward issues more closely related to the psychoses of early childhood (Boullin, Coleman, and O'Brien, 1970; Boullin, Coleman, O'Brien, and Rimland, 1971; Campbell, Friedman, DeVito, Greenspan, and Collins, 1974; Campbell, Friedman, Green, Collins, Small, and Breuer, 1975; Coleman, 1973; Coleman, Campbell, Freedman, Roffman, Ebstein, and Goldstein, 1974; Ritvo, Yuwiler, Geller, Ornitz, Saeger, and Plotkin, 1970).

At our present state of knowledge, no specific drug is available for reliable treatment of any diagnostic categories of psychoses in early life. Currently used drugs are most effective in reducing symptoms such as insomnia, hyperactivity, impulsivity, irritability, disorganized behavior, psychotic thought disorder, and certain types of aggressivity. Thus far, lithium appears to represent the first psychoactive agent that is specific in the treatment of a well-defined condition such as the manic phase of the manic-depressive illness. It should be noted, however, that psychotic children do not necessarily respond to lithium or to the other drugs in the same manner as psychotic adults.

Experience indicates that drug treatment is an essential component of the total treatment of the psychotic child of preschool age. Such a child may no longer be as responsive to the same drug treatment at a later age as during the course of his first years of life. The severity of illness and generally poor prognosis appear to warrant the risks related to psychoactive agents. Hopefully, a more rational psychopharmacologic approach, which would consider the entire developing organism of the individual child, will lead us to more effective therapies for psychotic children.

Finally, the basic need for uniformity in the classification of childhood psychoses is still with us. We suggest that certain biochemical and neuro-endrocrine parameters will facilitate the delineation of categories in the mixed population of psychotic children. There are reasons to hope that this would be of considerable value in predicting whether a child can benefit from a specific drug.

ACKNOWLEDGMENTS

Part of this paper was read on November 1, 1973 at the First International Leo Kanner Colloquium on Child Development, Deviations, and Treatment, Chapel Hill, North Carolina. Part of the work was supported by Public Health Service Grant MH-04665 from the National Institute of Mental Health. The author wishes to thank Dr. Loren Wissner Greene for her assistance in the literature search.

REFERENCES

Ajuriaguerra, J. de. *Manuel de Psychiatrie de l'Enfant*. Paris: Masson et Cie, 1971.

Anderson, W., McC., and Dawson, J. The variability of plasma 17-hydroxycorticosteroid levels in affective illness and schizophrenia. *Psychosomatic Research*, 1965, *9*, 237–248.

Angrist, B., Sathananthan, G., and Gershon, S. Behavioral effects of L-dopa in schizophrenic patients. *Psychopharmacologia*, 1973, *31*, 1–12.

Annell, A. Insulin shock treatment in children with psychotic disturbances. *Acta Psychotherapeutica Psychoanalytica Orthopoedica*, 1955, *3*, 193–205.

Annell, A. L. Manic-depressive illness in children and effect of treatment with lithium carbonate. *Acta Paedopsychiatrica*, 1969, *36*, 292–361. (a)

Annell, A. L. Lithium in the treatment of children and adolescents. *Acta Psychiatrica Scandinavica*, 1969, *207* (Supp.), 19–30. (b)

Anton-Tay, F., and Wurtman, R. J. Brain monoamines and endocrine function. In L. Martini and W. F. Ganong (Eds.), *Frontiers in neuroendocrinology*. London: Oxford University Press, 1971.

Arbit, J., Boshes, B., and Blonsky, R. Behavior and mentation changes during therapy. In A. Barbeau and F. H. McDowell (Eds.), *L-dopa and Parkinsonism*. Philadephia: Davis, 1970.

Arnold, L. E., Kirilcuk, V., Corson, S. A., and Corson, E. O'L. Levoamphetamine and dextroamphetamine: Differential effect on aggression and hyperkinesis in children and dogs. *American Journal of Psychiatry*, 1973, *130*, 165–170.

Arnold, L. E., and Wender, P. H. Levoamphetamine's changing place in the treatment of children with behavior disorders. *Pediatrics*, 1975.

Arnold, L. E., Wender, P. W., McCloskey, K., and Snyder, S. H. Levoamphetamine and dextroamphetamine: Comparative efficacy in the hyperkinetic syndrome. *Archives of General Psychiatry*, 1972, *27*, 816–822.

Balázs, R., Kovács, S., Cocks, W. A., Johnson, A. L., and Eayrs, J. T. Effect of thyroid hormone on the biochemical maturation of rat brain: Postnatal cell formation. *Brain Research*, 1971, *25*, 555–570.

Ban, T. A. Nicotinic acid in psychiatry. *Canadian Psychiatric Association Journal*, 1971, *16*, 413–431.

Ban, T. A., and Lehman, H. E. *Nicotinic acid in the treatment of schizophrenias. Progress Report I*. Toronto: Canadian Mental Health Association, 1970.

Bender, L. One hundred cases of childhood schizophrenia treated with electric shock. *Transactions of the American Neurological Association*, 1947, *72*, 165–169.

Bender, L. Theory and treatment of childhood schizophrenia. *Acta Paedopsychiatrica*, 1967, *34*, 298–307.

Bender, L. The life course of children with schizophrenia. *American Journal of Psychiatry*. 1973, *130*, 783–786.

Bender, L., Cobrinik, L., Faretra, G., and Sankar, D. V. S. The treatment of childhood schizophrenia with LSD and UML. In M. Rinkel (Ed.), *Biological treatment of mental illness*, New York: L. C. Page & Co., 1966.

Bender, L., and Cottington, F. The use of amphetamine sulfate (Benzedrine) in child psychiatry. *American Journal of Psychiatry*, 1942, *99*, 116–121.

Bender, L., Goldschmidt, L., and Sankar, D. V. S. Treatment of autistic schizophrenic children with LSD-25 and UML-491. In J. Wortis (Ed.), *Recent advances in biological psychiatry.* New York: Plenum Press, 1962.

Bender, L., Faretra, G., and Cobrinik, L. LSD and UML treatment of hospitalized disturbed children. In J. Wortis (Ed.), *Recent advances in biological psychiatry,* New York: Plenum Press, 1963.

Bender, L., and Keeler, W. R. The body image of schizophrenic children following electroshock therapy. *American Journal of Orthopsychiatry,* 1952, *22,* 335–355.

Bender, L., and Nichtern, S. Chemotherapy in child psychiatry. *New York State Journal of Medicine,* 1956, *56,* 2791–2795.

Boullin, D. J., Coleman, M., and O'Brien, R. A. Abnormalities in platelet 5-hydroxytryptamine efflux in patients with infantile autism. *Nature,* 1970, *226,* 371–372.

Boullin, D. J., Coleman, M., O'Brien, R. A., and Rimland, B. Laboratory predictions of infantile autism based on 5-HT efflux from platelets and their correlation with the Rimland E-2 score. *Journal of Autism and Childhood Schizophrenia,* 1971, *1,* 63–71.

Bradley, C. The behavior of children receiving benzedrine. *American Journal of Psychiatry,* 1937, *94,* 577–585.

Bradley, C., and Bowen, M. Amphetamine (Benzedrine) therapy of children's behavior disorders. *American Journal of Orthopsychiatry,* 1941, *11,* 92–103.

Brambilla, F., and Penati, G. Hormones and behavior in schizophrenia. In D. H. Ford (Ed.), *Influence of hormones on the nervous system.* Basel: Karger, 1971.

Butcher, L. L., Engel, J., and Fuxe, K. L-dopa induced changes in central monoamine neurons after peripheral decarboxylase inhibition. *Journal of Pharmacy and Pharmacology,* 1970, *22,* 313–316.

Burk, H. W., and Menolascino, F. J. Haloperidol in emotionally disturbed mentally retarded individuals. *American Journal of Psychiatry,* 1968, *124,* 1589–1591.

Campbell, J. D. Manic-depressive disease in children. *Journal of the American Medical Association,* 1955, *198,* 154–157.

Campbell, M. A psychotic boy with self-mutilating behavior and the antiaggressive effect of lithium. Paper presented at the 20th Annual Meeting of the American Academy of Child Psychiatry, Washington, D. C., October 18–21, 1973.

Campbell, M., Fish, B., Shapiro, T., and Floyd, A., Jr. Thiothixene in young disturbed children. A pilot study. *Archives of General Psychiatry,* 1970, *23,* 70–72.

Campbell, M., Fish, B., Shapiro, T., and Floyd, A., Jr. Study of molindone in disturbed preschool children. *Current Therapeutic Research,* 1971, *13,* 28–33. (a)

Campbell, M., Fish, B., Shapiro, T., and Floyd, A., Jr. Imipramine in preschool autistic and schizophrenic children. *Journal of Autism and Childhood Schizophrenia,* 1971, *1,* 267–282. (b)

Campbell, M., Fish, B., David, R., Shapiro, T., Collins, P., and Koh, C. Response to triiodothyronine and dextroamphetamine: A study of preschool schizophrenic children. *Journal of Autism and Childhood Schizophrenia,* 1972, *2,* 343–358. (a)

Campbell, M., Fish, B., Korein, J., Shapiro, T., Collins, P., and Koh, C. Lithium–chlorpromazine: A controlled crossover study in hyperactive severely disturbed young children. *Journal of Autism and Childhood Schizophrenia,* 1972, *2,* 234–263. (b)

Campbell, M., Fish, B., Shapiro, T., and Floyd, A., Jr. Acute responses of schizophrenic children to a sedative and "stimulating" neuroleptic: A pharmacologic yardstick. *Current Therapeutic Research,* 1972, *14,* 759–766. (c)

Campbell, M., Fish, B., David, R., Shapiro, T., Collins, P., and Koh, C. Liothyronine treatment in psychotic and nonpsychotic children under six years. *Archives of General Psychiatry,* 1973, *29,* 602–608.

Campbell, M., Friedman, E., DeVito, E., Greenspan, L., and Collins, P. J. Blood serotonin in disturbed and brain damaged children. *Journal of Autism and Childhood Schizophrenia,* 1974, *4,* 33–41.

Campbell, M., Friedman, E., Green, W. H., Collins, P. J., Small, A. M., and Breuer, H. Blood serotonin in schizophrenic children. A preliminary study. International Pharmacopsychiatry, 1975.

Campbell, M., and Hersh, S. P. Observations on the vicissitudes of aggression in two siblings. *Journal of Autism and Childhood Schizophrenia*, 1971, *1*, 398–410.

Campbell, M., and Shapiro, T. Therapy of psychiatric disorders in childhood. In R. I. Shader (Ed.), *Manual of Psychiatric Therapeutics*. Boston: Little, Brown and Company, 1975.

Campbell, M., Small, A. M., Collins, P. J., Friedman, E., David, R., and Genieser, N. B. Levodopa and levoamphetamine: a crossover study in schizophrenic children. Current Therapeutic Research, 1976, 18.

Cerletti, V. Old and new information about electroshock. *American Journal of Psychiatry*, 1950, *107*, 87–94.

Cleckley, H. M., Sydenstricker, V. P., and Geeslin, L. E. Nicotinic acid in the treatment of atypical psychotic states. *Journal of the American Medical Association*, 1939, *112*, 2107–2110.

Coleman, M. Serotonin levels in infant hypothyroidism. *Lancet*, 1970, *2*, 365.

Coleman, M. Serotonin and central nervous system syndromes in childhood: A review. *Journal of Autism and Childhood Schizophrenia*, 1973, *3*, 27–35.

Coleman, M., Campbell, M., Freedman, L. S., Roffman, M., Ebstein, R. P., and Goldstein, M. Serum dopamine-B-hydroxylase levels in Down's syndrome. *Clinical Genetics*, 1974, *5*, 312–315.

Conners, C. K. Deanol and behavior disorders in children: a critical review of the literature and recommended future studies for determining efficacy. *Psychopharmacology Bulletin:* Special Issue, Pharmacotherapy of Children, 1973, 188–195.

Corson, S. A., Corson, E. O'L., Kirilcuk, V., Knopp, W., and Arnold, L. E. Differential interaction of amphetamines and psychosocial factors in the modification of violent and hyperkinetic behavior and learning disability. *Federal Proceedings*, 1972, *31*, 820.

Crane, G. E. Clinical psychopharmacology in its 20th year. *Science*, 1973, *181*, 124–128.

Creak, M. Schizophrenic syndrome in childhood. Progress report of a working party. *Cerebral Palsy Bulletin* 1961, *3*, 501–504.

Danziger, L. Thyroid therapy of schizophrenia. *Diseases of the Nervous System*, 1958, *19*, 373–378.

Danziger, L., and Kindwall, J. A. Thyroid therapy in some mental disorders. *Diseases of the Nervous System*, 1953, *14*, 3–13.

DiMascio, A., Soltys, J. J., and Shader, R. I. Psychotropic drug side effects in children. In R. I. Shader, and A. DiMascio (Eds.), *Psychotropic Drug Side Effects*, Baltimore: Williams & Wilkins Company, 1970, 235–260.

Dostal, T. Antiaggressive effect of lithium salts in mentally retarded adolescents. In A. L. Annell (Ed.), *Depressive states in childhood and adolescence*. Stockholm: Almquist & Wiksell, 1972.

Durell, J., Libow, L. S., Kellam, S. G., and Shader, R. I. Interrelationships between regulation of thyroid gland function and psychosis. *Association for Research in Nervous and Mental Diseases*, 1963, *43*, 387–399.

Dutton, G. The growth pattern of psychotic boys. *British Journal of Psychiatry*, 1964, *110*, 101–103.

Dyson, W. L., and Barcai, A. Treatment of children of lithium responding parents. *Current Therapeutic Research*, 1970, *12*, 286–290.

Eayrs, J. T. Developmental relationships between brain and thyroid. In R. P. Michael (Ed.), *Endocrinology and human behavior*. Oxford University Press, 1968.

Effron, A. S., and Freedman, A. M. The treatment of behavior disorders in children with benadryl. *Journal of Pediatrics*, 1953, *42*, 261–266.

Eisenberg, L. The course of childhood schizophrenia. *Archives of Neurology and Psychiatry*, 1957, *78*, 69–83.

Eisenberg, L. Role of drugs in treating disturbed children. *Children,* 1964, *2,* 167–173.

Eisenberg, L. The classification of childhood psychosis reconsidered. *Journal of Autism and Childhood Schizophrenia,* 1972, *2,* 338–342.

Eisenberg, L., and Conners, C. K. Psychopharmacology in childhood. In N. B. Talbot, J. Kagan, and L. Eisenberg (Eds.), *Behavioral Science in Pediatric Medicine.* Philadelphia: W. B. Saunders Company, 1971, 397–423.

Engelhardt, D. M., Polizos, P., and Margolis, R. A. The drug treatment of childhood psychosis. In W. L. Smith (Ed.), *Drugs, development and cerebral function,* Springfield, Ill.: Charles C. Thomas, 1972.

Engelhardt, D. M., Polizos, P., Waizer, J., and Hoffman, S. P. A double-blind comparison of fluphenazine and haloperidol in outpatient schizophrenic children. *Journal of Autism and Childhood Schizophrenia,* 1973, *3,* 128–137.

Everett, G. M., and Borcherding, J. W. L-dopa: Effect on concentrations of dopamine, norepinephrine and serotonin in brains of mice. *Science,* 1970, *168,* 849–850.

Feldmesser–Reiss, E. E. The application of triiodothyronine in the treatment of mental disorders. *Journal of Nervous and Mental Disease,* 1958, *127,* 540–545.

Fish, B. Drug therapy in child psychiatry: Pharmacological aspects. *Comprehensive Psychiatry,* 1960, *1,* 212–227.

Fish, B. The influence of maturation and abnormal development on the responses of disturbed children to drugs. *Proceedings of the Third World Congress of Psychiatry,* 1963.

Fish, B. Drug use in psychiatric disorders in children. *American Journal of Psychiatry,* 1968, *124,* 31–36.

Fish, B. Methodology in child psychopharmacology. In D. H. Efron, J. O. Cole, J. Levine, and J. R. Wittenborn (Eds.), *Psychopharmacology, Review of Progress* (Public Health Service Publication No. 1836). Washington, D.C.: United States Government Printing Office, 1968.

Fish, B. Psychopharmacologic responses of chronic schizophrenic adults as predictors of responses in young schizophrenic children. *Psychopharmacology Bulletin,* 1970, *6,* 12–15.

Fish, B. The "one child, one drug" myth of stimulants in hyperkinesis. Importance of diagnostic categories in evaluating treatment. *Archives of General Psychiatry,* 1971, *25,* 193–203.

Fish, B., Campbell, M., Shaprio, T., and Floyd, A., Jr. Comparison of trifluperidol, trifluoperazine and chlorpromazine in preschool schizophrenic children: The value of less sedative antipsychotic agents. *Current Therapeutic Research,* 1969, *11,* 589–595. (a)

Fish, B., Campbell, M., Shapiro, T., and Floyd, A., Jr. Schizophrenic children treated with methysergide (Sansert). *Diseases of the Nervous System,* 1969, *30,* 534–540. (b)

Fish, B., Campbell, M., Shapiro, T., and Weinstein, J. Preliminary findings on thiothixene compared to other drugs in psychotic children under five years. In H. E. Lehmann and T. A. Ban (Eds.), The thioxanthenes: *Modern problems of pharmacopsychiatry* (Vol. 2). Basel, Switzerland: S. Karger, 1969. (c)

Fish, B., Shapiro, T., and Campbell, M. Long-term prognosis and the response of schizophrenic children to drug therapy: A controlled study of trifluoperazine. *American Journal of Psychiatry,* 1966, *123,* 32–39.

Fox, W., Gobble, I. F., Clos, M., and Denison, E. A clinical comparison of trifluperidol, haloperidol and chlorpromazine. *Current Therapeutic Research,* 1964, *6,* 409–415.

Freedman, A. M., Ebin, E. V., and Wilson, E. A. Autistic schizophrenic children. An experiment in the use of D-lysergic acid diethylamide (LSD-25). *Archives of General Psychiatry,* 1962, *6,* 203–213.

Freeman, R. D. Drug effects on learning in children. A selective review of the past thirty years. *Journal of Special Education* 1966, *1*, 17–43.

Freeman, R. D. Psychopharmacology and the retarded child. In F. Menolascino (Ed.), *Psychiatric Approaches to Mental Retardation in Childhood.* New York: Basic Books, 1970.

Freeman, W. Psychosurgery. In S. Arieti (Ed.), *American handbook of psychiatry* (Vol. II). New York: Basic Books, 1959.

Frommer, E. Depressive illness in childhood. In A. Coppen and A. Walk (Eds.), *Recent developments in affective disorders. A symposium, British Journal of Psychiatry,* 1968, Special Publication No. 2, 117–136.

Gallant, D. M., and Bishop, M. P. Molindone: A controlled evaluation in chronic schizophrenic patients. *Current Therapeutic Research,* 1968, *10,* 441–447.

Gallant, D. M., Bishop, M. P., Nesselhoff, W., Jr., and Sprehe, D. J. Further observations on trifluperidol: A butyrophenone derivative. *Psychopharmacologia,* 1965, *7,* 37–43.

Gallant, D. M., Bishop, M. P., and Shelton, W. A preliminary evaluation of P-4657B: A thioxanthene derivative. *American Journal of Psychiatry,* 1966, *123,* 345–346.

Gallant, D. M., Bishop, M. P., Timmons, E., and Gould, A. R. Thiothixene (P-4657B): A controlled evaluation in chronic schizophrenic patients. *Current Therapeutic Research,* 1966, *8,* 153–158.

Gershon, S., Holmberg, G., Mattson, E., and Marshall, A. Imipramine hydrochloride. Its effects on clinical, autonomic and psychological functions. *Archives of General Psychiatry,* 1962, *6,* 96–101.

Gjessing, R. Beiträge zur Kenntniss der Pathophysiologie des katatonen Stupors. *Archive für Psychiatrie und Nervenkrankheiten,* 1932, *96,* 319–392.

Gjessing, R. Disturbances of somatic functions in catatonia with a periodic course, and their compensation. *Journal of Mental Science,* 1938, *84,* 608–621.

Gjessing, R. Beiträge zur Somatologie der periodischen Katatonie. *Archive für Psychiatrie und Zeitschrift Neurologie,* 1953, *191,* 191–326.

Goldfarb, W. *Childhood Schizophrenia.* Cambridge, Mass.: Harvard University Press, 1961.

Goodwin, F. K., Murphy, D. L., Brodie, H. K. H., and Bunney, W. E. L-dopa, catecholamines, and behavior: A clinical and biochemical study in depressed patients. *Biological Psychiatry,* 1970, *3,* 341–366.

Gram, L. F., and Rafaelsen, O. J. Lithium treatment of psychotic children and adolescents. A controlled clinical trial. *Acta Psychiatrica Scandinavica,* 1972, *48,* 253–260.

Greenbaum, G. H. An evaluation of niacinamide in the treatment of childhood schizophrenia, *American Journal of Psychiatry,* 1970, *127,* 129–132.

Gurewitz, S., and Helme, W. H. Effects of electroconvulsive therapy on personality and intellectual functioning of the schizophrenic chiid. *Journal of Nervous and Mental Disease,* 1954, *120,* 213–226.

Hartlage, L. C. Effects of chlorpromazine on learning. *Psychological Bulletin,* 1965, *64,* 235–245.

Helper, M., Wilcott, R. C., and Garfield, S. L. Effects of chlorpromazine on learning and related processes in emotionally disturbed children. *Journal of Consulting Psychology,* 1963, *27,* 1–9.

Heuyer, G., Lang, J. L., and Rivaille, C. J. Aspects cliniques des schizophrenies traitees par l'insuline. *Revue de Neuropsychiatrie Infantile et d'Hygiene Mentale de l'Enfance,* 1956, *4,* 390–396.

Himwich, H. E., Kety, S. S., & Smythies, J. R. *Amines and schizophrenia.* New York: Pergamon Press, 1967.

Hoffer, A. Childhood schizophrenia: A case treated with nicotinic acid and nicotinamide. *Schizophrenia,* 1970, *2,* 43–53.

Hoffer, A. Mechanisms of action of nicotonic acid and nicotinamide in the treatment of schizophrenia. In D. Hawkins and L. Pauling (Eds.), *Orthomolecular psychiatry.* San Francisco: W. H. Freeman, 1973.

Hoskins, R. G. *The biology of Schizophrenia.* New York: Norton & Co., 1946.

Kanner, L. Autistic disturbances of affective contact. *Nervous child,* 1943, *2,* 217–250.

Kety, S. S. Toward hypotheses for a biochemical component in the vulnerability to schizophrenia. *Seminars in Psychiatry,* 1972, *4,* 233–238.

Klein, D., and Fink, M. Psychiatric reaction to imipramine. *American Journal of Psychiatry,* 1962, *119,* 432–438.

Kraft, I. A., Ardali, C., Duffy, J. H., Hart, J. T., and Pearce, P. A clinical study of chlordiazepoxide used in psychiatric disorders of children. *International Journal of Neuropsychiatry,* 1965, *1,* 433–437.

Krantz, J. C., Jr., Truitt, E. B., Jr., Speers, L., and Ling, A. S. O. New pharmacoconvulsive agent. *Science,* 1957, *126,* 353.

Kurtis, L. B. Clinical study of the response to nortriptyline on autistic children. *International Journal of Neuropsychiatry,* 1966, *2,* 298–301.

Lapin, I. P., and Oxenkrug, G. F. Intensification of the central serotoninergic processes as a possible determinant of the thymoleptic effect. *Lancet,* 1969, *1,* 132–136.

LaVeck, G. D., and Buckley, P. The use of psychopharmacologic agents in retarded children with behavior disorders. *Journal of Chronic Diseases,* 1961, *13,* 174–183.

LeVann, L. J. Chlordiazepoxide, a tranquilizer with anticonvulsant properties. *Canadian Medical Association Journal,* 1962, *86,* 123–126.

LeVann, L. J. Haloperidol in the treatment of behavioral disorders in children and adolescents. *Canadian Psychiatric Association Journal,* 1969, *14,* 217–220.

Lipman, R. S. Methodology of drug studies in children. Annual Meeting of the American Orthopsychiatric Association, Chicago, Illinois, March 21, 1968.

Lipman, R. S. The use of psychopharmacological agents in residential facilities for the retarded. In Frank J. Menolascino (Ed.), *Psychiatric Approaches to Mental Retardation.* New York: Basic Books, Inc., 1970, Chapter 15.

Lipton, M. A., Ban, T. A., Kane, F. J., Levine, J., Mosher, L. R., and Wittenborn, R. *Megavitamin and orthomolecular therapy in psychiatry.* Washington, D.C.: American Psychiatric Association, 1973.

Loranger, A. W., Goodell, H., Lee, J. H., and McDowell, F. Levo-dopa treatment of Parkinson's syndrome. Improved intellectual functioning. *Archives of General Psychiatry,* 1972, *26,* 163–168.

Martini, L., and Ganong, W. F. *Frontiers in neuroendocrinology,* 1971. London: Oxford University Press, 1971.

McAndrew, J. B., Case, A., and Treffert, D. A. Effects of prolonged phenothiazine intake on psychotic and other hospitalized children. *Journal of Autism and Childhood Schizophrenia,* 1972, *2,* 75–91.

McCann, S. Mechanism of action of hypothalamic-hypophyseal stimulating and inhibiting hormones. In L. Martini and W. F. Ganong (Eds.), *Frontiers in neuroendocrinology.* London: Oxford University Press, 1971.

McGrath, S. D., O'Brien, P. F., Power, P. J., and Shea, J. R. Nicotinamide treatment of schizophrenia. Report of a multihospital controlled trial. *Schizophrenia Bulletin,* 1972, *5,* 74–76.

Moniz, E. *Tentative operatoires dans le traitement de certaines psychoses.* Paris: Masson et Cie, 1936.

Mosher, L. R. Nicotinic acid side effects and toxicity. A review. *American Journal of Psychiatry,* 1970, *126,* 1290–1296.

Murphy, D. L. Amine precursors, amines and false neurotransmitters in depressed patients. *American Journal of Psychiatry*, 1972, *129*, 141–148. (a)

Murphy, D. L. L-dopa, behavioral activation and psychopathology. In I. J. Kopin (Ed.), *Neurotransmitters*. Baltimore: Williams & Wilkins, 1972. (b).

Ng, K. Y., Chase, T. N., Colburn, R. W., and Kopin, K. J. L-dopa-induced release of cerebralmonoamines. *Science*, 1970, *170*, 76–77.

O'Brien, C. P., DiGiacomo, J. N., Fahn, S., and Schwarz, G. A. Mental effects of high-dosage levodopa. *Archives of General Psychiatry*, 1971, *24*, 61–64.

Oettinger, L. Chlorprothixene in the management of problem children. *Diseases of the Nervous System*, 1962, *23*, 1–4.

Osmond, H., and Hoffer, A. Massive niacin treatment in schizophrenia. Review of a nine-year study. *Lancet*, 1962, *1*, 316–319.

Osmond, H. The background to the niacin treatment. In D. Hawkins and L. Pauling (Eds.), *Orthomolecular psychiatry*. San Francisco: W. H. Freeman, 1973.

Pauling, L. Orthomolecular psychiatry. *Science*, 1968, *160*, 265–271.

Persky, H., Zuckerman, M., and Curtis, G. C. Endocrine functions in emotionally disturbed and normal men. *Journal of Nervous and Mental Disease*, 1968, *146*, 488–497.

Piggott, L. R., and Gottlieb, J. S. Childhood schizophrenia—what is it? *Journal of Autism and Childhood Schizophrenia*, 1973, *3*, 96–105.

Pilkington, T. L. Comparative effects of librium and taractan on behavior disorders of mentally retarded children. *Diseases of the Nervous System*, 1961, *22*, 573–575. (a)

Pilkington, T. L. The effects of librium and taractan on the behavior of psychotically disturbed mentally retarded children. *Psychopharmacology Abstracts*, 1961, *61*, 575. (b)

Polizos, P., Engelhardt, D. M., Hoffman, S. P., and Waizer, J. Neurological consequences of psychotropic drug withdrawal in schizophrenic children. *Journal of Autism and Childhood Schizophrenia*, 1973, *3*, 247–253.

Pollack, M., Klein, D. F., Willner, A., Blumberg, A., and Fink, M. Imipramine-induced behavioral disorganization in schizophrenic patients: Physiological and psychological correlates. In J. Wortis (Ed.), *Recent advances in biological psychiatry*. New York: Plenum Press, 1965.

Prange, A. J., Jr., Wilson, I. C., Rabon, A. M., and Lipton, M. A. Enhancement of imipramine antidepressant activity by thyroid hormone. *American Journal of Psychiatry*, 1969, *126*, 457–469.

Prange, A. J., Jr., and Lipton, M. A. Hormones and behavior: Some principles and findings. In R. I. Shader (Ed.), *Psychiatric complications of medical drugs*. New York: Raven Press, 1972.

Ramsey, R. A., Ban, T. A., Lehmann, H. E., Saxena, B. M., and Bennett, J. Nicotinic acid as adjuvant therapy in newly admitted schizophrenic patients. *Canadian Medical Association Journal*, 1970, *102*, 939–942.

Reiss, M. Correlations between changes in mental states and thyroid activity after different forms of treatment. *Journal of Mental Sciences*, 1954, *100*, 687–703.

Reiss, M. (Ed.) *Psychoendocrinology*. New York: Grune & Stratton, 1958.

Reiss, M. Clinical and basic neuroendocrine investigations in some states of mental retardation. In D. H. Ford (Ed.), *Influence on hormones on the nervous system*. Basel: Karger, 1971.

Rimland, B. *Infantile Autism*. New York: Appleton-Century-Crofts, 1964.

Rimland, B. High-dosage levels of certain vitamins in the treatment of children with severe mental disorders. In D. Hawkins and L. Pauling (Eds.), *Orthomolecular psychiatry*. San Francisco: W. H. Freeman, 1973.

Ritvo, E. R., Yuwiler, A., Geller, E., Kales, A., Rashkis, S., Schicor, A., Plotkin, S., Axelrod, R., and Howard, C. Effects of L-dopa in autism. *Journal of Autism and Childhood Schizophrenia,* 1971, *1,* 190–205.

Ritvo, E. R., Yuwiler, A., Geller, E., Ornitz, E. M., Saeger, K., and Plotkin, S. Increased blood serotonin and platelets in early infantile autism. *Archives of General Psychiatry,* 1970, *23,* 566–572.

Rolo, A., Krinsky, L., Abramson, H., and Goldfarb, L. Preliminary method study of LSD with children. *International Journal of Neuropsychiatry,* 1965, *1,* 552–555.

Ruttenberg, B. A., and Steg, N. Vulnerability and risk—a continuum of etiology in the clinical syndrome of infantile autism. Paper presented at 51st Annual Meeting of the American Orthopsychiatric Association, Workshop 53, San Francisco, California, April 8–12, 1974.

Rutter, M. Childhood schizophrenia reconsidered. *Journal of Autism and Childhood Schizophrenia,* 1972, *2,* 315–337.

Sachar, E. J. Psychoendocrine aspects of acute schizophrenic reactions. *Psychosomatic Medicine,* 1963, *25,* 510–537.

Sachar, E. J., Harmatz, J., Bergen, H., and Cohler, J. Corticosteroid responses to milieu therapy of chronic schizophrenics. *Archives of General Psychiatry,* 1966, *15,* 310–319.

Sachar, E. J., Hellman, L., Roffwarg, H. P., Halpern, F. S., Fukushima, D. K., and Gallagher, T. F. Disrupted 24-hour patterns of cortisol secretion in psychotic depression. *Archives of General Psychiatry,* 1973, *28,* 19–24.

Safer, D. J., and Allen, R. P. Factors influencing the suppressant effects of two stimulant drugs on the growth of hyperactive children. *Pediatrics,* 1973, *51,* 660–667.

Sakel, M. *The pharmacological shock treatment of schizophrenia.* New York: Nervous and Mental Diseases Publishing Co., 1938.

Schain, R. J., and Freedman, D. X. Studies of 5-hydroxyindole metabolism in autistic and other mentally retarded children. *Journal of Pediatrics,* 1961, *58,* 315–320.

Schapiro, S. Influence of hormones and environmental stimulation of brain development. In D. H. Ford (Ed.), *Influence of hormones on the nervous system.* Basel: S. Karger, 1971.

Schaub, C. L., Soulairac, A., and Franchimont, P. Action of chlorpromazine on the hypothalamo-somato-tropic and the hypotholamo-corticotropic axis in man. In D. H. Ford (Ed.), *Influence of Hormones on the Nervous System.* Basel: Karger, 1971. Pp. 121–139.

Schildkraut, J. J., and Kety, S. S. Biogenic amines and emotion. Pharmacological studies suggest a relationship between brain biogenic amines and affective state. *Science,* 1967, *156,* 21–30.

Schou, M. Lithium in psychiatric therapy and prophylaxis. A review with special regard to its use in children. In A. L. Annell (Ed.), *Depressive states in childhood and adolescence.* Stockholm: Almquist & Wiksell, 1972.

Sheard, M. H. Behavioral effects of p-chlorophenylalanine in rats: Inhibition by lithium. *Communications in Behavioral Biology,* 1970, *5,* 71–73. (a)

Sheard, M. H. Effect of lithium on foot shock aggression in rats. *Nature,* 1970, *228,* 284–285. (b)

Sheard, M. The effect of lithium on behavior. *Communications in Contemporary Psychiatry,* 1971, *1,* 1–6. (a)

Sheard, M. H. Effect of lithium on human aggression. *Nature,* 1971, *230,* 113–114. (b)

Sherman, L., Kim, S., Benjamin, F. and Kolodny, H. D. Effect of chlorpromazine on serum growth—hormone concentration in man. *New England Journal of Medicine,* 1971, *284,* 72–74.

Sherwin, A. C., Flach, F. F., and Stokes, P. E. Treatment of psychoses in childhood with triiodothyronine. *American Journal of Psychiatry*, 1958, *115*, 166–167.

Silver, A. A. Management of children with schizophrenia. *American Journal of Psychotherapy*, 1955, *9*, 196–215.

Simeon, J., Saletu, B., Saletu, M., Itil, T. M. and DaSilva, J. Thiothixene in childhood psychoses. Paper presented at the Third International Symposium on Phenothiazines, Rockville, Maryland, 1973.

Simmons, J. Q., III, Leiken, S. J., Lovaas, O. I., Schaeffer, B., and Perloff, B. Modification of autistic behavior with LSD-25. *American Journal of Psychiatry*, 1966, *122*, 1201–1211.

Simon, G. B., and Gillies, S. M. Some physical characteristics of a group of psychotic children. *British Journal of Psychiatry*, 1964, *110*, 104.

Simpson, G. M., Cranswick, E. H., and Blair, J. H. Thyroid indices in chronic schizophrenia. *Journal of Nervous and Mental Disease*, 1963, *137*, 582–590.

Simpson, G. M., Cranswick, E. H., and Blair, J. H. Thyroid indices in chronic schizophrenia. II. *Journal of Nervous and Mental Disease*, 1964, *138*, 581–585.

Simpson, G. M., and Igbal, J. A preliminary study of thiothixene in chronic schizophrenics. *Current Therapeutic Research*, 1965, *7*, 310–314.

Simpson, G. M., and Krakov, L. A preliminary study of molindone (EN-1733A) in chronic schizophrenia. *Current Therapeutic Research*, 1968, *10*, 41–46.

Skynner, A. C. R. Effect of chlordiazepoxide. *Lancet*, 1961, *1*, 1110.

Snyder, S. H., Taylor, K. M., Coyle, J. T., and Meyerhoff, J. L. The role of brain dopamine in behavioral regulation and the actions of psychotropic drugs. *American Journal of Psychiatry*, 1970, *127*, 199–207.

Sokoloff, L., and Roberts, P. Biochemical mechanism of the action of thyroid hormones in nervous and other tissues. In D. H. Ford (Ed.), *Influence of hormones on the nervous system*. Basel: Karger, 1971.

Sprague, R. L., and Werry, J. S. Methodology of psychopharmacological studies with the retarded. In N. R. Ellis (Ed.), *International Review of Research in Mental Retardation* (Vol. 5). New York: Academic Press, 1971. Pp. 147–219.

Sugerman, A. A., and Herrmann, J. Molindone: An indole derivative with anti-psychotic activity. *Clinical Pharmacology and Therapeutics*, 1967, *8*, 261–265.

Sugerman, A. A., Stolberg, H., and Hermann, J. A pilot study of P-4657B in chronic schizophrenics. *Current Therapeutic Research*, 1965, *7*, 310–314.

Taylor, K. M., and Snyder, S. H. Amphetamine: Differentiation by D- and L-isomers of behavior involving brain norepinephrine or dopamine. *Science*, 1970, *168*, 1487–1489.

Tupin, J. P., and Smith, D. B. The long-term use of lithium in aggressive prisoners. Paper presented at the Meeting of the Early Clinical Drug Evaluation Unit, Psychopharmacology Research Branch, NIMH, Catonsville, Maryland, June 1972.

Waizer, J., Polizos, P., Hoffman, S. P., Engelhardt, D. M., and Margolis, R. A. A single-blind evaluation of thiothixene with outpatient schizophrenic children. *Journal of Autism and Childhood Schizophrenia*, 1972, *2*, 378–386.

Weischer, M. L. On the antiaggressive effect of lithium. *Psychopharmacologia*, 1969, *15*, 245–254.

Werry, J. S., Weiss, G., Douglas, V., and Martin, J. Studies on the hyperactive child III: The effect of chlorpromazine upon behavior and learning ability. *Journal of American Academy of Child Psychiatry*, 1966, *5*, 292–312.

Whitehead, P. L., and Clark, L. D. Effect of lithium carbonate, placebo and thioridazine on hyperactive children. *American Journal of Psychiatry*, 1970, *127*, 824–825.

Williams, J. M., and Freeman, W. Evaluation of lobotomy with special reference to children. Association for Research in Nervous and Mental Disease, Proceedings, 1953, *31*, 311.

Wilson, M. B., Prange, A. J., Jr., McClane, T. K., Rabon, A. M., and Lipton, M. A. Thyroid hormone enhancement of imipramine in nonretarded depressions. *New England Journal of Medicine,* 1970, *282*, 1063–1067.

Wilson, I. C., Prange, A. J., Jr., and Lara, P. P. T_3 alone in depressed adults. Paper presented at the Annual Meeting of the American College of Neuropsychopharmacology, San Juan, Puerto Rico, December 1972.

Wittenborn, J. R., Weber, E. S. P., and Brown, M. Niacin in the long-term treatment of schizophrenia. *Archives of General Psychiatry,* 1973, *28*, 308–315.

14

Perceptual Training:
A Critical Retrospect

LESTER MANN and LIBBY GOODMAN

Present-day concern with perceptual* adequacy is one facet of a larger trend currently in vogue in special education, that of diagnostic prescriptive teaching. The diagnostic–prescriptive approach seeks to maximize the efficiency of the teaching–learning process, by matching instructional methods with individual characteristics of the learner. According to a variety of current models, a child's functioning levels in specific ability or "process" domains; i.e., his strengths and weaknesses, are assessed. This information, in turn, is used to design or direct instructional strategies appropriate to the child's educational needs and personal learning style. Ideally, one would exploit the child's strengths and remediate his weaknesses, so as to attain the greatest educational benefits for the child. Diagnostic–prescriptive teaching is not restricted to perceptual assessment alone. It is directed to other processes as well; e.g., auditory memory, language, and encoding skills. However, while there are many dimensions in diagnostic–prescriptive teaching, the perceptual has been most emphasized and popularized by clinicians and teachers.

Is there sufficient evidence supporting the utilization of either diagnostic or remedial instruments in the perceptual realm? We believe that the answer to this question is largely negative. It is to this belief that we shall address ourselves in

---

*Perceptual motor functioning is subsumed under perception and often used interchangeably.

LESTER MANN and LIBBY GOODMAN · Department of Special Education, Montgomery County Intermediate Unit, Blue Bell, Pennsylvania 19422.

this paper, dealing first with some conceptual issues of concern, and then with research directly bearing on the practical application of the perceptual–motor hypothesis.

THE PERCEPTUAL MOTOR HYPOTHESIS

The authors have written a variety of conceptual critiques of perceptual–motor evaluation and training, and of the entire psychoeducational testing–training programs of the past decades (Goodman and Hammill, 1973; Hammill, Goodman, and Wiederholt, 1973; Mann, 1971a; Mann, 1971b; Mann, 1970; Mann and Phillips, 1967). We shall address ourselves in this paper to some of the more pressing issues relevant to the practical application of the perceptual hypothesis.

1. *Perception is an abstraction: Abstractions cannot be trained.* Perception is not legitimately a localized "process"—it or its subparts—that the proponents of perceptual training can isolate and train. "Its" stimulus and response parameters are arbitrarily defined by researcher and testmaker, and the "O's" in the equation are hypothetical. "It" is a concept that does not exist to be trained. There are indeed behaviors that we can deem perceptual and that have significance in the management and training of learning-impaired children. This would include alternating illumination levels in a classroom, utilizing books with distinctive print, teaching the child more effective discrimination of letters and words and in scanning pages. Such types of common-sense management and training are a far cry from training "perceptual functioning" as a set of processes, such as are carried out in the Kephart and Frostig programs (Kephart, 1971; Frostig and Horne, 1964).

2. *It is not clear what perceptual assessment measures.* Certain types of behaviors can comfortably be conceptualized and demarcated as being "perceptual." We can subdivide perceptual behavior into visual perceptual, perceptual–gross motor, and perceptual–fine motor activity. While we may not still be sure what organismic domains we are assessing in so proceeding, and how definitively we are assessing them, we can nevertheless utilize such constructs without excessive splitting of hairs and with a reasonable feeling of intellectual and empirical consensus.

Such constructs help to clarify our thinking and organize our teaching and training and research efforts. We can even be more precise if we narrow research and training efforts to those within a laboratory context (Fleishman, 1972). But the perceptual training movement by and large depends on the utilization of poorly validated and unreliable instruments such as the Frostig, the Winterhaven, and the Purdue rating scales to determine *their* parameters of "perception" and to assess children's strengths and weaknesses in this or that perceptual process.

The perceptual assessment proponents confuse test names with the actual behaviors and processes these tests elicit. The names they have assigned to various perceptual tests are in fact arbitrary and established largely on the basis of intuitive logic, common-sense conceptualizations, and unsubstantiated borrowed concepts from experimental psychology and other investigatory realms; they are usually face valid and no more. Perceptual assessors in fact have not in any way definitively demonstrated the ways their perceptual assessment instruments are related to the latent behavioral domains they presume to measure. Yet, they proceed to recommend training for their perceptual "its" or "thems" on the basis of their tests.

Compounding their miscontributions to evaluation and training, the perceptual assessment proponents insist that they can precisely delineate subdomains of perceptual functioning. One may simply point to the reliabilities of Frostig's Development Test of Visual Perception and to a myriad of factorial studies that have not supported her claims, to realize the futility of any attempt at precise measurement along the lines she proposes (Hammill, Colarusso, and Wiederholt, 1971; Boyd and Randle, 1970; Allen, 1968; Cawley, Burrow and Goodstein, 1968; Ohnmacht and Olson, 1968; Corah and Powell, 1963). "Perceptual training must penetrate even into the ultimate elements on which the individual perceptions depend. It should analyze, dissect and investigate," said Descoeudres in 1928. Our attempts to proceed along these lines, now as in her days, are based on wishful thinking, rather than upon the facts.

Some other points should briefly be made against perceptual assessment, keeping in mind that perceptual training efforts are by and large directed by results of perceptual tests. First, perceptual assessment approaches presume to assess major areas of perceptual function and dysfunction. Assuming for the moment that indeed they can delineate specific subareas of strength and weakness in perception, it would not follow that such subareas are the areas of major relevance to the child's behavior or achievements. When we teach arithmetic and reading, there is certainly agreement that these are valid goals for almost every child, but are figure-ground perception and object constancy the major areas upon which to focus our diagnostic and intervention efforts? Why should we focus, as Frostig suggests, on the five areas of perception that she offers us? What other more important areas of perception are we ignoring? How about distal versus proximal perception, or inner versus outer figure contours? How about a signal detection approach to stimuli (it has probably been tried somewhere)? In short, by focusing on the perceptual functioning variables offered us by the popular perceptual tests, we may be focusing on the wrong variables, ignoring other significant ones, and otherwise proceeding down the path of irrelevant and futile practices.

In any case, it is invalid to use perceptual test results as indicators of quantitative strength and weakness in perceptual areas. The current perceptual tests are normative, not criterion-referenced ones. Their scores indicate relative success or failure as compared to those of normative populations, not amounts of this or that perceptual ability. Yet, in practice such test scores are treated quantitatively by perceptual assessment proponents, as indicating degrees of strength and weakness within this or that perceptual function. Attempts to increase or optimize perceptual functioning, proceeding on this basis, necessarily are incorrectly directed.

A final point: We are willing to concede that perceptual tests may reveal that something is right or wrong with a child's functioning. In the same vein, we are willing to concede that perceptual tests can indeed identify children with problems. Low scores on them are probably indicative of something wrong with the low scorer. However, we contend that what is wrong is not clearly identified by the tests. For example, the same score on a Frostig subtest may represent a failure of comprehension, impaired attention, or limited motivation, rather than an impaired perceptual process—certainly not specific perceptual impairment. To proceed to train on the basis of such test results is not likely the optimum way of helping a child.

3. *Perceptual training represents artificial regression.* A fundamental assumption for the legitimacy of perceptual training is that such training (directed to essentially preschool levels of training) is essential to effective functioning in more advanced spheres of behavior, e.g., athletic functioning, reading, arithmetic, and the like. Because of this insistence on developing fundamentals in perception, perceptual training consigns many children to activities developmentally far below their capacities, based on the results of perceptual tests, which as we know have less and less relevance to school achievement with advancing age. It has forced bead-stringing, parquet-block assembly, and jigsaw puzzle expertise upon children whose maturity levels, abilities, and interests are beyond such activities. One has only to attend the conferences for learning disabilities and exceptional children to see the preschool toy fair that their exhibits usually represent. Is this all special and remedial education can accomplish? If so, performance contracting, with *Creative Playthings*, is recommended by these writers. We do not believe that much can be gained in such developmental regression. The more intelligent and legitimate approach to failure in a given subject or task area is to determine the highest entry skills of the disabled child and to proceed from there. This is developmental training of a sort, too, but the developmental sequence here is based on instructional objectives the child must achieve, rather than on his presumed developmental status.

4. *Perceptual training may focus on the wrong activities.* We have earlier discussed the narrowed focus of perceptual tests. We reiterate our criticisms for perceptual training. If we proceed on the basis of the recommendations provided by perceptual assessors and trainers, we may well be overlooking essential

"perceptual" functions and training unessential areas. Just as important, we may be overtraining perceptually and end up with a stimulus-bound, visually fixated nonreader. Certainly, reading is more than vision and perception; it is cognitive decoding, utilizing the eyes but not fully dependent upon them.

5. *Perceptual training is irrelevant.* Everything that we do has perceptual inputs and outputs. Whether we are drinking coffee, reading a book, or participating in a sport, perception is there. It is entirely unnecessary to single out it or its components for specific training.

If we train a child in the areas essential to his successful living, we will be training him perceptually. Further, if indeed we can train for reading by perceptual training, we can assume that if we have taught the child to read we have also trained him perceptually. If, in fact, we are training him in meaningful adaptive behavior, we can disregard perception as a consequential area of intervention and instead focus our teaching on what the child needs to know. It will be true, of course, that not every child will be able to acquire all the skill areas we will try to impart. Not all will become competent readers, mathematicians, or athletes. We may have to focus on other realms of skill that a child can manage. Perceptual training, however, will not, in any case, make the difference between success or failure.

RESEARCH REVIEW

The discussion to follow is concerned with the research evidence pertaining to the efficacy of perceptually based training programs for young children. No attempt has been made to carry out an exhaustive or all-inclusive review of the literature. Instead, we have drawn from literature reviews compiled by other authors and we have utilized a number of selected references in order to highlight trends.

Correlation Studies

An extensive number of descriptive studies of perceptual ability in young children are available in the literature. The nature—i.e., samples, variables, time lapse—varied considerably among these investigations. Studies that focused on the relationship of perceptual competencies to intellectual ability, school readiness and achievement in preprimary and school-aged children were of greatest interest.

Goodman (1973) in a review of visual—motor skills and school achievement, was specifically concerned with perceptual—motor functions of the sort embodied in the Kephart and Getman—Kane training program. Further, her review was restricted to studies that employed young preacademic children as subjects. In all, 14 studies, of which 6 dealt with concurrent and 8 with the long-term predictive relationship between perceptual and performance variables, were located. Goodman found evidence of a highly significant and consistent relationship between perceptual—motor skills and school readiness in kindergarten children; however, with increasing age, the relationships noted at the preschool level weakened and were only partially maintained. The apparent relationship of perceptual—motor skills and readiness at the kindergarten level may be due, in part, to the similarity that exists between perceptual—motor measures and readiness tests; i.e., matching, copying, as well as many other comparable tasks are frequently found on both types of tests. However, educationally speaking, the relationship between perceptual—motor ability over time and academic ability is of special importance.

Studies that reported correlations between children's test scores on the Frostig Developmental Test of Visual Perception (DTVP) and intelligence and school performance have been reviewed by Hammill and Wiederhold (1973). They categorized the reported correlation coefficients into three areas: intellectual, readiness, or achievement variables. Overall, the results are noteworthy for the consistency of significant relationships within all three categories. Twelve correlations were given for measures of intelligence and all of the coefficients were statistically significant (range from .18 to .59; median correlation was .39). Of 29 separate analyses between DTVP scores and measures of achievement, 23 were significant (range from .01 to .65; median correlation was .40). Only 3 studies that correlated DTVP test results and readiness measures could be located. The coefficients in all 3 instances were significant beyond the .05 level and were generally higher than those associated with measures of intelligence or academic performance. However, the magnitude of the coefficients was probably due, in part, to the considerable similarity that exists between the subscales of readiness test and the subtests of the DTVP; e.g., copying on the Metropolitan Readiness Test and the Eye—Hand Coordination Subtest of the DTVP. By applying the statistical guidelines for interpretation of correlation coefficients recommended by Guilford, the authors determined that many of the significant relationships were too weak to be practically significant. Hammill and Wiederholt concluded, therefore, that early perceptual ability, as measured by the DTVP, was only "minimally useful" in the prediction of future school achievement. A similar conclusion regarding the potential utility of the Frostig Test materials has been reported by Bortner (1974).

For educators, the contribution of perceptual ability to reading is of primary concern as reading competency is the foremost academic goal of the early school years. Hammill (1972) has summarized the research pertaining to reading achievement in first- and second-grade children. In addition to restricting his review to studies that employed first- and second-grade pupils, he distinguished between reading comprehension and word-calling. Only studies that assessed the former type of reading performance were examined in detail. Of the 12 research reports (of an original 42 investigations) that met the prestated criteria, 8 failed to find any statistically significant relationships or reported correlations so low that they were of little value for predictive purposes. Of the 4 studies that did report significant findings, 2 had serious methodological flaws. On the basis of these data, Hammill concluded that the cumulative findings of the studies provided little evidence of a practical or meaningful relationship between perception and reading for first- and second-grade children.

Regarding the issue of the interdependence of perceptual abilities and reading achievement, Bortner (1974) maintains that it is necessary to distinguish between tests of perceptual–motor ability and tests of perceptual discriminative ability. After categorizing a group of studies according to this dimension, he repeatedly found significant relationships between measures of perceptual discriminative ability and reading but inconsistent results between perceptual–motor and reading tests. He concluded that there was an undeniable relationship between perceptual discrimination and reading, but that the extent of a relationship of perceptual–motor ability and reading remains questionable. Bortner's conclusions hold some implications for assessment and evaluation; the diagnostician should not review pure perceptual and integrated perceptual–motor tasks as one and the same thing but should, if a perceptual–motor dysfunction is suspected, attempt to separate the perceptual and motor components of the problem.

While Bortner's conclusions are more optimistic than those of Hammill, they are not necessarily contradictory. Each author has approached the literature with a different frame of reference. Hammill focused on reading comprehension at a restricted age level and applied a statistical standard by which to evaluate the utility of reported correlation coefficients. Bortner, on the other hand, was more concerned with the specification of the nature of the perceptual tasks and did not direct his attention to word comprehension but rather to the "pure" perceptual aspects of reading. However, reading is more than letter discrimination or word-calling. Therefore, the implications of Hammill's review bear more relevance for the classroom.

Studies of long-term predictive power of early perceptual–motor assessment is of particular interest and has been investigated by Goodman and Wiederholt (1973), Keogh and Smith (1967), and deHirsch, Jansky, and Langford (1966). Goodman and Wiederholt (1973) used multiple regression techniques to determine the relative power of visual perception; readiness (for kindergartners), achievement (for first graders), and intelligence measures to predict future reading success among urban, disadvantaged children. Of the three measures used with kindergarten subjects (Developmental Test of Visual Perception, Metropolitan Readiness Test, Slosson Intelligence Test), perception was the only significant predictor. However, the relationship, while statistically reliable, was too weak to be practically useful. For first-grade subjects, only the Metropolitan Achievement Test results, of the three measures used (Metropolitan Achievement Test, Developmental Test of Visual Perception, Slosson Intelligence Test), proved to be a significant and useful predictor. Inclusion of the perceptual testing did not strengthen the predictor battery.

DeHirsch *et al.* (1966) in a 2-year longitudinal study examined the relationship of 37 preschool variables to reading ability at the end of second grade. Of the 10 perceptual–motor tests included in the original battery only 3 (Pencil Memory, Bender–Gestalt Test and Figure Ground) variables yielded significant coefficients when related with measures of achievement. Further, of the three variables, only the correlation of the Bender–Gestalt Test and achievement ($r = 44$) was strong enough to be educationally useful. The predictive power of kindergarten Bender–Gestalt Test Scores over a period of 7 years has been documented by Keogh and Smith (1967). However, they pointed out that the test was a more accurate predictor for students who initially received good rather than poor scores. Therefore, it would seem that the Bender–Gestalt is of limited value for remedial purposes.

In summary, there appears to be a definite and generally consistent significant relationship between perceptual and perceptual–motor skills and performance on tests of intelligence, readiness, and school performance. On the whole, the studies that reported statistically significant relationships far outnumber studies that failed to find significant relationships between perceptual and performance variables. Additionally, the absolute values of the reported coefficients tend to range from weak to moderate. But, if some standard of practicality is applied, many of the significant correlations reported prove to be too weak for practical application. Therefore, it would appear that overreliance on perceptually based test devices for the prediction of future school performance or cognitive development is unwise. More important, the use of these correlation results as substantiation of a causal relationship between the early perceptual–motor ability and later cognitive–academic achievement is totally unwarranted. Evidence relative to the trainability of perceptual–motor functions and the transferability of such training to other performance areas can only be derived from the results of experimental, i.e., intervention, studies.

Intervention Studies

Of the many perceptual and/or motor training systems that are commercially available, the most popular and widely used are those developed by Kephart (1971), Frostig–Horne (1964), and Getman–Kane (1964). These programs vary from highly structured training systems (Frostig–Horne) to loose collections of recommended remedial activities (Kephart). Both the Frostig–Horne and Kephart systems are test related; Frostig's Developmental Test of Visual Perception (1961) evaluates the child's performance on five different perceptual and/or motor skills that correspond to the five series of developmental worksheets that comprise the remedial program. Kephart's Purdue Perceptual Motor Survey (Roach and Kephart, 1960) points out perceptual–motor dysfunction in any of 11 performance areas. The Getman–Kane program does not incorporate a diagnostic device; rather, the authors maintain that the training program can be used for both remedial and developmental instruction and suggest that it be used as a general supplement to kindergarten and first-grade curricula.

Over the past several years special education periodicals have published a continuous stream of papers dealing with the efficacy of perceptual–motor training. The training systems of Frostig, Kephart, and Getman–Kane, more than any others, have been cited as the sources, totally or in part, for training procedures employed in most published research reports. As these training systems do, in fact, represent the state of the art of perceptual–motor training as it is practiced in special education today, we feel justified in limiting our discussion to the research relative to these programs.

The research pertaining to the Frostig–Horne training methodology has been presented by Hammill, Goodman, and Wiederholt (1974). The authors found that the Frostig–Horne training was used most often for the express purpose of bringing about improvements in reading skill and achievement. However, in 13 of 14 studies (Buckland and Balow, 1973; Wiederholt and Hammill, 1971; Arciszewski, 1968; Bennett, 1968; Fortenberry, 1968; Jacobs, 1968; Jacobs, Wirthlin, and Miller, 1968; Lewis, 1968; O'Connor, 1968; Sherk, 1968; Linn, 1967, 1968; Forgone, 1966; Rosen, 1966; and Mould, 1965), which investigated the effect of Frostig–Horne type training on reading achievement, failed to find significant improvements for the children who received such training. The single contradicting study reported by Lewis (1968) had serious methodological flaws that essentially negated his positive findings. In the area of readiness, 7 relevant studies were found. Of these, 4 investigators reported that perceptual training did not measurably influence children's performance on readiness tests (Buckland and Balow, 1973; Wiederholt and Hammill, 1971; Simpkins, 1970; McBeath, 1966). The remaining 3 studies did yield significant improvements in readiness scores (Frostig, 1970; Alley, Snider, Spencer, and Angell, 1968; Cowles, 1968). The conflicting nature of these research findings does not permit definitive statements, pro or con, regarding the efficacy of the Frostig–Horne materials when used as a supplement to school-readiness programs.

In light of the preponderantly negative findings regarding reading and readiness, the authors asked a more fundamental question: What degree of effectiveness do the Frostig–Horne materials have on the more basic perceptual–motor skill development. Of 7 studies that investigated this question (Wiederholt and Hammill, 1971; Alley, 1968; Alley *et al.,* 1968; Arciszewski, 1968; Cawley, Burrow, and Goodstein, 1968; Jacobs, 1968; Jacobs, Wirthlin, and Miller, 1968) 6 reported no statistical differences between trained and nontrained subjects, while only 1 (Mould, 1965) found such training to be beneficial in training perceptual processes.

On the whole, the results were disappointing. The negative trend is definite for both reading and, surprisingly, for perceptual skills as well. The increases in readiness do not offset these other results. The cause of the readiness improvements is questionnable; i.e., treatment effect or similarity or pretest and posttest measures. The implications of the cumulative research data are quite clear. Young children derive little if any educational benefits from participation in Frostig training programs.

The studies pertaining to Kephart and Getman–Kane training have been summarized by Goodman and Hammill (1973). Of 42 intervention studies, only 16 met minimal methodological criteria (Goodman, 1973; Halliwell and Solan, 1972; Hiers, 1970; Keim, 1970; McRaney, 1970; Falik, 1969; Lipton, 1969; O'Connor, 1968; Okada, 1969; Pryzwanski, 1969; Turner and Fisher, 1969; Faustman, 1967; Wimsatt, 1967, McBeath, 1966; Garrison, 1965; and Getman–Kane, 1964). Of these studies, 11 were concerned with the effects of visual–motor training on visual–motor performance. In all, 25 measures of visual–motor ability were included in the posttest batteries of these studies and the results were, for most part, insignificant. The experimental subjects performed significantly better than the control subjects in only 4 instances. But in 1 of these studies, O'Connor (1968), the significant result is suspect due to a difference in the teacher–pupil ratio between the experimental and control groups (1:10 versus 1:30 respectively).

The effects of visual–motor training on school readiness were investigated in 8 studies in which 9 posttest criteria of readiness were used. Significantly better readiness scores favored the trained subjects on 3 of the 9 posttests (Hiers, 1970; Turner and Fisher, 1969; Lipton, 1969). The results of 2 of the "positive" studies are puzzling, however. Hiers (1970) noted improvement on the cognitive and auditory subtests but not on the visual–motor subtests of the Metropolitan Readiness Test, and Turner and Fisher (1969) found improved readiness without a concommitant improvement in visual–motor skills. In the later instance, the authors themselves suggest that the positive treatment effect may have been due to confounding variables and not the treatment variable under investigation.

The effects of visual–motor training on intelligence, school achievement, and language functioning were investigated in 10 studies. Fifteen different posttest analyses were reported but the experimental subjects performed significantly better in only 6 instances. Wimsatt (1967), using kindergarten, first and second-grade students, found that the experimental kindergarten children made significant gains in reading aptitude but not in intelligence, while the first and second-graders apparently did not benefit at all from the training program. In light of the limited treatment effect, he concluded that there is little evidence that visual—motor training benefits general learning abilities. In contrast, significantly better performance on tests of reading comprehension for first graders who received supplemental perceptual—motor training in addition to their regular reading program were found by Getman and Kane (1964) and by Halliwell and Solan (1972). Faustman (1967) reports significantly greater gains in word-recognition ability for the experimental group, and Okada (1969) found that treatment produced significant improvements in the psycholinguistic functioning of first-grade experimental children.

Goodman and Hammill's review of the literature related to the application of the Kephart and Getman—Kane training programs yielded only 1 study in which training of this sort had been used with orthopedically handicapped children (Hendry, 1970). In this study, a small group of multiply handicapped children demonstrated improvements on selected perceptual—motor skills after participation in a 6-week training program. However, the results reported by Hendry are suspect due to the study's inadequate research design; i.e., lack of a control group, small number of experimental subjects, short training period. The lack of intervention studies for the orthopedically handicapped is unfortunate. Presumably, children with permanent physical limitations would have a compelling need for remedial perceptual and/or motor training. Goodman (1973) subsequently applied the Kephart—Getman techniques in a program for 44 preschool physically handicapped youngsters. Criteria were selected to measure improved performance in the three areas of visual, motor, and integrated visual—motor ability. Contrary to expectations, the experimental subjects did not perform significantly better than the control subjects on any of these tests at the end of the five-month training period. In fact, the group differences did not even consistently favor the experimental children. It would appear then that participation in the supplemental visual—motor program was no more effective than participation in the regular preschool program regarding the enhancement of visual—motor functioning. While the results of this study by itself cannot be viewed as conclusive evidence of the efficacy or nonefficacy of the Kephart and Getman—Kane training activities, it does, however, take on added significance when combined with other intervention studies.

The method of analysis employed in the reviews of Hammill *et al.* (1974) and that of Goodman and Hammill (1973) were based on the prevailing trend of significant and nonsignificant results, and a distinction was made between adequate and inadequate research; positive findings in the absence of adequate procedures were generally discounted. One may argue, as Bortner (1974) has done, that "if only one good study demonstrated a positive result, then the trainability of perception would have to be viewed as a viable concept." We must disagree. The credibility of educational research of the type we have been discussing lies in the experimental rigor and the demonstrable replicability of the results. Considering the lack of control that characterizes the research in our field, it seems to us that it would be wiser to view isolated instances of positive research findings, especially when faced with a number of reports to the contrary, as due to other, rather than intended, treatment effects. Bortner further questioned the adequacy of current training programs as embodiments of perceptual theory, and suggests that the proof of the theory not be based on utilization of "primitive technologies." While his point is well taken, at this time we can only respond to what has been done, not what might be forthcoming in the future.

To conclude, then, the results of attempts to implement the Frostig–Horne materials and the Kephart–Getman techniques in the schools have for the most part been unrewarding. The readiness skills of children were improved in only a few instances. The effect of training on intelligence and academic achievement was not clearly demonstrated. Particularly disappointing were the findings that pertained to the effects of such training on perceptual–motor performance itself. In light of the cumulative research data, one must seriously question the validity of the theory upon which these training programs rest.

The intervention studies reviewed by us this far have involved comparative analysis of various treatments (perceptual–motor training versus traditional school activities, different perceptual–motor training systems, etc.) among similar groups of children. A second type of intervention study, not mentioned to this point, is designed to assess the effects of different treatment methods when they are provided for groups of children who differ in certain basic abilities. The research paradigm is based on the conception of aptitude–treatment–interaction (ATI); i.e., learning efficiency is enhanced when children are assigned to alternative instructional programs congruent with their individual learning characteristics. In the past several years, increasing numbers of ATI studies have been conducted in both regular and special education. ATI studies in the field of special education have almost exclusively focused on children's modality functioning as the basis for classification of youngsters into different ability groups. Typically, children are assessed and categorized as auditory or visual learners and instruction is then fitted to the preferred information processing mode: auditory-based instruction for auditory-preferred learners and visual-based instruction for visual-preferred learners. The expectations are that visual learners will function more efficiently via the visual mode, and that auditory learners will function more efficiently via the auditory channel. Investigations of the modality-based ATI effects in Special Education settings include the works of Newcomer and Goodman (1975), Lilly and Kelleher (1973), Waugh (1973), Sabatino, Ysseldyke, Woolston (1973), Ysseldyke (1973), Sabatino and Ysseldyke (1972), Janssen (1971), Freer (1971), and Bateman (1968). The study of

Lilly and Kelleher was the only investigation reported to date in which children performed significantly better when instruction was presented through their preferred information processing channel.

While the research efforts thus far have provided little evidence to support the benefits of the ATI paradigm in special education (a similar finding has been reported by Ysseldyke, 1973a, and Bracht, 1970, for the literature in all areas of education), the ATI approach, nevertheless, holds considerable appeal and we do anticipate continued interest and effort in this direction in the future. Such research is the best hope for identifying perceptual inputs in learning—if indeed they can be effectively isolated.

CONCLUSIONS AND RECOMMENDATIONS

In the light of the evidence against perceptual training, except as a busy work maneuver or a parent palliative, what do we have as alternatives, in the face of so many children who have failed to learn because of handicaps mild and severe? We do believe that there are answers, though they will not have the charismatic appeal of perceptual training, and they will not undo handicaps. Rather, they promise to assist us in training handicapped children to the best of their abilities.

What are these answers? They are: (1) behavioral, or more properly, instructional objectives and (2) criterion-referenced measurement.

We will not enter into any extended discussion of them here. Those who are not fully acquainted with the subjects are referred to Popham (1972) and Kibler (1970) for satisfactory accounts of the one, and to Jackson (1970), Kriewall (1969), and Johnson (1971) for the other. Behavioral objectives simply allow us to state, with narrowed precision, what the specific goals of our instruction are. We can thus chart and direct the training and learning processes in a definite unambiguous way. Criterion-referenced measurement can help to determine how much an individual has achieved in a specific area of behavior or academics, in contrast to norm-referenced measurement, the traditional standardized mode in education where an individual's score on a test is compared to the norms established for that test. CRM (criterion-reference tests) and NRM (norm-reference tests) are not incompatible, but they do aim for different purposes: the one for determining how much a child has gained in a given area, the other for how well he did compared to others. There are many criticisms raised against both the behavioral objective-based instruction as being mechanistic and narrow, and even sterile. Accusations have been made that criterion-referenced measurement is naïvely simplistic, when one considers the vast domains of behavior that we are interested in. How can any instrument with a finite number of test items measure the total behavioral realm effectively? And are we really assessing learning quantitatively by using it? We believe that such objections are indeed appropriate for "higher" realms of instruction. But we, in remedial and special education, are involved in far simpler and more basic areas where indeed the items to be taught tend to be mechanical, as, for example, in shoe-tieing or word-decoding, and where the domain of behavioral items we wish to sample may not be a finite range of self-care skills rather than the complexities of more advanced knowledge. There will be many domains of behavior for which criterion-referenced objective approaches are not successful—the affective domain is one where we and others question their value. But, for many areas of essential behavior, they have already proven effective when combined in a program of mastery learning.

Mastery learning is a recent development, or modification of earlier similar practices introduced or reintroduced by Benjamin Bloom (1968) in recent years. It refers to teaching toward criterion in given subject-matter areas, and, if the individual student has not succeeded in one attempt, he must try, try again. Bloom has increased achievement and knowledge enormously in his college classes by its application. It does not necessarily depend on instructional objectives or criterion-referenced measurement, though these clarify and accelerate the process—at least for handicapped children.

Proger and Mann have adapted the mastery learning approach, using a variant of instructional objects or curriculum-embedded instructional objectives; i.e., one's referent to a specific curriculum. They have utilized the Palo Alto reading series to successfully teach nonreading, learning-disabled children, who failed miserably to learn to read in some of the finest schools. In the system called Individual Achievement Monitoring, one simply proceeds by teaching through 2-week instructional units of the Palo Alto Curriculum. At the close of each unit, a child is tested on a criterion-referenced test assessing mastery of that unit. If he passes, he proceeds to the next unit. If he fails, he repeats the unit. Tested against the pass–fail criteria set on his unit test, he again proceeds through the same curriculum unit or passes on. If he fails at this time, specialized teaching is brought to bear. But this has rarely been required. Given enough exposure, almost all move through the curriculum. The speed with which they do it, not their perceptual competency or auditory decoding skills, is the critical variable relating to success. Contrary to the claim by some that the curriculum has not been shown successful with the learning-disabled, Proger and Mann have demonstrated that curriculum can be taught if properly managed. The details of the original system have been published recently in the *Journal of Learning Disabilities* (Proger and Mann, 1973). We have altered the original approach and concepts somewhat, since that period, and a more recent version of the program applicable for regular grades is currently available from Harcourt Brace Jovanovitch, Inc.

Libby Goodman and Don Hammill proceeded along similar lines toward developing a competency-based inventory of basic school skills. Rather than tell teachers what they ought to be looking for in the classrooms, Goodman and Hammill have depended on the teachers, rather than theories or a process orientation, as the source for items that have been included in their test measure. The instrument emphasizes the skills and behaviors that teachers expect first-grade children to possess and that are necessary for school success. The results, thus far, are quite promising. Teachers heartily approve of this approach and have found that the instrument is practical, relevant, and adaptable for both remedial and/or developmental instruction. Statistically, preliminary results indicate that the test is valid and possesses a higher degree of reliability and predictive power than most of the readiness tests currently in use (Goodman and Hammill, 1974).

To sum up, perceptual training has digressed training for the child with problems into irrelevancies and mispractice. It is time that we return to training children in the skills functional for their living. One way to do this is with instructional objectives and criterion-referenced measurement. Thorndyke in 1948 reviewed the investigations of Hotelling and Thurstone in their search for abilities similar to those of Guilford in our day (Ebel, 1974). He concluded that this work "has not so far increased our equipment of adequate tests of pure abilities much, if at all." Then he added, "I do not require them of the future partly because I do not believe the mind is composed of such and partly because in any case there are more urgent needs." Here he meant tests of practical and utilitarian abilities, ones that contribute to success in life—reading, writing, and shoelace-tieing. They are presumably the abilities that schools were intended to teach—not those of perception. We can only concur.

REFERENCES

Allen, R. M. Factor Analysis of the Developmental Test of Visual Perception performance of educable mental retardates. *Perceptual and Motor Skills,* 1968, *26,* 257–258.

Alley, G. Perceptual–motor performance of mentally retarded children after systematic visual-perception training. *American Journal of Mental Deficiency,* 1968, *73,* 247–250.

Alley, G., Snider, W., Spencer, J., and Angell, R. Reading readiness and the Frostig–Horne training program. *Exceptional children,* 1968, *35,* 68.

Arciszewski, R. A. The effects of visual perception training on the perceptual ability and reading achievement of first grade students. *Dissertation Abstracts,* 1968, *29,* 4174-A.

Bateman, B. The efficacy of an auditory and a visual method of first grade reading instruction with auditory and visual learners. In H. K. Smith (Ed.), *Perception and reading.* Newark, Delaware: International Reading Association, 1968.

Bennett, R. M. A study of the effects of a visual perception program upon school achievement, IQ and visual perception. *Dissertation Abstracts,* 1968, *29,* 3864-A.

Bloom, B. S. Learning for Mastery. *Evaluation Comments,* 1968, *1,* No. 2.

Bortner, M. Perceptual Skills and early reading disability. In L. Mann, and D. Sabatino (Eds.) *The second review of special education.* Philadelphia: Journal of Special Education Press, 1974, 79–101.

Boyd, L., and Randle, K. Factor Analysis of the Frostig Developmental test of Visual Perception. *Journal of Learning Disabilities,* 1970, *3,* 253–255.

Bracht, G. H. Experimental factors related to aptitude-treatment interactions. *Review of Educational Research,* 1970, *40,* 627–645.

Buckland, P. and Balow, B. Effects of visual percentual training on reading achievement. *Exceptional Children,* 1973, *39,* 299–304.

Corah, N. L., and Powell, B. J. A factor analytic study of the Frostig Developmental Test of Visual Perception. *Perceptual and Motor Skills,* 1963, *16,* 59–63.

Cawley, J. F., Burrow, W. H., and Goodstein, H. A. An appraisal of Head Start participants and non-participants (Research report, Contract OEO4177, Office of Economic Opportunity). Storrs, Conn.: University of Connecticut, 1968.

Cowles, J. D. An experimental study of visual-perceptual training and readiness scores with certain first grade children. Unpublished doctoral dissertation. University of Alabama, 1968.

De Hirsch, K., Jansky, J., and Langford, W. S. *Predicting reading failure.* New York: Harper and Row, 1966.

Ebel, R. L. And still the dryads linger. *American Psychologist,* 1974, *29,* 485–492.

Falik, L. H. The effects of special training in kindergarten with second grade reading. *Journal of Learning Disabilities,* 1969, *2,* 325–329.

Faustman, M. N. Some effects of perception training in kindergarten on first grade success in reading. International Reading Association Conference (Seattle, May, 1967), ERIC ED 017–397.

Fleishman, E. A. On the relation between abilities, learning, and human performance. *American Psychologist,* 1972, *27,* 1017–1032.

Forgone, C. Effects of visual perception and language training upon certain abilities of retarded children. Unpublished doctoral dissertation, George Peabody College for Teachers, 1966.

Fortenberry, W. D. Effectiveness of a special program for development of word recognition by culturally disadvantaged first grade pupils. ERIC ED 027–368, 1968.

Freer, F. J. Visual and auditory perceptual modality differences as related to success in first grade reading word recognition. Dissertation Abstracts, 6193-A. Unpublished doctoral dissertation, Rutgers University, 1971.

Frostig, M. Pilot program in early childhood education, Compton, City School District, 1970. Unpublished report, Project 75-E. 1. A.

Frostig, M., and Horne, D. *The Frostig program for the development of visual perception.* Chicago: Follett, 1964.

Frostig, M., Maslow, P., Lefevre, D. W., and Whittlesey, J. R. B. *The Marianne Frostig Developmental Test of Visual Perception,* Palo Alto, California: Consulting Psychologists Press, 1961.

Garrison, E. B. A study in visual-motor perception training in first grade, ERIC ED 031–292, 1965.

Getman, G. N., and Kane, E. R. The physiology of readiness: An action program for the development of perception for children. Minneapolis, Minnesota: Programs to Accelerate School Success, 1964.

Goodman, L. Efficacy of visual motor training for orthopedically handicapped children. Unpublished doctoral dissertation, Temple University, Philadelphia, 1973.

Goodman, L., and Hammill, D. The effectiveness of Kephart–Getman activities in developing perceptual–motor and cognitive skills. *Focus on Exceptional Children,* 1973, *4,* 1–9.

Goodman, L., and Hammill, D. *The Goodman-Hammill Basic Schools Skills Inventory.* Follett, 1975.

Goodman, L., and Wiederholt, J. L. Predicting reading achievement in disadvantaged children. *Psychology in the Schools,* 1973, *10,* 181–185.

Halliwell, J. W., and Solan, H. A. The effects of a supplemental perceptual training program on reading achievement. *Exceptional Children*, 1972, *38*, 613–621.

Hammill, D. Training visual perception processes. *Journal of Learning Disabilities*, 1972, *5*, 552–559.

Hammill, D., Colarusso, R. P., and Wiederholt, J. L. Diagnostic value of the Frostig test: A factor analytic approach. *Journal of Special Education*, 1970, *4*, 279–282.

Hammill, D., Goodman, L., and Wiederholt, J. L. Visual-motor processes: Can we train them? *Reading Teacher*, 1974, *27*, 469–478.

Hammill, D., and Wiederholt, J. L. Review of the Frostig Visual Perception Test and the related training program. In L. Mann and D. Sabatino (Eds.), *The first review of special education*. Philadelphia: Journal of Special Education Press, 1973.

Hendry, B. C. The effects of gross-motor movements on the perceptual–motor development of primary age multiply handicapped children. *Dissertation Abstracts*, 1970, *31*, 5231-A.

Hiers, M. H. A comparison of the readiness test performance of a group of primary level educable mentally retarded children instructed on visual-motor perception tasks and a comparable group receiving no prescribed instruction. *Dissertation Abstracts*, 1970, *31*, 6440-A.

Jackson, R. Developing criterion-referenced tests. Princeton, New Jersey. Educational Testing Service, 1970. ERIC Clearinghouse on Tests, Measurement, and Evaluation, ED 041–052.

Jacobs, J. N. An evaluation of the Frostig visual-perception training program. *Educational Leadership*, 1968, *25*, 332–340.

Jacobs, J. N., Wirthlin, L. D., and Miller, C. B. A follow-up evaluation of the Frostig visual perceptual training program. *Educational Leadership Research Supplement*, 1968, *4*, 169–175.

Janssen, D. R. Effects of visual and auditory perceptual attitudes and letter discrimination pretraining on word recognition. Unpublished doctoral dissertation, The Pennsylvania State University, 1971.

Johnson, M. S., and Kress, R. A. Task analysis for criterion-referenced tests, measurement, and evaluation, ED 041 052, 1971.

Keim, R. P. Visual-motor training, readiness, and intelligence of kindergarten children. *Journal of Learning Disabilities*, 1970, *3*, 256–259.

Keogh, B. K., and Smith, C. E. Visuo-motor ability for school prediction: A seven year study. *Perceptual and Motor Skills*, 1967, *25*, 101–110.

Kephart, N. C. *The slow learner in the classroom* (2nd ed.). Columbus, Ohio: Charles E. Merrill, 1971.

Kibler, R. T. (Ed.). *Behavioral objectives and instruction.* Boston: Allyn and Bacon, 1970.

Kriewall, T. E., and Hirsch, E. The development and interpretation of criterion-referenced tests. Madison: University of Wisconsin Research and Development Center for Cognitive Learning, 1969. ERIC ED 042–815.

Lewis, J. N. The improvement of reading ability through a developmental program in visual perception. *Journal of Learning Disabilities*, 1968, *1*, 652–653.

Lilly, S. M., and Kelleher, J. Modality strengths and aptitude–treatment interaction. *Journal of Special Education*, 1973, *7*, 5–13.

Linn, S. H. From the classroom: Visual perceptual training for kindergarten children. *Academic Therapy Quarterly*, 1967, *4*, 255–258.

Lipton, E. D. The effects of physical education programs to develop directionality of movement on perceptual–motor development, visual perception, and reading readiness of first grade children. *Dissertation Abstracts*, 1969, *30*, 2362-A.

Mann, L. Perceptual training: Misdirections and redirections. *American Journal of Orthopsychiatry*, 1970, *40*, 30–38.

Mann, L. Perceptual training revisited: The training of nothing at all. *Rehabilitation Literature,* 1971, *32,* 322–237, 335. (a)

Mann, L. The ground game in special education. *Journal of Special Education,* 1971, *5,* 53–58. (b)

Mann, L. and Phillips, W. A. Fractional practices in special education: A critique. *Exceptional Children,* 1967, *33.* 311–317.

McBeath, P. M. The effectiveness of three reading preparedness programs for perceptually handicapped kindergarteners. *Dissertation Abstracts,* 1966, *27,* 115-A.

McRaney, K. A. A study of perceptual motor exercises utilized as an early grade enrichment program for the improvement of learning activity and motor development. *Dissertation Abstracts,* 1970, *31,* 2935-A.

Mould, R. E. An evaluation of the effectiveness of a special program for retarded readers manifesting disturbed visual perception. Unpublished doctoral dissertation, Washington State University, 1965.

Newcomer, P. L., and Goodman, L. Effect of modality of instruction on the learning of meaningful and non-meaningful material by auditory and visual learners. *Journal of Special Education,* 1975, *9,* 261–268.

O'Connor, C. Effects of selected physical activities upon motor performance perceptual performance and academic achievement of first graders. *Perceptual Motor Skills,* 1968, *29,* 703–709.

Ohnmacht, F., and Olson, A. V. Canonical analysis of reading readiness measures and the Frostig DTVP. *Educational and Psychological Measurement,* 1968, *28,* 479–484.

Okada, D. M. The effects of perceptual and perceptual motor training on the visual perception, auditory perception, and language performance of institutionalized educable mental retardates. *Dissertation Abstracts,* 1969, *30,* 2857-A.

Popham, W. T. Objectives-based management strategies for large educational systems. *Journal of Educational Research,* 1972, *66,* 4–9.

Proger, B. B., and Mann, L. Criterion-referenced measurement: The world of gray versus black and white. *Journal of Learning Disabilities,* 1973, *6,* 18–30.

Pryzwanski, W. E. The effects of perceptual-motor training and manuscript writing on reading readiness skills in kindergarten. *Dissertation Abstracts,* 1969, *31,* 384-B.

Roach, E. C., and Kephart, N. C. *The Purdue Perceptual–Motor Survey.* Columbus, Ohio: Charles E. Merrill, 1960.

Rosen, C. L. An experimental study of visual-perceptual training and reading achievement in first grade. *Perceptual and Motor Skills,* 1966, *22,* 979–1086.

Sabatino, D. A., and Ysseldyke, J. E. An evaluation of diagnostic-prescriptive teaching with handicapped children. Mimeograph, The Pennsylvania State University, University Park, Pa., 1972.

Sabatino, D. A., Ysseldyke, J. E., and Woolston, J. Diagnostic–prescriptive teaching utilizing perceptual strengths of mentally retarded children. *American Journal of Mental Deficiency,* 1973, *78,* 7–14.

Sherk, J. K. A study of the effects of a program of visual perception on the progress of retarded readers. *Dissertation Abstracts,* 1968, 4392-A.

Simpkins, K. W. Effect of the Frostig program for the development of visual perception on the readiness of kindergarten children. *Dissertation Abstracts,* 1970, *30,* 4286-A.

Turner, R. V., and Fisher, M. D. The effects of a perceptual motor training program upon the readiness and perceptual development of culturally disadvantaged kindergarten children. ERIC ED 041–663, 1969.

Waugh, R. P. Relationship between modality preference and performance. *Exceptional Children,* 1973, *39,* 465–496.

Wimsatt, W. R. The effects of sensory-motor training on the learning abilities of grade school children. *Dissertation Abstracts,* 1967, *28,* 347-B.

Wiederholt, J. L., and Hammill, D. D. Use of the Frostig—Horne Perception Program in the urban school. *Psychology in the schools.* 1971, *8,* 268–274.

Ysseldyke, J. Diagnostic—prescriptive teaching: The search for aptitude—treatment interactions. In L. Mann and D. A. Sabatino (Eds.), *The First Review of Special Education.* Philadelphia: Journal of Special Education Press, 1973. (a)

Ysseldyke, J. E. Aptitude—treatment interaction research with learning-disabled children. Paper presented at the 1973 annual meeting of the American Educational Research Association, New Orleans, February 27, 1973. (b)

15

A Behavior Modification Approach
to the Treatment of Autistic Children

O. IVAR LOVAAS, LAURA SCHREIBMAN, and
ROBERT L. KOEGEL

When we talk about *autistic children* we are describing children who manifest several characteristic pathological behaviors (e.g., social withdrawal, self-stimulation, ritualistic behavior, echolalic and psychotic speech, apparent sensory deficit, affective impoverishment). When using such a diagnostic label one is typically conceptualizing *autism* as a distinct entity; an underlying process that is seen as the cause of these deviant behaviors. Indeed, a great deal of research has focused on this one underlying process as the basis for the psychopathology. From a behavioristic viewpoint, it is quite unnecessary to postulate such an underlying *disease* or entity, and indeed it is quite possible that the different autistic behaviors are related to several different kinds of antecedent conditions. For example, we do know that many if not all of the behaviors one observes in autistic children exist in other children as well; retarded and blind children self-stimulate as do normal children if they have nothing else to do. Brain-damaged children sometimes echo while some retarded children have unusually well-developed rote memories, and so on.

In our treatment we have felt that we could develop procedures to help these children overcome their pathological behaviors and develop healthy ones with-

O. IVAR LOVAAS · Department of Psychology, University of California, Los Angeles, California 90024.
LAURA SCHREIBMAN · Department of Psychology, Claremont Men's College, Claremont, California 91711.
ROBERT L. KOEGEL · Department of Speech, University of California, Santa Barbara, California 93106.

out having to postulate an underlying process such as autism. Instead, we have thought that we may be able to isolate the controlling conditions for each one of their various pathological behaviors, taken one at a time. It would of course be desirable, if for no other reason than treatment efficiency, if we could discover that their various behaviors interacted in the sense that if we changed one behavior, then certain others would change concurrently. But one may also be prepared for the possibility that these behaviors are relatively independent of each other so that as one gains some control over one of them, one does not necessarily gain control over the others. For example, as one established the kind of relationship with a child that makes him affectionate to adults, he might not simultaneously show any improvement in his language. However, should a speech therapist be successful in teaching language to such a child, then one might observe a concurrent decrease in psychotic speech. Needless to say, we hope for large interacting response classes, since our treatment efforts would then become proportionately more efficient.

Given the uncertainty both in regard to etiology and prognosis of the diagnostic label *autism*, we would prefer to provide a diagnosis of the child in terms of the specific behaviors he does or does not have. Such a behavioral diagnosis may be productive for several reasons. First, if the variables that control a particular behavior are known, then the treatment is suggested by the diagnosis. If we do not know how to alter the behavior, then the diagnosis would suggest that further research must be attempted before these behaviors can be treated. Therefore, a prognosis is also included in the behavioral diagnosis. Finally, describing a child in terms of specific behaviors, since these are relatively public and visible to all, should help to facilitate communication between those who produce research and those who consume it.

BEHAVIOR THEORY AND AUTISM

The first succinct attempt to understand the behavior of autistic children within a behavioristic framework was carried out by Ferster (1961). Ferster presented a very convincing argument of how it was that in the absence of acquired symbolic rewarding aspects of social stimuli (and with a general deficiency in acquired reinforcers), one might expect the very impoverished behavioral development one sees in autistic children. The primary contribution of Ferster's theoretical argument lies in the explicitness and concreteness with which he relates learning principles to behavioral development. There have been some general efforts to relate learning theory to psychopathology in the past, but perhaps none presented the argument as directly as did Ferster.

Shortly thereafter, Ferster and DeMyer (1962) reported a set of experiments in which they exposed autistic children to very simplified but controlled environments where they could engage in simple behaviors such as pulling levers or matching to sample, for reinforcers that were significant or functional to them. The Ferster and DeMyer studies were the first to show that the behavior of autistic children could be related in a lawful manner to certain explicit environmental changes. What the children learned in these studies was not of much practical significance, but the studies did show that by carefully programming certain environmental consequences, these children could in fact be taught to comply with certain aspects of reality.

These early studies and others had certain features in common. They explicitly arranged certain relationships between their patient's behavior and his surroundings and immediate environment. The data that emerged from these studies were on the whole very regular and lawful, which is another way to say that one could understand the patient and be of help to him. Finally, because the majority of the patients whom these investigators worked with had been so difficult to help before, a wave of optimism and enthusiasm was communicated about what might be done for severely disturbed, such as psychotic and retarded children. It seemed, in these early studies, that the problem that faced us could be solved if we paid attention to perfecting our educational techniques for teaching appropriate behaviors, rather than making research efforts into some hypothetical entity within the child, such as brain damage or psychosis.

Let us now turn to a very brief summary of the essential points within that part of learning theory that we have relied upon to help us in our treatment projects with psychotic children. Using the concepts of learning theory, one can view a child's development as consisting of the acquisition of two events: (a) behaviors and (b) stimulus functions. If we look at the behavioral development of autistic children, perhaps the most striking feature about them centers on their behavioral deficiency. They have little if any behavior that would help them function in society. If one was going to treat autistic children based on this perspective, then one would try to strengthen behaviors, such as appropriate play and speech, by reinforcing their occurrence. When their occurrence is initially absent, those behaviors should be gradually shaped by rewarding successive approximations to their eventual occurrence. Similarly, one might attempt to treat certain behaviors, such as tantrums and self-destruction, by either systematically withholding those reinforcers that may be maintaining these behaviors or by the systematic application of aversive stimuli contingent on their occurrence. In other words, it would be possible to develop a treatment program where one worked directly with the child's behaviors, using whatever reinforcers were functional for that child. In the programs we have developed so far, we have usually developed behaviors through primary reinforcers such as food.

The child not only acquires behaviors as he develops, but his environment also acquires *meanings* (stimulus functions) for him. One part of the meaning that the world has for a person centers on its perceived reward and punishment attributes. We speak here of symbolic rewards and punishments, which technically are referred to as secondary or conditioned reinforcers. That is, certain parts of the child's environment that were neutral when he was born come to acquire the function of rewarding and punishing him. One can think of many good examples to illustrate this point, and it is particularly obvious that within the social area much of this kind of learning takes place. The presence or absence of an approving smile, while neutral to the newborn infant, gradually assumes reinforcing functions as the child interacts with his parents. The primary reason that the acquisition of these secondary reinforcers is so important lies in their control over the acquisition of behavior. Normal children appear to acquire much of their behaviors on the basis of secondary reinforcers. If autistic children do not respond to or become minimally affected by praise, smiles, hugs, interpersonal closeness, correctness, novelty, and other such secondary reinforcers that support so much behavior in normal children, it would be logical to argue that their behavioral development should be accordingly deficient. Thus, much of an autistic child's failure to develop appropriate behavior could be viewed as a function of a more basic failure of his environment to acquire meaning for him; that is, his environment failed to acquire secondary reinforcers. This was the essence of Ferster's (1961) theoretical analysis of autism.

Since these early papers, several studies have applied behavior modification procedures in an attempt to treat or educate autistic children. These studies have been characterized by relatively sophisticated research designs, which have allowed the investigators to draw conclusions about the effectiveness of their interventions; most of the potential thrust in behavior modification research derives from this adherence to sound research designs. Most of the behavioral studies have relied upon single-subject (or within-subject) replication designs, so that one could be reasonably certain that the treatment that was given did in fact help that child. But since the studies were limited to single children, the effect of the treatment across several children was not known. In one of the first and better known studies, Wolf, Risley, and Mees (1964) used reinforcement principles and a reversal design to treat a 3½-year-old autistic boy who would not eat properly, lacked normal social and verbal repertoires, was self-destructive, and refused to wear glasses necessary to preserve his vision. The child's behavior improved markedly and a subsequent follow-up study (Wolf, Risley, Johnston, Harris, and Allen, 1967) showed that he continued to improve after discharge from the program, to the point where he was able to take advantage of a public school education program.

In another early study, Hewett (1965) described a procedure for building speech in children who were initially mute. He used a shaping procedure to increase the child's attending behavior, then systematically rewarded the child for vocalizations that eventually matched those modeled by the therapist. Using this procedure, the child acquired the beginnings of meaningful language.

What the studies of Wolf, Risley, and Mees (1964) and of Hewett (1965) showed was that it was quite possible to take learning-theory principles that had been discovered in a laboratory setting, to move outside the laboratory and into the child's day-to-day environment, and to begin to work with behaviors that were directly and clinically relevant, such as to reduce tantrums and atavistic behavior and to establish meaningful social behaviors. These studies relied on what was known already within learning theory to carry out their therapeutic programs. Their use of extinction, shaping by successive approximations, and similar principles had all been isolated in animal research.

When one works with children who have severe behavioral deficiencies, it soon beomes apparent that there are some real limitations in the degree to which one can build complex behavior repertoires into children by using direct shaping procedures. Observations of the development of normal children suggested that the acquisition of complex behaviors was facilitated through imitation of such behaviors in adults and peers (Bandura, 1969). In work with autistic children, it was soon discovered that these children were greatly deficient in imitative behavior and seemed to learn little if anything on an observational basis. Therefore, to make significant progress in the acquisition of complex repertoires, we needed to know more about the conditions under which imitation occurred. Fortunately, Baer and Sherman (1964) published a very important study that showed that if one reinforced a child for imitating some of a model's behavior, the child would also begin to imitate other behaviors of the model, even though he had not been explicitly reinforced for imitating these. They viewed imitation as a discrimination, a situation in which the child discriminates the similarity between his and the model's behavior as the occasion for reinforcement. Although the Baer and Sherman study dealt with normal children who already imitated, its results gave rise to procedures for building imitative behavior in nonimitating children. Thus, Metz (1965), using reinforcement-theory principles, presented the first study to show how one could use reinforcement theory principles to build nonverbal imitative behavior in nonimitating autistic children. Lovaas, Berberich, Perloff, and Schaeffer (1966) showed how it was possible, through the use of a discrimination-learning paradigm, to build imitative verbal behavior in previously mute autistic children.

In reviewing the history of this development, it is apparent that barely fifteen years have elapsed since Ferster (1961) published the first theoretical article that attempted a behavioral analysis of autism and that not more than twelve years have elapsed since the first treatment study was published. Obviously, this is a very new field that has experienced a promising start.

RECENT DEVELOPMENTS

We will now go on to illustrate some of the more recent developments within the behavior modification approach to autistic children. As we do so, it will become apparent that a behavioral approach to autism has not addressed itself to the *total* child or *autism* as an entity, whatever that means. Neither has this behavioristic approach committed itself to a particular etiology of autism. It is important to point out that it would be very significant to discover whether there is a phenomenon called autism and to discover a specific etiology of such a problem. However, the search for answers to such questions is severely restricted because of limitations on research methodology. So, for the time being, we refrain from posing questions to which it seems impossible to obtain answers today. On the other hand, the children present certain immediate problems that we can attempt to ameliorate on the basis of what we know today.

Analysis of Self-Destructive Behavior

One of the most bizarre and most profoundly sick behaviors that one will ever encounter is self-mutilation, which is characteristic of so many psychotic and retarded children. One can see children who tear with their teeth large amounts of tissue from their shoulders and arms, who chew off part of their fingers, hit their heads so violently against the wall that they detach their retinas, and accidentally would kill themselves unless they were somehow sedated or restrained. Many of these children, although they may be only 8 or 9 years old, have spent most of their lives in restraints, tied down both by their feet and arms.

Irrational as these behaviors may appear, the studies that were conducted to better understand these behaviors show self-mutilation to be a very "lawful," understandable phenomenon. Rather than the self-destruction being an expression of some tenuous internal state, such as a shattered, guilty, worthless self, we found it to be rather straightforward learned behavior. That is, we first attempted to treat self-destruction using the treatment procedure most often prescribed at the time. This treatment, based on the psychodynamic model of psychopathology, suggested delivering affection, understanding, and sympathetic comments to reassure the child of his self-worth, etc. We carefully measured the amount of self-destructive behavior emitted by the child and found that when we gave sympathetic comments contingent upon the child hurting himself, his self-destruction increased in strength, only to return to baseline when these comments were no longer administered. Figure 1 presents the data for one child, Gregory, indicating the change in his self-abusive behavior as a function of the attention he received for such behavior. His data are presented as cumulative curves. This means that if he did not hit himself, the line is flat (i.e., horizontal); and each time he injured himself, it is recorded on a pen that makes one small step upward for each response. The steeper the curve, the more hits. that we have in sessions 1 and 2 baseline data that tell us that his self-destructive

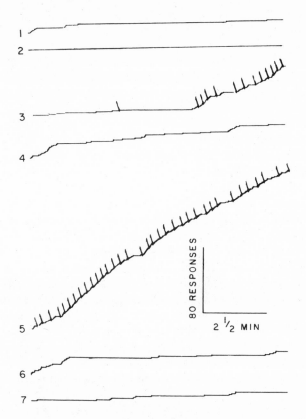

Figure 1. Gregg's self-destruction, as cumulative response curves, over successive sessions (1 through 7). The upward-moving hatchmarks in Sessions 3 and 5 mark delivery of sympathetic comments, play, etc., contingent on self-destruction.

behavior is very low; the curves are almost flat. In session 3, we started our treatment with him, expressing our concern and affection for him when he hit himself. Note also that each time we treated him in this manner the pen on the graph gave a signal by an upward-moving stroke or hatchmark. In session 3, he showed a marked increase in the rate of self-destruction when we treated him like that. In session 4, we removed the treatment and the curve flattened out; he got better. In session 5 we reintroduced the treatment and he hit himself some 200 times in the short period of 10 minutes. When we again removed the treatment (sessions 6 and 7), we recovered his baseline. This, then is an ABABA design. Incidentally, it would have been quite possible for us to have killed Greg through this treatment. All we needed to do was to thin out the reinforcement schedule a bit (i.e., follow self-destructive acts by sympathetic comments less than 100% of the time) and to have given love contingent on more vicious blows, closer to the eyes or other vulnerable spots. In other words, it looked like the self-mutilation was reinforceable, like operant behavior. It is noteworthy that this is the first instance reported in the literature where objective measures were taken to carefully assess the effects of treatment for self-destruction. Clearly, the emphasis on a research framework has enabled us to see quite vividly the dangerous prospects of this form of treatment.

We hypothesized that if self-destruction were reinforceable, as operant behavior is, then it should extinguish if we made certain that no social consequences were administered contingent upon its occurrence. This is exactly what happened. When the children were left free to injure themselves without parents or nursing staff intervening, the self-destructive behavior fell off in a very gradual but lawful manner from, for example, a high of some 4,000 self-destructive acts in the first hour to 3,500 the second hour, then 300, and then slowly to zero by the tenth session. What most convinced us that self-mutilation was in fact operant behavior pertained to its highly discriminated nature. For example, the child would not hurt himself in a room where he had been "run to extinction" but would resume self-destruction at full strength in another situation only feet and seconds away if he had been comforted for self-destructive behavior there. Clinically speaking, the children did not waste any blows unless there was a payoff for it, and our data showed that they were incredibly discriminating as to which situations paid off. Technically speaking, we say that self-mutilation was under the control of discriminative stimuli (S^D).

Although extinction may work to reduce self-destruction, there are serious limitations to extinction procedure since some of the children hurt themselves severely during extinction. Clearly, the child who hits himself thousands of times in an hour's time, or a child who tears flesh off his shoulder, is in danger, and one takes too many chances letting such a child undergo extinction runs as we have described them. Therefore, we tried out ways of delivering aversive stimuli (such as painful electric shock) contingent upon self-destruction, in the hope of stopping it more quickly. The data we reported (Lovaas and Simmons, 1969) showed an immediate and very dramatic termination of the self-destructive behavior, even in children who had been self-destructive for years. It is unclear why a relatively innocent aversive stimulus should terminate self-destruction, considering the very severe physical abuse the children inflicted upon themselves. It is possible that the children had adapted themselves to the pain from their self-inflicted injuries, while the electric shock was new, offering no opportunity for adaptation. Several people have now published on the control of self-destructive behavior (Bucher and Lovaas, 1968; Risley, 1968; Tate and Baroff, 1966) and the data are remarkably consistent.

It is likely that we understand self-destructive behavior better than any other of the behaviors that psychotic children bring to treatment. It is also significant to point out that the analysis we have presented for self-destructive behavior is the kind of analysis that behavior modifiers undertake; that is, trying to understand one behavior at a time, identifying the conditions that control the behavior, and observing how changes in one behavior may alter others. Surprisingly, and disappointingly, the reduction in self-destructive behavior did not bring with it a simultaneous change in large classes of other behaviors. The children who stopped mutilating themselves did not simultaneously become normal.

Self-Stimulatory Behavior

By far the most common form of behavior exhibited by psychotic and retarded children centers on the self-stimulatory behavior we mentioned earlier. This includes a great deal of spinning, twirling, rocking, and gazing as well as other very repetitive and stereotyped movements that seem to have no particular relationship to what is happening in the child's day-to-day life.

Our understanding of this behavior class is very limited. From clinical observation, and not so much based on systematic research, it appears that this behavior disappears or is supplanted when more normal behaviors are acquired. We do know also that the presence of certain forms of self-stimulation makes the child more difficult to teach, apparently because he is less attentive to external cues. For example, in a study by Lovaas, Litrownik, and Mann (1971) autistic children were taught to respond to an auditory input in order to obtain candies and other sweets. If the child was presented with this auditory stimulus when he was involved in self-stimulatory behavior, then frequently he would fail to respond to the auditory input, either completely missing the opportunity to obtain his reinforcer or responding after some delay. In another study by Koegel and Covert (1972), autistic children were taught a very simple discrimination task such as responding on a machine (depressing a lever) in the presence of a light stimulus. They observed that the children failed to acquire this very simple discrimination as long as they were allowed to self-stimulate. When given disapproval (either verbal or with a slap of the hand) resulting in the suppression of self-stimulation, the children did learn. It appears, then, that the self-stimulatory behavior may interfere with one's efforts to teach these children; for the sake of helping them acquire new behaviors, one may initially decrease self-stimulatory behavior.

Recent research in our lab, largely under the direction of Arnold Rincover and Crighton Newsom, has proceeded on the notion that self-stimulatory behavior is operant behavior and that it is different from other kinds of operants in the sense that the reinforcement for such behavior consists of the sensory feedback (kinesthetic, visual, auditory, etc.) that the behavior itself produces. In that sense it is the child himself who controls that reinforcement, hence shaping his own behavior. Given the extensive and durable self-stimulatory repertoires of autistic children, we suspect that these self-stimulatory reinforcers must be very strong, and we are exploring ways of using self-stimulatory reinforcers instead of food, etc., to build appropriate behaviors. So far, research shows self-stimulatory reinforcers to be much less satiable than the primary, appetitive ones.

The Teaching of Appropriate Behaviors

Since these children have such limited repertoires and since many are essentially without any social or intellectual behavior, they present a great challenge to educators. In a sense, one has the opportunity to start building a person from the beginning in regard to social and emotional development as well as intellectual development. In the short amount of space allotted here, we can only point to certain examples to illustrate the techniques that have been employed in our attempts to build new behaviors.

Simultaneously with the suppression of self-stimulatory behaviors, the teacher generally begins her work by attempting to establish some early forms of stimulus control. The teacher may request of the child some simple behavior such as sitting quietly in a chair. Since even such a minimal request often evokes tantrums of self-destructive behavior, the establishment of this basic stimulus control and the reduction of aggression and self-destructive behaviors generally proceed together. It is generally impossible to work on the acquisition of appropriate behaviors until one has achieved some reduction of the pathological behaviors.

When one attempts to educate children who are so deficient in behavioral development, theoretically one has two alternate paths to follow. For example, instead of building behaviors piece by piece, one could decide to teach a child to value interpersonal interactions, intellectual achievement, curiosity about the world, and so on. Technically speaking, one could attempt to place these children in a situation where one optimized the child's motivational system to help them acquire conditioned reinforcers. We have pointed out before (Lovaas, Freitag, Kinder, Ruberstein, Schaeffer, and Simmons, 1966) that in many ways this would be an optimal strategy because the child, being properly motivated, would learn much without explicit attempts to teach him. To illustrate this point, if a child were strongly reinforced by a large range of social reinforcers, he would probably learn to behave in social ways, that is, to talk, play with peers, and so on, so as to come in contact with these stimulus events. It is unfortunate that this alternate path to teaching is not open to us since we do not know how to establish conditioned reinforcers or to build motivation in autistic children. No doubt one of the great challenges in the years ahead will be to achieve a better understanding of how motivation is acquired.

Given this limitation on the child's motivational system, the alternative is to proceed to build behaviors with the reinforcers that are functional. One can always fall back upon basic reinforcers that are functional. One can always fall back on basic reinforcers such as food and pain, and as one works with any one child, one discovers idiosyncracies in his motivational structure, such as a particular liking for a certain piece of music, a toy, etc., that can be partitioned in various ways and delivered to the child contingent upon certain desirable behaviors. The acquisition of new behaviors is accomplished in a step-by-step program. Let us turn to efforts to build language to illustrate how these programs have worked out.

Building Language

Using a shaping procedure, several investigators (Hewett, 1965; Lovaas, 1966) have provided procedures for developing speech in previously mute autistic children. The procedure relied heavily on developing imitative speech. Let us illustrate the procedures from our language program. This program has been presented on film (Lovaas, 1969) and will appear in a book (Lovaas, in press). Briefly described, the verbal imitation training involves four steps of successive discriminations. In Step 1 the therapist increases the child's vocalizations by reinforcing him (usually with food) for such behavior. In Step 2 the child's vocalizations are reinforced only if they are in response to the therapist's speech (e.g., if they occur within five seconds of the therapist's speech) until he can match the particular sound given by the therapist (e.g., "a") In Step 4 the therapist replicates Step 3 with another sound (e.g., "m"), demanding increasing fine discriminations and reproduction from the child. In this manner, starting with sounds that are discriminably different (such as "m" and "a"), the child is taught to imitate an increasingly large range of sounds, words, and sentences. Imitation, then, is a discrimination where the response resembles its stimulus. Once he can imitate, the previously mute child becomes similar to echolalic autistic children; they both imitate the speech of others, but neither knows the meaning of the words he utters. Their speech exists without a context.

A program for the establishment of meaningful speech involves establishing a context for speech that consists of two basic discriminations. In the first discrimination the stimulus is nonverbal and the response is verbal, as in *expressive* speech (e.g., the child may be taught to label a food). In the second discrimination the stimulus is verbal but the response is nonverbal, as in language *comprehension* (e.g., the child learns to follow instructions, obey commands, and so forth). Most language situations involve components of both discriminations: The stimulus and response have both verbal and nonverbal components. The speech program, based on these two discriminations, begins with simple labeling, which is made functional as soon as possible. For example, as soon as a child knows the label for a food, he is fed contingent upon asking for food. The program gradually moves on to make the child increasingly proficient in language, including training in more abstract terms (such as pronouns, time, etc.); some grammar, such as the tenses; the use of language to please others, as in recall or storytelling, and so forth. These later levels are only rarely reached by mute children, but are almost always reached by echolalic children. Other investigators using similar procedures report similar data on language training (Risley and Wolf, 1967).

Throughout the treatment program, there is an emphasis on teaching the child behaviors that are both socially desirable and useful to him. Thus, while the majority of the research has focused on attempts to build language, there have also been several attempts to facilitate social and self-help skills. Lovaas, Freitas, Nelson, and Whalen (1967) published a procedure for building nonverbal imitation that proved particularly useful for the purpose of developing social and self-help skills. It includes methods for building those behaviors that make the child easier to live with, such as friendly greetings and shows of affection, dressing himself, feeding himself, brushing his teeth, and so on. Again the method is based on shaping procedures where the child is rewarded for making closer and closer approximations to the attending adult's behavior. As the children learn to discriminate the similarity in their own and the model's behaviors, they acquire imitative behavior, as they did in the speech program.

GENERALIZATION AND FOLLOW-UP RESULTS

We now have some data that provide an estimation of the changes one might expect in autistic children undergoing behavior therapy (Lovaas, Koegel, Simmons, and Long, 1973). We examined three measures of the generality of treatment effects: (a) stimulus generalization, the extent to which behavior changes that occur in the treatment environment transfer to situations outside that treatment; (b) response generalization, the extent to which changes in a limited set of behaviors effect changes in a larger range of behaviors; and (c) generalization over time (or durability); that is, how well the therapeutic effects maintain themselves over time.

Let us illustrate the kinds of treatment changes and follow-up data we have collected by presenting certain data on the first 10 children we treated. We recorded 5 behaviors in a free-play situation that was different from the treatment environment, and in the presence of people who had not treated the child. Two of these behaviors were "sick" behaviors—self-stimulation and echolalia, which we have described earlier. Three of the behaviors were "healthy"—

appropriate verbal behavior, which was speech, related to an appropriate context, understandable, and gramatically correct; social nonverbal, which referred to appropriate nonverbal behavior that depended on cues given by another person for its initiation or completion; and appropriate play, which referred to the use of toys and objects in an appropriate, age-related manner. The recordings were made before treatment started, at the end of treatment (after 12 to 14 months), and in a follow-up some 1 to 4 years after treatment. The children were divided into two groups—those who were discharged to a state hospital and those who remained with their parents.

The data are presented in Figure 2. Percent occurrence of the various behaviors is plotted on the ordinate for before *B* and after *A* treatment and shows the latest follow-up *F* measures. *I* refers to the average results for the 4 children who were institutionalized (discharged to a state hospital), and *P* refers to the 6 children who lived with their parents after their discharge from treatment. For all the 5 behaviors the trends are the same: the children who were discharged to a state hospital lost what they had gained in treatment with us: They increased in their psychotic behavior (self-stimulation and echolalia),

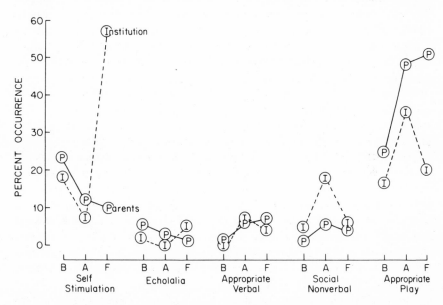

Figure 2. Multiple response follow-up measures. Percent occurrence of the various behaviors is plotted on the ordinate for Before (B) and After (A) treatment, and for the latest Follow-up (F) measures. "I" refers to the average results for the 4 children who were institutionalized, and "P" refers to the average results for the 9 children who were discharged to their parents' care. Percent occurrence of the behaviors is presented on the ordinate.

they appear to have lost all they had gained of social nonverbal behavior, and they lost much of their gains in the area of appropriate verbal and appropriate play. The children who stayed with their parents, on the other hand, maintained their gains or improved further. For the children who regressed in the state hospital, a brief reinstatement of behavior therapy could temporarily reestablish the original therapeutic gains.

Since we assessed these behaviors in environments other than that of the treatment, we know that our procedures produced stimulus generalization. The children's Stanford–Binet IQ scores and Vineland Social Quotient scores also showed large gains during the course of treatment, and since we did not train the children on these tests, they provide explicit measures of response generalization.

These findings clearly emphasize an important point underlying the use of principles of behavior modification. That is, there may be important differences in the procedures for the production and maintenance of behavior. Thus, it does not appear to be enough to help the child acquire appropriate behaviors and to overcome the inappropriate ones; it is also important to provide maintaining conditions that ensure that the improvements will last. Our follow-up paper (Lovaas *et al.*, 1973) discusses several of the strengths and weaknesses of a behavior modification approach to the treatment of autistic children.

CONTEMPORARY RESEARCH

Behavior therapy for severely psychotic children requires extensive teacher involvement; it is incremental and slow and the therapeutic gains are reversible. Many very important questions still remain unanswered. Why do certain autistic children show much larger improvements than others? Why does a given autistic child show relatively large and rapid improvements in some areas and slow, minimal gains in other areas? Why do so few autistic children become normal? Can autistic children function in public schools? Let us conclude this chapter by reviewing some current research that will hopefully suggest improvements in the use of behavior modification with autistic children.

Many researchers and clinicians have emphasized the extreme inconsistency with which autistic children respond to sensory input. At one time they appear to be blind and deaf, while at another time they show extremely fine visual and auditory acuity. In one situation they respond correctly to an instruction, while at another time they appear to have learned nothing about how to respond. Such peculiarities in the children's responding led us to conduct the following studies.

In the first study (Lovaas, Schriebman, Koegel, and Rehm, 1971) we trained normal children and autistic children to respond to a complex stimulus involving the simultaneous presentation of auditory, visual, and tactile cues. Once this discrimination was established, elements of the complex were presented separately to assess which aspects of the complex stimulus had acquired control over the child's behavior. We found that the autistic children had primarily come under the control of only one of the cues; the normal children responded uniformly to all three cues. We also found that we could arrange conditions so that a cue that had remained nonfunctional when presented in association with other cues could be established as functional when trained separately; thus, the autistic children did not appear to show a deficit in any particular sensory modality. Rather, when presented with multiple sensory input, a restricted range of that input gained control over their behavior.

In a teaching situation, when the child can both see the teacher's face as well as hear him talk, the autistic child may solve the verbal imitation problem by attending only to the teacher's face. We referred to this finding as *stimulus overselectivity* and pointed out that it had many implications for understanding the behavior and learning problems of autistic children. For example, if autistic children are generally overselective in their response to multiple cues, they may be functionally blind in those situations where they are "hooked" on auditory cues and functionally deaf in those situations where they are "hooked" on visual cues. In a related study (Schreibman and Lovaas, 1973), autistic children were trained to discriminate between a boy doll and a girl doll. The results showed that for some children this discrimination would diminish to chance level when a specific stimulus (such as the shoes) was removed from the dolls, pointing out the extreme selectivity with which autistic children respond to their environment. Such stimulus overselectivity also has implications for understanding why autistic children learn certain tasks so slowly. A necessary condition for much learning involves a contiguous or near contiguous presentation of two or more stimuli. If autistic children do not respond to one of the stimuli, certain acquisitions may then fail to occur; for example, their acquisition of affect may be retarded, as well as their development of meaningful speech. The establishment of meaningful speech involves establishing a context for speech and thus requires response to multiple inputs. For example, in attempting to teach a child to say the word *book*, the most common training procedure ("this is a book") involves a cross-modality shift. If the child responds to the auditory input, he may fail to perceive the visual referent and hence not associate the appropriate label.

We now have data that bear directly on this problem of shifting stimulus control. These data show that autistic children often selectively respond to prompt stimuli to the exclusion of training stimuli (Koegel, 1971). Two groups of children, autistic and normal, were pretrained on a color discrimination task. Later, the colors were presented simultaneously with training stimuli (e.g., two geometric forms, two tones) in a prompt-fading procedure. Gradually fading the color prompt generally produced acquisition of the training discrimination for normal Ss but not for autistic Ss. The autistic Ss continued to selectively respond to the prompt until it was entirely faded out, at which point they began to respond at chance level. They had learned nothing about the training stimuli (e.g., forms). Surprisingly, the autistic Ss acquired these same training discriminations when prompts were not used. That is, the usual technique of providing the children with extra stimuli to guide their learning may be exactly what makes it so difficult for them to learn.

It is interesting to note that while the autistic children generally failed to transfer from the color prompt to the training stimuli, they became very good at discriminating minute differences in the color prompts. That is, perhaps stimulus overselectivity may have benefited the autistic children's acquisition of the very difficult faded-color discrimination. Once trained on the color cue in the initial pretraining, stimulus overselectivity may have functioned to decrease the children's acquisition of discriminations along continuums other than color but to increase their acquisition of discriminations along the color continuum. Thus, it might be a better procedure to use a training technique such as transfer along a continuum (Lawrence, 1952) that would actually take advantage of an autistic child's overselectivity. A study from our lab (Schreibman, 1975) examined this hypothesis. Results showed that when the prompt stimuli fell along the same continuum as the training stimuli, prompting facilitated the acquisition of a very difficult discrimination that the children showed no evidence of acquiring, either without a prompt or with a prompt, in a continuum other than the training stimuli.

CLASSROOM TREATMENT

Little if any systematic research has been carried out on the education of autistic children in classroom settings. Research to date has focused primarily on the treatment of autistic children in a one-to-one teacher-child ratio. Economically, this makes the treatment unfeasible in many hospital and school situations. Therefore, we recently began a research program concerned with the teaching of autistic children in groups (Koegel and Rincover, 1974). Let us illustrate this research by citing a study where the emphasis is on establishing a teacher as a discriminative stimulus (S^D) for appropriate behavior even though the child is in a large group of children. To achieve this end, we began working with two children, using one teacher and two teacher aides. The teacher provides commands and instructions and the aides deliver contingent rewards and punishments. As the children become more and more proficient, reinforcement for appropriate behaviors becomes increasingly intermittent and additional children are introduced into the group, one at a time. If behaviors deteriorate at any one time, the size of the class is immediately reduced, reinforcements become more dense, and shortly thereafter we begin building again. Through a process like this, then, it is hoped that the autistic child will be able to behave appropriately in a more average (normal) classroom.

NEW DIRECTIONS

The systematic manner in which we have evaluated our treatment procedures has allowed us to carefully plan the future directions of our work in some detail. We have varied the age of the children we have treated, and the data clearly show that the younger the autistic child, the more progress he will make in treatment. In fact, we treated 4 children who were under 3 years of age. Of the 4 children, 3 made substantial gains and at this time appear headed toward normalcy. We are currently involved in a large-scale operation testing age as a variable in treatment.

Another important implication of the follow-up work is that in order to provide for the maintenance and generalization of treatment gains, it is necessary to provide for the continuation of treatment outside the clinic. Thus, our main emphasis now is on training the parents in the application of the behavior therapy techniques. We have developed a systematic, detailed, and intensive program for training parents of autistic children to become behavior modifiers (Koegel, Schreibman, and Lovaas, 1973). To place the therapy in the hands of the parents assures generalization of the treatment effects to the child's natural environment and helps maintain the treatment gains.

Finally, we have to design teaching procedures that are more efficient than the ones we now have. We are now very careful in our use of prompt and attempt to use those prompts that will facilitate rather than interfere with learning. Thus, we avoid using prompts that require the child to attend to multiple cues and instead use prompts that fall within the same dimension of the training stimulus. For example, this may involve exaggerating the relevant stimulus of a discrimination (or presenting it alone) and gradually fading in the irrelevant or incorrect stimulus; the child need respond to only the relevant stimulus throughout training.

SUMMARY COMMENT

We know more about some behaviors than others. For example, we know more about self-destructive behavior than self-stimulation. We were of more help to some children than to others. If the child possessed a verbal topography at the beginning of treatment, even if it was socially nonfunctional (such as echolalia), then we could help him substantially in developing a meaningful language. But we were less proficient in establishing new behavioral topographies in autistic children when none existed. For example, if the child was mute, his progress with behavior modification procedures was very limited. Follow-up data showed that in order to maintain the gains that the child made in treatment, he had to remain within an extension of the therapeutic environment. For example, for the child to continue showing improvement, his parents had to be taught behavior modification principles. The delivery of contingent, functional reinforcers has repeatedly been demonstrated to be a most significant feature both in providing for learning and in maintaining the behavioral gains.

As we worked with these children, it became more apparent that they possessed certain deviations in perceptual functioning, particularly in responding to multiple stimulus inputs, which necessitate revisions of the usual manner of presenting educational material. Only additional research will enable us to structure such optimal learning environments.

The first 12 years in behavior modification relied heavliy on learning principles derived from the animal laboratory and their ready application resulted in rapid progress. It is likely that the next 10 years will demand considerable new research directed specifically to the autistic child in order to help him develop appreciably further.

ACKNOWLEDGMENTS

The research in our laboratory was sponsored by USPHS Research Grant No. 11440 from the National Institute of Mental Health, and EHA Title VI-B, No. 42-00000-0000832/025, from the California Department of Education to the Office of the County Superintendent of Schools, Santa Barbara, California.

Portions of this paper have previously appeared in Chapter VII of the Seventy-second Yearbook of the National Society for the Study of Education: *Behavior Modification in Education*, 1973.

REFERENCES

Baer, D. M., and Sherman, J. Reinforcement of generalized limitation in young children. *Journal of Experimental Child Psychology*, 1964, *1*, 37–39.

Bandura, A. *Principles of Behavior Modification*. New York. Holt, Rinehart, & Winston, 1969.

Bucher, B., & Lovaas, O. I. Use of aversive stimulation in behavior modification. In M. R.

Jones (Ed.), *Miami symposium on the prediction of behavior 1967: Aversive stimulation.* Coral Gables: University of Miami Press, 1968.

Ferster, C. B. Positive reinforcement and behavioral deficits of autistic children. *Child Development,* 1961, *32,* 437–456.

Ferster, C. B., and DeMyer, M. A method for the experimental analysis of the behavior of autistic children. *American Journal of Orthopsychiatry,* 1962, *32,* 89–98.

Hewett, J. M. Teaching speech to an autistic child through operant conditioning. *American Journal of Orthopsychiatry,* 1965, *35,* 927–936.

Koegel, R. L. Selective attention to prompt stimuli by autistic and normal children. Unpublished doctoral dissertation. University of California, Los Angeles, 1972.

Koegel, R. L., and Covert, A. The relationship of self-stimulation to learning in autistic children. *Journal of Applied Behavior Analysis,* 1972, *5,* 381–387.

Koegel, R. L., and Rincover, A. Treatment of psychotic children in the classroom environment. I. Learning in a large group. *Journal of Applied Behavior Analysis,* 1972.

Koegel, R. L., Schreibman, L., and Lovaas, O. I. A manual for training parents in behavior modification with autistic children. Technical article, Institute for Applied Behavioral Science, University of California, Santa Barbara, 1973.

Lawrence, D. H. The transfer of a discrimination along a continuum. *Journal of Comparative and Physiological Psychology,* 1952, *45,* 511–516.

Lovaas, O. I. A program for the establishment of speech in psychotic children. In J. Wing (Ed.), *Childhood autism.* London: Pergamon Press, 1966.

Lovaas, O. I. *Behavior modification: Teaching language to psychotic children.* (Instructional film, 45 min., 16 mm. sound) New York. Appleton-Century-Crofts, 1969.

Lovaas, O. I. Teaching language to psychotic children. Unpublished manuscript, University of California, Los Angeles, 1972.

Lovaas, O. I. *Teaching Language to Autistic Children.* New York: Irvington Publishers, in press.

Lovaas, O. I., Berberich, J. P., Perloff, B. F., and Schaeffer, B. Acquisition of imitative speech by schizophrenic children. *Science,* 1966, *151,* 705–707.

Lovaas, O. I., Freitag, G., Kinder, M. I., Ruberstein, B. D., Schaeffer, B., and Simmons, J. Q. Establishment of social reinforcers in two schizophrenic children on the basis of food. *Journal of Experimental Child Psychology,* 1966, *4,* 109–125.

Lovaas, O. I., Freitas, L., Nelson, K., and Whalen, C. The establishment of imitation and its use for the development of complex behavior in schizophrenic children. *Behaviour Research and Therapy,* 1967, *5,* 171–181.

Lovaas, O. I., Koegel, R. L., Simmons, J. Q., and Long, J. Some generalization and follow-up measure on autistic children in behavior therapy. *Journal of Applied Behavior Analysis,* 1973, *6,* 131–166.

Lovaas, O. I., Litrownik, A., and Mann, R. Response latencies to auditory stimuli in autistic children engaged in self-stimulatory behavior. *Behaviour Research and Therapy,* 1971, *9,* 39–49.

Lovaas, O. I., Schreibman, L., Koegel, R., and Rehm, R. Selective responding by autistic children to multiple sensory input. *Journal of Abnormal Psychology,* 1971, *77,* 211–222.

Lovaas, O. I., and Simmons, J. Q. Manipulation of self-destruction in three retarded children. *Journal of Applied Behavior Analysis,* 1969, *2,* 143–157.

Metz, J. R. Conditioning generalized imitation in autistic children. *Journal of Experimental Child Psychology,* 1965, *2,* 389–399.

Risley, T. The effects and side effects of punishing the autistic behaviors of a deviant child. *Journal of Applied Behavior Analysis,* 1968, *1,* 21–34.

Risley, T., and Wolf, M. M. Establishing functional speech in echolalic children. *Behaviour Research and Therapy,* 1967, *5,* 73–88.

Schreibman, L. Within-stimulus versus extra-stimulus prompting procedures on discrimination learning with autistic children. *Journal of Applied Behavior Analysis,* 1975, *8,* 91–112.

Schreibman, L., and Lovaas, O. I. Overselective response to social stimuli by autistic children. *Journal of Abnormal Child Psychology,* 1973, *1,* (2), 152–168.

Tate, B. G., and Baroff, G. S. Aversive control of self-injurious behavior in a psychotic boy. *Behaviour Research and Therapy,* 1966, *4,* 281–287.

Wolf, M. M., Risley, T., Johnston, M., Harris, F., and Allen, E. Application of operant conditioning procedures to the behavior problems of an autistic child: A follow-up and extension. *Behaviour Research and Therapy,* 1967, *5,* 103–111.

Wolf, M. M., Risley, T., and Mees, H. Application of operant conditioning procedures to the behavior problems of an autistic child. *Behaviour Research and Therapy,* 1964, *1,* 305–312.

16

On the Structure of Inner and Outer Spielraum— the Play Space of the Schizophrenic Child

RUDOLF EKSTEIN and ELAINE CARUTH

> Der Mensch *braucht freien Spielraum, um spielend eigenes Denken und Wissen, eigene Kultur,* Menschen*kultur zu gebären. Ein weiter Spielraum sei* dem Menschen *die Welt. . . . Jedwed Ding sei ihm ein Spiel, und das Spiel sie ihm heiliger Ernst.*
>
> —frei nach Georg Groddeck, 1902

> [Man *requires free play space in order to give birth playfully to his own thinking and knowledge, his own culture,* man's culture. *The world be a wide play space to* man. . . . *Everything be a play to him, and play be to him holy and serious.*]
>
> —Freely after Georg Groddeck, 1902.

Play has been described as the language of the child and, like the adult's dream, may be considered the royal road to his unconscious (Erikson, 1950). Play, like language, serves an intrapsychic as well as an interpersonal function; it is a means by which the child resolves inner conflicts; it enables him to master the passively experienced traumatic events of his macrocosmic real world by actively repeating them in his microcosmic play world. Play is also a means of communicating

---

RUDOLF EKSTEIN · Childhood Psychosis Project, Reiss–Davis Child Study Center and Department of Medical Psychology, University of California at Los Angeles, California 90024.
ELAINE CARUTH · Department of Child Psychiatry, University of California at Los Angeles, California 90024.

these inner events and is thus object-directed, particularly in instances where the child has already achieved the capacity for more advanced object relations. Play helps develop and strengthen structures capable of delay functions, and thus furthers the future development of adaptive goal-oriented behavior. Play can be described in terms of its content—the play, as well as its structure—the *Spielraum*, or play space (Erikson, 1940). Through his play and through his playing, the child recreates his life space, the meaningfully cathected experiences of both his inner and outer worlds, in the microcosmos of the play space. The child's earliest autoplay with his body can be understood in terms of the beginning individuation experience, and his playing, with the notion that there is a self and object; fingers and toes that are "me-here," a nipple and milk that are "her-there." Somewhat more advanced play was described when Freud (1955) observed a child roll a spool of thread back and forth, accompanied by the words, "gone; there," thus reflecting the child's attempts to master the notions of separation and reunion. Such playing indicated that the child had begun to establish a capacity for object constancy, so that out of sight was not completely out of mind; in fact, was helped to remain in mind, so to speak, through the very act of playing. Parenthetically, that play was expressed on a particular level of communication—that of play action—(Ekstein and Friedman, 1966) in which fantasies are woven around a toy. Such play reflects a fairly advanced level of psychic structure and functioning that is not always available to the schizophrenic child. Ekstein and Friedman (1966) refer to a schema for ordering different levels of communication, indicating the progressive development of the capacity for goal-oriented thought as it evolves and advances from the initial phase of pure impulse expression to higher levels, such as acting out, role play, and rational fantasy.

The play of the schizophrenic child reflects his unique inner disturbances; is action dominated, impulse ridden, and driven by delusional rather than illusional fantasies as yet undifferentiated from both external reality and internal psychic structures. The schizophrenic child's play reveals core difficulties around individuation and separation, autism and symbiosis, boundaries and differentiation, all of which are empirically described and theoretically elaborated in Mahler's (1968) classic work. From a historical standpoint, Freud (1954) called attention to the mother's role in the child's development as conveyed through her response to the baby's cry of hunger. He pointed out that the screaming of the baby, a discharge taking place along the path of an internal change "thus acquires an extremely important secondary function, that is, of bringing about an understanding with other people; and the original helplessness of human beings is thus the primary source of all moral motives." Freud describes the first understanding to be brought about with the mother, an understanding that restores her, overcomes the trauma of birth—actually that of separation—and provides the link between mother and baby that is the prototype of language, the mother tongue. Thus, at a later stage the child will be capable of both separating painlessly from the mother, and restoring the object loss. Language helps to establish contact with people as well as to keep them at a distance (Peller, 1966).

An eternal theme, in literature and poetry, in mythology and religion, in the comic books and the science fiction that are today's mythology, is the playing-out of individuation and separation, of loss and restoration of the love object. When the poet Heine (1844) wrote of his delight in returning to Germany from exile and of touching Mother Earth again, he referred to the myth of Heracles and the giant, Antaeüs. As long as he could maintain his strength by keeping constantly in touch with Mother Earth, Antaeüs was able to defeat Heracles. Consequently, when Heracles pinned Antaeüs down, quite naturally anticipating destruction if the giant, his victory was turned into defeat; he had in fact aided Antaeüs to restore his strength. The giant only lost his life after Heracles, discovering the secret, held him high in the air, thereby depriving him of that universal wellspring of his strength—contact with the mother. In many ways this is similar to the truly Herculean task of the therapist with a schizophrenic child patient. The usual psychotherapeutic means of conquering mental illness, and the attendant personal isolation, is to establish contact. Yet, with the schizophrenic child, at the very moment the therapist seems to succeed, he simultaneously loses, because such contact turns into that devouring fusion state that restores the strength of the truly giant illness. For some children the autistic retreat becomes the only means of retaining some element of self, albeit at the expense of giving up the object world.

Such is the slight of the schizophrenic and autistic child: To reach out for the therapist is to risk regaining the object at the price of losing the self. The autistic and symbiotic child struggles between the need for restoring, for fusing with the object, and the need to flee from the reunion that at the moment of fulfillment becomes a nightmare of annihilation.

Therapeutic work with schizophrenic children and adolescents must take into account their special problems around the need for optimal distance in the struggle for and against autonomy; the struggle to merge once more with the object, only to lose the self; and their struggle to free the object and retain the self. Problems with establishing self and object constancy underlie this inability to resolve the struggle to attach and detach, to connect and disconnect. They are comparable to the normal child's struggle for separation from the earlier ana-clitic position, the resolution of which leads to optimal separation and growth. For the autistic child, however, such problems lead only to a stagnation of psychic growth that is manifested in all aspects of his psychic development, in his unneutralized, undifferentiated love—hate; in his incapacity to differentiate thought from act; in his inability to restrain the act, the immediate impulse discharge. Such work must allow for the difficulties attendant upon making contact with a child unable to establish contact, one for whom there does not yet exist two separate people since he can neither experience the therapist nor even at times the playroom as separate from himself. For example, an 8-year-old schizophrenic child may spend one session in the office violently erupting and the next session as a kind of miniature Macbeth anxiously erasing the mess he had made the previous hour that represented the fragmented, bad self-image that had dirtied/fused with the office walls.

The authors' stance on psychotherapy for schizophrenic and autistic conditions clearly indicates that they do not believe in affixing labels to such patients that would place them in an unalterable, diagnostic category. Rather, they regard autism as perhaps a transitory stage in the normal growing-up of children, referring specifically to the developmental line of object relations (A. Freud, 1965). Autism may be an expression of a molar illness, a state of a broader disease process such as schizophrenia. Or, at the present state of our knowledge, it may be a seemingly immovable and unchangeable fixation based on some individual intractable deficits.

Different authors, searching for the cause of that dilemma, may stress the maturational lag, the physiological and neurological happenings before and after birth, the environmental dilemma, the mistakes of the parents. These authors' position has been to seek and define the nature of the illness and to search for the causes of the cure (Ekstein and Friedman, 1968), occasionally identifying certain necessary, but as yet never sufficient, causes of the illness. Their version of the analytic definition of schizophrenia has developed from a unified system of psychopathology permitted by Freud's introduction of the concepts of the unconscious and the two principles of mental functioning—the pleasure principle and the reality principle (Freud, 1958). These concepts have allowed for the recognition of similarities as well as differences between normality, neurosis, and psychosis.

Regardless of the therapeutic optimism or pessimism about psychotherapeutic interventions, what is suggested here is that the therapist must take into account the problems that he seemingly creates for the schizophrenic child even as the child tries to allow and achieve what little autonomy he can without giving up the fragmented parts of himself that in illness can only be maintained through the autistic megalomanic withdrawal. It is necessary to learn how to identify the optimal distance necessary for each individual child. Optimal play space must be developed in which the child may gradually make contact with both the self and the object, with inner and outer reality, whatever his biological or psychological deficits.

Sometimes the illness writes its own prescription and the impression is gained that the autistic children are warning against intimacy and interpersonal contact; that such interpersonal contact should be replaced by automaton contact that comes from the environment as positive or negative stimuli emanating from a robotlike source. These children seem to seek the deanimated techniques—the cow prod—as they seek to recreate the outer world in the image of an echo of their inner world, thus wiping out differentiation.

There is no question that a treatment model of positive and negative reinforcement, dedicated to behavior modification, will have results inasmuch as it responds to certain demands of the patient. In such instances, all too often the therapist has become but a tool or an extension of the patient's self.

In psychoanalytic therapy the demand for the deanimated automaton therapist is frequently expressed in the child's arranging a psychotherapeutic dialogue that is really a monologue, and is often not even a monologue but a monolithic massive retreat. A plot is written by the patient and the therapist simply acts and talks out the role that is given to him. There is seemingly no place for interpretation or true participation, only for the patient's creation of a robot, his outer self with whom he now conducts a quasidialogue. Whatever language exists appears to be a dream language, like inner communication, like talking to oneself and with oneself, the forerunner of a true conversation and of a true dialogue. But the language may have verbal overtones. Frequently, with the small child who has not yet reached verbal language except in its most primitive beginnings, such forerunners of language as echolalia and echopraxia will have to be dealt with.

In some instances the therapist has to work in an infinitesimally small play space, metaphorically speaking, so that there is no true place for him. This unbelievably small play space, like a dream, does not exist in the external world, although representations of reality may enter in the same way that the day residue enters into the normal person's dreams. The play space, like the life space, is guarded and offers no entry for the therapist. Whatever cues the therapist gives from outside are responded to merely like echoes. If the therapist does become a part of the inner world, he does so by becoming the automaton to whom a role is assigned—by becoming echolalic and echopraxic in the service of the therapy.

An example comes from the therapy of a schizophrenic adolescent (Ekstein and Caruth, 1965) who permitted the therapist to enter his obsessive fantasies in which the patient was the chairman of a meeting of fictional characters, such as Superman and Donald Duck—personalities from cartoons and stories he had read. A decision had to be made in the meeting concerning whether or not he should masturbate. The patient and his therapist were the only real people in this delusional world, where within his organization of a quasidemocratic meeting he felt able to imitate what he had observed of interpersonal situations. After many attempts, the therapist was allowed to enter the inner play space of the patient's fantasies. In his fantasies he permitted the therapist to intervene in the balance of power between the different participants, all of them introjects in his own personality. The odds, or votes, were against the therapist, however, since the powerful majority followed the recommendations of Mr. Punishment rather than those of Mr. Prudence, the patient's synonym for the therapist. Nevertheless, the therapist found his way into the patient's inner world by being a quasiautomaton. He preserved his independence to the extent that the patient remembered, imitated, and projected his words into the fantasy of the therapist within the fictitional fantasy-gathering.

Despite the peculiar nature of this psychotic transference, it allowed a system of communication. While autistic private dialogue is almost a monologue, this system of communication does have a touch of the external world, as would be true for the dreamer who dreams that his analyst says certain things that he, the dreamer, had projected into him. This device of allowing the beginnings of a dialogue, which is not truly interpersonal but intrapsychic, keeps intact the residuals of the patient's individuality and permits the kind of distance that avoids symbiotic fusion. The therapist's task is to be satisfied with a play space that gives him almost no room in which to play, to interpret—indeed, to function. It seems that the behavior modifiers are satisfied, not just temporarily, but permanently, with establishing contact with this kind of place space. Thus, rather than aiming at changing the patient's self-prescription, they identify with him and assume vis-à-vis him a quasiautistic position. The new dilemma is experienced in the countertransference that leads the therapist to regress to manipulation, although in reality he has been manipulated. This psychological manipulation is the prototype of the autistic child's physical manipulation of the therapist by using him as a mere tool or as an extension of his own body. Such therapists avoid the patient's inner world as if to suggest there is no inner life, only behavior. This is the position of the autistic child vis-à-vis external objects whom he triggers like teddy bears with electric buttons for negative and positive reinforcements.

When allowing the patient to define the conditions of the play space, to define the distance, a temporary concession is made in order for him to become incorporated into the play situation. Parenthetically, for some patients, the inner and outer distances required in the actual physical play space almost seem to have an inverse correlation to the psychological play space. This has been described as a stop, take, touch, and run patient (Cooper, 1972), who establishes contact and then flees; who can tolerate only minimal contact; who cannot accept a regular therapeutic structure but nevertheless maintains the therapist internally. In some instances, the schizophrenic child may be unable to experience as alive either himself or the therapist in the intimacy of the office where he retreats into silence. He is, however, able to converse for an entire session over the telephone. For such patients the therapist's task becomes that of wait, be available, give, and remain; to allow an infinitely large outer "play space" in reality to counterbalance the infinitesimally small inner one.

The patient has many other ways to guarantee distance, such as the communication of his problems through metaphors, allusions, similes. In the interpretation of the metaphor, it can be shown that insight can only be acquired by him if distinct enough to be neither threatening to his integrity nor to trigger premature acting-out, fusion experience, and/or depersonalization. The patient not only assigns predictable roles to the therapist and writes his dialogue, but at times deals with the self in the same way. He permits the self to emerge and to achieve some form of self-constancy by assigning roles to himself, by pretending certain roles, by pretending to be understood as a play rehearsal for future identities—that is, he may pretend feelings, roles, intentions; he may make promises he will be unable to keep. An example is the patient (Ekstein and Friedman, 1971) who pretended adulthood by ordering a taxi to enable him to attend his therapy hour and on arrival refusing to pay the fare because he felt his caretaker or therapist should pay it. When he finally paid the fare, he asked the taxi driver for a Christmas present. He was unable to maintain the role of the independent negotiator and regressed into a child who wanted to be rewarded for good behavior.

These presented roles, attempted prematurely, are prewritten in the sense that they represent the first attempt to absorb interpretations and implied demands from the educating world or the therapist. Frequently, the patients request to be made into well-adjusted automatons: again a plea for behavior modification rather than for the achievement of an inner self. In each of these situations, it is essential to match the interpretive space of the therapist with the play space of the patient. The therapist's space may either be infinite or unbelievably small so that he must carefully measure the distance by which he can become an acceptable object, at least around those areas in the child's life where he is most ready.

Psychotic transference conditions sometimes threaten to be flooded by the reappearance of powerful negative introjects as expressed in murderous impulses, the wish to escape or to break up therapy. In such instances it is useful to establish a support system, such as casework that, combined with the other part of the transference, operates by maintaining the focus on the outer reality while the therapist keeps the focus on inner reality (Ekstein, Friedman, Caruth, and Cooper, 1971). It is also necessary to supplement psychotherapeutic work with educational work and day treatment in residential centers, as well as psychopharmalogical assistance when necessary; arrangements in which different forces effect hand-in-hand cooperation. With such arrangements, behavior modification, and other means of education, reality orientation must have as much space as the analytic interventions because psychoanalytic therapy is not considered to constitute *the* cure but merely to be one of the parameters necessary to achieve optimum results. As in all aspects of work with children, child psychotherapy was never meant to be the exclusive instrument to help them get well and to grow up.

The goals in treatment are to allow for the development of the unique individual rather than to merely train the patient for external adjustment. Neither love nor destructive hate is enough, and treatment plans must evolve from a scientific understanding of the total intrapsychic structure and interpersonal functioning of the individual rather than from a limited moralistic or humanistic value system that concerns itself only with symptoms. Scientific understanding in the service of restoration of the patient's capacity for autonomy and self-control remains the primary goal, which must not be sacrificed to expediences of control and conformity.

REFERENCES

Cooper, B. On self-prescription of instant psychotherapy: stop, touch, take, and run. *The Reiss–Davis Clinic Bulletin*, 1972, *9* (2), 116.

Ekstein, R., and Caruth, E. To sleep but not to dream: on the use of electrical tape recording in clinical research. *The Reiss–Davis Clinic Bulletin*, 1965, *2* (2), 87.

Ekstein, R., and Friedman, S. The function of acting out, play action, and play acting in the psychotherapeutic process. In R. Ekstein (Ed.), *Children of time and space, of action and impulse.* New York: Appleton-Century-Crofts, 1966. P. 169.

Ekstein, R., and Friedman, S. Cause of the illness or cause of the cure? *International Journal of Psychiatry,* 1968, *5* (3), 224.

Ekstein, R., and Friedman, S. Do you have faith I'll make it? *The Reiss–Davis Clinic Bulletin,* 1971, *8* (2), 94.

Ekstein, R., Friedman, S., Caruth, E., and Cooper, B. Building of and work with the support systems. In R. Ekstein (Ed.), *The challenge: despair and hope in the conquest of inner space.* New York: Brunner/Mazel, 1971. P. 239.

Erikson, E. Studies in the interpretation of play, I. Clinical observations of play disruption in young children. *Genetic Psychological Monographs*, 1940, *22*, 557.

Erikson, E. *Childhood and society.* New York: Norton, 1950.

Freud, A. *Normality and pathology in childhood.* New York: International University Press, 1965.

Freud, S. (1895). Project for a scientific psychology. In *Origins of psychoanalysis.* New York: Basic Books, 1954. P. 397.

Freud, S. (1920). *Beyond the pleasure principle,* standard edition, 1955, *18,* 3.

Freud, S. (1911). *Formulations on the two principles of mental functioning,* standard edition, 1958, *12,* 213.

Heine, E. (1844). Deutschland, ein Wintermärchen. Heine's Sämtliche Werke - Der Tempel Verlag, Leipzig.

Mahler, M. *On human symbiosis and the vicissitudes of individuation.* New York: International Universities Press, 1968.

Peller, L. French contribution to language development. *Psychological Study of the Child,* 1966, *21,* 459.

17
Educational Strategies
for the Autistic Child

JAMES J. GALLAGHER and RONALD WIEGERINK

Of all of the many puzzles related to the development of the young child, none seems to be more fascinating or frustrating than the behavior of the child diagnostically labeled "autistic." One of the authors of this paper recently returned from a tour of special schools for handicapped children in the Soviet Union. In one of these auxiliary schools for the "debile" or educable mentally retarded, he was shown a youngster whom the Soviets identified as schizophrenic, but whom we would designate autistic. This experience was particularly unnerving because the child resembled, to a great degree, autistic children seen in the United States. He did not engage in meaningful social contact; he had a number of stereotyped ritualistic behaviors; he liked his environment to be orderly and in place and got very upset if things were moved around. He talked some, but did not respond verbally to social contact; rather, his verbalizations were self-initiated. The translator told us that she could not understand the words the boy was saying. To see an obviously autistic child in such a different culture is to cause one to be thoughtful about etiology.

In planning an educational program for autistic children, it is important to have close communication between the scientific community and the educational community. Since autistic children differ from the norm in almost every conceivable dimension, from social contacts to expressive communication to

JAMES J. GALLAGHER · Frank Porter Graham Child Development Center, University of North Carolina at Chapel Hill, North Carolina 27514.
RONALD WIEGERINK · Developmental Disabilities Technical Assistance System, University of North Carolina at Chapel Hill, North Carolina 27514.

problem-solving to attention, the educator does not really know where to begin. What is the basic problem? Does it lie in the emotional domain? If so, perhaps play therapy or emotional reeducation is the treatment of choice. The work of Bettelheim (1950) and Kanner (1943) stressed this presumption. If it is in the basic cognitive process of attention or sensory processing as Rimland (1964) claims, then a totally different remedial program stressing cognitive exercises is called for.

The importance of identifying the key dimension that should receive educational focus is illustrated by Gallagher (1973) who pointed out that much wasted effort was spent in educating children with "minimal brain dysfunction" through a variety of visual perceptual exercises on the assumption that this was a fundamental problem with these children. Apart from the fact that many children with this diagnostic label did not have perceptual motor problems at all, further research identifed the visual-motor coordination as the key area of defect in many cases, rather than visual interpretation per se. A goodly amount of educational energy that was expended on the development and presentation of a variety of visual perceptual tasks could have been saved with proper identification of the problem at hand. A not dissimilar quandary faces us with the autistic child, and the educator must rely on the scientist to uncover the root causes of this strange disorder.

THE PRIMARY PROBLEM?

What characterizes the fundamental problem of autism and what are the secondary consequences stemming from it? Some recent work helps to provide new suggestions. Pribram (1970) has related the behavioral characteristics of autistic children to brain injury in the frontolimbic core area. He believes that the basic defect in the autistic child rests in short-term memory defects and the failure to register experience in cognitive tasks and interpersonal relationships. All these factors would seem to indicate that the frontolimbic core may be involved. Pribram distinguishes further between context-free and context-sensitive behaviors, which appeared distinctively different in ablation studies with primates. He points out that *signs* are context-free attributions signifying constant aspects of the environment, whereas symbols are context-dependent constructions symbolizing the organism's sensitivity to changes in the environment. It is these symbolic skills that are sensitive to brain injury in this area. Language, for example, would be context-dependent and likely to be difficult to develop under conditions of early damage (see also Luria, 1966).

Bryson (1970, 1972) has pursued the identification of the basic cognitive defect in autistic children. In a series of experiments with a small number of autistic children, she explored the possibility that short-term memory was at the heart of supposed perceptual problems. Previous experiments have reported auditory and visual information-processing problems, and it was considered possible that the cross-modal deficits (auditory–visual) were due to the inability of the youngster to hold an auditory signal in his short-term memory long enoug to match it to the visual stimuli.

Accordingly, Bryson presented a series of matching and sequence tasks to six autistic youngsters, ages 3 to 6. In the visual–visual dimension, the child had to correctly match a color, shape, or object presented to him with an identical one from among four alternatives. When presented the pictures of a sink, tub, comb, and brush, for example, the child had to take the picture of the tub and match it to the one of four choices that was correct. In the auditory–visual dimension an auditory cue was given, such as the word "tub," and the child's task was to respond and match that cue to the appropriate picture.

Bryson found that serious impairment in functioning was obtained by merely delaying the presentation, the matching or sequencing tasks for three seconds, after the presentation of the original stimulus. It appears then that there are two specific deficits that are identifiable. One is visual–visual short-term memory. The second deficit was in the auditory–visual information processing. This remained uniformly difficult for most of the children under both delayed and immediate presentation.

Other researchers have pointed to difficulties in modality preference. Ornitz's (this volume) research indicated that autistic children prefer visual over auditory stimuli. Lovaas, Schreibman, Koegel, and Rehm (1971) found an overselection of responding to only one stimulus complex from an auditory, visual, and tactile array. Hermelin and O'Connor (1970) found that the autistic children in their studies were dependent on motor feedback for learning. In a series of studies (Hermelin and O'Connor, 1970; Frith and Hermelin, 1969), motor tracking and card arrangments were used to show that autistic children learned through cues that were primarily manipulative, and benefited little from additional visual information. They concluded that autistic children relied more upon perceptual activity that perceptual analyses. These findings have profound implications for educators who are concerned with building educational programs that circumvent learning difficulties and accentuate the positive.

It should not be imagined that the cause of the autism is unidimensional or that there is wide agreement on the specific dimensions involved. Problems in the auditory channel information processing of the autistic child have been noted by a number of researchers. Their inability to code and store auditory signals effectively would seem to be a major problem. Fassler and Bryant (1970) used ear-muff type protectors in an attempt to guard against auditory confusion in 20 autistic children. These children showed unusual attachment to objects and a desire for sameness characteristic of classic autistic children. The results of the use of ear protectors were revealed in the children's becoming calmer and more attentive to lessons in their classroom situation. This suggested that random auditory input had a least a contributing influence in confusing the information processing of the child.

Frith (1972) and Hermelin and Frith (1971) concluded that autistic children are insensitive to temporal structure and respond to external rule-governed sequences as if they were random. On the other hand, they follow internal rules in producing musical sequences of equal complexity to normal children. Hermelin (1972) found autistic children more responsive to visual than tactile cues, as did Schopler (1970).

Ornitz (1973) compared four contrasting theories regarding the underlying sensory problems of autistic children. The first was that physiologic overarousal leads to motor activity designed to reduce stimulus bombardment (Hutt, Hutt, Lee, and Ornsted, 1965). The second was the opposite, that insufficient sensory stimulation resulted in the need for additional sensory input. The third accounts for the seemingly contradictory findings supporting the previous two theories. It states that sensory motor behaviors are a result of inadequate moderation of sensory input: that under- and overreactions to sensory inputs are a result of disfunctioning gating mechanisms (Ornitz, 1973). Ornitz concludes that the primary disorder appears to be one of disorder in sensorimotor integration. These findings account for the erratic behavior that autistic children show within educational environment and during educational programming. They would indicate the need for educational environments in which there is controlled sensory input that is responsive to inter- and intra-individual differences.

EDUCATIONAL STRATEGIES

Given this array of findings, what kind of educational strategies should be devised? What to teach, how to teach and where to teach? One of the educational modifications necessary for educating autistic children has to be in the minds of the educators themselves. There is an unwritten assumption behind most educational programming that the child should first understand the concept, and having understood it, he will then be moved to change his behavior. In this instance, we are reversing that sequence and proposing that the most important thing for the autistic child to do is to behave properly first, and then hope that he will understand why later. As Wing (1966) states:

It is possible to teach an autistic child to hug his father when he comes home from work, to kiss his mother, to form his mouth into a smile, to say "please" and "thank you," to have reasonable table manners and not steal packets of detergent from the supermarket, without the child understanding why he has to behave in such ways. This, of course, is how a normal child learns to behave socially, except that much of it happens spontaneously by imitation at an earlier age.

If we assume that the fundamental defect in the autistic child lies in the neural mechanisms controlling the short-term memory, or in the complex reticular system controlling sensory input as Rimland suggests, then we might go back to the developmental beginnings of the child to see the implications that such a defect would have on early and subsequent development.

Learning Mechanism. While most children learn about the world around them through either reinforcement or social imitation, both of these learning mechanisms lose their power in a situation where there is a temporal sequence necessarily involved between stimulus and response.

Linguistic Code. The linguistic concepts that are most often used by adults and by the child bridge such temporal lags between stimulus and response are not present because language itself is absent. If language originally is based on the categorizing of a set or group of experiences, such categorizations become difficult for an autistic child who would have to hold in his memory such a grouping, while attaching a label to it.

Affective Behavior. Also, the development of affective behavior and social linkages require tying experiences with one another in some *temporal* order. Thus, the mother's affection and hugging becomes tied to physical rewards of food and drink. If no connection is made between the physical affection and the rewards, then the child remains affectively unmoved. Parents seeing this "coldness" may then develop secondary negative reactions of their own, further increasing the distance between the child and social rewards.

Memory. If every day is a new experience for the child because of his sievelike memory, then it is little wonder that he wants to create some order out of the daily cacophony of experiences. He wishes to place his toys in an exact order and becomes very upset if one is moved. The world has little enough structure without his own imposed structure being disturbed.

Assuming these statements to be true, we are left with the question of how does the child learn anything? It would appear that his major learning is through contiguity, the visual linking of two experiences that occur at the same time. Such learning can be extraordinarily inefficient as when a child bangs his toy on the floor at the same time the electric power goes out. The normal child, even with his supply of magical thinking, can tell him as well that he did not put the lights out by banging his toy on the floor. However, the autistic child may have more difficulty abandoning such seemingly bizarre associations.

The work that has already been done in this area provided a useful set of clues concerning appropriate educational strategies. Hewitt (1965) was one of the first investigators to use behavior modification techniques in teaching speech to a nonverbal autistic boy of 5 years old. Hewitt's contention was that the problem with retraining the youngsters lay primarily in the therapist's inability to retreat developmentally to the earliest stage where the problem could be reached and dealt with. In the case of autistic children, the retreat must be made developmentally to the very earliest and most primitive levels.

Hewitt used food rewards to condition the youngsters to maintain *eye contact* with another human being. Following that level of attention, he then moved to a second phase of *social imitation* where the child would imitate gestures and hand movements. He then moved to the third phase to the use of *expressive language* to obtain food reinforcement, and finally, to *transfer* those expressive skills to other social situations. By starting at the very earliest levels and by moving slowly through these sequences, Hewitt was able to produce a 32-word working vocabulary on the part of the 5-year old youngster who had been mute.

Risley and Wolf (1967) demonstrated how it was possible to alter the echoic behavior of autistic children. Through a careful application of behavioristic principles of fading, shaping, and reinforcement, they were able to change the speech of an autistic child from echoic to responsive. Whereas previously the child would simply repeat the questions of the questioner, the child developed a repertoire of meaningful answers. Champlin (1970) was later able to apply similar principles in a natural environment and develop spontaneous speech in autistic children. He developed a program that utilized a three-room apartment. Three autistic children were exposed to the natural but controlled environment and through a process of stimulus fading were taught to ask for items (food, water, toothbrush, etc.) that were present. This movement from echoic speech to meaningful responses to spontaneous speech was a significant breakthrough for these children.

Hartung (1970) used verbal imitation as the key to development of functional speech in autistic children. He reported that echolalia was both a positive sign that signified the presence of potential expressiveness but later, in treatment, a sign of resistance.

In view of the distinction made by Pribram on context-free versus context-dependent learning, it is interesting to note the experience of Miller and Miller (1973) using a training program for autistic children with elevated boards and sign language. They used signs that are traditional in the field of the deaf and linked these signs with activities that the youngster engages in, such as walking on a 10-inch board elevated three to six feet off the ground. These educators were able to obtain success linking words with action.

As Miller and Miller stated, there was a tendency for the youngsters to generalize the signs such as *eat* and *drink* not only to their eating situation in a dining hall, but on picnics and in restaurants as well. The authors found the use of elevated boards stimulated understanding in use of action signs such as *come* and *stop*. Since these systems could be easily adapted to home use, parent training programs would seem to profit by this approach.

Nordquest and Wahler (1973) have reported on a parent training program using the skills of behavior modification to alter and reduce such autisticlike behavior as rituals, crying, and whining, and have encouraged imitative nonverbal and verbal behavior.

They point out that once the parents have learned the basic principles and received supervision in their use—

The professional can then direct his attention to the design of the treatment package, making changes and advising the parents as new problems arise. Such a home-based program would considerably reduce treatment costs incurred by the family and diminish concern for the generalization of treatment from the laboratory to the child's natural environment. (p. 85)

Schopler and Reichler (1970) have used a parent training program to improve the relationship of parent and child and provide for a closer relationship between usually frustrated family members.

The Regional Intervention Program, Nashville, Tennessee (Ora and Wiegerink, 1970), has trained parents of autistic children in language, motor, and cognitive developmental educational sequences so that they could effectively elucate their own children during the preschool years. The parents were instructed while working individually with their own children in tutoring rooms. The staff of the project modeled the teaching behaviors to be learned and instructed the parents in basic behavior modification strategies and concepts. The parents were successful at learning and performing the teaching sequences and became the instructors of other parents. At this time parents of autistic children and children who display autisticlike behaviors do all of the direct parent instruction in that program.

In public school classrooms established by the Regional Intervention Program, a variety of teaching techniques proved to be effective. Each took into account the importance of the sensorimotor skills and inclinications of autistic children. A reading program for one child was devised in which an electric typewriter was utilized, similar to the talking typewriter program of O. K. Moore (1960). During phase 1 the child was simply allowed to play with the typewriter, an activity in which he engaged with much energy and seeming delight. During phase 2, as the child pressed keys, a teacher sitting beside him called out the names of the letters typed. During phase 3, the teacher called out selected letters (turning on the electric switch only when the child selected the correct key). Much prompting was necessary during the early stages of this phase. Once the child learned a set of letters, the teacher presented alphabet cards and called out the letters. Soon the names of objects were presented and finally pictures of objects and the child would type the appropriate name. While the program developed over a 6-month period, the child did develop a typing and reading vocabulary of 30 words.

Another program was devised in which the autistic children's manipulative abilities were also taken into account (Strain and Wiegerink, 1976) in teaching the children to socially interact. Four activities were used to induce proximity behaviors and eventually social play between two autisticlike isolated children. The activities were water play, peg-placement, ball-rolling, and block-building. During controlled 20-minute sessions, the two children were reinforced for engaging in parallel play and finally social interactions increased significantly and water play proved to be the most effective in developing sustained interaction.

Other children who did not demonstrate verbal control were taught nonoral reading. Through a procedure of presenting a picture of an object with its name (ball), children were taught to select the objects to go with their names and names to go with objects. These words were later used to construct requests (I want ball) and still later as parts of stories. Through this method, verbally mute children were taught to read and express themselves using printed and written language.

Despite the "where to teach" the autistic child remains an issue as well as what and how to teach. Rutter (1970) suggests three aims of education of the autistic child. These are:

1. Preventing the development of secondary handicaps;
2. Finding approaches to education that circumvent the primary handicaps;
3. Finding techniques to aid the development of functions involved in the primary handicaps.

He suggests that a mixture of speaking and nonspeaking children is essential and proposes a flexible arrangement whereby groups may be homogeneous for certain educational purposes and heterogeneous for others.

What general educational principles can be drawn fm the literature and the experiences of educators directly attempting to improve the development of autistic children?

Reduction of Stimuli

The reduction of extraneous stimuli seems to be one general principle underlying educational strategy coming from both research and experience. A bare room with few extraneous elements seems required in the initial stages of training so that the only stimulus presented is the one that has to be responded to.

Simultaneous Presentation of Stimuli

Both stimuli to be linked are presented at the same time in temporal space. If there is a defect in short-term memory as severe as described in many young autistic children, then linkages have to be formed with close temporal conjunction. This means that parental affection must be given *simultaneously* with the application of food, not sometime before or sometime after; the auditory stimulus should be provided at the same time as the visual stimulus, not before or after. After having achieved success at linking simultaneously presented stimuli, slow extension of stimulus presentations on a temporal dimension would seem called for.

Developmentally Based

Training should be done on strict developmental lines with care being taken to start from the earliest level or stage of performance. In the area of social contacts, this might take the form initially of establishing eye contact and simple imitative behaviors.

Memory

In the area of memory, tasks can be designed to match forms with minimal temporal disjunction while gradually increasing the complexity of the item and length of time elapsed as the child gains competence. It cannot be said, with even the severe cases, that there is *no* memory, particularly for the many other children with major communication problems that are not as severe as the classic autistic child.

Content Channel

The autistic child appears generally to avoid those dimensions that have temporal aspects to them, such as the kinesthetic and auditory. The visual dimension seems to be the one that has the least impairment from a receptive standpoint. It should be used as one of the least dimensions under the most circumstances in the learning task.

SUMMARY

The autistic child presents a unique and complex instructural problem for today's educator. In days past many of these children, considered uneducable, would have simply been excluded from educational opportunities. However, in today's world of a broader understanding of the concept of education, and a clearer understanding of the individual's rights to an education (Gilhool, 1973), education must address the issue of how best to provide a quality education for autistic children.

It is the fate of educators that they cannot wait for certainty before trying to educate children to the best of their ability. The puzzle of the autistic child is still far from solution, as the other papers in this volume point out. Nevertheless, the educator must operate on the best of current knowledge.

The general educational philosophy in such instances is to attempt to focus the educational program either (1) on attempts to improve the central process or processes that seem to be deficient, or (2) on those developmental dimensions that seem most amenable to modification. As this paper has indicated, the information-processing skills that seem central to the problem are short-term memory processes, and reception through the auditory channel. These two major deficiencies then cause extensive subsequent deficiencies in expressive performance of the child.

One of the educational strategies noted here is to focus the educational program on eliciting the appropriate behavior on the part of the child. This can be done through a variety of operant techniques without the intervening necessity of having the child consciously will that behavior. As habits increase for the proper behavior, then the child can begin thinking about and willing the behavior to happen. This is the reverse of the usual educational procedures that try to convince the child that it is the "proper thing to do" and then rely on the child's own "motivation to please" to direct that behavior to happen through internal control of his own mental processes.

Another educational emphasis, trying to take into account limited memory, is on the visual contiguity or visually associating the objects or actions you wish the child to connect cognitively. Also, immediate rewards for desired behavior, both social and cognitive, seem to be required. With these techniques simple to learn, the parent can be a powerful ally and has been so used successfully to supplement the educational program in a number of instances.

It is likely that with the new "right to education" legal suits around the country (Gilhool, 1973), which demand public education for all children, much more attention will be paid to the effective ways of educating autistic children than in the past.

The authors believe that progress can be made if special education is based on the following understandings:

1. Autistic children are educable.

2. Their unique learning characteristics are due to basic cognitive deficits in information processing.

3. Such deficits can be compensated for, in part, by carefully structured educational programs with specified developmental learning sequences and enhanced reinforcing stimuli.

4. Structured ecuation programs should begin early in life, with the parent or parent surrogate as the primary teacher.

5. Educational programs for these children are feasible, and in the long run, less costly than institutional care.

6. The provision of appropriate educational programs for these children is not a manifestation of public generosity but rather a reflection that these children, too, have a clear right to an appropriate education.

ACKNOWLEDGMENTS

Special appreciation is expressed by the authors for the contribution of Lucretia Kinney for her editorial and general assistance in the preparation of this paper.

REFERENCES

Bettelheim, B. *Love is not enough*. Glencoe: Free Press, 1950.

Bryson, C. Systematic identification of perceptual disabilities in autistic children. *Perceptual and Motor Skills*, 1970, *31*, 239–246.

Bryson, C. Short term memory and cross-modal information processing in autistic children. *Journal of Learning Disabilities*, 1972, *5*, 25–35.

Champlin, J. *The efficacy of home settings in the language training of low-functioning echoic children*. George Peabody College (unpublished doctoral dissertation), 1970.

Fassler, J., and Bryant, N. *Task perfromance, attention and classroom behavior of seriously disturbed, communication-impaired, "autistic"-type children under conditions of reduced auditory input*. U. S. Office of Education Project #422001. Teachers College, Columbia University, New York, 1970.

Frith, U. Cognitive mechanisms in autism: experiments with color and time sequence production. *Journal of Autism and Childhood Schizophrenia*, 1972, *2*, 160–173.

Frith, U., and Hermelin, B. The role of visual and motor cues for normal, subnormal, and autistic children. *Journal of Psychological Psychiatry*, 1969, *10*, 153–163.

Gallagher, J. New educational treatment models for children with minimal brain dysfunction. *Annals of the New York Academy of Sciences*, 1973, *205*, 383–389.

Gilhool, T. Education: An inalienable right. *Exceptional Children*, 1973, *39*, 597–610.

Hartung, A review of procedures to increase verbal imitation skills in autistic children. *Journal of Speech and Hearing Disorders*, 1970, *35*, 203–217.

Hermelin, B. Locating events in space and time: Experiments with autistic, blind and deaf children. *Journal of Autism and Childhood Schizophrenia*, 1972, *2*, 288–298.

Hermelin, B., and Frith, U. Psychological studies of childhood autism: Can autistic children make sense of what they see and hear? *Journal of Special Education*, 1971, *5*, 107–117.

Hermelin, B., and O'Connor, N. *Psychological Experiments with Autistic Children.* Oxford, Pergamon Press, 1970.

Hewitt, F. Teaching speech to an autistic child through operant conditioning. *American Journal of Orthopsychiatry*, 1965, *35*, 927–936.

Hutt, C., Hutt, S. J., Lee, D., and Ornsted, C. A behavioral and electroencephalographic study of autistic children. *Journal of Psychiatric Research* 1965, *3*, 181–197.

Kanner, L. Autistic disturbances of affective content. *Nervous Child*, 1943, *2*, 217–250.

Lovaas, O. I. Considerations in the development of a behavioral treatment program of psychotic children. In Don Churchill (Ed.), *Infantile Autism: Proceedings of Indiana University Colloquium.* Springfield, Ill.: Charles C. Thomas, 1968.

Lovaas, O. I., and Litvownik, A. Response latencies to auditory stimulus in autistic children engaged in self-stimulatory behavior. *Behavior Research & Therapy*, 1971, *9*, 39–50.

Lovaas, O. I., Schreibman, L., Koegel, R., and Rehm, R. Selective responding by autistic children to multiple sensory input. *Journal of Abnormal Psychology*, 1971, *77*, 211–222.

Lovaas, O. I., and Simmons, J. Manipulation of self-destruction in three retarded children. *Journal of Applied Behavior Analysis*, 1969, *2*, 143–157.

Luria, A. *Higher cortical functions in man.* New York: Basic Books, 1966.

Miller, A., and Miller, E. Cognitive developmental training with elevated boards and sign language. *Journal of Autism and Childhood Schizophrenia*, 1973, *3*, 65–85.

Moore, O. K. *Autmoated responsive environments.* Hemden, Conn.: Basic Education, Inc., 1960.

Nordquist, V., and Wahler, R. Naturalistic treatment of an autistic child. *Journal of Applied Behavior Analysis*, 1973, *6*, 79–87.

Ora, J., and Wiegerink, R. Regional intervention project for parents and children. Bureau of Education for the Handicapped, U. S. Office of Education, Progress Report, 1970.

Ornitz, E. M. The modulation of sensory input and motor output in autistic children. This volume.

Pribram, K. Autism: A deficiency in context-dependent processes? *Proceedings of the National Society for Autistic Children.* Rockville, Md.: Public Health Service, U. S. Department of HEW, 1970.

Rimland, B. *Infantile Autism.* New York: Appleton-Century-Crofts, 1964.

Risley, T., and Wolf, M. M. Establishing functional speech in echolalic children. *Behavior Research and Therapy*, 1967, *5*, 73–88.

Rutter, M. Autism: Educational issue. *Special Education*, 1970, *59*, 6–10.

Schopler, E. Visual versus tactile receptor preference in normal and schizophrenic children. *Journal of Abnormal Psychology*, 1966, *71*, 108–114.

Schopler, E., and Reichler, R. Developmental therapy by parents with their own autistic child. *Colloquium on Infantile Autism.* London: Ciba Foundation, 1970.

Strain, P. S., and Wiegerink, R. Social play of two behaviorally disordered preschool children during four activities: a multiple baseline study, *Journal of Abnormal Psychology,* 1975, in press.

18

Residential Care for Normal and Deviant Children

SPYROS A. DOXIADIS

RESIDENTIAL CARE FOR NORMAL BABIES AND SMALL CHILDREN

Residential care of infants deprived of a normal family—and associated problems such as adoption and fostering—have been the concern of religious leaders, lawmakers, kings, and emperors for thousands of years.

Thus, in the code of Hammurabi (2250 B.C.) we find articles protecting the rights of an adopted child: An adopted child could not be claimed by anyone. If unfairly treated, he could return to his father's home; he could not be disinherited unless he received one-third of a son's portion in advance.

Many centuries later the legal code of Justinian conferred absolute liberty on foundlings, while the same emperor had endowed a big institution for children in Constantinople with a fleet of ships, the profits of which were used for the maintenance of the asylum.

Another striking example of the interest of the powerful of the times in matters concerning the development of children comes to us from Salimbene, a chronicler of the thirteenth century describing the reign and actions of Frederick II, king of Germany, king of Sicily, and emperor of the Holy Roman Empire:

> ... He wanted to find out what kind of speech and what manner of speech children would have when they grew up if they spoke to no one beforehand. So he bade foster

SPYROS A. DOXIADIS · Institute of Child Health, Aghia Sophia Children's Hospital, Athens, Greece.

mothers and nurses to suckle their children, to bathe and wash them, but in no way to prattle with them or to speak to them. For he wanted to learn whether they would speak the Hebrew language or Greek or Latin or Arabic, or perhaps the language of their parents of whom they had been born. But he labored in vain, because the children all died. For they could not live without the petting and joyful faces and loving words of their foster mothers. [Doxiadis, 1970]

One can hardly find a more conclusive example of the effects of "maternal deprivation."

Scientists, however, became really interested in this problem only in the nineteenth century and then only because of excessive mortality in the institutions. This kind of interest, i.e., only in physical survival, continued until World War II. The decrease in the death rate of infants both in the general population and in institutions, resulting from the application of public health measures and advances in treatment, provided the conditions for the development of interest in the other aspects of residential care of infants and led to the pioneer work of Spitz and Anna Freud. Thus, when Bowlby, at the request of the World Health Organization, wrote his famous monograph in 1951 (Bowlby, 1951), he could rely on a good number of original papers to document the view that the long stay of infants in an impersonal institution may mean permanent damage to the development of their intellect and personality. Eleven years later, new evidence was collected and reviewed again at the request of WHO by Ainsworth and others (Ainsworth, Andry, Harlow, Lebovici, Mead, Prugh, and Wootton, 1962).

Ten years later, Rutter (1972) wrote a thorough, comprehensive, and critical review of maternal deprivation, examining not only the outcome but also the possible mechanisms operating to bring about the described results. Since the publication of his work in 1972, nothing has been reported to alter his review in a substantial way.

The present paper mentions only briefly the effects upon the infant of life in a residential institution, since these have been so excellently described and analyzed by Rutter. There are, however, other aspects of residential care of normal infants and small children that are more of a sociological and organizational nature, and it is with these that the present paper will deal primarily.

Since my purpose is not to cover the literature but only to describe some aspects that I consider important, I refer to the work of only a few authors, and I present my own experience, conclusions, and recommendations.

I feel more emphasis should be placed on sociological and organizational aspects of residential care. The reader of a psychological study of the problems of life in an institution, of separation, of deprivation, or privation is left, quite rightly, with many questions. There is no doubt that there still exist in this field many problems requiring for their solution much systematic work, and some of the approaches are full of ethical or methodological difficulties. It will take a long time until we get the answers we desire. This, however, should in no way delay action on the basis of what we already know. There is a risk that new research and further discussion may become plausible excuses for avoiding the pain of decision and the effort of action. We should not consider that everything scientific must be measured. There are things that are obvious and others that are obviously inhuman. To act upon evidence that is not complete, foolproof, and measurable is, I think, permissible, provided we do not go back to the prescientific era of believing uncritically all observations and of acting blindly from personal impressions.

Four points will be discussed here: (1) Which child needs residential care and why? (2) Does it matter if he lives in an institution? (3) Are all institutions the same? (4) What is the gain from intervention?

Which Children Need Residential Care and Why?

Social and cultural factors influence the reasons why a child may be placed in an institution. These differ from country to country, and it is therefore important to investigate conditions in each country and in each type of region (urban, rural) to find out why a child may lose its natural family environment and be in need of some type of custodial care. Examples from two countries illustrate this point. In a survey conducted by Tizard and Tizard (1969)* in England, based on admissions to the care of three voluntary societies, it was shown that, excluding children admitted specifically for adoption, in 60% of the cases the principal reason for admission was illegitimacy. Less frequent reasons for admission were, in descending order, the desertion of a parent or the breakup of a marriage, the long illness of a parent, and neglect or cruelty by a parent. In infants admitted under the age of 6 months, illegitimacy formed a much higher proportion, 91%. After the age of 2 years, the most frequent cause was the desertion of a parent or the breakdown of a marriage.

Figures from Greece, a country less technologically developed than England, where the extended family has not completely disappeared, show a slightly different picture. Thus, in the Babies Center Metera, a modern residential nursery, 99% of the infants admitted in the three years 1971 to 1973 were born to unmarried mothers. This picture is biased in the sense that before an infant is admitted a thorough search is made by the social workers to find another solution before the decision for admission is made. When the mother is married, in almost all cases admission in infancy does not become absolutely necessary.

The above are statistical data and are therefore helpful in determining general policy by the agencies, the communities, or the state. It should, for

---

*I am grateful to Professor J. Tizard and Dr. Barbara Tizard for their kind permission to report extensively on their work.

example, be possible to investigate and determine by cross-cultural studies the effect of modern contraceptive measures on the number of illegitimate children, or the effect of the migration of workers (as in the last 15 years has been happening from southern to more industrialized nothern European countries) on family breakup and desertion and the fate of the children of these marriages. These examples are mentioned to demonstrate first how much we need to know about the sociological aspects of the need for residential care, but also to show how many causes and factors may participate to bring about the need for custodial care. No attempt to solve the problem is complete if it does not combine the cultural and the socioeconomic, even the political approach with the psychological, aimed at the best solution for a particular child. And this is the second need: Parallel with the investigation of the general factors operating on groups of children, there is a need for a thorough investigation of the circumstances of each particular child before deciding what is best. In the past, and even quite often now, in many countries there is a tendency to place the infant or small child in an institution without exploring other possibilities and their advantages or disadvantages. As we should not consider that every institution is necessarily damaging, so we should not think that we should try at all costs to keep a child in his family. It has been shown by many workers that antisocial behavior in adolescents depends more on a damaging family environment before the child is taken into care than on the quality of care as such (see Rutter, 1971).

A second factor that has to be investigated in each country in general, and that has to be considered in the decision for each child in particular, is the likely outcome. Is the child likely to remain in the institution for a long time or not? Since residence for years, even in the best of institutions, may be damaging, it is important to be able to foresee what the fate of a child, once admitted, will be. And if there are special groups more likely to remain for long in an institution, special attention should be given there, either to avoid admission or to plan quickly for discharge to a more permanent environment. Here again the statistics provided by Tizard and Tizard (1969) are useful. Surveying the fate of children admitted to the care of three large voluntary agencies, and excluding those admitted specifically for adoption, they found that at the end of five years 18% were adopted and 46% had been restored to the care of a relative. Placement with a foster family occurred early for about one-third of the children, and the more likely to be fostered were illegitimate babies under the age of 6 months. These were likely to be placed "with a view to adoption," hence 95% of those adopted in general were adopted by their foster parents. Nonwhite children and especially boys were less likely to be adopted, and this constitutes the "vulnerable" group; i.e., those more likely to stay for a long time in residence.

In our institution in Athens, the children more likely to stay in residence above the age of 1 year were, excepting the physically or mentally handicapped, those with a very unstable mother unable to make up her mind about the future of her child or considered unfit to take care of it, or a mother coming from a disturbed or disrupted family environment. Of those discharged, 70% were adopted and 22% returned to their natural parent(s). Thus, in a country like Greece in which it is, for legal reasons, very difficult to take away from a mother the legal custody of her child, the children more likely to need residential care for a long time do so for reasons arising out of their mother's problems. Furthermore, again in countries in which adoption is becoming only recently socially acceptable, adoptive parents are much less likely to accept children with even small physical handicaps. This is therefore the second group likely to stay longer in residential care.

Does It Matter if a Child Lives in an Institution?

Before proceeding to the discussion of the possible ill effects of life in an institution, some consideration should be given to the alternatives. Otherwise, although the theoretical discussion may be useful, the decision for each individual child will be unrealistic if we do not face the question of what alternative solution exists if he is not admitted. Here again sociocultural factors are important.

There are countries or areas where unmarried motherhood is becoming more and more socially acceptable, and therefore a child's life with an unmarried mother does not constitute a social stigma with the ensuing psychological trauma. In such countries, more facilities also exist for day care while the single mother is working. Where social customs are very condemning of unmarried motherhood and illegitimacy, the disadvantages of staying with the mother might be greater than those of institutional life. This is only an example to warn against generalizations and against adopting conclusions from one country for application in another. There are, of course, alternatives, such as intense marital discord, that are detrimental to healthy development in all countries.

The decision to take a child into care and place it in an institution has therefore to be weighed against all likely alternatives in addition to the factors mentioned in the previous section. But to do this, we need to know more about the effects of life in an institution, away from the natural parents.

Two things have to made clear here. The first is that we are not talking here about the old type of institution with the entirely impersonal care and the generally accepted results of gross retardation. This is not because such institutions do not exist any more, but because no one any longer doubts these ill effects. What we are investigating here are the effects of institutions with a better staff-child ratio, with at least partially trained personnel, and with a social service able to take care of the child before and after residential care.

The second is that no better substitute has yet been found for life in a normal, loving, middle-class family with few children. This continues to be the best environment we know for normal physical, mental, and emotional development.

The whole subject of "maternal deprivation," the commonest cause of which is residential care, has been so admirably reviewed by Rutter than nothing more can be added in this paper. For the general reader, however, it is worthwhile to abstract some of the work of the staff of the Child Development Unit at the Institute of Education of London University (Tizard, 1970; Tizard, Cooperman, and Tizard, 1972). I have singled out this work among a large number of papers on the topic of cognitive development in institutionalized children for two reasons. First, the young children studied were living in residential nurseries well above what we may call the average. These nurseries were characterized "not only by a high standard of physical care but by a concern for the psychological well-being of the children." They had no shortage of staff and no rapid staff turnover. Furthermore, these nurseries had responded to earlier criticisms and tried to "deinstitutionalize" the environment and make it more stimulating. Second, the authors have used a sociological approach and correlated their findings on cognitive development, mainly language development, with the organizational structure of the nurseries.

Children aged 24 months scored a mean of 22 months on the Cattell Mental Age test. On the Reynell Language tests, there was a tendency for the children under 30 months to score slightly lower than the average. For example, the mean Reynell Comprehension score for this group was 98.07 (S.D.8.6), while for older children up to 5 years it was 106.68 (S.D.8.7). It can thus be seen that there was very little evidence of retardation in the development of the speech of these children living in a modern type of institution. Differences between nurseries will be discussed later.

In addition to the assessment of cognitive development, the same workers studied the development of social behavior in 2-year-old children reared in long-stay residential nurseries (Tizard and Tizard, 1971). They specifically studied the response to strangers, the response to separation, the attachment and the behavior patterns. They used as controls home-reared children of working-class families in the London area. The main difference found between the two groups was in the behavior toward caretakers and toward strangers. The nursery children, under certain circumstances, were more dependent on familiar adults and less willing to approach or to stay alone with strangers. Their behavior resembled that of an 18-months-old, but their attachment behavior was to a wider range of adults than those of a home-reared child. However, within this range they had preferences so that their attachment, although more diffuse, was not indiscriminate. In general, the authors did not see any gross disturbance of behavior in the type of nurseries they studied.

From these and similar studies it can be concluded that in the modern residential nurseries, where the children are divided into small family-size groups, where a good staff-children ratio is provided, and where staff members are trained to be sensitive to the needs of the children for normal cognitive and emotional development, we do not see the gross retardation or the gross disturbances in behavior that we used to see in the old type, impersonal institutions.

We should not, however, make the same mistake that was made in the past in lumping together all modern residential nurseries without trying to analyze the various components of residential care, and without trying to relate the results we are measuring in the cognitive and emotional development to certain parameters in the environment. Yarrow (1961, 1968), in a series of papers, was among the first to conceptualize the various types of mother-substitute care with emphasis on the type of caretaking and the possibility of attachment of each infant to one or more adults. Thus he described the usual types of residential institutions: (a) those having a major but frequently changing mother figure; (b) those dispersing care among a multitude of caretakers giving insufficient care; (c) those providing discontinuous care given by many caretakers; and (d) those dispersing care among few adults but with sufficient continuity.

The London researchers (Tizard, 1976; Tizard, Cooperman, Joseph, and Tizard, 1972) approached the study of the environment on a different basis, since in the institutions they were studying the great errors of the past had been eliminated. The staffs were adequate in number, with reasonable continuity and trained to recognize and respect the needs of small children.

Thus, the nurseries studied were divided according to the degree of autonomy each family-size group (usually six children) had within the organization of the whole nursery. In the least autonomous nurseries the units were in fact "run by the matron from the center," while in the most autonomous there was a much closer approximation to a family setting and the caretaker in charge had a great degree of freedom in planning the program, the menu, and the timetable of her "family." There was also an intermediate type.

The authors found a very definite relationship between the degree of autonomy and the nurseries and the development of the children. Thus, in the three most autonomous the mean language comprehension score was close to that of children of professional families (social class I and II, according to the English Registrar's General Classification), i.e., 115, while the score for the least autonomous group was 99.4 (1.5 standard deviation lower) and similar to that of children of working-class families. One of the main differences found between the most and the least autonomous group was the quality of the talk of the staff; there was no difference in the amount. Thus, the staff in the most autonomous group, in which, as reported above, the children had a most satisfactory language comprehension score, "spoke in longer and more complex sentences, made more informative remarks, gave more explanation with their commands, gave fewer negative commands, answered the children more often, and were more often answered by the children." In examining to what the "quality of staff behavior" was related, the group concluded that this was determined more by the perception of the caretaker regarding her position within the authority system, i.e., the degree of autonomy, and less by her qualifications or, within limits, by the ratio of staff to children.

The authors were careful to point out that the degree of autonomy was not the only difference between the nurseries they studied; neither was it the only factor responsible for the differences in language development of the children. It is clear, however, that other things being equal (for example, the number and training of the staff), the internal organization of the nursery can significantly contribute to much better child development.

This approach is, I think, of extreme importance because we have reached in our thinking and planning—if not, unfortunately, in universal application—a stage where we know how to avoid the old errors of institutional upbringing with the resulting retardation in cognitive development and deviations in emotional development. What we need now is the knowledge of more subtle influences that will lessen the difference between the development of the child of low socioeconomic status and the child of high socioeconomic status.

In this respect one should not ignore the fact that the quality of staff behavior is not independent of educational, cultural, economic, and family background of the nurses—caretakers, especially in less developed countries.

Education has in many countries been too much influenced by the training of hospital nurses. Devoting a large part of time to medical problems and wearing identical uniforms and caps are two of the obvious effects of such influence. We have found, for example, in our institution a great resistance from lay members of the board to abolishing nurses' caps. My personal feeling is that schools for the training of infants' caretakers (nursery nurses in Britain) should in the future be less and less influenced by the mentality and the practices of schools for sick children's nurses and be more like schools for teachers. This is consistent with getting away from the main institutional task of the past, which was physical health and survival, and facing the real task of the present, which is mental health. In the countries of the world—and there are still many— where the training of young girls to work in institutions for healthy infants and young children is now beginning or about to begin and where there is therefore an absence of senior staff, my advice would be to recruit the staff not from the nursing profession, as is the first impulse, but from the teaching profession or from psychology.

The importance of the cultural and economic background becomes evident when one examines nurses in different countries or from different socioeconomic backgrounds in the same country. Girls who have grown up in small, poor, rural communities are less likely to acquire the sensitivity to the infant's cognitive and emotional needs. It seems that their early experiences with a lack of essentials for their physical well-being (food, adequate housing) makes them less able than their more fortunate colleagues to understand needs less evident, such as stimulation, a one-to-one personal relationship, and attachment.

One further point from our experience with the school for nurses affiliated with the Babies Center Metera is how deeply ingrained are habits regarding infant rearing acquired at home compared with the later practical and theoretical training acquired during three years at the school.

A practical conclusion to be drawn from the above is the need to study cultural habits of infant rearing in the community where the student nurses come from. Only then can we reinforce what we consider desirable and try to uproot what we consider undesirable.

Are All Institutions the Same?

As the result of the work conducted mainly in the postwar years, of the two books commissioned by WHO (Ainsworth, Andry, Harlow, Lebovici, Mead, Prugh, and Wootton, 1962; Bowlby, 1951) and of the dissemination to professional and lay people of knowledge of child development, of maternal deprivation, and of institutionalism, there are more modern institutions such as those studied by the Tizards, in which the gross ill effects of privation are no longer present. In such institutions one does not see children of 18 months unable to walk or of 24 months unable to say a single world. Neither does one see body-rocking or head-banging as common manifestations or the anxious, depressed, or apathetic children described in the old type of institution. This very welcome progress has made assessment of the quality of care provided more difficult because we have not had to measure so much cognitive development as the effects of the environment on the development of emotional stability or more generally on the personality.

To measure these environmental effects, one may use tests directed toward assessment of individuality to see whether a certain environment may stifle individual differences and lead to undesirable uniformity. Or, one may use tests directed toward assessment of social adjustment or emotional stability or other characteristics of personality deemed by the investigator as desirable or undesirable. Obviously, measurements based on the development of children while in the institution and a follow-up many years later, when possible, constitute the best criterion of the performance of that institution. Needless to say, in such a study all other factors likely to influence the development should be taken into consideration.

Such a measurement, however, is very laborious and for the results to have some value many years must pass for an adequate follow-up. We need therefore another approach as well, which will give in a brief period of time a measurement of the standard of work of an institution. This can be done by using a scale assessing various aspects of the work in an institution on the assumption that certain practices will be more and others less beneficial for the development of the children.

Such a scale has been constructed and used by King, Raynes, and Tizard (1971). It is called the Child Management Scale and it comprises four groups of items as shown in Table 1. The scale includes the results of the assessment of four institutions, showing a great difference in scores from 1.43 and 2.41 for two children's homes to 19.60 for a pediatric hospital and 26.07 for a hospital for subnormal children (the lower the score, the better the standard of care). In studying the factors contributing to the differences among the institutions, the authors concluded that they could not be attributed to the varying reasons for the children being in each institution, to the size of the institutions or the living units, to *assigned* (as distinct from *effective*) staff ratios, or to the proportion of trained staff. They thought the differences could be partly related to the kind of training received by the staff and the type of organization of the units inside each institution; i.e., whether they were approaching a type of household organization.

Such a scale will prove to be, I think, extremely useful because it enables the staff from inside or any observer from outside to obtain a picture of the standard of care provided and to effect the necessary improvements within a short period of time. Furthermore, by providing a numerical assessment and the possibility of comparison to other institutions, it will be a useful tool in the hands of people who must convince the various administrative authorities of the need for change. This Child Management Scale is constructed for institutions for children. With my associates at the Babies Center Metera we try to construct and use a similar one for residential nurseries for babies and children up to 24 months.

The Gain from Intervention

It has been established that infants living in institutions may show a gain in their cognitive development if given extra attention (Sayegh and Dennis, 1965; Schaffer and Emerson, 1968). We have been experimenting with a type of intervention addressed to the caretakers and not directly to the infants. At the Babies Center Metera, a residential nursery near Athens, in which infants live in groups of 12 in separate pavilions, an experienced pediatrician has been spending 90 minutes daily talking to nurses and student nurses about the babies and young children they are looking after, pointing out their individual needs and

Table 1

Revised Child Management Scale[a]

Rigidity
1 (AC)   Do children get up at same time at weekends?
2 (AC)   Do children go to bed at same time at weekends?
3 (AC)   Do they use the yard or garden at set times?
4 (AC)   Do they use their bedrooms at set times?
5   Are there set times when visitors can come to visit?
6   Which children are routinely toileted at night?

Block treatment
7 (AC)   After dressing do children wait around doing nothing?
8 (AC)   Do they wait in line before coming in for breakfast?
9 (AC)   Do they wait together as a group before bathing?
10 (AC)   Do they wait together as a group after bathing?
11 (AC)   How do they return from the toilets?
12 (AC)   Do they wait at tables before the meal is served?
13 (AC)   Do they wait at tables after meals before next activity?
14 (AC)   How are they organized for walks?

Depersonalization
15   What is done with their private clothing?
16   What is done with their private toys?
17   How many possess the following articles of clothing?
18   Whereabouts do they keep their daily clothes?
19   How many have toys or books of their own?
20   Do they have pictures, photos, etc., in their rooms?
21   How much time do the children have for playing?
22   How are children's birthdays celebrated?
23   How are tables laid for meals?

Social distance
24 (AC)   Do the children have any access to the kitchen?
25 (AC)   Do the children have any access to other areas?
26   How do staff assist children at toilet times?
27   How do staff assist children at bath times?
28   Do staff on duty eat with the children?
29   Do staff sit and watch television with children?
30 (AC)   How many children have been on outings with staff?

[a]Items marked (AC) relate to ambulant children only.
From *Patterns of Residential Care* by R. D. King, N. V. Raynes, and J. Tizard, Copyright 1971 by Routledge and Kegan Paul. Reprinted by permission.

attributes and discussing their observations. This was in addition to whatever other medical needs existed in that pavilion. Two likely effects of such an intervention were studied and compared with a control pavilion: the behavior of nurses and the development of the infants, measured on the Bayley scale. At the time of the writing of this report we have witnessed a statistically significant improvement in the way the nurses have worked with the children. Since warmth and affection were not lacking before the intervention, what we found that did improve, with structured observations, was the nurses' understanding of the different needs of each infant according to his developmental and individual characteristics (rhythm, activity, general temperament). What has not been as yet evident is an improvement in the infants' scores on the Bayley scale. This may be due either to the fact that a small number of children have been followed so far, or to the likely need of a long latent period until the changed behavior of caretakers has some effect on the measured development of the infants.

RESIDENTIAL CARE OF DEVIANT CHILDREN

What has been said about institutional care for normal babies and small children applies also to deviant children. The problems and the risks are the same, although they are magnified by the special condition of the child. Furthermore, the great individual variability in assets and liabilities and in the needs and vulnerability of normal children is even greater among deviant children so that they need even more individualized management and decision concerning their care. For these reasons, regarding the care of deviant children in or out of institutions, there is perhaps more divergence of opinion and we need more data than for normal children.

One additional and perhaps the most important difference between the residential care of normal and deviant children is that in the first case there is in the great majority of children no choice: The child is unprotected because of illegitimacy or disruption of his family or similar reasons, and life in an institution for short or long periods is the only solution. In the case of deviant children—and in the context of the present symposium, mainly autistic children—we can choose between life in a "normal," undisrupted family and life in an institution. The question, in other words, is whether there are data to support the view that in addition to the educational help, i.e., attendance at special schools, there is any reason for these children to be boarders rather than day pupils. There are no hard research findings, i.e., controlled studies, to support either view. Only incidental findings can be quoted and one of the most recent is that reported by Rutter and Bartak (1973), who studied the type of educational treatment most likely to help the scholastic progress of autistic children. In one of the three units studied (unit C), in which also the best educational results were attained, a number of children were weekly boarders, i.e., they spent the weekends at home. A comparison between day pupils and boarders showed that although there were no significant differences in social responsiveness or behavior in class, *when at home* the boarders tended to exhibit more deviant behavior and to have a greater social handicap. The authors point out that no general conclusion is justified from this difference, since the groups were not comparable in the sense that some of the children were boarded specifically because the parents could no longer cope with their problems at home. It is therefore a matter for individual decision, since some children behaved better at school and even a few of them at home, after they became residents, but "this was not generally the case."

In the absence therefore of any definite research findings that lead to general conclusions concerning the best policy, the decision in each case should be taken after examining three factors: the child, the family, and the institution.

The Child

The main question regarding residential care of the deviant child is how to combine the feeling of warmth and security with the necessary environmental stimulation that can be provided by specialized personnel. It is of interest to note that Rutter and Bartak (1973), in the work that has been mentioned previously on the relative value of three educational units for autistic children, observed that the strength of two units lay in the warm interaction of staff to children, while that of the third lay in the provision of systematic teaching. They concluded that "the results for units A and B could be improved by the provision of more systematic teaching and those for unit C by the greater use of warmth and praise."

It is now commonplace to say that in many institutions children suffer emotional and sensory deprivation in such a way as to make the initial handicap worse. On the other hand, we cannot say that we have explored all the possibilities for cognitive development among deviant children. Every person responsible for the decision concerning the home or institutional management of the deviant child must weigh the advantages and disadvantages of the two factors and strike a balance between the family environment and the special stimulations of the institution.

During the preschool years, unless the institution is of a particularly high standard or unless the family has proved that it cannot cope, the best environment is that of the family. After the first few years, when special educational treatment becomes necessary, the best solution for most children will be attendance at a day school.

The Family

The presence of a deviant child in a family may create great problems, sometimes bringing the members closer together, but more often increasing preexisting stresses and weaknesses. No decision should be taken in ignorance or in disregard of the effect on the family. Placing the child in an institution relieves the parents of a heavy burden, but it may considerably increase their feelings of guilt and it may in other cases make them feel that they have no further responsibility for the future of their child. Thus, in each case a thorough study of the family by experienced persons should be undertaken. If it is felt that the family can provide a warm, secure, supporting environment, then day attendance at a special institution or school is the best answer. However, even in these circumstances there should always be available auxiliary staff to help the parents in emergencies and arrangements to take care of the child in his home or in a foster family should the mother be absent or exhausted and in need of help. For this reason, it is advisable to establish in educational institutions small boarding units so that the child does not have to go, if the need arises, to an entirely strange environment.

The Institution

The institution is mainly the staff that works in it. Here we have two types of questions: The first is how to select and train the staff, and the second is how to avoid boredom and maintain the interest of the staff in the care of deviant children.

One way to accomplish these goals is to have different staff members responsible for the physical and family-type care of the children and for their special education. In such a way, part of the staff can be relieved from the burden of being continuously responsible for a deviant child. Furthermore, the above-mentioned system of day care of five-day-a-week care gives to the staff of the institution the opportunity to rest.

In the past such institutions had the tendency to become isolated, and this increased the indifference and boredom of the staff. It is therefore essential for any such institution to be in very close contact with a university, a medical school, or any similar institution of higher learning with frequent visits from outside staff and frequent discussions and conferences. One additional factor for success is a very well-developed social and educational service for follow-up and for family counseling. In such a way, the mother substitutes and the teachers will be continuously informed of the family situation of each child while in residence and for his subsequent fate after he leaves the institution. There will thus be a feedback to help the staff to assess their work.

REFERENCES

Ainsworth, M. D., Andry, R. G., Harlow, R. G., Lebovici, S., Mead, M., Prugh, D. G., and Wootton, B. *Deprivation of maternal care*. Geneva: World Health Organization, 1962.

Bowlby, J. *Maternal care and mental health*. Geneva: World Health Organization, 1951.

Doxiadis, S. Mothering and Frederick II. *Clinical Pediatrics*, 1970, *9*, 565–566. Quotation on p. 565 from J. B. Ross and M. M. McLaughlin (Eds.), *A portable medieval reader*. New York: Viking, 1959. P. 366.

King, R. D., Raynes, N. V., and Tizard, J. *Patterns of residential care*. London: Routledge and Kegan Paul, 1971.

Rutter, M. Parent–child separation: Psychological effects on the children. *Journal of Child Psychology and Psychiatry*, 1971, *12*, 233–260.

Rutter, M. *Maternal deprivation reassessed*. Harmondsworth, England: Penguin Books, 1972.

Rutter, M., and Bartak, L. Special educational treatment of autistic children: A comparative study - II. Follow-up findings and implications for services. *Journal of Child Psychology and Psychiatry*, 1973, *14*, 241–270.

Sayegh, Y., and Dennis, W. The effect of supplementary experiences upon the behavioral development of infants in institutions. *Child Development*, 1965, *36*, 81–90.

Schaffer, H. R., and Emerson, P. E. The effects of experimentally administered stimulation on development quotients of children. *British Journal of Social and Clinical Psychology*, 1968, *7*, 61–67.

Tizard, B. Varieties of residential nursery experience. In R. V. Clarke, I. Sinclaire, and J. Tizard (Eds.), *Varieties of residential experience*. London: Routledge and Kegan Paul, 1976 in preparation.

Tizard, B., Cooperman, O., Joseph, A., and Tizard, J. Environmental effects on language development: A study of young children in long-stay residential nurseries. *Child Development*, 1972, *43*, 337–358.

Tizard, B., and Joseph, A. Cognitive development of young children in residential care: A study of children aged 24 months. *Journal of Child Psychology and Psychiatry*, 1970, *11*, 177–186.

Tizard, J., and Tizard, B. *Preschool children in residential care*. Report from the Department of Child Development, Institute of Education, University of London, 1969. Mimeographed.

Tizard, J., and Tizard, B. The social development of two-year-old children in residential nurseries. In H. R. Shaffer (Ed.), *The origins of human social relations*. New York: Academic Press, 1971.

Yarrow, L. J. Maternal deprivation: Toward an empirical and conceptual re-evaluation. *Psychological Bulletin*, 1961, *58*, 459–490.

Yarrow, L. J. Conceptualizing the early environment. In C. Chandler, R. S. Lourie, and A. DeHuff Peters (Eds.), *Early child care*. New York: Atherton Press, 1968.

19
Developmental Therapy: A Program Model for Providing Individual Services in the Community

ROBERT J. REICHLER and ERIC SCHOPLER

In this paper we discuss some of the problems of bringing therapeutic services to children. It is by now clear that our understanding of both normal development and developmental abnormalities is seriously incomplete. We have neither a coherent body of knowledge nor a comprehensive theory, and most treatments available for an abnormally developing child do not adequately utilize what knowledge we do have. In the first part of this paper some basic reasons for the lack of adequate services will be explored, with special reference to the problems of autistic and other severely deviant children. The purpose of this exploration is to identify issues that have interfered with the development of adequate care, and to suggest some essential elements for the provision of appropriate services for children and their families. In this discussion, autism and psychosis are used interchangeably, both referring to rating systems (Reichler and Schopler, 1971) based on the Creak (1964) criteria.

In the second part of the paper, we present the North Carolina program for autistic children (Division TEACCH—Treatment and Education of Autistic and related Communications handicapped CHildren) as a model for developmental services involving both family and community. We identify aspects of the

ROBERT J. REICHLER and ERIC SCHOPLER · Department of Psychiatry, School of Medicine, University of North Carolina at Chapel Hill, Chapel Hill, North Carolina 27514.

program that evolved in an attempt to counteract or resolve the problems presented in the first part.

PROFESSIONAL ISSUES

Professional specialists are often ready to claim ultimate expertise on one or another aspect of children's development or dysfunctions. Experience suggests, however, that often the specialist, whether psychiatrist, psychologist, teacher, or speech therapist, has certain professional sets and specialized skills that make him respond to a child's difficulty in terms of his specialized knowledge rather than the needs of the individual and his family. Such occupational investment frequently pits professionals against each other as they defend their respective roles: A social worker defends the family against a child psychiatrist who is protecting the child; an educator insists on educational priorities against the psychotherapist's "emotional" concerns; the organically oriented clinician opposes one psychogenically trained. The investment is not surprising, considering that it takes from six to fifteen years to train a professional, and that specialized training by its very nature tends to narrow perspective. This is most clearly spelled out by McLuhan (1966) discussing specialization in *Understanding Media*:

> Perfect adaptation to any environment is achieved by a total channeling of energies and vital force that amounts to a kind of status terminus for a creature. Even slight changes in the environment of the very well adjusted find them without any resource to meet new challenge. Such is the plight of the representatives of "conventional wisdom" in any society. Their entire stake of security and status is in a single form of acquired knowledge, so that innovation is for them not novelty but annihilation. p. 74

Professional narrowness leads directly to a highly focused orientation toward specific *but limited* aspects of the patient, depending on the specialist's interest in certain symptoms, diseases, organ systems, or special methodologies. Inevitably this focus expresses itself in fragmentation of the patient into different problems and discontinuity of the services available to him. Even in this day of concern with the "whole person," different professionals appear to see different whole persons and furnish contradictory advice. Treatment techniques tend toward similar specialization, and therapy offered a child may be more determined by the portal he walks through and the setting he finds himself in than by the particular requirements of his problem.

When children with similar problems are seen in different settings, from disparate diagnostic perspectives, it adds significantly to the nosological confusion discussed in the next section, but one of the most serious results of this professional segmentation is its effect on availability of services. The more specialized the professional's concern, the longer and more expensive is his training, and the fewer are the professionals trained in it. And, with fragmentation and duplication of services, professional efforts are used inefficiently (Reichler, Babigian, and Gardner, 1966). The overall result is services that are scarce, expensive, and incomplete.

The toll such professional narrowness and protectiveness has exacted from children and their families is amply recorded in the published accounts by parents (Wilson, 1968; Park, 1967; Eberhardy, 1967; May, 1950). One paper, written by a parent who is a psychiatrist (Kysar, 1968), describes, with appropriate anger, the travail of his family through the professional jungle and the conflict between two professional camps. The conflicting opinions of professionals and the nightmarish inconsistencies between the recommendations and their actions are vividly documented. Even more poignant is the description of the destructive impact of this experience on the members of his family, and their need ultimately to fall back upon their own resources. He says:

> Many parents do not want to institutionalize their children. We have found in the course of establishing our new school that there are many parents, especially those with some stability and warmth, who struggle for years with little help with the daily ordeals of a seriously disturbed child. We have also heard over and over again the stories of sincerely cooperative parents being bounced back and forth between the two camps in child psychiatry, i.e., being told "There's no evidence of organicity; it's entirely emotional" by one group and then the opposite for another group. *It is small wonder that these parents go shopping around for repeated evaluations.* p. 146 [italics added]

DIAGNOSTIC ISSUES

Nosological confusion contributes heavily to the persistence of separate professional camps and the contention between them. Each adversary in the clinical–scientific conflict over "approaches" supports particular diagnostic criteria for autism and other developmental handicaps as if there were some ultimate, definitive schema that his particular system best approximates (Kanner, 1971). Diagnosis relates to the essential "3 P's" of medical care: prevention, prescription, and prognosis. Prevention is based on understanding of causative factors. Prescription refers to all interventions that cure, improve, or moderate any dysfunction. Prognosis requires a judgment of the probable course and outcome of a problem, and is especially important when the condition is fatal or chronic, or when interventions may be inadequate. Diagnosis in itself serves no purpose unless it leads to some rational action. What is often not adequately appreciated is that a particular nosology may serve one purpose effectively but have little relevance for another. In addition, different purposes lead to different strategies. For instance, a classification for preventive purposes would attempt to produce homogeneous clusters of patients with the goal of discovering a common etiology, since an etiological nosology may lead to specific interventions, to preventive counseling as in genetics, or other public health measures.

A therapeutic nosology, on the other hand, brings together problems that require similar interventions but do not necessarily share a common cause, since it seeks to develop the facilities and personnel for skilled and efficient care.

Prognostic nosologies are important for the development of extended-care facilities and for planning the personal, social, and fiscal future.

In the absence of a nosology based on any coherent and systematic ideas, we must rely on a descriptive classification that may not be incompatible with the other basic schemes. It is often useful even when etiology or treatment is known and may lead to recognition of subgroups or previously unapparent aspects of a dysfunction. There are, however, almost as many ways of classifying children as there are purposes to be served; any symptom, historical antecedent, or theoretical issue may provide the primary framework. The more idiosyncratic the classification, the more confusion there is in communication, and the professional environment then begins to approximate the Tower of Babel. A descriptive classification must at best be consistent and systematic. Theoretical notions should not influence the description of primary characteristics of behavior. Accurate descriptive classifications allow comparisons between different research reports and facilitate the systematic evaluation of different treatments.

Much cogent criticism of psychiatric classification has regularly appeared in the literature (Menninger, Ellenberger, Pruyser, and Mayman, 1958; Stengel, 1960; Rutter, 1968; Rutter, Lebovici, Eisenberg, Sheznevskij, Sadoun, Brooke, and Lin, 1969; Strauss, 1973). The current nosology offered by the American Psychiatric Association (1968) in DSM II is clearly a compromise between conflicting points of view. It offers a scheme based inconsistently on theory, on conjectured etiology, and on vague description. Childhood disorders are assigned to limited categories that do not refer to developmental processes. The only other current official alternative, the GAP (Group for the Advancement of Psychiatry, 1969) Classification of Psychopathological Disorders in Childhood, describes itself as relying "heavily upon psychoanalytic theory." It is backed up by a list of literally hundreds of symptoms, almost precluding classification in any sense. Neither the APA nor the GAP has any clear relevance to treatment.

Frustration over the failure of prolonged and repeated attempts to arrive at an adequate diagnostic model has led to a surge of nihilistic denigration of diagnosis per se, intensified by concerns about the misuse and abuse of labeling. In addition, antidiagnostic sentiment is expressed by some behaviorists whose primary focus has been the individual symptoms. They argue that diagnosis is irrelevant and that for treatment it suffices to identify individual and specific troubling behaviors and then apply appropriate techniques. What is ignored in these discussions is the essential function of diagnosis. Nosology is not supposed to be definitive, but only to provide a changing, developing language for communication. For prescriptive purposes, a diagnosis should also imply a preferential hierarchy of treatments. Some diagnostic system is necessary to allow comparison among the various interventions available, to evaluate therapeutic efforts, and to foster development of new treatments. Even a non-nosological behavioristic approach to treatment must ultimately specify which techniques are most effective for what behaviors and under what conditions.

Despite the need, there exists no uniform or generally accepted classification scheme for the severe developmental disorders. The present state of confusion is vividly represented by the many overlapping diagnostic terms abounding in the literature (psychosis, autism, atypical child, childhood schizophrenia, to name a few). It results in part from confusion regarding the purpose of diagnosis, in part from ignorance concerning causation, significant descriptive features, and prognosis. For instance, Rimland (1964) makes a strong argument for an attempt at a concise, narrow definition of autism. While he does not state it explicitly, he clearly supports an *etiological* classification, in this case a biological one. He argues:

> A failure to differentiate cannot help but impede progress toward solution of the problems both diseases present. For example, pooling autistic children, who almost never show any somatic problems, with schizophrenic children, who consistently do show such problems, will almost certainly becloud the findings from metabolic studies or other investigations of bodily function (e.g., Loegler, Colbert, and Eiduson, 1961).

The particular clustering of symptoms arrived at relates more meaningfully to a specific etiology than an alternative cluster might. In our opinion, such closure is premature when the etiology is not definitely known.

The problem with available nosology in children's dysfunctions is not the attempt at classification per se, but the lack of therapeutic interventions that are both specific and effective. If specific and effective interventions are developed, as lithium was for adult manic-depressive disorders, differential diagnosis will become more meaningful and the focus will change from a simple descriptive exercise to identification of patient parameters that point to specific treatment.

Regardless of the lack of adequate nosology, professionals continue to be preoccupied with diagnosis. To evaluate child development, increasing numbers of clinics and screening programs are appearing that offer elaborate diagnostic services but little or nothing in the way of treatment. Since these facilities often serve as a learning environment for professionals in training, there is a continued reinforcement of attention on pseudoetiological diagnoses rather than on creative and pragmatic intervention. Similarly, in child psychiatry, obsession with extensive diagnostic evaluation persists. This is often performed within so limited a theoretical framework that many problems remain obscured and only a limited range of interventions are even considered. The orientation to diagnosis that is based on different theories and techniques, taught to different professionals trained in different settings, perpetuates the separation of the profession into separate camps. The focus on classification implies to those outside the profession that the right diagnosis will lead to the right treatment or prognostic advice, and drives parents from center to center and professional to professional in search of it.

PARENTAL AND PROFESSIONAL SOCIAL ROLES

The question of the proper role of parents in achieving appropriate services for their psychotic children is a matter of confusion and mistrust. Parents of retarded children, as well as of children with serious physical illnesses, have long been organized on local and national levels into cohesive forces organizing money, research, and educational support for their children's needs. In contrast, parents of autistic or psychotic children for a long time tended to avoid public identification, individually or collectively. Their lack of social support is explainable in terms of scapegoating by professionals (Schopler, 1971). It may also be understood in terms of conflicts in social role between parents and professionals. Professionals are sometimes referred to as "the authorities." To be an authority is to possess special information, knowledge, and access to other authorities. To fill this social role, it is necessary to have expert knowledge of a field, an exclusiveness that is sometimes underlined by the use of special terminology and jargon. Because of lengthy educational preparation, apprenticeship, and professional certification, it has become part of the professional's social role to maintain that these preparations are both necessary (and, by implication, sufficient) for attaining authority. To have one's professional role evaluated, to be held accountable to anyone, other than perhaps one's professional peers, is not usually part of the authority's self-concept.

The role of parent, on the other hand, is generally defined as the responsibility for child rearing. To hold responsibility means to be morally, legally, and mentally accountable. Not too many generations ago the division between parental responsibility and parental authority was negligible, but today with the increase in population, the division of labor, and specialized bureaus, the split between parental responsibility and authority has often reached painful and ludicrous proportions.

In attempting to deal with autistic children, the professional's role is often enveloped in confusion and myth. This arises when he is obliged by it to pretend to specialized knowledge that he does not have. There is no denying the practical values of any professional role, but when the role is played too vehemently the effects are often unproductive or socially harmful. The fact that the contrast between professional and parental roles is not simply the contrast between authority and responsibility appears to be another major source of parental disability in rearing autistic children.

Both parents and professionals have contributed to the creation of the incongruity between parental responsibility and professional authority. Parents want and need someone to search for causes and tell them probable causes and outcome. Professionals want and need to fulfill this role. The trouble has been that there are many conflicting doctrines on cause and cure that pass for facts. Most causal theories have some plausibility and most treatments are at least partially successful, at least with some children. It is interesting that since infantile autism was first published as a diagnostic entity (Kanner, 1943) with constitutional implications, the least plausible causal emphasis (i.e., parental psychopathology and mismanagement) has had the most sustained support. It is the least plausible from the point of view of empirical clinical research and observation. Perhaps it has endured because it assigns roles to people that they are prepared to play. Parents are supposed to love and sustain their children and assume responsibility for what happens to them, and it is natural for them to question themselves when confronted with obscure peculiarities of development.

The professional role, on the other hand, is to give authoritative responses to questions of causative probability and treatment of choice. When the answers to these questions are unknown and professional consensus is lacking, then the hypothesis of parental guilt and its consequences for treatment seem to be the best match for sustaining both parent and professional in their social roles. Parents of autistic children, like many others—including parents of the "learning disabled" and the "emotionally disturbed"—often find themselves thrust into the role of those responsible for their children's condition. This has the effect of intimidating parents, as does the use of denigrating diagnostic labels such as "schizophrenogenic," "double-binding," "emotionally cold," "obsessive-compulsive," "refrigerator," "smothering," and "rejecting."

As parents have become organized in response to these inequities they have inadvertently tended to foster inadequate services for their children. Parents come to think of themselves as "mental-retardation parents," "autism parents," "learning-disability parents," "cerebral-palsy parents," etc. They become professionalized. They then identify themselves with the professional group most actively involved in the care of their own group of children and lobby for these professionals. That they do this is both natural and understandable. Unfortunately, however, it leads to duplication of programs, wasteful competition for overlapping funds, and fragmentation of services.

ESSENTIAL ELEMENTS OF A SOLUTION

We have reviewed some of the current difficulties in delivering services for children. In discussing solutions to these obstacles, we are emphasizing a developmental perspective; that is, children's needs change with age. These changes manifest themselves in observable behavior. In fact, whether a child's behavior falls within the normal or deviant range, his needs are also developmentally determined. Moreover, even the most difficult abnormal children, the autistic, are more readily understood via the similarities to their behavior found also in younger normal children. Because of the importance of this developmental orientation, we have referred to our own program as "developmental therapy."

Before the problems of comprehensive service delivery for children can be resolved, they must first be frankly recognized. It does no good for professionals to dismember children's problems into speciality areas, whether they reflect methods of clinical practice or the organization of state and national agencies. What is needed is a generalist viewpoint with primary attention to the needs of children and their families rather than to the needs of the specialist. Such reorientation to the child fosters a functional, *rehabilitative* intervention.

A nosology that develops from the rehabilitative orientation requires a careful, quantitative assessment of function. It cuts across the categorical attempts to label and pigeonhole children, which, while valid for certain research issues, has little relationship to the needs of the child and his parents. It is not antagonistic to classification, but its categories develop from clustering of individuals who share similar arrays of function. For different purposes, different typographies may be developed, but each must have its foundation in *measured levels of discrete function.* Such an approach to diagnosis serves the communicative purpose of nosology well. No matter what particular typographical clustering is being used by any individual clinician or investigator, accurate comparison of various endeavors is still possible if descriptive quantitative data are available.

Primary attention to the needs of the child and his family and a sympathetic recognition of their plight do much to eliminate the scapegoating tendency identifiable in professional practice. A rehabilitative intervention lends itself to the direct involvement of parents, family, and community in solving the child's problems. In such a process the training of parents, the experience of developing effectiveness with their child, and their development of broader understanding of the child's needs all serve to destigmatize parents, encourage effective action, and decrease the degree of their "professionalization." Each of these issues will be discussed at greater length and detail in the context of the development of the program for autistic children in North Carolina.

HISTORY AND RATIONALE OF THE PROGRAM

The initial problem confronting the professional treating severely dysfunctional children, if institutionalization is not immediately considered, is the management of the child at home. Following a pilot study in 1966, using parents of psychotic children as co-therapists, a five-year study, the Child Research Project, was begun (Schopler and Reichler, 1971b), and later evolved into a state-wide program. The lack of professionals and facilities to serve these children demanded it. Initial success by ourselves and others in teaching parents home management suggested it should be possible to teach parents the other training and educational techniques we were finding useful with their children. The parents' enthusiastic response and success were encouraging.

Despite the evident need, the concept of helping parents to interact more effectively with their psychotic child ran counter to prevailing theory in the field. Clinical observations of parents ascribed to them emotional and intellectual deviations far more frequently (Bettelheim, 1967) than these characteristics had been demonstrated through controlled research. Myers and Goldfarb (1961) found mothers imposing their perplexities on their "schizophrenic" offspring, and parents' aberrant thinking had been repeatedly linked to the thought structure found in them. Such "schizophrenogenic" influences had been measured in studies with the Goldstein Scherer Object Sorting Test (Singer and Wynne, 1965; Lovibond, 1954; Lidz, 1958, 1962; Wild, 1965; and Rosman, 1964). In each of these studies parents showed more disordered thinking than did control groups. The primary interpretation of these findings placed the emphasis on parental thought disorder as generating similar impairment in the child. These views were maintained despite reports like that of Pitfield and Oppenheim (1964), who found that some of the stereotyped characteristics were not present in their sample of 100 mothers of psychotic children. These studies were extended by Schopler and Loftin (1969a,b). The results showed that parents were impaired in their thinking when tested in association with their psychotic child in the context of a psychodynamic evaluation. However, when another group of parents of psychotic children were tested in the context of an interview asking them how they were able to successfully raise their normal children with a problem child in the family, they showed no more impaired thinking than a control group of parents of retarded children. It was increasingly clear that parents of psychotic children are disorganized in *reaction* to their disorganized psychotic child.

Further supportive data was produced as work with these families continued and the nature of the children's problems came into focus (Reichler and Schopler, 1971). Despite the experience that parents could be helped to foster their children's development, and the slowly accumulating evidence that childhood autism or psychosis is primarily due to some form of biochemical or neurophysiological brain abnormality rather than parental psychopathology (Ornitz and Ritvo, 1968; Schopler and Reichler, 1971c; Rimland, 1964; and Schopler, 1965), clinicians persist in their inappropriate distrust of parents. Parents' opinion, records of developmental history, and accounts of experiences with their child were, and still are, frequently reinterpreted by clinicians and disbelieved without adequate evidence. In contrast to the unjustly held view that parents of psychotic children misperceive their child to the detriment of his development, staff of the Child Research Project were impressed with the parents' ability to assess their own child quite realistically. Since this view of the parents was a clinical impression, it was tested in more controlled conditions (Schopler and Reichler, 1972). Prior to any diagnostic procedures or formal testing, parents were asked to estimate in years and months their psychotic child's level of functioning in areas such as language, motor, and social development. These estimates were compared with the results of formal testing on standard psychological tests. The results showed significant overall correlations.

These data clearly supported the clinical evidence that parents were capable of realistically assessing their children's current level of functioning. Similar findings have been reported for parents of retarded children (Schulman and Stern, 1959; Wolfensberger and Kurtz, 1971). Despite understanding their children's current functioning, the parents often give the *impression* of denying or not understanding their child's limitations. They appear to be uncertain about the meaning of current functioning and limitations for the child's future and for his potential to achieve relative independence in his own life. Wolfensberger and Kurtz's (1971) review of this topic with respect to the mentally retarded and cerebral palsied children reported a similar discrepancy between parents' ability to assess current functioning, and their ability to formulate future expectations. It is not completely obvious why the implications of a child's handicaps are so unclear to parents, but we suspect, in agreement with Wolfensberger and Kurtz (1971), that it is in part the expression of parents' hope, heavily contaminated by the overzealous optimism of many therapists and teachers. A study directly examining parents' future expectations, as well as the current assessment and future expectations of children by referring professionals, is currently underway. It is a disheartening task for most professionals, especially those with an investment in treatment, to communicate limited or poor prognoses to parents; most will delay or avoid the issue as much as possible. Furthermore, it would appear easier for professionals, and more consistent with some of their theories, to maintain parents in their overexpectations rather than admit their own limited understanding and ability to predict.

Description of the Program

The state-supported program for the Treatment and Education of Autistic and related Communications handicapped CHildren (TEACCH) was legislatively established in 1972. It developed from the Child Research Project, supported initially by the U.S. Office of Education, the National Institute of Mental

Health, and the Department of Psychiatry of the School of Medicine at the University of North Carolina at Chapel Hill.

The program currently consists of three clinical diagnostic and treatment centers, located in the three major population regions of the state, and special education classrooms carefully distributed throughout each region. Each center is directed by a doctorate-level psychologist who supervises three to four psychoeducational therapists. The administrative design of the program maintains centers of this size in order to allow the flexibility necessary for the individualized management and special education program needed for each family. More than half of the referrals to the program come from Developmental Evaluation Clinics, special education programs, mental health clinics, and psychiatrists. A third of the referrals are self-referred or come from a variety of service programs and professionals.

An appointment for the child and both his parents is given after the referral is received. This first diagnostic visit lasts about four hours. While parents discuss concerns about their child with a staff member, the child is seen for a psychoeducational evaluation. Parents are also asked to bring along some toys and play material from home, familiar to the child. They use their materials in interacting with their child in order to help the staff understand the child's relationships with the people with whom he is most familiar. The parents are told the staff's impressions of their child. Their questions are answered at the conclusion of the first visit and recommendations are made. All information about the child is shared with the parents.

If this brief study of the child indicates he might benefit from admission to the program, a trial period of appointments is offered to the family for six or eight weeks. This period enables parents to learn what the program expects of them and to make a realistic commitment based on their estimate of what they can expect from the program. At the end of this period, the findings and recommendations of the staff are discussed with the parents. A contract for working together is made that is reevaluated for possible renewal at regular intervals. Even if families do not continue after this trial period, parents usually leave with a better understanding of their child and how to manage him.

Eleven classrooms, each providing an educational program for five to eight children, are located throughout the state. A cooperative effort with local school systems enables these classes to be located in community public schools. A modified self-contained special-education classroom helps to provide a tailored developmental program for each child. Opportunity is available for children in the program to participate in certain regular classrooms when this is appropriate to their needs and abilities. The class also functions as a resource room for other children in the school, which means that children from the regular grades not only receive services but provide stimulation for the autistic children. Often treatment continues at the clinical center, but this is determined according to the need of each child and his family. The staff of each classroom, a teacher and assistant teacher, are specially trained by TEACCH. This preparation in the unique work of the program is further employed to prepare additional professionals for working with autistic children. Teachers, parents, and the staff of the center determine when a child is to be enrolled and the duration of his daily program. The class operates according to the local school's daily schedule. Most children attend for a full school day, but adjustments are made as a child's developmental level dictates. Parents continue working with their children through home programs and direct participation in the classroom.

Regular meetings are held at each center to enable parents to meet each other and discuss common concerns and experiences, or to further their education regarding their children's problems through films or speakers.

Theoretical Framework

Since we still have little knowledge of the specific causes of childhood psychosis, it may be helpful to explain the theoretical framework and the focal propositions that guide our program.

Some prevalent theories of autism are locked tightly for their verification to a prescribed therapy. Thus, Bettelheim's (1967) therapy involves separating the child indefinitely from his parents and replacing them with warm, accepting parent surrogates. This therapy by parentectomy and the psychogenic theory are often presented as justification of one for the other. A similar relationship exists between the position taken by many learning theorists and their procedures for operant conditioning. The therapist assumes that behavior can be shaped if the right reinforcement contingencies can be found. Ferster (1961) proposed that autistic behavior is *caused* by parental inability to provide proper reinforcement for the child. Such circular reasoning is not the link between developmental therapy and the propositions formulated above under *History and Rationale*.

In developmental therapy, it is assumed that the directions of a child's development are largely determined by the interactions with his parents. By and large, the normal child's behavior is shaped around parental expectations; the child in turn has an effect on the parent's behavior. The human infant is born with a biologically determined set of reflexes and responses that appear in regular sequence, *relatively* unaffected by learned experience. Some of these responses are basic to social development. Some infants, for example, smile much more than others. An infant's smile increases his mother's involvement, and infants who smile frequently tend to be fatter than infrequent smilers (Freedman, 1966). Similar studies of the infant's contributions to the developing dyadic interactions with its parents are increasingly being reported in relation to vocal, gaze, and affective behaviors (Stern, 1973; Kaye, 1975; Tronick, 1975;

Osofsky, 1975; Als, 1975; Parke, 1975). For an autistic infant with impaired responses, the mother is negatively or inconsistently reinforced for her mothering efforts. The interaction cycle is directed more by the biological limitations than it is for the normal child.

The presence of such rigidities of constitutional adaptation was alluded to in Kanner's original discovery of autism (Kanner, 1943), which has subsequently been elaborated and clarified in the reviews of Eisenberg (1967) and Rutter (1971). In these reviews a consensus about the nature of childhood psychosis appears to be evolving. Learned experience has less effect on preschool children than on older children, increasing the likelihood that for the younger child adaptational difficulties involve biological processes. Our own studies (Schopler, 1965, 1966; Schopler and Reichler, 1971c; Reichler and Schopler, 1971) agree with those of others (Ornitz and Ritvo, 1968; Rutter, 1968) in suggesting that the primary defect in autism or childhood psychosis involves impairment in communication and understanding with manifestations in both cognitive and perceptual processes.

With this developing biological perspective, and the evidence that parents can function appropriately and effectively with their own psychotic child, the following propositions were formulated as a basis for developmental therapy:

1. Since the causes of autism are as yet unknown, and probably vary, the classification must, for the time being, remain broad but descriptively explicit;

2. The most likely causes are those involving biochemical and neurological brain abnormalities, resulting in perceptual inconsistencies and impairment of speech and communication as well as other integrative dysfunctions;

3. Parents' personalities fall within the "normal range," differing from the general population only in that they have reacted with perplexity and confusion to their unresponsive or inconsistently responsive children.

Once the parents' difficulties are recognized as largely reactive, the need for educating, training, and supporting them is evident. Although clinical evidence is sometimes offered for theories that the parents make a significant causal contribution to their child's problems, this is usually a misinterpretation. Poor parental attitudes and management are most often the consequence of ineptness and ignorance rather than the expression of purposeful or malignant psychopathology. Why else are they seeking help! The direct involvement of parents in the rehabilitation and development of their children requires that they be respected and accepted as collaborators and co-therapists.

Professional Issues: Staff

The ability to involve parents as collaborators and accept their role as major therapeutic agents requires a special openness on the part of the staff. We have found clear advantages to both children and their parents when the therapists who work with them are not highly trained and specialized professionals. As indicated in our introductory remarks, occupational investment, identity, and training often create biases and limitations of skill that make the specialist respond in terms more of his specialized knowledge than of the needs of an individual child and his family. In our program, effective therapists have come from various educational backgrounds, including linguistics, education, speech, child development, Chinese history, and art. They are selected for their interest and sensitivity in teaching autistic or psychotic children and their parents rather than according to their professional identity.

We have discovered that the best method for selecting potential therapists, after initial interview, is to observe them in interaction with a psychotic child and then with a parent. The applicant is then asked to write a report of the interaction, and briefly outline plans for working with the child. A similar interaction is sampled with a parent. The applicant is asked to hold a brief interview with a parent in order to assess the parent's struggles and concerns about his situation. The purpose is to formulate initial ideas on how to help the parent, and to write a report with recommendations based on evidence from the interview. This procedure allows us also to get parental reaction to the suitability of a potential therapist. This brief "job" sample gives a most reliable evaluation of the applicant's suitability for the job and provides the potential therapist with a clearer idea of the nature and demands of the task.

All staff members function both as therapists to children and consultants to parents, though usually not with the same family. This dual role encourages a balanced perspective on the parent–child interactions and tends to temper any biases toward parents or children. The resulting acceptance of parents as reasonable people, earnestly struggling with a very difficult problem, is reciprocally reflected in the parents' attitude toward the therapists. The parents are willing to try new, sometimes difficult, suggestions offered by therapists, and are motivated to persist. The overall effect is one of mutual acceptance and identification between parent and therapist as people with a shared experience and some knowledge of what it is like to be in the other's position. Both the selection process and the training of therapists foster a generalist viewpoint with primary attention to the needs of the child and his particular family.

In addition, certain of our operational practices encourage attitudes that are communicated during training. The goal of therapeutic intervention is to help the whole family, not only the psychotic child. Progress is measured as much by increased competence in the parents as in the child. Increased competence is expressed by more active participation in the development of programming for the child, often to the point of disagreement with and criticism of the therapist's suggestions. These changes are associated with decreased guilt and depression, improved self-esteem, and better organized family lives.

Therapists are encouraged to become interested in the families even before entering on the therapeutic program. It is a stated rule in the procedure handbook of the program that all patients seen for evaluation continue to be the responsibility of the program until a more appropriate resource or agency has *accepted* clinical responsibility for them. Such a commitment prevents the tendency, practiced in many other programs, of selecting mildly disturbed patients who are most easily treated. It also fosters active advocacy by therapists, encouraging an aggressive search for appropriate services for clients if and when they have less need of our program. Families' response to this built-in sense of dedication adequately compensates staff for the extra effort. Therapists tend to generalize this commitment to a concern with helping the families with any problems that may hamper their function. This may include help in obtaining a wide range of services, including medical care and social services for other members of the family. An encompassing concept develops that anything that supports improved function of the family also benefits the psychotic child.

A second attitude, related to the first, affects the way in which counseling or advice is generated. We recognize the ease with which advice can be given, often based only on plausible theory or beliefs. When such advice fails, the cause is too easily ascribed to parental failure rather than to inadequacy of the advice. We moderate this tendency by requiring, whenever possible, that therapists personally demonstrate the effectiveness of a particular intervention before asking parents to adopt it. This procedure has the effect of modifying initially unrealistic advice, and creating empathy with the parents. These attitudes are maintained and practiced from the director's level down, thus producing a sense of acceptance and cooperation in all staff and families.

Diagnostic Issues: Autism and Psychosis

We have alluded to the confusion in the field regarding description and diagnosis, and mentioned that there is increasing evidence for a biological basis of the primary dysfunctions in childhood psychosis. Considerable clarity was brought to the problem of diagnosis by the British Working Party led by Creak (1961, 1964). We use a 14-point objective rating system, based on the nine points worked out by Creak's working party and elaborated by Reichler (Reichler and Schopler, 1971), to measure the degree of psychosis in each child referred. These 14 criteria, offering only a broad descriptive classification, have the advantage of avoiding premature closure, which impedes the subsequent identification of more discrete subgroups as more specific knowledge became available. Each child is rated on observations made during a semi-standardized interaction. While it is recognized that all children receiving similar ratings of severity of psychoses do not necessarily share the same "disease" or even necessarily the same major handicap, the rating scale does offer some measure of the severity of behavioral and learning impairment. It also provides a substantial observational basis for communication among professionals and, more importantly, with parents. The objective ratings also help focus therapeutic attention to problem areas as opposed to the diffuse, global sense of disorder often fostered by more allegorical or theoretical diagnostic views (Schopler and Reichler, 1971a,b).

With observation of children in the program over time, we have become increasingly aware of how unevenly some children develop in functions and skills. The staff must consistently examine each child's skill in several areas and program individually for each function. It is not possible to predict a child's ability in one skill, given the level of ability in another. We have found most available tests and scales inadequate for the comprehensive assessment required at the low developmental level at which most of the children functioned. Therapists have therefore been obliged to invent tasks by which to evaluate each child. It was apparent early that development of an evaluation instrument specifically designed to assess children developmentally across discrete modalities would facilitate individualized programming for each child, and improve the ability to communicate the child's specific dysfunctions to his parents. We were encouraged to do so by the analysis of scores on the Psychosis Rating Scale, which indicated that problems in human relatedness were the effect of impaired perceptual functions (Reichler and Schopler, 1971). Such an effort was also suggested by the observations of other workers in the field (Churchill, 1969).

An evaluation instrument, the Psychoeducational Profile (PEP) was created out of task items that had been found to be useful in teaching developmentally dysfunctional children in our program. This procedure, as opposed to one based on a priori or theoretical notions, allows developmental programs to be evolved from the child's performance on the PEP. The instrument consists of five principal scales measuring imitation (motor and vocal), sensory modalities (vision, hearing), motor development (fine, gross, and visual-motor integration), cognitive functions (auditory, vocal, advanced), and language (imitation, vocabulary, verbal comprehension, reading, and visual comprehension). In addition, there is a "Pathology Scale" (affect; relating, cooperation, and human interest, play and interaction materials; and pathological sensory modes), which measures abnormal or unusual patterns of development in contrast to "pathologically" delayed development. While "normal" performance curves have been constructed for the PEP, they serve primarily to assess developmental sequence and to allow appropriate developmental alignment of individual scales. The objective is not to assign a *normalized score* to a child, but rather to compare *his* level of function in one modality with *his* level of function in another. This quantitative developmental instrument fits the requirements mentioned in the introduction for a diagnostic procedure oriented to a functional, rehabilitative treatment.

The diagnostic procedure described here overcomes most of the problems associated with nosological issues. It allows a pragmatic therapy that focuses on the individual child's needs, taking into account his strengths and weaknesses and relatively unencumbered by professional and theoretical issues. The selection process and training of therapists prevents most of the difficulties associated with professional issues. It fosters a generalist viewpoint with primary attention to the needs of the child and his particular family. For these components to be utilized effectively, a program must embody structure and procedures that overcome the problem of confusion in parent roles, and incongruity and conflict between parental responsibility and professional authority.

Parental Issues: Parents as Co-Therapists

Often families are referred to our program only after they have taken their child to several centers, usually receiving only diagnostic services and getting brief and superficial advice, with their confusion increasing at each evaluation. More often than not, information received from these centers is stamped "confidential," with the explanation "not to be shown to patient or relatives."

Parents are unable to develop an appropriate, consistent developmental relation with their child under these circumstances. Sometimes there are uncertain indications of brain damage or retardation, and the confidentiality of the records is an attempt to shield parents from the shock of unpleasant possibilities. The data on parental estimates have already indicated that parents are acutely aware of their children's disabilities. *But they are unable to organize this awareness in the face of professionally imposed ignorance. For parents to act effectively with their children as developmental agents, they must be fully informed.* In our experience, unpleasant information or lack of clear knowledge are never as stressful as continued uncertainty. We share all available information openly with parents. This requires reasonable time to interpret it clearly. *It also demands frank acknowledgment of professional ignorance.* These are the first steps of honest involvement of parents as co-therapists. We avoid the choice between hopelessness and unrealistic optimism by concentrating on the child's and the parent's immediate needs and providing a specific program to facilitate his development.

When our program is considered appropriate for a child, an agreement is made with the parents to collaborate for a definite period of time. Parents optimally attend twice weekly for 45-minute sessions, with fathers often alternating in their visits. Variations and adaptations of this pattern are made realistically, depending on the needs and limitations of the family and child. During these visits parents may observe the therapist's demonstration, discuss problems in other areas of their home life with the parent consultant, or demonstrate their home program with the child. Occasionally other family members working with the child are invited.

Therapy Demonstration

During demonstrations by a therapist, parents observe through the one-way screen with their parent consultant. The consultant focuses their attention on relevant aspects of the demonstration and answers questions they may raise. There are several important advantages of this technique. (1) It avoids the mystique and unfounded authority of the therapist who reports to parents from only private observations of the child. (2) It guards the parents against recommendations that are more easily made than carried out. (3) It provides stimulation stemming from constructive competition between parents and therapist, and also affords an opportunity for parents to copy the actions of the therapist. (4) Direct demonstrations have a more immediate impact than verbal interpretation. They are more easily understood, especially by unsophisticated parents, than are verbal explanations. (5) By allowing the parent to see the therapist's struggles, frustrations, and occasional mistakes, the parents become less self-critical and are better able to resume the bond of responsibility for their own child. (6) The demonstrations play a key role in encouraging parents to use as guidelines their knowledge of successful experience in normal child rearing, but to apply this knowledge in the special way required in their autistic child.

The therapist confers with the parent consultant prior to the demonstration, and they agree on the session's focus. For example, parents often have unusual difficulty in controlling the child's behavior, and adopt an air of resignation in accepting anything the child does. The therapist will show how to get the child seated at the table, when to give him a helpful swat on the behind, and how to maintain a meaningful interaction when the child withdraws.

Specific interventions are evolved appropriate to the child's development, based on the Psychosis Rating Scale, the Psychoeducational Profile, parents' identification of specific problem areas, and any other relevant information. Both experience and the results of a study of the effect of treatment structure (Schopler, Brehm, Kinsbourne, and Reichler, 1971) indicate that psychotic children learn more adaptive behavior patterns in a structured situation. This is not a surprising finding, though it is not yet accepted by all child professionals. It is in general accord with results in other brain dysfunctional children (Wender, 1971). Even *play* is learned by the child in a structured interaction.

The Home Program

Concurrent with their observation sessions, parents are also given home programs, which are revised at regular intervals. These describe objectives, methods, and materials for working with the child in daily sessions. The content of the home program is based on the therapist's assessment of the child and the parents' experience at home. At regular intervals, parents demonstrate the home program with their child while therapist and consultant observe. Parents bring along the materials they have made or bought for home use. They are aware of being observed and occasionally filmed. Although many of them are at first nervous about performing behind a one-way screen, the nervousness disappears after they have observed the therapist for awhile. In fact, sooner or later most parents request additional demonstration sessions to show new developments of which they are especially proud. Not only do spontaneous demonstrations of new progress boost the parental ego, these sessions also maintain some motivating competition for understanding and improving the interaction with the child.

Generally the parents' daily home program sessions are more easily organized into an enjoyable and successful interaction than are problems in other areas of home life. To work out solutions to these problems, the parent meets with his consultant in an office rather than the observation room. The problems discussed often involve issues not practical or feasible for demonstration, such as difficulties with sleeping, eating, and toilet training. One child did not go to bed until eleven o'clock. He sat in the living room rocking himself for half an hour every night, after which he slept in his parents' bed. This had been going on for several years. The parent consultant helped the parents to divide this bedtime problem into several units. First they moved the rocking chair into the child's bedroom and near a radio he liked listening to. After he became accustomed to this change, he was moved from the parents' bed to his own bed. A difficult struggle ensued, requiring parents to move the child 15 times to his own bed during the first few nights. Within three weeks, however, he was sleeping in his own bed.

At the end of each contract period, all data relating to the child's development are formally shared with parents and a new working agreement is mutually arrived at. Perhaps the most important aspect of the program is the effect of the central recognition that parents are responsible for their children and are the people most likely to have their children's well-being at heart. Parent involvement has been greater and more consistent than was initially expected. In the beginning of the Child Research Project, many parents had to drive for one to five hours for each visit. Nevertheless, attendance has been regular and punctual with only a few cancellations. Home program sessions with the children and daily logs were maintained with great regularity, including some periods when parents felt discouraged or hopeless. At the beginning of therapy sessions, parents usually ask for a very specific home program and then follow it to the letter. After a period of successful work, they become more resourceful. At this stage the therapist's role is primarily to help identify areas of functioning requiring further development in the child and techniques to do this. As parents increase in their capacity to use and participate in setting these directions, the therapist lends his support to their initiative.

Many parents, especially mothers, have developed a degree of objectivity, investment, and skill found only in the best teachers. For example, the director of an educational program for autistic children visited the Child Research Project. She was observing an adult–child interaction. After a brief time of observation, she remarked that this was an unusually skillful therapist and wondered why the parents were not observing. She was astonished and gratified to learn that it was the mother herself who was working with the child.

IMPLICATIONS FOR SOCIAL ACTION

In the field of mental health, there is a gradual but increasing acceptance that para-professional and relatively untrained workers are performing important therapy. This is usually acknowledged with the explanation that increasing demand for services accompanied by shortage of trained personnel makes use of such subprofessionals necessary. Our experience suggests that it is not only expedient to use parents to supplement the shortage in manpower, but that they are also frequently the most effective developmental agents for their children. Others have now effectively used parents as co-therapists or developmental agents with their children. We have experimented with the use of a parent as a child therapist and parent consultant to other families with success. Ora and Wiegerink (1970) have extended our initial concept by using parents as their major staff, but in our program, distance precludes a complete move in this direction.

With improved self-esteem based on their success with their children and their acceptance as colleagues, our parents of psychotic children are no longer socially invisible. They formed the North Carolina Society for Autistic Children (NCSAC) in 1970 as a chapter of the National Society for Autistic Children. With increased knowledge of their children's needs they initiated two model experimental classes. With new confidence in themselves, they successfully lobbied the state legislature and produced the first state-wide, state-supported program for their children. The legislation reflects their new sense of effectiveness. Not only does it not have a minimum age for admission, but it mandates the active involvement of the parent as participant in the classroom. NCSAC has organized summer camps for its children and is planning a permanent camp. The camp plan may best speak for the mature, healthy, and realistic understanding these parents have of their children. They recognize that many of the children may never be able to live fully independent lives. Rather than assuming the hopeless and self-pitying attitude so often expected and projected by professionals, they are using the camp as a basis for planning a structured community for their children. To this degree, the parents' effective action for their children resembles what parents of other handicapped children have done, but they have managed to avoid most of the narrow "professionalization" of some other parent organizations.

As the words contained in TEACCH indicate, the parents and we have recognized that the same programming efforts that have been useful for their children have broader application. The name reflects a sense of commonality with children with severe communication and language impairments. But the parents have not stopped there. Their increased understanding and sophistication have made them aware of the needs their children share with all handicapped children: adequate evaluation centers, appropriately staffed and equipped treatment services, and perhaps most importantly, educational opportunity. To this end, they have initiated a coalition of parent groups of handicapped children called Parents and Professionals for Handicapped Children (PPHC). Their success is already dramatic. They have been recognized as the constituency for the state Child Advocacy Program and are being consulted on legislation concerning children.

Through various experiences in dealing with state and local agencies, the parents and we have become aware of a serious obstacle to planning comprehensive services for children: There is no one who speaks for them. The bureaucratic structure is primarily a direct extension of the professional model discussed in the beginning of this article. It therefore suffers all the constraints and problems of those specialized professional identifications.

This problem is clearly identified by a quote from the *Schizophrenia Bulletin* (Mosher and Gunderson, 1973).

> The study of childhood psychoses is another area which has seen a tremendous upsurge of interest in recent years. While this evidence of increased commitment has provided a measure of relief to the families of psychotic children, their ordeal, though perhaps a little less lonely now, remains a formidable one. Because their children's problems are so special and so severe, programs for dealing with them are often either unavailable or exorbitantly expensive. The two institutions to which parents most frequently appeal for help—Medicine and Education—sometimes seem to be trying to outdo each other in their attempts to disclaim responsibility for the care of these children. "Your child has a *medical* problem," say the schools. "He needs special *education*," respond the hospitals and clinics. Parents begin to feel that they are doomed to hear an ever-recurring dialogue in which only one message is clear: "There is nothing we can do for your child." In the end, parents whose children are rejected by existing special classes or special treatment centers are left with a choice of keeping the child at home or relegating him to custodial care in a State institution; both choices seem unreasonable. To alleviate this situation, a better coordination of education and medical services is mandatory. If shared responsibility is ultimately considered unrealistic, it would seem preferable that the child's care be the primary responsibility (with medical backup, of course) of the educational systems so that he can stay as nearly within the usual school—and family—based life of

most children as is feasible. This is the course which has been followed in Great Britain and which was recently adopted in North Carolina. Perhaps the program developed in North Carolina will serve as a pilot program in which problems can be worked out before the system is introduced elsewhere. (pp. 47–48)

The parents and we have recognized that bureaucratic structures, be they funding or administrative, inevitably influence the very structure, goals, and operations of a service program. The PPHC coalition has been making forceful and persistent efforts to modify these bureaucratic structures so they reflect the principles identified in this paper and elaborated elsewhere (Reichler, 1974). These endeavors have led to several improvements in services for children. A bill for mandatory education for all handicapped children is now in effect. An attempt to legislate a new single agency to serve all the needs and control all funds related to handicapped children failed, but did produce an Office for Children with responsibility to provide coordinated planning, set priorities across agencies, and control distribution of funds for all human resource programs related to children. The Department of Public Instruction now, for the first time, has an advisory council, including parents, to which it is accountable. Most significantly, at the state level, there is a palpable increase in awareness and concern for handicapped children, and a growing discomfort with the fragmenta- tion of services for them. Reflecting this, the major priorities of the Department of Human Resources include a state-wide early screening program, improved developmental evaluation services, and a commitment to the development of a "single portal of entry" for services at the local level. This would mean a single agency or clinic where any handicapped child could go to receive the wide variety of coordinated services he needs. Further action is attempting to provide a wide continuum of services such as respite care and group homes as alternatives to institutionalization. Much of this continues to be a struggle in overcoming ignorance, fear, and well-ingrained prejudices. Lorna Wing (n.d.) said it as well as anyone: "The way in which handicapped people are provided for is one index of the degree of civilization of a community. Ours still has some way to go" (p. 31).

SUMMARY

In this paper we have reviewed the problems involved in developing compre- hensive, therapeutic, developmental services to children in general, and autistic children in particular. Professional specialization was identified as a major cause of the disjointed, uncoordinated, and often overlapping services that now exist. Nosological confusion was shown to derive from and to support professional dismemberment of children's problems into speciality areas. And lastly, parents, both as victims of professional scapegoating and in a more active role of "professionalized" parents, were examined for their role in supporting this system.

The Division for the Treatment and Education of Autistic and related Communications handicapped CHildren (TEACCH) was discussed in detail as one model for the delivery of comprehensive developmental services for children. The essential components of such a program are:

1. That a single theoretical or professional viewpoint cannot predominate in an effective developmental system. The program must be accountable to the child and his family.

2. That parents are responsible for their children and are the people most likely to have their children's well-being at heart. This requires an open, honest program with active and equal parent involvement.

3. That professional overspecialization often fosters narrow perspectives, with a shift of focus from child-oriented concerns to professional concerns. This suggests that specialists who supply detailed and specific knowledge must be balanced by generalists and parents with a more pragmatic focus on the whole child.

4. That bureaucratic structure directly affects the operations, goals, and the very nature of programs it influences. The implication is that the bureaucratic structure itself must contain all of the elements elaborated and have a primary responsibility and concern for children, if programs are to enable professionals from various fields, working together with parents, to best serve all our children.

This program allows coordinated services for children, whatever they may need, instead of forcing the child to fit a preconceived definition. It fosters effective development and comparative evaluation of a variety of techniques so the most effective help for our children can be delivered to all.

REFERENCES

Als, H., and Lewis, M. The contribution of the infant to the interaction with his mother. Reported at the Biennial Meeting of the Society for Research in Child Development, Denver, Colorado, 1975.

American Psychiatric Association. *DSM-II, Diagnostic and statistical manual of mental disorders* (2nd ed.). Washington, D.C.: APA, 1968.

Bettelheim, B. *The empty fortress: Infantile autism and the birth of the self.* London: Collier-Macmillan, 1967.

Churchill, D. Psychotic children and behavior modification. *American Journal of Psychiatry*, 1969, *125*, 1585–1590.

Creak, M. Schizophrenic syndrome in childhood: Progress report of a working party. *Cerebral Palsy Bulletin*, 1961, *3*, 501–504.

Creak, M. Schizophrenic syndrome in childhood: Further progress report of a working party. *Developmental Medicine and Child Neurology*, 1964, *6*, 530–535.

Eberhardy, F. The view from "the couch." *Journal of Child Psychology and Psychiatry*, 1967, *8*, 257–263.

Eisenberg, L. Psychotic disorders in childhood. In L. D. Eron (Ed.), *Classification of behavior disorders*. Chicago, Illinois: Aldine Press, 1967.

Ferster, C. B. Positive reinforcement and behavioral deficits in autistic children. *Child Development*, 1961, *32*, 437–456.

Freedman, D. G. The effects of kinesthetic stimulation on weight gain and on smiling in premature infants. Paper presented at the annual meeting of the American Orthopsychiatric Association, San Francisco, California, 1966.

Group for the Advancement of Psychiatry. Psychopathological Disorders in Childhood: Theoretical Considerations and a Proposed Classification. Formulated by the Committee on Child Psychiatry, G.A.P., New York, New York, 1969.

Kanner, L. Autistic disturbances of affective contact. *Nervous Child*, 1943, *2*, 217–250.

Kanner, L. Approaches: Retrospect and prospect. *Journal of Autism and Childhood Schizophrenia*, 1971, *1*, 453–459.

Kaye, K. Gaze direction as the infant's way of controlling his mother's teaching behavior. Reported at the Biennial Meeting of the Society for Research in Child Development, Denver, Colorado, 1975.

Koegler, R. R., Colbert, E. G., and Eiduson, S. Wanted: A biochemical test for schizophrenia. *California Medicine*, 1961, *94*, 26–29.

Kyser, J. The two camps in child psychiatry: A report from a psychiatrist–father of an autistic and retarded child. *American Journal of Psychiatry*, 1968, *125*, 141–147.

Lidz, T. Intrafamilial environment of the schizophrenic patient: IV. The transmission of irrationality. *Archives of Neurology and Psychiatry*, 1958, *79*, 305–316.

Lidz, T. Thought disorders in the parents of schizophrenic patients A study utilizing the object sorting test. *Journal of Psychiatric Research*, 1962, *1*, 193–200.

Lovibond, S. The object sorting test and conceptual thinking in schizophrenia. *Australian Journal of Psychiatry*, 1954, *5*, 52–70.

McLuhan, M. *Understanding media*. New York: Signet Books, New American Library, 1966.

May, J., *A physician looks at psychiatry*. New York: John Day, 1950.

Menninger, K., Ellenberger, H., Pruyser, P., and Mayman, M. The unitary concept of mental illness. *Bulletin of the Menninger Clinic*, 1958, *22*, 4–12.

Mosher, L., and Gunderson, J. Special report: Schizophrenia, 1972. *Schizophrenia Bulletin*, 1973, *7*, 47–48.

Myers, D. I., and Goldfarb, W. Studies of perplexity in mothers of schizophrenic children. *American Journal of Orthopsychiatry*, 1961, *31*, 551–564.

Ora, J., and Wiegerink, R. *Regional intervention project for parents and children*, Progress Report. Washington, D.C.: Bureau of Education for the Handicapped, U.S. Office of Education, 1970.

Ornitz, E. M., and Ritvo, E. R. Perceptual inconstancy in early infantile autism. *Archives of General Psychiatry*, 1968, *18*, 76–98.

Osofsky, J. D. Neonatal characteristics and directional effects in mother–infant interaction. Reported at the Biennial Meeting of the Society for Research in Child Development, Denver, Colorado, 1975.

Park, C. *The siege*. New York: Harcourt, Brace & World, 1967.

Parke, R. E., and Sarvin, D. B. Infant characteristics and behavior as elicitors of maternal and parental responsibility in the newborn. Reported at the Biennial Meeting of the Society for Research in Child Development, Denver, Colorado, 1975.

Pittfield, M., and Oppenheim, A. Child-rearing attitudes of mothers of psychotic children. *Journal of Child Psychology and Psychiatry and Allied Disciplines*, 1964, *1*, 51–57.

Reichler, R. J. Comprehensive services for children: A program model, in *Resources, education and the law: Resources for autistic children*, Proceedings of the 6th Annual Meeting and Conference of the National Society for Autistic Children. Washington, D.C.: NSAC, 1974, 28–36.

Reichler, R. J., Babigian, H. M., and Gardner, E. A. The mental health team: A model for a combined approach to the problems of the poor. *American Journal of Orthopsychiatry*, 1966, *36*, 434–443.

Reichler, R. J., and Schopler, E. Observations on the nature of human relatedness. *Journal of Autism and Childhood Schizophrenia*, 1971, *1*, 283–296.

Rimland, B. *Infantile autism*. New York: Century Psychology Series, Appleton-Century-Crofts, 1964. Chapter 4, 67–76.

Rosman, B. Thought disorders in parents of schizophrenic patients: A further study utilizing the object sorting test. *Journal of Psychiatric Research*, 1964, *2*, 211–221.

Rutter, M. Concepts of autism: A review of research. *Journal of Child Psychology and Psychiatry*, 1968, *9*, 1–25.

Rutter, M. The description and classification of infantile autism. In D. W. Churchill, G. D. Alpern, and M. K. DeMyer (Eds.), *Infantile autism*. Springfield, Illinois: Charles C. Thomas, 1971.

Rutter, M., Lebovici, S., Eisenberg, L., Sneznevskij, A. V., Sadoun, R., Brooke, E., and Lin, T. Y. A tri-axial classification of mental disorders in childhood (Report of the Third WHO Seminar on Psychotic Disorders). *Journal of Child Psychology and Psychiatry*, 1969, *10*, 41–61.

Schopler, E. Early infantile autism and receptor processes. *Archives of General Psychiatry*, 1965, *13*, 327–335.

Schopler, E. Visual versus tactual receptor preferences in normal and schizophrenic children. *Journal of Abnormal Psychology*, 1966, *71*, 108–114.

Schopler, E. Parents of psychotic children as scapegoats. *Journal of Contemporary Psychotherapy*, 1971, *4*, 17–22.

Schopler, E., Brehm, S., Kinsbourne, M., and Reichler, R. J. Effects of treatment structure on development in autistic children. *Archives of General Psychiatry*, 1971, *24*, 415–421.

Schopler, E., and Loftin, J. Thinking disorders in parents of young psychotic children. *Journal of Abnormal Psychology*, 1969, *74*, 3281–3287. (a)

Schopler, E., and Loftin, J. Thought disorders in parents of psychotic children: A function of test anxiety. *Archives of General Psychiatry*, 1969, *20*, 174–181. (b)

Schopler, E., and Reichler, R. J. Developmental therapy by parents with their own autistic child. In M. Rutter (Ed.), *Infantile autism: Concepts, characteristics, and treatment*. London: Churchill-Livingston, 1971. (a)

Schopler, E., and Reichler, R. J. Parents as co-therapists in the treatment of psychotic children. *Journal of Autism and Childhood Schizophrenia*, 1971, *1*, 87–102. (b)

Schopler, E., and Reichler, R. J. Psychobiological referents for the treatment of autism. In D. W. Churchill, G. D. Alpern, and M. K. DeMyer (Eds.), *Infantile autism*. Springfield, Illinois: Charles C. Thomas, 1971.

Schopler, E., and Reichler, R. J. How well do parents understand their own psychotic child? *Journal of Autism and Childhood Schizophrenia*, 1972, *2*, 387–400.

Schulman, J. L., and Stern, S. Parents' estimates of the intelligence of retarded children. *American Journal of Mental Deficiency*, 1959, *63*, 696–698.

Singer, M., and Wynne, L. Thought disorder and family relations of schizophrenics. *Archives of General Psychiatry*, 1965, *12*, 201–212.

Stengel, E. Classification of mental disorders. *Bulletin WHO*, 1960, *21*, 601–663.

Stern, D. Mother and infant at play: The dyadic interaction involving facial, vocal, and gaze behaviors. In M. Lewis and L. Rosenbaum (Eds.), *The origins of behavior* (Vol. I). New York: Wiley, 1973.

Strauss, J. S. Diagnostic models and the nature of psychiatric disorder. *Archives of General Psychiatry*, 1973, *29*, 445–449.

Tronick, E., Adamson, L., Wise, S., and Als, H. Infant emotions in normal and perturbed interactions. Reported at the Biennial Meeting of the Society for Research in Child Development, Denver, Colorado, 1975.

Wender, P. *Minimal brain dysfunction in children.* New York: Wiley, 1971.

Wild, C. Disturbed styles of thinking: Implications of disturbed styles of thinking manifestations on the object sorting test by the parents of schizophrenic patients. *Archives of General Psychiatry*, 1965, *13*, 464–470.

Wilson, L. *This stranger, my son: A mother's story.* New York: Putnam, 1968.

Wing, L. *Children apart: autistic children and their families.* A Family Doctor Booklet. London: British Medical Association, n.d.

Wolfensberger, W., and Kurtz, R. A. Measurement of parents' perceptions of their children's development. *Genetic Psychological Monographs*, 1971, *83*, 3–92.

Discussion of Intervention Section

The seven chapters in this section all concern themselves with improving learning and adaptation in deviant children. There are important differences in the authors' definitions of clinical phenomena and the changes their particular intervention strategies are most suited to effect. However, regardless of their differences, at this time the main criteria for using any one of these interventions are the extent to which the desired behavioral changes are effected in the child and in his environment.

Not only do these chapters represent significant differences in intervention targets, they also develop quite different relationships between theory and clinical data. No doubt these theoretical linkages play a more prominent role in clinical research than they do in the more "basic research" on normal development and biological structures. After all, the social scientist dedicated to "basic research" has relative freedom in the selection of the questions he studies. He does not have to study questions for which he has difficulty in finding subjects or appropriate research methodology. The clinician, on the other hand, has accepted the role of struggling with problems of social and personal adjustment, regardless of what is known about the causes and cures of such problems. It has been the social-role pressure of being expected to have expertise on the handling and solving of complex adjustment problems, combined with not having scientifically established solutions, that has made theoretical explanations almost as important to clinicians as empirical data are to scientists. For these reasons it has been almost impossible for clinicians to develop interventions independently of theories and assumptions about causation.

Our discussion of this section will be focused on comparing these seven chapters for differences in their intervention targets and for their linkages between their theoretical explanations and their clinical data.

The biological interventions reviewed by Campbell are not established for any specific diagnostic category of children. Much of the drug research has been done with institutionalized children in metropolitan medical centers. Accordingly, many of the subjects suffered from psychosis, brain damage, and mental retardation in varying degrees and numbers. Even though no specific drug treatment has been established for any specific pathological behavior or diagnostic category, Campbell has suggested some noteworthy success. This includes effectiveness for changing and regulating the sleep–wake cycle; normalizing activity level as in impulsivity, hyperactivity, and aggressivity; and generally reducing such related behavior as psychotic disorganization.

In the past many clinicians believed that for patients whose psychoses were caused by biological deficits, their treatment may best be sought pharmacologically. Campbell does not rely on such simplistic relationships, nor does she attempt to rely on theoretical explanations for the selection of one agent over another. Although such explanations no doubt are available, Campbell's presentation suggests an empirical approach. Different drugs are simply tried out. In those cases when the drug is effective, continued use is stimulated; if ineffective, it may be dropped. In either case, both psychiatrist and patient must generally get along without adequate explanations for improvement.

The chapters by Mann and Goodman and by Gallagher and Wiegerink both refer to special education interventions. While Gallagher focuses his discussion on autistic children, Mann and Goodman present a critique of perceptual training recently used for a wide spectrum of children who have in common reading and related language problems. Mann and Goodman's critique responds to an educational fad in the use of "perceptual training for ameliorating" all kinds of learning difficulties. Although most of this chapter is devoted to critiquing the excesses of one technique, they also suggest positive special education strategies. These include the formulation of clear educational objectives or actual skills for living. Such competency training is based on directly relevant behavioral procedures, with repetition as needed for the individual child. While both of these chapters appear to share an impatience with "perceptual training" as a widely usable special education intervention, the Gallagher chapter grapples with the special education needs of autistic children in particular.

Gallagher and Wiegerink attempt to connect the optimum educational strategy with the most likely biological causes of autism. Although they conceded that there is no consensus in the field on the causes of autism, they nevertheless do not believe that a meaningful educational intervention can be developed independently of knowing the biological root cause of the condition. Among the different causal explanations for autism in the literature, they focus on impaired short-term memory and deficits in auditory–visual information processing. These causal explanations are used to focus on intervention techniques aimed at remedying these same deficits. These techniques, including the use of balancing beams and the reduction of complex stimuli, have been reported as effective with various children. However, it is probably an oversimplification to expect that the success or failure of any special education intervention is dependent on its relationship to underlying biological deficits. Specific physiological or biochemical impairment does not usually result in specific behavior. Moreover, it does not follow that when a specific impairment is identified that it can or should be retrained by a related technique. Some impairments have to be compensated by training other modalities, others have to be accepted while existing strengths are developed. When and how to follow either direction can only be determined through individualized educational assessment.

Different views on the relationship between causation and intervention are expressed in the two chapters as they criticize "perceptual training." Gallagher and Wiegerink see the lack of success with this educational strategy on diagnostic grounds. Most of the children treated with perceptual training simply did not suffer from perceptual defects. Mann and Goodman, on the other hand, emphasize the inappropriateness of training perception as an abstraction. In theory the child's reading skills are dependent on his perceptual skills. It then seemed to follow that impaired reading could be corrected by training the underlying perceptual impairment. When this did not happen, the problem was not only diagnostic; according to Mann and Goodman, more likely the failure was due to the confusion between theoretical construct and actual learning processes. Recommending a nontheoretical, direct-line approach to special education problems, Mann and Goodman remind us that, practically speaking, perceptual training in education for reading involves levels of illumination, letter and word discrimination, and scanning pages. When perceptual training is used as a broader theoretical construct, it simply may not have application to the special education of individual children.

In contrast to the special education discussions, Lovaas, Schreibman, and Koegel do not address themselves to the complex questions of the possible causes of autism, nor to the complicated issues of the "total" child who is considered autistic. Rather than attempting to deal with the range of special training and special help such children may require, their behavioristic approach is intended to modify any specific behavioral problems manifested by autistic children. However, no basis is given for selecting the behavior to be modified. There is only the guideline to ask just those questions that can be answered with present-day research methodology. Accordingly, behavior modification with autistic children has been especially aimed at self-destructive behavior, self-stimulation, and certain speech deficits.

In their chapter Ekstein and Caruth deal with psychoanalytic play therapy applied to schizophrenic and autistic children. While these children are not described either by behavioral characteristics or etiological assumptions, the authors are clearly referring to those children who are capable of recreating the events of their life space within the microcosm of the play world. Such activity, even when impaired, relies on symbolic behavior and mental representation. Accordingly, the children treated with this strategy would mainly be confined to those described by DeMyer as high-level autistics. It would also include other children whose mental deficiencies are not greater than borderline. The play of these children reflects their inner disturbance. They are impulse dominated, unable to differentiate internal from external reality, and they have difficulty with separation and individuation.

If the relationship between causal theory and intervention is a major concern with educational strategies, it is even more obviously so in psychoanalytic play therapy. In the Ekstein and Caruth chapter, for example, one of the causal assumptions about childhood schizophrenia is identified. They refer to the concept of "individuation and separation" that had been developed by Mahler as a full-scale explanation of childhood schizophrenia. This theoretical construct is pursued by Ekstein and Caruth through literature, poetry, mythology, religion, comics, and science fiction. Although the cosmic presence of the construct may be both interesting and aesthetically moving to the reader, it is related only tangentially to the treatment of the schizophrenic child as a metaphor for the difficulty of establishing meaningful contact. In this chapter psychoanalytic play therapy is presented mainly as a theory or metaphor for one of the generalized human dilemmas, i.e., separation and individuation. Perhaps it is for this reason that the specific or unique significance of the psychoanalytic treatment parameters do not become clear on their own terms. Possibly the recognition of play therapy as a metaphor leads Ekstein and Caruth to accord equal importance to education, residential treatment, psychopharmacology, and behavior modification in the treatment of schizophrenic children. It is of interest that Campbell's atheoretical or pragmatic review of biological interventions arrives at the same conclusion regarding the need for the other intervention modalities. Perhaps this represents an acknowledgment that no single optimum intervention has as yet been demonstrated, and that only individualized treatment plans can reasonably be justified at this time.

In contrast to psychoanalytic play therapy, Lovaas, Schreibman, and Koegel in their discussion of behavior modification go to some pains to avoid the use of theoretical speculation to justify their intervention methods. It is, of course, one of the obvious strengths of operant conditioning that the application of appropriate positive and negative reinforcements can change the behavior of children and other living creatures. The potential pitfalls of theorizing are further decreased by cautioning the clinical investigator to confine his efforts to questions that can be answered by existing methodology. This has meant shaping or controlling one behavior at a time, such as self-destructiveness, self-stimulation, and certain language behavior. Although the modification of such behaviors are well demonstrated, the changed behaviors do not usually generalize to other classes of behavior, nor do they necessarily maintain the improved direction over time. The authors express their disappointment at the limitations of success. Rather than theorizing about the nature of the autistic condition, they develop experimentally an explanatory construct of stimulus overselecting. This mechanism is used to attempt an explanation for the learning peculiarities of autistic children. Although stimulus overselectivity may be the best explanation for the data of the Lovaas, Schreibman, and Koegel study, it may become a misleading theoretical construct if used to direct curriculum for all autistic children. Likewise it is a limited construct for trying to understand the many complex questions facing parents and professionals concerned with disturbed children. These include problems of motivation, hierarchies of learning tasks, questions that the behaviorist may feel he should officially ignore until he can find an experimental paradigm.

The previously mentioned treatment strategies are all aimed at improving the functioning of individual children by decreasing maladaptive, pathological, or undesirable behavior and conversely improving their adaptive, functional, desirable characteristics. Only Doxiadis's chapter deals with an intervention that is primarily aimed at changing the child's environment. Residential care or treatment is used with the most dependent of children, not only because they are in the youngest age group, but also because for various reasons they do not have a family to supply adequate care and nurturance for the child's growth and development. The most common reasons for institutionalization include illegitimacy, desertion, parents' death, and other forms of family breakdown. Doxiadis demonstrates how the most common reasons for institutional care vary from one culture to another, and how decisions for residential care must be arrived at on an individual basis, relative to the options available to the child. While it is not to be expected that long-term residential care is capable of fostering the child's development equally well as an adequate family, it may be the best available alternative.

There are some similarities between the behaviorists' position and Doxiadis's chapter on institutional care. Like the behaviorists, he addresses himself to basic practical issues, such as what constitutes good institutional treatment? And what is a good placement decision? Although his approach is empirical, like the behaviorists, unlike them he is willing to tackle the complex and important questions even before research proof can be demonstrated. Moreover, he insists that we have an obligation to act on the best information we have until research data are established. He refrains from seeking behavioral laws and principles to govern institutional placement and treatment. Instead, he emphasizes the variations of cultural and individual considerations that will shape the relatively best decision for each child.

Similar to the Doxiadis discussion of residential care and unlike the other intervention papers, the Reichler and Schopler chapter includes both considerations of community organizations and individual treatment structures for meeting the needs of severely disturbed children. While their formulations are based on experience (their Developmental Therapy Program for autistic or psychotic children and those with related communications disorders), they develop clear implications for other behavioral disorders of childhood. The main thrust of this chapter is an organizational one. That is, it starts with identifying the problems of disturbed or disabled children and their families and current deficiencies in meeting these problems. This is followed by a discussion of how such deficiencies may be remedied, considering individual needs in a humane, economically feasible, and effective manner, using the limited knowledge we now have available. Answers to some of these shortcomings are suggested through reorganization of existing knowledge. This includes changing nosology from theoretical and professional bases to a problem-need basis and changing professional roles so that highly specialized and expensively trained professionals can appropriately be replaced by well-trained generalists. Parents are regarded as co-therapists rather than patients or causal agents, and children are treated with an educational emphasis at a developmentally appropriate level, regardless of the degree or severity of their impairment.

Similar to the other behaviorally oriented discussions, Reichler and Schopler emphasize empirically defined and individualized treatment solutions. Toward this aim a dual perspective is used. The first involves the developmental assessment of strengths and weaknesses of the impairment within the child and his family. Based on individual assessment, weaknesses are trained either directly or through strengths in other functions. Parents, siblings, and relatives are involved according to their resources and abilities. The second perspective involves assessing the community and helping parents and professionals to develop different feasible resources that will also allow a greater range of optimum individualized intervention. It is perhaps the unique contribution of this chapter to pursue optimum individualized treatment modalities across a wide range of intervention activities. The authors show how treatment objectives can be blocked by classification procedures based on theory and professional territoriality rather than the needs of the child. They also discuss how rigidly maintained professional roles and the resulting duplication of services can reduce the achievement of individual growth. Their demonstration for overcoming these modern impediments was made in an empirically based program, through a combination of social reorganization and developmental therapy evolved in the North Carolina state program for autistic children.   .

In conclusion, some of the important differences between experimental and clinical research were eloquently illustrated in the three sections of this volume. For experimental research, whether with normal children or with animals, the aim is to learn about specific regularities of behavior and function characterizing the subjects represented by the experimental sample. Individual variations often contribute to the obscurity of results, and are identified by the researcher as "noise" or "error." For the clinician, individual differences are usually the basis for planning interventions and even social change. In a clinical population such individual differences among people, regardless of their source, tend to offer the main clues for improving adaptation.

The experimental researcher has some greater degrees of freedom in selecting experimental hypotheses, subjects, and procedures than does the clinician, who is expected to help with any adjustment problems appropriate to his place of service. The researcher, on the other hand, need only ask those questions that he believes he can answer empirically.

These two examples of basic differences between clinical and experimental research are the source of much lack of communication and friction across professions with related interests. However, the chapters in this volume offer clear evidence that similar kinds of differences and frictions occur within the same areas of research as well. Opposite conclusions were discussed by Mandell and Rosenzweig because, among other reasons, different neurological systems were under consideration for each of them. Disagreements over intervention strategies may be traceable to whether the target is self-destructive behavior, the child's play sequences, or complex individual–community interaction. Each one of the areas reviewed was limited and defined by the investigator's theories, the questions he asked, the subjects studied, the procedures used, and the rules of logic or statistics by which the results and their implications were derived.

Perhaps one of the most dramatic examples of the delicate relationships between these various parts, was Kaye's review of the sucking reflex, apparently one discrete unit of infant behavior. Even when such an explicit and observable behavior unit is defined, the investigator's theoretical stance, the analysis of behavioral sub-units, and the procedures available, all have a determining effect on the results. The researcher's intellectual requirements call for the statement of results, relative to the research conditions. The clinician's treatment requirements call for the immediate application of the best knowledge available at the time.

Both areas of endeavor are subject to similar errors of judgment and logic. These include the application of a theory beyond the data it has been demonstrated to explain, as for example the psychoanalytic theory applied to normal child development or conversely the overgeneralization of experimental data to theories defined by other data. For example, the direct application of Rosenzweig's findings on environmental effects on the rat cortex applied directly to culturally deprived children. The overgeneralization of data and theory is not to be confused with the stimulation of new hypotheses across different research domains. For example, hypotheses on the effects of early deprivation on the human child's neurological development may be stimulated by Rosensweig's research, but can only be formulated specifically on the basis of knowledge of infant neurobiology, specific conditions of deprivation, and possible methodology for assessing the interaction between the two. Perhaps we have learned anew that you can't add apples and pears. Specific findings from one research context do not apply equally to another, unless by some unusual coincidence. On the other hand, you have to add apples and pears if you need to know the number of fruit.

Standing back far enough from the complex variability presented by each participant, some important categories of overlap emerge anew.

1. That the clinician concerned with deviant children cannot ignore the important complex developmental processes demonstrated empirically from research with animals and with normal children. Despite the difficulties in the direct application of findings in animal studies to the human condition, models generated should sensitize the clinician to a vast array of developmental information that is usually ignored because it does not fit into current theories of psychopathology or because its relevance to particular problems is not immediately apparent. It is striking that even the simplest measures of biological studies, routinely obtained in other medical settings, is inevitably absent from psychiatric records. Developmental histories concerning early biological development, including activity levels, perceptual responsiveness, sleep—wake cycles, and temperamental characteristics, if queried at all, are done in a cursory manner. In addition, environmental parameters suggested from normal developmental studies such as peer effects need greater attention than they have generally received in the clinical setting.

2. The developmental investigator can profitably attend to clinical experience to suggest some aspects of behavior for appropriate and relevant research. The study of psychopathology, despite its still inadequate models, nevertheless identifies behaviors and events that are of obvious significance to the adequate functioning of the developing human. At the same time, care must be exercised to recognize the limitations of data derived in the context of specific theories from studies utilizing a specific methodology. The casual mixing of different conceptual frameworks, under the banner of eclecticism, leads to confusion in the developmental and clinical arenas. The developmental scientist needs to understand information generated from studies of biological processes in order to better define his own units of behavioral investigation, to suggest appropriate areas of study and potential integration, and to suggest factors that must be accounted for in developmental studies. In particular, attention must be given to the characteristics, the level of development, and maturation of those biological systems that appear to relate to the behaviors under investigation, since the state of the system will affect the impact of the environmental conditions that interest him.

3. Finally, the neurobiologist has much to gain from attention to the studies of both the clinical and developmental investigator. As with the developmental-

ist, data from pathological syndromes can usefully guide the biologist into relevant areas of study and suggest models of interactive processes not necessarily apparent in animal studies. This may lead to animal and other biological models that might not be directly generated from current studies. In addition, the awareness of the complexity of the human condition should caution over-interpretation of findings generated from one species to another or the simplistic application of such data to human problems.

Awareness of research on normal development should similarly sensitize the biologist to the complexity and diversity of human development. The study of individual differences and variability within individuals during maturation should flow from such interactions. In the processes a sharpening of techniques for the identification and measurement of significant biological and behavioral units should evolve.

We are a long way from a clinically applicable theory of biological and psychological development. However, there appears to be much potential for working out closer connections between these areas.

This kind of cross-fertilization is primarily on the level of stimulating thought rather than specific information. It is to the continuation of the process of speculation, careful observation, and appropriate inferences, a process so well exemplified by Leo Kanner's professional contribution, that this volume has been dedicated.

E.S. and R.J.R.

Author Index

Subject Index

Acetylcholinesterase (*See* Brain enzymes)
Adaptation, 2-3, 55-56, 64-65, 136-137
Adoption, 331-332
Adrenergic system (*See* Catecholamine system)
Aggression and socialization, 206-207, 237 (*See also* Symptoms of psychosis)
Amblyopia ex anopsia (*See* Sensory experience)
Amphetamine (*See* Drug treatment, stimulants)
Animal models, 33, 37, 41
Anxiety and social involvement, 210-211 (*See also* Symptoms of psychosis)
Aphasia (*See* Language deviance)
Assumptive reality (*See* Egocentrism)
Auditory defects (*See* Autism, sensory and perceptual processes)
Autism
  characteristics, 106-113, 121, 160, 219-220, 231-233, 243, 249, 291-292, 305-307, 314, 319, 321, 354, 374-377
  compared to aphasia, Down's Syndrome, blind-deaf, and normal, 160
  compared to retardation, 98, 99
  diagnostic criteria, 96-98
  early behaviorist studies of, 292-293
  educational programs for, 219, 357
  etiology, 243, 291-292, 296, 314, 319-321, 347, 355, 358, 359, 361, 362
  home programs for, 358, 365
  intelligence and mental abilities, 93-95, 99-100
  lack of services for, 347-353

Autism (*cont'd*)
  language development in, 95, 100-103, 160
  parental and professional social roles, 352-353
  and parents, 95-98 (*See also* Parents of psychotic children)
  and performance profile, 107-111
  sensory and perceptual processes, 95, 115, 116, 117, 121, 122, 124, 125, 139, 160, 272-284, 321, 322
  in Soviet Union, 319
  symptoms and age, 239, 307
  treatment of (*See* Behavior therapy; Biological treatments; Developmental therapy; Drug treatment; Educational treatment; Learning therapy and treatment of autism; Psychoanalytic play therapy; Psychoeducational treatment)
Aveyron, savage boy of, 10, 12
Axoplasmic flow, 28

Behaviorism, 188-189, 193-194, 236
Behavior therapy or treatment and behavioral modification, 314, 317, 376-377
  fading, 305-306
  free play, 302-304
  home management, 354-356
  imitation techniques, 232, 295, 302, 305
  language training, 301-302
  maintenance, 304
  reinforcement of nonverbal behavior, 295